THE DEATH OF
CHRISTIAN BRITAIN

—— ·◆· ——

PRAISE FOR THE FIRST EDITION

'A tremendously impressive book and wonderful social history.'
Niall Ferguson, *Start the Week, Radio 4*

'This book should be read by anybody who cares about the future of religion. [Brown's} statistics are convincing and disquieting. The personal testimonies he quotes are moving and revealing. He shows clearly that Christianity, as we have known it in this country, is in its death throes.'
Karen Armstrong, *The Independent*

'A very brave, readable book, and a marvellous social history lesson … this is a powerful wake-up call.'
Antonia Swinson, *Scotland on Sunday*

'Callum Brown plunges bravely into one of the most complex debates of our era in this engaging book. He does not claim that we are all atheists now, but asserts that a massive shift in our self-understanding as a nation has occurred, which has reduced Christianity to the status of an eccentric and irrelevant sub-culture in a dynamically plural society.'
Richard Holloway, former Bishop
of Edinburgh, *The Scotsman*

'Church leaders should not ignore this book.'
Patrick Comerford, *Irish Times*

'A study which deserves the attention of all who are seriously concerned either with the history or with the future of British Christianity.'
David L. Edwards, *Tablet*

'*The Death of Christian Britain* is a *tour de force* in the social history of religion ... This most provocative of historians has pulled off an extraordinary double feat. He has simultaneously rejected more strenuously than ever before the long tradition of British historiography that sought to apply the concept of secularization to the late nineteenth and early twentieth centuries and at once reapplied the concept exclusively and dramatically to the last forty years. ... The novelty of Brown's argument lies not only in his new chronology of secularization, but in his use of a range of evidence formerly untouched by historians.'

Jeremy Morris, *Historical Journal*

'[Callum Brown] is one of the most thought-provoking religious historians in Britain today. ... This is a bracing book, and a stimulating read ... a bold attempt to try to explain what happened to Christianity in our land in our lifetime, and it deserves to be taken seriously.'

Frances Knight, *Theology*

'This is one of the most entertaining, moving and stimulating works which I have read upon its subject, modern British Christianity. It has the ring of authenticity to me ...'

Sheridan Gilley, *Reviews in History*

'This 250-page book offers a highly controversial approach to the subject of the decline of Christianity in Britain. ... I thoroughly recommend this book to anyone who has an interest in the decline of religion in the industrialised world generally and of Christianity in particular.'

Frank Pycroft, *Catholics for a Changing Church* website

'Here is a radical and highly readable account of the fortunes of Christianity in modern Britain. ... whether or not one agrees with Brown's conclusions, it is imperative that this highly stimulating book is read widely. I believe it shows beyond doubt that traditional ways of interpreting Victorian religiosity are in their death throes.'

Sarah Williams, *Gospel-culture.org* newsletter

'... this book should be read by anybody who cares about the future of religion. His statistics are convincing and disquieting. Brown argues that within a generation Christianity will merely be a minority movement ... As we face the "death of Christian Britain" may God give us the courage to change.'

Scottish Bulletin of Evangelical Thought

'For anyone who is genuinely interested in the future and mission of the Christian Church at the start of the new millennium, Callum Brown's book should be essential reading . . . this is quite simply a remarkable, courageous and deeply illuminating book. And it is so for a number of crucial reasons. First of all because Brown imagines what for many of us is the unthinkable, namely the complete eradication of the Christian faith from our contemporary social habitat if the decline in religious practice and belief continues in this country unabated into the not too distant future. Secondly because he breaks with the accepted thesis that this is due to an invidious process of secularisation that started some 200 years ago and introduces new insights from cultural theory and gender studies to throw light on the role of public religion in contemporary society. Thirdly because Brown claims, I believe quite rightly, that for too long we have accepted the analysis of social science that investigates only the roles or functions religion exercises in a democratic society.'

Colin Greene, Head of Theology and
Public Policy at The Bible Society,
The Bible in Transmission

'This may be a text book, but it engages the mind and the soul . . . many might even take issue with the title, and refuse to read on. But to do so would be folly: a week spent immersed in Brown's book could reap substantially more fruit than a series of revival meetings.'

Brian Draper, *Amazon.co.uk* review

'Brown's book is full of insight, and his appeal to the cultural forces of late modernity as a corrosive influence on religious adherence is much more nuanced than those one would normally encounter in sociological studies.'

The Revd Canon Professor Martyn Percy,
Ripon College, *Church Times*

'Brown's argument is persuasive and important. As someone who was born in 1945, was sent by non-churchgoing parents to Sunday school and relentlessly bombarded by Christian narratives throughout both primary and grammar schools, who studied the Bible both at school and university and who then experienced the Sixties as an antidote to the stultifying narrow-mindedness and respectability-worship of the Fifties, I repeatedly recognise elements of his analysis as realities I have lived through.'

Richard Poole, *Planet*

'Callum Brown has written a defining text in the debate about secularisation, and a text that every Christian leader should read, then read again.'

Crawford Gribben, *Christianity and Society*

CHRISTIANITY AND SOCIETY IN
THE MODERN WORLD
General editor: Hugh McLeod

THE DEATH OF CHRISTIAN BRITAIN

Understanding secularisation
1800–2000

SECOND EDITION

Callum G. Brown

Routledge
Taylor & Francis Group

LONDON AND NEW YORK

First edition published 2001
by Routledge

This edition published 2009
by Routledge
2 Park Square, Milton Park, Abingdon, Oxon OX14 4RN

Simultaneously published in the USA and Canada
by Routledge
711 Third Avenue, New York, NY 10017

Routledge is an imprint of the Taylor & Francis Group, an informa business

© 2001, 2009 Callum G. Brown

Typeset in Stempel Garamond by
Florence Production Ltd, Stoodleigh, Devon

British Library Cataloguing in Publication Data
A catalogue record for this book is available from the British Library

Library of Congress Cataloging in Publication Data
Brown, Callum G., 1953–
The death of Christian Britain: understanding secularisation, 1800–2000/
Callum G. Brown. – 2nd ed.
p. cm. – (Christianity and society in the modern world)
Includes bibliographical references (p.) and index.
1. Secularism – Great Britain – History – 19th century.
2. Great Britain – Church history – 19th century.
3. Secularism – Great Britain – History – 20th century.
4. Great Britain – Church history – 20th century
I. Title.
BR759.B76 2010   274.1′08–dc22
                        2008045899

ISBN10: 0–415–47133–8 (hbk)
ISBN10: 0–415–47134–6 (pbk)
ISBN10: 0–203–87943–0 (ebk)

ISBN13: 978–0–415–47133–6 (hbk)
ISBN13: 978–0–415–47134–3 (pbk)
ISBN13: 978–0–203–87943–6 (ebk)

CONTENTS

——— •◆• ———

— Contents —

ILLUSTRATIONS

——— .◆. ———

FIGURES

TABLES

ACKNOWLEDGEMENTS

—— ·◆· ——

Secularisation is happening, yet secularisation theory is wrong. It is wrong for different reasons to those I suggested in my previous publications. Where before I believed that better social science would solve the problem of a theory in error, I now understand that the social science was the problem. I took the theory to be apart from the object of study; I see now it was a part of it. As a result, I apologise to my editor, Hugh McLeod, for not writing the book he first suggested in 1994. The presumptions I then held about religion, society and the nature of the social historian's craft suffered a 'reality' slip a year later when Lynn Abrams entered my home. From contesting her blessed discourses, I 'turned' (rather too violently for her liking, I suspect) to a reconception of the issues for this book. She may not have enjoyed living through this one (preferring the one on the Vikings much more), but she has been both inspiration and the post-evangelical companionate partner to it.

I have had to cross much unfamiliar, terrifying but enriching theoretical terrain in this book, and I fear that in striving for the big answer I may not have covered every nook and cranny in argument and method. Readers from diverse specialisms – from religious history, literary linguistics, oral history, women's and gender history, and cultural history – read an early draft in whole or in part in an attempt to save me from my own short-comings. They were: Lynn Abrams (for whom this is a new duty of the domestic angel), Nigel Fabb, Matthew Hilton, Sue Morgan and Penny Summerfield. I am so incredibly indebted to each one for their frank and challenging critiques. My editor, Hugh McLeod, deserves special praise for commenting on so many drafts, correcting so many errors, and manag-ing to be so supportive about the design despite misgivings about the argument. I am also grateful to the fruitful ideas from scholars I met on a visit to the University of Guelph, Ontario, including Elizabeth Ewan and Peter Goddard who introduced me to the work of mediaevalists and Northrop Frye respectively. I have also had most productive discussions on aspects of my interest with David Bebbington, Stewart J. Brown and Mary Heimann, and with the honours history students at Strathclyde

University who took my Popular Culture class over ten years. I alone, of course, bear responsibility for what follows.

In conducting the research, I have been well served by libraries and librarians: Birmingham Central Library, the Harris Library in Preston, and the Stirling Council Library Headquarters where Alan Muirhead kindly guided me to their Drummond Collection. Thanks are also due to the staff at Stirling University Library for striving to meet my access needs to the nineteenth-century Drummond Collection, Peter Nockles at the John Rylands Library of the University of Manchester for guidance on the Methodist collection, and the library staff of New College (Edinburgh), Glasgow, Strathclyde, Lancaster and Central Lancashire universities. I am grateful to Mr A. Halewood of Halewood & Sons Bookshop in Friargate, Preston, for indulging my notetaking from his immense collection of Victorian improving magazines. I must also thank Paul Thompson and the staff of the ESRC Qualidata Archive at the University of Essex, and Elizabeth Roberts of the Centre for North West Regional Studies at the University of Lancaster, for their permission to use oral testimony from their collections.

Finally, I acknowledge the permission of Music Sales Ltd for quoting from the lyrics of 'She's Leaving Home' by John Lennon and Paul McCartney.

ADDENDUM FOR SECOND EDITION

Thanks go to all those audiences – religious, humanist and academic – at home and abroad who have responded to my talks on this book both critically and supportively for seven years. I have benefited especially from intellectual exchange with Lynn Abrams, David Bebbington, Olaf Blaschke, Jan Bremmer, Wim Damberg, Michael Gauvreau, Colin Greene, Lucian Hölscher, Stuart Macdonald, Hugh McLeod, Arie Molendijk, Marit Monteiro, Patrick Pasture, Peter van Rooden, Erik Sidenvall, Michael Snape, Jo Spaans, and Yvonne Maria Werner. I pay tribute to Gerald Parsons, the finest of commentators, and John Wolffe of the Open University who have been supportive of the creation of the second edition, and who contributed much to extending the readership and analysis of the first edition. To Gerald and Hugh, the series editor, go special thanks for reading an earlier draft of chapter 10 and saving me from some grievous errors. All remaining ones are my fault.

Callum Brown
September 2008

ABBREVIATIONS

———— ·◆· ————

CNWRS, SA	Centre for North West Regional Studies, Sound Archive, University of Lancaster
FAM	Family Intergenerational Interviews, Qualidata Archive
FLWE	Family Life and Work Experience before 1918 Collection, Qualidata Archive
QA	Qualidata Archive, ESRC Qualitative Data Archival Resource Centre, University of Essex
SOHCA	Scottish Oral History Centre Archive, Department of History, University of Strathclyde

NOTE ON
ORAL HISTORY

—— ·◆· ——

The oral-history testimonies from the FAM, CNWRS and SOHCA collections bear pseudonyms in the text. At the request of the Qualidata Archive,
the testimonies in the FLWE collection (of persons born in the late nineteenth century) bear the interviewees' real names. In all cases, notes provide
full archival reference numbers.

And when I look at a history book and think of the imaginative effort it has taken to squeeze this oozing world between two boards and typeset, I am astonished. Perhaps the event has an unassailable truth. God saw it. God knows. But I am not God. And so when someone tells me what they heard or saw, I believe them, and I believe their friend who also saw, but not in the same way, and I can put these accounts together and I will not have a seamless wonder but a sandwich laced with mustard of my own.

Jeanette Winterson, *Oranges Are Not The Only Fruit*, London, Vintage, 1991, p. 93.

CHAPTER ONE

INTRODUCTION

—— .•. ——

This book is about the death of Christian Britain[1] – the demise of the nation's core religious and moral identity. As historical changes go, this has been no lingering and drawn-out affair. It took several centuries (in what historians used to call the Dark Ages) to convert Britain to Christianity, but it has taken less than forty years for the country to forsake it. For a thousand years, Christianity penetrated deeply into the lives of the people, enduring Reformation, Enlightenment and industrial revolution by adapting to each new social and cultural context that arose. Then, really quite suddenly in 1963, something very profound ruptured the character of the nation and its people, sending organised Christianity on a downward spiral to the margins of social significance. In unprecedented numbers, the British people since the 1960s have stopped going to church, have allowed their church membership to lapse, have stopped marrying in church and have neglected to baptise their children. Meanwhile, their children, the two generations who grew to maturity in the last thirty years of the twentieth century, stopped going to Sunday school, stopped entering confirmation or communicant classes, and rarely, if ever, stepped inside a church to worship in their entire lives. The cycle of inter-generational renewal of Christian affiliation, a cycle which had for so many centuries tied the people however closely or loosely to the churches and to Christian moral benchmarks, was permanently disrupted in the 'swinging sixties'. Since then, a formerly religious people have entirely forsaken organised Christianity in a sudden plunge into a truly secular condition.

This book sets out on an ambitious and probably controversial journey to understand what happened. It is not merely a chronicle of what befell the churches or the faith of the British people; nor is it a foray into conventional social history to seek social causes of declining popular religiosity; nor is it a sociology of modern British religion, or what's left of it. The story being told here is not to be found in books on 'the church in crisis', religious history or sociology of religion. What is attempted is rather different. The aim is to look at how the British people in the past – in the nineteenth and first half of the twentieth centuries – absorbed Christianity

I

into their lives and then, from the 1960s, stopped doing so. The techniques deployed in this book are new, drawn from modern cultural theory, and they provide a fresh and different interpretation of what makes a society Christian in the first place and what happens when it dechristianises. The techniques allow us to revise the narrative of religious decline, or what is commonly called secularisation, and to appreciate anew its causes, nature and timing. What emerges is a story not merely of church decline, but of the end of Christianity as a means by which men and women, as individuals, construct their identities and their sense of 'self'. This breach in British history, starting in the 1960s, is something more fundamental than just 'failing churches'. What is explored and analysed is a short and sharp cultural revolution of the late twentieth century which makes the Britons of the year 2000 fundamentally different in character from those of 1950 or 1900 or 1800, or from peoples in many other countries.

There is no pleasure in proclaiming the death of Christian Britain. Some people will be able to catalogue tremendous losses – of faith, of succour in worship, of social activity in church organisations, of a sense of spirituality. There is the loss of old certainties, that fixed moral core which Britons as a whole used to recognise even when they deviated from it. Christianity was, to borrow a metaphor of one scholar, like a banister upon which a person leaned when climbing or descending stairs.[2] It was a fixture in our lives, conservative by instinct and little changing in nature, by which individuals knew and trusted others by their respectability in family behaviour and conformity to the Christian Sunday. On the other hand, many people will be able to identify gains from the decentring of rigid moral codes – such as increased sexual freedom and freedom for diverse sexualities, greater gender equality, and a new tolerance of religious and ethnic difference. One could say, not altogether flippantly, that the decline of Christian certainty in British society since the 1950s has meant that respectability has been supplanted by respect – in which moral criticism of difference has been replaced by toleration and greater freedom to live our lives in the way we choose.

Indeed, one of the hallmarks of Britain in the year 2000 is the recent growth of ethnic diversity, largely through immigration, and the rise of a multi-faith society in which Christianity has been joined by Islam, Hinduism and the Sikh religion, amongst others. However, what has been noticeable to all observers is that the strength of attachment to other religions in Britain has not, in the main, suffered the collapse that has afflicted the bulk of the Christian churches. In the black and Asian communities of Britain, non-Christian religions are in general thriving. Moreover, one of the few sections in our society where Christian churches are thriving is in the predominantly black communities. Yet, it must be emphasised that the haemorrhage of British Christianity has not come about as a result of competition from or conversion to other churches. No new religion, no new credo, not even a state-sponsored secularism, has been there to displace it.

It is not especially novel to proclaim that the Christian churches are in decline in Britain. But what is new is the idea of the death of Christian Britain. To propose that this is possible, let alone happening or happened, will be disturbing to many people. Christians may find it controversial, especially church leaders and clergy who, despite watching the inexorable decline of members year-on-year for the last four decades, still in the main hold to an optimistic outlook for their religion. Some clergy, especially of the liberal mainstream Christian denominations, locate the future of their religion within a 'multi-faith' vision of society in which ecumenism and church union introduce a new acknowledgement of the validity of religious experience and belief derived from other religious traditions. Many church-people may find the claim excessive, especially since the *UK Christian Handbook* suggests that in 1995 as many as 65 per cent of Britons were 'Christian'.[3] More widely, the death of Christian Britain will be controversial to others because the 'death' of a religion has hitherto been unimagined – except when a secular socialist state, state repression, religious 'reformation', or military-supported religious imperialism has threatened a faith, none of which apply to Britain in the new millennium. It will also be controversial to a large group of scholars in the social sciences and humanities (including sociology, church history and social history) for whom the decline of religion is not something new but something very, very old. For most scholars, Christian religion in Britain, Europe and North America has been in almost constant decay for at least a century, and for some sociologists and historians for even longer – for between two hundred and five hundred years. They have imagined religious decline as one of the characteristics of the modern world, caused by the advance of reason through the Protestant Reformation and the Enlightenment, and through the social and economic dislocation of the industrial revolution. What scholars have imagined is religious decline as a long-term process that has left today's Britons with a residual Christian belief but no churchgoing habit. In all of these cases, Christian decay in Britain has been perceived as a decline without an imagined end. This book imagines the end.

The first and most obvious manifestation is the Christian churches in crisis. In the year 2000 less than 8 per cent of people attend Sunday worship in any week, less than a quarter are members of any church, and fewer than a tenth of children attend a Sunday school. Fewer than half of couples get married in church, and about a third of couples cohabit without marriage. In England only a fifth of babies get baptised in the Church of England, and in Scotland one estimate is that about a fifth are baptised in either the Church of Scotland or the Roman Catholic Church. By some calculations, as few as 3 per cent of people regularly attend church in some counties of England, and in most the non-churchgoers represent over

90 per cent of the population. If church participation is falling, all the figures for Christian affiliation are at their lowest point in recorded history. Christian church membership accounts for less than 12 per cent of the people and is falling. There is now a severe crisis of Christian associational activity: religious voluntary organisations, which formerly mushroomed around congregations and independent missions, account for a minuscule fraction of recreational activities. Most critical is the emerging evidence of the decay of Christian belief. Though 74 per cent of people express a belief in the existence of some kind of God or 'higher power', 50 per cent or fewer subscribe to the existence of sin, the soul, heaven, hell or life after death – while the numbers having specific faith in Jesus Christ as the risen Lord are considered so statistically insignificant that opinion pollsters do not even ask the question.[4] Whilst some non-Christian religions are growing in Britain as they are elsewhere – notably Islam and comparatively small 'new religions' like Mormonism – growing religions are not filling the spiritual vacuum being deserted by Christianity.[5]

So weak are the demographics of church connection that the government is now contemplating disestablishing the Church of England (the last state church in the countries of the UK), whilst the Church of Scotland is contemplating destroying its historic status as the National Kirk by a union with three other denominations.[6] Church authorities every week deal with the disposal of church buildings by selling them off as carpet showrooms or for conversion into 'des. res.' flats, while older cathedrals and minsters survive by transformation into heritage sites for historical–religious tourism rather than religious worship.[7] In such ways, Christianity is becoming Britain's past, not its present. The Christian churches have not only fallen in size but also in moral standing. They were once a safe and unmoveable fixture at the heart of national standards, but now confidence in the probity of church leaders is almost weekly challenged by scandal. In the last five years, at least one Catholic bishop and a seemingly endless line of priests have admitted to having sex with women, a significant minority of priests and nuns stand accused of child abuse, Protestant ministers and elders (of both sexes) are accused of extra-marital relations, gay priests are starting to 'come out', and even accusations of financial impropriety have been levelled at some clergy.[8] To be sure, these are small minorities in each of these categories, but such public scandals are destabilising the moral certainty formerly vested in Christian churches.

Also under threat are the Christian churches as fixtures in the landscape of British institutions. Ecclesiastical statisticians are now routinely predicting the disappearance of churches. Major denominations, ranging from the Roman Catholic Church to the Church of Scotland, are short of recruits to be priests and ministers.[9] Britain's leading church statistician, Peter Brierley, has warned that declining popular support will cause some denominations to disappear during this century. The Church of Scotland in 1997 even put a date on its own demise through membership loss – in the year 2033.[10] As never before, church leaders are being forced to think the unthinkable as every statistic, and every balance sheet of income and expenditure, forces them not just to close church buildings, but to think about where this inexorable 'down-sizing' is leading. Crumbs of comfort have come in the last decade from evidence that the British people still recognise the existence of God even if they do not attend church. As Grace Davie, a leading religious sociologist has put it, the people are 'believing without belonging'. However, even she acknowledges that 'the content of belief is drifting further and further from the Christian norm'.[11]

The situation was not always like this, and it is surprising how recent that was. Between 1945 and 1958 there were surges of British church membership, Sunday school enrolment, Church of England Easter Day communicants, baptisms and religious solemnisation of marriage, accompanied by immense popularity for evangelical 'revivalist' crusades (the most well-known being those of the American Southern Baptist preacher, Dr Billy Graham). Accompanying these was a vigorous reassertion of 'traditional' values: the role of women as wives and mothers, moral panic over deviancy and 'delinquency', and an economic and cultural austerity which applauded 'respectability', thrift and sexual restraint. Not since the late Victorian period had there been such powerful evidence of a professing Christian people in Britain. Nor was Britain unique. In the United States between 1942 and 1960, popular religiosity and institutional church strength not only continued to grow, but earlier denominationalism gave way to a vigorous and inclusive religious culture which – as in Britain – nurtured conservatism and traditional values, whilst church membership *per capita* grew faster than at any time since the recording of statistics began in 1890.[12] In Australia, the period 1955 to 1963 has been described as a 'modest religious boom' which affected every denomination across all the measurable indices of religious life, characterised by the same crusading evangelism and social conservatism as in Britain and the United States.[13] In most regions of West Germany between 1952 and 1967 there was a modest rise in church-going amongst the Protestant population, whilst in France, Spain, Belgium and the Netherlands in the 1950s a resilient religious observance underpinned confessionalist politics.[14] National experiences varied greatly, and there were exceptions (notably in Scandinavia), but there is clear evidence that in the mid-twentieth century there was a significant resilience to Christianity in Britain and much of the Western world.

On a surface level, the 1950s appeared to be the beginning of our modern and contemporary condition. Britons then were appreciating the beginnings of the new technology which presaged our world of 2000: nuclear power (which went on stream in 1957), television (which spread quickly to most homes after the broadcast of Queen Elizabeth II's coronation in 1953), and labour-saving kitchen appliances (like refrigerators and modern electric cookers). The welfare state was under full construction, cities were being modernised by comprehensive town planning (slum-clearance and the building of peripheral housing estates and new towns), and there was a start being made to the expansion of higher education. But to perceive a modern 'feel' to the 1950s is merely to probe skin-deep. It is a measurement made overwhelmingly in terms of things, not in terms of what the British people felt, did or thought. In its cultural climate, the 1950s was in fact a deeply old-fashioned era, so old that it has often been described as the last Victorian decade. Nearly 2 million people came to hear Billy Graham preach in London in a short religious crusade in 1954, and a further 1.2 million came in Glasgow in 1955, with 100,000 worshippers packing Hampden Park football stadium for a single religious service. Nothing like it had been seen before in British Protestantism, and nothing like it has been seen again. The mental world which produced this in the 1950s was not just a world of a tiny minority, held together by the sub-culture of a closeted and defensive Christian community. The mental world which drew in those worshippers was a national culture, widely broadcast through books, magazines and radio, and deeply ingrained in the rhetoric with which people conversed about each other and about themselves. It was a world profoundly conservative in morals and outlook, and fastidious in its adherence to respectability and moral standards. Many people may have been hypocritical, but that world made them very aware of their hypocrisy.

A vast chasm separates us from the mid-twentieth century condition. Religious statistics show how far away that world of the 1950s was from ours in the year 2000, and how much closer it was to the world of 1900. Take the types of marriage – religious or civil – which couples undertook. In 1900, 85 per cent of marriages in England and Wales (and 94 per cent in Scotland) were religiously solemnised. By 1957, 72 per cent of marriages in England and Wales (and 83 per cent in Scotland) were still by religious rites. But in the 1960s, decline was rapid. In England and Wales, religious marriage fell from 70 per cent in 1962 to 60 per cent in 1970, and continued to decline to 39 per cent in 1997. In Scotland, the fall over the same period was from 80 per cent in 1962, to 71 per cent in 1970, and then to 55 per cent in 1997. The position has been even worse for Christianity than these figures suggest, because an increasing proportion of religious nuptials has been by non-Christian rites. These statistics might appear bad for the state of religious marriage, but in the year 2000 they actually constitute the highest indicator of religiosity there is. All the other measures of Christian activity and adherence are markedly worse in both absolute terms and in terms of rate of decline. Take the proportion of infants baptised in the nation's largest Christian church, the Church of England. Out of every 1,000 live births, 609 baptisms were performed in the Church in 1900; by 1927 the proportion had actually risen to 668, the highest ever, and even by 1956 the figure was 602. But then it fell dramatically – to 466 in 1970,

365 in 1981 and 228 in 1997. Or take the level of church membership in the population at large. Between the 1840s (when data become available) and the year 2000, the best estimates indicate that the peak year of church adherence per head of population came in 1904 for England and Wales and 1905 for Scotland. After some decline over the next forty years, the proportion rose again to a peak in England and Wales in 1959 only 11 per cent lower than at the start of the century; in Scotland the peak came in 1956, and was only about 6 per cent lower than in 1900. This relatively minor decline was followed after 1963 by steep decline. In Scotland total church adherence *per capita* was 46 per cent lower in 1994 compared to 1905, whilst the proportion of the population who were Easter communicants in the Church of England had halved by the end of the 1980s compared to the start of the century.[15]

These dry, impersonal statistics reveal an important thing. They show that people's lives in the 1950s were very acutely affected by genuflection to religious symbols, authority and activities. Christianity intruded in very personal ways into the manner of people's comportment through their lives, through the rites of passage and through their Sundays. Religion mattered and mattered deeply in British society as a whole in the 1950s. But it started to stop mattering in the 1960s. Something happened to change the destiny of these statistics of church connection and activity, statistics which had moved up and down only slowly for over a hundred years but which very suddenly plunged.

There is a need for imagining this 'endgame' of Christian decline in Britain. It is needed for reasons of scholarship, for reasons of understanding our contemporary society and its future, or for simply needing to know whether church buildings and church schools are going to be needed for much longer. At a simple level, it is not acceptable – logically – to continue perceiving Britain's (or any other country's) principal religion as 'in decline' without conceptualising where the decline is heading (or has already arrived). At a more complex level, whilst commentators concentrate attention on the continuing statistical evidence of church decline at the start of the twenty-first century, it may be more imperative to pose the question whether the meaningful event – the destiny-shaping turning-point – has already passed. Was there some perceptible change of a much wider and more profound nature in around 1963 which triggered the downward march of all statistical and related evidence of popular religiosity? To declare Christianity dead, do you wait until the proportion of people who attend church, who pray to a living personal Christian God, who get married in a church or who baptise their children, falls below 50 per cent, 25 per cent, or 10 per cent? Alternatively, do you wait until the last church closes or the last Christian dies? When dealing with a society, its Christian construction depends on not just the existence of churches or Christians within it. Muslims, Jews and many other non-Christian faiths exist in

Britain in the year 2000, but nobody attributes them with defining the character of the nation's culture. The point here is that the mere presence of Christian churches or Christian people in Britain does not make, and never has made, Britain Christian, and their mere gradual disappearance does not in itself make it unchristian. What made Britain Christian was the way in which Christianity infused public culture and was adopted by individuals, whether churchgoers or not, in forming their own identities. Before getting to religious decline, the conception of religiosity must be made wider and deeper.

What happened at the point of secularisation helps us to grasp what constitutes Christian religiosity. What is 'ending' in Christian Britain as we start a new millennium is something more elemental than merely the churches failing to attract the people to worship. The 1960s' revolution was about how people constructed their lives – their families, their sex lives, their cultural pursuits, and their moral identities of what makes a 'good' or 'bad' person. For example, Christianity has been challenged not just by the decline of religious marriage, but by the decline of marriage itself as cohabitation rises steeply. Similarly, the transformation is not just to be measured in the growth of sexual activity with multiple partners, contrary to traditional Christian rules on sex with nobody but a spouse, but by the decriminalisation of homosexuality in 1967 and the overt pride displayed since by those in gay relationships. This is a most fundamental change in morality since the 1950s. Similar changes have happened to women since the 1960s – changes that have gone further in this country than almost any other: the increasing proportions of women who never marry, never have children, and the increasing age at which those who do have children start their families. This does not infer that unmarried sexually-active people, gays, older mothers of young children, and childless spinsters cannot be Christians. That is not the point. The point is that the complex web of legally and socially accepted rules which governed individual identity in Christian Britain until the 1950s has been swept aside since the 1960s. Secularisation is to be located, in part at least, in the changing conditions which allowed previously regarded Christian and social 'sins' to be regarded as acceptable and moral, at least by many, in British society in 2000.

Consequently, identifying the end of Christian Britain – its date – is bound up with defining what Christian Britain was before it died. Much of this book is concerned with this task. What actually constitutes the 'end' of the religious nation can only be truly appreciated by taking a vantage point from which we can perceive what has been lost and when it was lost. This is why an historical perspective is most important. To be aware of the magnitude and character of such fundamental cultural and religious change, we have to look at the starting point and reassess its character.

The starting point for any study of British secularisation has traditionally been the birth and rise of British urban and industrial society.

Historians have evolved a rather pessimistic view of religion's role in Britain between 1800 and 1963, based on two major hypotheses. The first of these is that the growth of industrial cities in the nineteenth century caused a decline in religiosity. The second hypothesis is that within cities (and smaller towns as well), the working classes became in broad terms alienated from organised religion and were the leading edge of secularisation. These two notions have been deeply ingrained in both ecclesiastical and historical understanding of British Christianity over the last two hundred years. In this book, both arguments will be challenged in their own terms by a re-examination of the evidence which supports them. But they will also be challenged by showing how the hypotheses have tended to foster very biased ways of constructing and 'reading' the evidence. The book offers an alternative religious history of modern Britain in which dispute is taken with the received wisdom that in the nineteenth and first half of the twentieth centuries Britain was a secularising place in which religious decline was a product of the social chasm between 'slum' and suburb, or between working and middle classes. In so doing, the dating of religious decline is shifted from the nineteenth century to the late twentieth century.

As a result, this book re-brands Britain of 1800 to 1963 as a highly religious nation, and the period as the nation's last puritan age. The Britain of our nearest forefathers is re-branded as a deeply Christian country of unprecedented churchgoing levels and the most strict religious rules of personal conduct. This puritanism was imposed not by the state but by the people themselves. Building on the work of some historians who have been 'optimistic' about religion in Victorian society, this task is undertaken through a reconception of what it meant to be a 'religious' person in a 'religious' society. In the chapters that follow the way in which Christian piety was imagined and represented between 1800 and 1950 is examined in some detail, to show the extent to which Christianity informed the individual woman and the individual man about their own identities. At the heart of this vision of Christian piety was evangelicalism which constructed a highly gendered conception of religiosity. Evangelical puritanism impinged mostly upon women rather than upon men. The book focuses considerable attention on how piety was conceived as an overwhelmingly feminine trait which challenged masculinity and left men demonised and constantly anxious. It was modern evangelicalism that raised the piety of woman, the 'angel in the house', to reign over the moral weakness and innate temptations of masculinity. Reversing pre-industrial society's privileging of male piety, this evangelical gendered framework for religion dominated public discourse and rhetoric, not just in the nineteenth century, but for the first six decades of the twentieth century as well. As a result, women, rather than cities or social class, emerge as the principal source of explanation for the patterns of religiosity that were observable in the nineteenth and twentieth centuries.

Most importantly, two other things will emerge. First, women were the bulwark to popular support for organised Christianity between 1800 and 1963, and second it was they who broke their relationship to Christian piety in the 1960s and thereby caused secularisation.

This account differs substantially from existing British religious history and narratives on secularisation. How British Christianity got to the state it is in at the year 2000 is currently understood almost universally in terms of the theory of long-term secularisation which was developed academically initially by sociologists, but since the 1950s has been adopted in whole or in part almost universally by historians. The theory of secularisation posits that religion is naturally 'at home' in pre-industrial and rural environments, and that it declines in industrial and urban environments. The rise of modernity from the eighteenth century – the growth of machines, rationality, class division and dissenting churches, and the supposed decline of primitive husbandry, superstition and harmonious social relations – destroyed both the community foundations of the church and the psychological foundations of a universal religious world-view. Secularisation, it is traditionally argued, was the handmaiden of modernisation, pluralisation, urbanisation and Enlightenment rationality. Consequently, the theory identifies the main origins of British secularisation in the industrial revolution and urban growth of the late eighteenth and early nineteenth centuries, which then accelerated in the later nineteenth and early twentieth centuries. For most investigative scholars of social history and sociology, British industrial society was already 'secular' before it had hardly begun.[16] This is referred to as the traditional, 'pessimist' view of religion in industrial society, an outlook which has dominated British academic life since around 1960.[17]

From the early 1970s, social historians of religion became progressively disenchanted with the theory of secularisation. Its sweeping claims made many uneasy when their empirical research revealed a complexity to the historical and social landscape that the theory seemed unable to encompass (leading some scholars into an ambivalence and sometimes an ambiguous silence about the theory), and when some research began to undermine – whether intentionally or not – the theory's causative explanations and traditional chronology of religious decline.[18] From the early 1980s, a revisionist school of 'optimist' scholarship became discernible – a growing scholarship which argued more directly that the theory of secularisation was wrong in whole or in part because it failed to account for the observable success of religion in nineteenth-century British industrial society.[19] Quite separately and simultaneously, scholars in other parts of the world also started to problematise and challenge secularisation theory with new empirical research – especially in the United States where pluralisation of urban denominations was re-assessed as correlating with increasing religiosity rather than its diminution as the theory predicts.[20] The accumulative effect of this work in Britain has been to push back the timing of religious decline from the late eighteenth and early nineteenth centuries to the late nineteenth and early twentieth centuries, and to make the early decline of popular religiosity appear more gradualist, nuanced and regionalised.[21]

However, the revisionism of scholars who are 'optimistic' about religiosity in urban society leaves two major problems. The first of these is empirical – the evidence already introduced briefly of sustained church growth and high religiosity among the British people in the 1940s and 1950s. The second problem is more fundamental. Whilst revision to the theory of secularisation has transformed understanding of the social history of religion in the eighteenth and nineteenth centuries through new methods[22] and model-building,[23] and has done much to destroy the validity and utility of the theory,[24] the way revisionism has gone about this task has been almost as flawed as secularisation theory itself. Scholars (including the present author) have been trying for years to qualify or disparage secularisation theory on its own terms – using the same methods and the same conceptualisation of the issue. But this has meant studying the nineteenth and early twentieth centuries in something close to obsessive detail, and has resulted in showing that secularisation took place more slowly, marginally later, and less completely than the theory originally suggested. But it has left the theory still in place, if not intact. This is a critical failing. By merely rescheduling the timing and gradient of secularisation, revisionism has left unmodified the core notion of religious decline as a prolonged, unilinear and inevitable consequence of modernity. By relying upon improved social-science investigation of religiosity to revise secularisation theory, revisionism has mistaken what the problem is.

The problem is social science itself and its definition of religion. The social-scientific study of religion has been one of the great projects of Enlightenment modernity. From the late eighteenth century to the present, religion has been defined, measured and 'understood' through 'empirical' evidence spawned by the supposed 'neutrality' of social science. Social science has privileged a 'rationalist' approach to religion which assigns importance to 'formal religion' and which denigrates or ignores 'folk religion', 'superstition' and acts of personal faith not endorsed by the churches. It privileges numbers, counting religion by measures of members or worshippers, and ignores the unquantifiable in argument and methodology. It makes religion an institutional 'thing' of society, in the form of the churches, religious organisations, the act of going to church, the act of stating a belief in God and so on. In doing so, social science dichotomises people: into churchgoers and non-churchgoers, into believers and unbelievers, those who pray and those who don't, into 'the religious' and 'the non-religious'. It is reductionist to bipolarities.

This chapter, of course, has already been guilty of this charge. In order to introduce discussion of religious decline, statistics have been cited in some profusion, dividing the people into churchgoers and non-churchgoers. This was deliberate and unavoidable. There is at present no well-developed alternative *modus operandi* in which to explore religiosity and its decline. To provide any analysis on religion in society in the last two centuries, scholarship (as well as church management) has demanded social-science method, and that demand continues today unabated as churches commission statistical projections of their own decline. But the argument of this book is that this social-science method obliterates whole realms of religiosity which cannot be counted. More than that, the argument is that the definitions of religiosity used by today's Christian churches rely on the social-science method initiated by evangelical churchmen of the 1790s and 1800s. Seduced by Enlightenment rationality, it was they who gave us the definitions of religion with which we today are still obsessed. One task of this book is to break this circular and enclosed form of reasoning, to bring the bipolarities of 'the churchgoing' and 'the non-churchgoing' under the microscope of examination, and to challenge the whole social-scientific project on religion.

Social science is not only reductionist in telling us what religion 'is', but what it 'does'. As thinking people interested in the state of religion in society, we talk about it in rhetoric, in the very language, created by social science. What social science did was give birth to the notion that religion has 'roles' or 'functions' in society. Broadly speaking, virtually all historical and sociological studies of religion and society have envisaged the 'role' of religion in four 'forms': *institutional Christianity* (the people's adherence to churches and practise of worship and religious rites), *intellectual Christianity* (the influence of religious ideas in society at large and of religious belief in individuals), *functional Christianity* (the role of religion in civil society, especially local government, education and welfare), and *diffusive Christianity* (the role of outreach religion amongst the people). These 'roles' have traditionally formed the basis for measuring the 'social significance of religion'[25] and are important matters for research. But the argument here is that the way each of these four 'functions' or 'roles' operates in a modern society depends on something more basic. There is a higher-level 'form' that religion takes. In this book it is called *discursive Christianity*.

Discursive Christianity is defined using modern cultural theory. Christian religiosity of the industrial era is defined as the people's subscription to protocols of personal identity which they derive from Christian expectations, or discourses, evident in their own time and place. Protocols are rituals or customs of behaviour, economic activity, dress, speech and so on which are collectively promulgated as necessary for Christian identity. The protocols are prescribed or implied in discourses on Christian behaviour. The discourses may be official ones from churches or clergy, public ones from the media, 'community' ones from within an ethnic group, a street or a family, or private ones developed by men and women themselves. The discourses will tend to be uniform, though the protocols need not be; indeed, they may be contradictory (as we shall see later). The discourses will be manifest in the protocols of behaviour (going to church on a Sunday, or saying grace before meals), but they will also be discerned in the 'voices' of the people. These voices are 'heard' as reported speech by contemporaries, as autobiography and oral-history testimony, and as biography and obituary (where the question of who is 'speaking' becomes a little complex). By listening to these voices, and by consulting the dominant media of the time (such as popular books, magazines and religious tracts), we can trace how the discourses circulated in society, how the protocols were derived from them, and how individual people in their testimony of autobiography and oral record show a personal adoption of religious discourses. This process is known by oral historians as 'subjectification' of discourse where people have been reflexive to the environment of circulating discourses. This is a personal process of subscription to often very public discourses, but can involve also very private (indeed sometimes intensely secret) protocols related to those discourses. This subscription is thus not necessarily an action which unifies individuals' behaviour or religious beliefs, but it creates a compelling religious culture (in the jargon a 'discursivity') to the construction of religiosity in the society at large. In this way, we reconstruct an individual's religious identity from how they in their own words reflected Christianity.

This fifth, discursive, conception of Christian religiosity is taken here as the prerequisite of all other roles of religion in society: of institutional, intellectual, functional and diffusive Christianity. For Christianity to have social significance – for it to achieve popular participation, support or even acquiescence – in a 'democratic' society free from state regulation of religious habits, it must have a base of discursivity. Otherwise, it is inconceivable. Concomitantly, secularisation – the decay of religiosity in all four traditional forms – is inconceivable without decay in discursive religiosity in which there is a loss of popular acceptance and recirculation of those discourses.

This method involves the relegation of social science as a method of inquiry. This is because the statistics and 'rational' measures of religion upon which historians and churchmen have traditionally relied are themselves products of that discursive Christianity. Christian discourse of the period 1800 to 1950 defined a 'religious person' in a variety of ways, but vital ones were as churchgoer and church member. Similarly, one key element in the definition of secularisation is the decline in churchgoing and church membership. These are not neutral measures of religiosity; they are highly specific ones in historical terms which applied in the nineteenth and twentieth centuries but not, for instance, in seventeenth-century England.[26] In this way, the theory of secularisation is constructed around the discourses of a specific age. As a consequence, critical to the method and the order of this volume is the relegation of social science to the status of a discursive constituent of the secularisation debate. The temptation to deal with the 'hard data' first in a book such as this is very great, even when the purpose is to show their shortcomings and inconsistencies. In Chapter 2, the discursive nature of religious statistics is shown through studying the intellectual origins of data collection on religion. But the data themselves have been relegated towards the end of the book so that they may be understood in the light of being themselves the product of Christian discourse on what protocols people should follow to establish their Christian identity. The bulk of the book – Chapters 3 to 7 – focuses on the period 1800 to 1950. It starts by examining the media, symbols and agencies for the circulation of religious discourses in Britain (Chapter 3). It proceeds to examine the discourses and their highly gendered construction (Chapters 4 and 5). Next, it turns to the subjectification of the discourses by individuals, following their penetration into people's accounts of their own lives (personal histories revealed through autobiography and oral history) and their translation into protocols of religious identity (Chapter 6). It is in the next chapter that the statistics of religiosity are interpreted, allowing a 'reading' of them as not neutral and social-scientific measures of religiosity, but as products of discourse (Chapter 7). Finally, the book turns to the period 1950 to 2000 to examine the final flourish of discursive Christianity in the religious growth of the late 1940s and 1950s, followed by its spectacular collapse in the 1960s and the secularisation of Christian Britain which ensued (Chapter 8).

The analytical heart of the book is Chapter 6. This is where we listen to people rather than counting them as numbers, as they speak about themselves and their lives. In the process, we 'hear' how the discourses of religious identity of the periods in which they lived were internalised and made personal, each constructing his or her idea of 'self' and structuring the stories of their lives in symmetry to the expectations of Christian life stories. This reflexivity of personal identities to discursive Christianity becomes the method to establish Britain as a Christian nation from 1800 to 1950, and the method to understand (or 'read') the 'hard data' of Chapter 7. In particular, it is through the individual's negotiation between discourses on religion on the one hand and discourses on other things (such as femininity, masculinity, respectability, parenting) on the other, and *then* in a negotiation between those discourses and the needs of day-to-day life, that some of the characteristics of the 'hard data' become intelligible. Where social-science 'structuralism' has one set of explanations for statistics of religiosity before 1950, the individual's personal subjectifying of Christian discourses can offer radical alternatives.

Chapter 8 focuses on the 1950s and 1960s and the issue of change to Christian discourse. It looks at how British people re-imagined themselves in ways no longer Christian – a 'moral turn' which abruptly under-mined virtually all of the protocols of moral identity. Ironically, it was at this very moment that social science reached the height of its influence in church affairs and in academe. Secularisation theory became the universally accepted way of understanding the decline of religion as something of the past – of the late eighteenth and early nineteenth centuries. The 1960s viewed itself as the end of secularisation. But by listening to the people themselves, this book suggests it was actually the beginning.

CHAPTER TWO

THE PROBLEM WITH 'RELIGIOUS DECLINE'

— .◆. —

THE WORLD WE HAVE LOST

'Religious decline' is an emotive, loaded term. It is the product of a long tradition which runs deep into the conceptual framework of social science and into the modern Christian church's construction of its 'mission'.

Religious decline in Britain is intellectually located in the distance between two 'worlds': the pre-industrial and the industrial. Pre-industrial society was the world we have lost – a world of innocence, humble spirituality, economic simplicity and social harmony.[1] Industrialisation and the growth of large cities started the rapid decline of the churches, religious belief and religious morality. Piety and machines were disconnected and opposing. By contrast, the world we have found was and remains a world of technology, competitiveness, and social dislocation, with piety a transient signifier of class identity.[2]

This secularisation narrative did not originate in the twentieth-century academy but in the late eighteenth-century world of changing power relations. To proclaim 'faith in danger' has been the perpetual task of churches in all historical ages to defend against backsliding, but it was only transformed into a perpetual thesis of 'religion in decline' in the special circumstances of agricultural improvement and industrial revolution. The thesis of decline has since been proclaimed by various interested parties. The first and by far the biggest group has been churchmen – parsons, ministers, priests and preachers – who have maintained an incessant clamour on the issue since the late eighteenth century. Within this group, the precise message has varied very significantly. Clergy of the established or state churches – the Church of England and the Church of Scotland – have had at the forefront of their minds the danger to their churches posed by the rise of alternative or dissenting churches. Pessimism about faith has for this group been closely related to a fear of loss of power. At national level within England and Wales, the Church of England has enjoyed privileged positions in the House of Lords and in the influencing of policy on a wide range of issues. Many of those issues have been to do with the devolved or local power of the state church: the exertion of influence in poor relief, education, moral control and so on. As established churches, the Church of England and the Church of Scotland exerted their power most effectively over the people directly, with the parish church the focus of considerable formal control over parishioners' lives. The rise of Methodism and Protestant dissenting churches in the eighteenth and early nineteenth centuries challenged that power and threatened the status of the vicar or minister.[3] Religious apathy or indifference also threatened that power, but only if the numbers of people got out of hand. Secularism, the concerted attachment to religious unbelief, was a similar threat. But of the three, established churchmen feared dissenters the most because they vastly outnumbered secularists and because they gave the indifferent the excuse not to submit to parish authority.

If established churchmen had immediate cause to shout loudly about religious decline, their message had a resonance with others. The 'establishment' – the political and social elites – were frequently heard joining in the clamour. Landowners relied on a combination of economic power (over tenants, tradesmen and the families reliant on them) and social power, and the latter depended significantly on the symbolic role of the parish church. The parish church and the manor house were the twin seats of local power, and the vicar and the lord or laird were the joint holders of that power. The parish churches were heavily dependent on the landowners for construction and maintenance, and the clergyman was usually selected by a member of the landowning classes (or by the Crown, which meant the same), and the minister relied for income derived from English tithes or Scottish teinds upon the produce of the land.[4] Church and land were tied together, whilst in towns municipality and church were also closely, though more complexly, bound. This made Sunday service immensely symbolic of local power. The English lord sat in his front-row boxed pew (and his Scottish equivalent in the 'laird's loft' at the back or side of the church), the clergyman was in his pulpit, and the parishioners sat in ranked pews allocated, rented or bought according to social and economic status.[5] To attend church was to participate in a parade of power, to submit symbolically to God and to Mammon. The two were not at odds, but in cahoots. Any threat to the one was a threat to the other, and for this reason the landed elites had immediate cause to wish their people in obedience to the church as they would have them in obedience to themselves.[6]

This system started to crumble in the eighteenth century. The disintegration was a slow process, and extended in some places until the middle decades of the nineteenth century. In a few places, such as the Highlands, Hebrides and Northern Isles, the eighteenth century actually witnessed the *rise* of the parish state as these inaccessible areas were brought within the national church and the national economy.[7] But elsewhere, Britain was being changed by new wealth, by increasing trading and manufacturing, creating a society with a sharpened awareness that the economic bonds which tied people to parish, land and landowner were dissolving. Agricultural improvement hastened that process, as landowners enclosed common fields and reorganised farming society as a hierarchy of rentiers, tenant farmers and farm workers. With new wealth and changing social sensibilities, the rich made country homes a place of retreat, not of permanent residence, and the lord's pew in the parish church was more often than not vacant at Sunday worship. The ecclesiastical bonding of plebs and lords in country and village was dissolving. This was a process hastened for many by the formation of textile villages in the eighteenth century where the rule of the landowner rarely held, and where, in many cases, distance from the parish church necessitated millowners or villagers to erect a church – usually not of the establishment but of dissent of one variety or another. Textile, mining and fishing villages became hotbeds of Methodism and dissent, and panic-stricken parish clergy started to equate the rise of dissent with the decline of religion. So the *idea* of religious decline was born in Britain within the notion of breaking social bonds, the decline of what E.P. Thompson called the 'paternalism–deference equilibrium'.[8] But if rural society begat the idea, it was quickly re-conceived within a new context – the industrial town.

THE MYTH OF THE UNHOLY CITY

From the outset of urban expansion and early industrialism in the late eighteenth century, British culture was developing doubts about the spiritual efficacy of the town. Literature, so important to the shaping of middle-class culture,[9] was dominated by texts – notably poetry – which located virtue and sensibility in pastoral scenes. Even before cities troubled the evangelical palate, change to rural society was anticipating urban concerns. The Scots poet Robert Fergusson (1750–74) eulogised the disappearing countryside of paternalism, and regretted the capitalistic improvements of the agricultural revolution,[10] whilst one character of novelist Tobias Smollett (1721–71), Matthew Bramble, expressed the fears of urban growth in Bath – that most 'genteel' and unthreatening of towns – where 'the mob is a monster ... a mass of ignorance, presumption, malice, and brutality'.[11] More influential and immensely popular amongst the English middle classes was the poet William Cowper (1731–1800), a converted evangelical who in the 1780s regarded 'London, opulent, enlarged, and still/Increasing London' as the pre-eminent source of vice and irreligion:

> Of holy writ, she has presumed to annul
> And abrogate, as roundly as she may,
> The total ordonance and will of God;

Advancing fashion to the post of truth,
And centering all authority in modes
And customs of her own, till sabbath rites
Have dwindled into unrespected forms,
And knees and hassocks are well-nigh divorced.
    God made the country, and man made the town.[12]

Walter Scott (1771–1832) and William Wordsworth (1770–1850), poets and novelists of enduring popularity with British people in the nineteenth century, centred much of their idylls in rural locations where charm and nature heightened sensibilities. Wordsworth wrote in 1805 that it was only in nature, 'Among the woods and mountains, where I found in thee a gracious Guide', that the 'High thoughts of God and Man' could be 'Triumphant over all those loathsome sights/Of wretchedness and vice' of London.[13] Robert Southey (1774–1843), the Poet Laureate, entered the debate over church extension in cities by the Church of England, highlighting the breakdown of the old parish system: 'Every parish being in itself a little commonwealth, it is easy to conceive, that before manufactures were introduced, or where they do not exist, a parish, where the minister and parochial officers did their duty with activity and zeal, might be almost as well ordered as a private family. . . . [This] cannot possibly be exercised in our huge city or manufacturing parishes.'[14]

The clergy accepted London as by its metropolitan nature to be a 'problem'. The Congregationalist John Blackburn told a mechanics' institute class in the capital in 1827:

> The metropolis of a great empire must necessarily be, in the present state of human society, the focus of vice. Such was Nineveh, such was Babylon, such was Rome – SUCH IS LONDON. Here, therefore, is to be found in every district, the theatre, the masquerade, the gaming-table, the brothel. Here are to be purchased, in every street, books that . . . tend to weaken all moral restraints, and to hurry the excited but unhappy youth who is charmed by them into the snares of pollution, dishonesty, and ruin.

Yet, though he considered 'the inhabitants of London be cursed with a moral plague', he acknowledged the capital to be well-endowed with evangelical agencies of spiritual and moral improvement: the various bible societies, mechanics institutes and the like. 'The materiel of moral improvement', he noted, 'is possessed here in greater abundance than in any other spot on the earth.'[15] But whilst London's vice was understandable if not excusable, that of the provincial city was not. Just as the poets eulogised rural piety and a lost golden age, so clergy translated to urban parishes quickly sensed the loss of the rural ecclesiastical system. The majority of British clergy continued to come from the countryside and villages probably until the early twentieth century.[16] And it was in the countryside where the hearts of the British clergy remained. Like no other profession, the clergy of Britain were the first to engage with the theoretical and practical problems of urbanity and the human condition. Even before doctors really contended with the great urban fevers of cholera and typhus in the 1830s, pastors were already engaging with overcrowded parishes and the flagging spiritual fibre of the nation.

The first and enduring implication of industrial urbanisation was the apparent decreasing churchgoing of the 'lower classes'. It was not especially new for clergy to berate one social group or another for poor morals or church-going habits. Indeed, the very essence of much eighteenth-century Methodist rhetoric in England was criticism of upper-class lukewarmness in religion, and an identical rhetoric was directed by evangelical clergy of the Church of Scotland at that country's landed and patrician orders. Absence of such elites from church was constantly criticised in the second half of the eighteenth century. What was new by the 1790s and 1800s was the linking of a new and very specific economic and physical environment – the industrial town – to the source of irreligion. The nature of industrial employment, including in the home, was seen as a problem for its removal of close paternalistic ties between social ranks and its pressure to profane the Sabbath in work or recreational release.

It was industrial work in home and mill that lay behind the development of Sunday schools by Robert Raikes of Gloucester in the early 1780s. Responding to the 'drunkenness, and every species of clamour, riot, and disorder' he witnessed at a local festival in the village of Painswick, he collected from the public the huge sum of £58 for the foundation of Sunday schools. Raikes explained that since homes were previously burgled during worship, the popularity of his scheme 'may be accounted for from the security which the establishment of Sunday schools have given to the property of every individual in the neighbourhood'. As a result, the Sunday schools quickly mushroomed in the village, providing child weavers with their only educational training: 'These children have no teaching but on the Sunday,' he said. 'Many have their books at their looms, to seize any vacant minutes, when their work is retarded by the breaking of threads.'[17] Sunday schools were initially perceived literally as schools on Sunday, as instructional agencies to be promoted within the framework of the established churches and, very often, municipal patronage. They were civic institutions of instruction and law and order; in Glasgow just as in Painswick, the inaugural 400 scholars walked through the streets to their schools on 18 November 1787 'in joyful procession' accompanied by multitudes 'applauding the benevolent design', and £210 was immediately subscribed.[18]

The mill and mining town was an even greater shock to evangelical action in the 1780s and 1790s. In the small town of Campbeltown on the Kintyre peninsula in the west highlands of Scotland, the development of commercial fishing, coal mining and whisky distilling drew the parish minister to comment in 1790: 'One circumstance in the general character of the lower class of people, both in town and country, according to the complaint and experience of their clergy, consists in the little attention paid to every thing beyond their worldly interest, and a woeful ignorance in matters of religion; . . . and . . . a more than usual neglect in attending public worship'.[19] When in 1785 the Adelphi cotton-spinning works opened in Perthshire and the new village of Deanston was spawned around it, a local remarked five years later that 'the consequence was very distressing. So many people collected in one house refined each other in all manner of wickedness. The duties of the family were neglected, the Sabbath was profaned; the instruction of youth was forgotten; and a looseness and corruption of manners spread, like a fatal contagion, every where around.'[20] Meanwhile, larger towns further south were objects of considerable anxiety. 'Sheffield is not the most irreligious town in the Kingdom', wrote one of the town's clergy in 1817; yet, he went on: 'Look at the families surrounding your dwellings, and you perhaps see a solitary instance where a whole household of several persons are regular attendants.'[21] In Manchester, J.P. Kay described the working classes as living 'precisely like brutes' seeking to gratify 'the appetites of their uncultivated bodies': 'Brought up in the darkness of barbarism, they have no idea, that it is possible for them to attain any higher condition'.[22]

Evangelical criticism of the emerging urban proletariat in the 1790s was especially strong in Scotland where clergy were most sensitive to the disintegration of the presbyterian parish-state.[23] But the Revolutionary Wars with secularist France from 1793 increased awareness of religious neglect at home: 'In vain shall we speak of the importance of good morals, while we are leaders in every species of dissipation, intemperance and debauchery. In vain shall we speak against French principles and French impiety, while our whole conduct manifests and promotes a disregard to the doctrines, laws and institutions of the Gospel.'[24] The war with a secularist foe had a cathartic effect on the British religious sense of the irreligious 'other', for in 1795–6 the two great schemes of British evangelicalism emerged in embryo simultaneously: the mission to the domestic 'heathen' of town and countryside, and the foreign mission to 'heathen' lands in the emerging empire. One minister prioritised action at home rather than overseas: 'When we see the tide of infidelity and licentiousness so great and so constantly increasing in our land, it would indeed be highly preposterous to carry our zeal to another, and far distant one.'[25] But the home mission had a problem; it depended too much on dissenters whose very existence implied criticism of the parish clergyman and challenge to the already shaky hierarchy of local power. The established churches did all they could to stall the home mission: they told government that dissent was 'democratical', 'seditious' and, in the case of Methodism, 'the miserable effusions of enthusiastic ignorance'.[26] Agricultural change, rural industrialism and radical politics came together in the 1790s to make the 'ecclesiastical republics'[27] of the dissenting congregation akin to the Jacobinical, and effectively stalled the home mission. So in the midst of war, the foreign mission won priority, and from 1795 British foreign missionary societies were founded upon the identification of an urgent and achievable Christian evangelisation of the country's maturing empire.

The home mission as a coherent idea did not really re-emerge until the end of war in the 1810s when a parallel discourse on the 'heathen' industrial city started to take shape. The most influential figure was the Revd Dr Thomas Chalmers (1780–1847), who in 1843 led the secession from the Church of Scotland to found the Free Church. Chalmers experienced what many clergy of his generation did. When he moved as minister from rural Fife to the Tron parish in central Glasgow in 1815, it was an immense shock. He struggled with the practicalities of being a minister in a town parish, finding that a visitation of every family – as was customary in rural areas – was near impossible in a slum area of some 11,000 people. Large numbers had no church connection, and he started to conceive the need for a variety to Christian agencies. 'The preaching of Christianity' he said in 1816,

> should be turned to meet the every style of conception and the every variety of taste or prejudice which can be found in all the quarters of society. The proudest of her recorded distinctions is that she is the religion of the poor – that she can light up the hope of immortality in their humble habitations . . . – that on the strength of her great and elevating principles a man in rags may become rich in faith. . . . Ay, my brethren, such a religion as this should be made to find its way into every cottage and to circulate throughout all the lanes and avenues of a crowded population . . .[28]

Chalmers started to organise day and Sunday schools in his parish on what was then a new and rigid principle: that they should be open to only children of the parish. Indeed, he went a step further in personally going with an elder to recruit twenty-eight children from a single lane, and appointed a day-school teacher for them. The 'principle of locality' was taking shape in Chalmers' designs. He told his congregation how the work of the urban church was now beyond the individual minister:

> It is not easy for me to describe my general feeling in reference to the population with which I have more immediately to do. I feel as if it were a mighty and impenetrable mass, truly beyond the strength of one individual arm, and before which, after a few furtive and unavailing exertions, nothing remains but to sit down in the idleness of despair. It is a number, it is a magnitude, it as an endless succession

of houses and families, it as an extent of field which puts at a distance all hope of a deep or universal impression . . .[29]

By 1817, Chalmers was developing a thorough fear of the large city. He told his congregation: 'I am surely not out of place, when, on looking at the mighty mass of a city population, I state my apprehension, that if something be not done to bring this enormous physical strength under the control of Christian and humanized principle, the day may yet become, when it may lift against the authorities of the land, its brawny vigour, and discharge upon them all the turbulence of its rude and volcanic energy.'[30] Four years later, Chalmers had advanced both his system and his ideas, publishing *The Christian and Civic Economy of Large Towns* as a two-volume social-scientific study of urban religion and morality which linked him to the ideas of Malthus and Ricardo. Deploying statistics of religiosity collected from his parish and Glasgow as a whole, he demonstrated just how far irreligion had taken a hold in working-class industrial towns. 'The atmosphere of towns, may at length become so pestilential, as to wither up the energies of our church.'[31] 'Profligacy,' he maintained, 'obtains in every crowded and concentrated mass of human beings.' People and clergy are separated, as are social classes.

> In a provincial capital, the great mass of the population are retained in kindly and immediate dependence on the wealthy residenters of the place . . . [which] brings the two extreme orders of society in to that sort of relationship, which is highly favourable to the general blandness and tranquillity of the whole population. In a manufacturing town, on the other hand, the poor and the wealthy stand more disjoined from each other. It is true, they often meet, but they meet more on an arena of contest, than on a field where the patronage and custom of the one party are met by the gratitude and good will of the other.

Chalmers thus saw the nature of economic relationships as differing between commercial and industrial towns. When the working classes were industrial and not service providers for the wealthy, there was no economic bond between them. Manufacturers, he said, were worthy people, but 'their intercourse with the labouring classes is greatly more an intercourse of collision, and greatly less an intercourse of kindliness, than there is that of the higher orders in such towns as Bath, or Oxford, or Edinburgh'. As a consequence, 'there is a mighty unfilled space interposed between the high and the low of every manufacturing city'. The solution to this void was 'to multiply the agents of Christianity amongst us, whose delight it may be to go forth among the people'.[32] However, when in the 1820s Chalmers moved to Edinburgh as professor of divinity, he quickly discovered that he had been too sanguine about the state of religion and moral degradation in a 'provincial capital'. He admitted to not understanding 'how the present and frightful degeneracy and disease should have ever taken place, breaking out into the frequent and ever-enlarging spots of a foul leprosy, till at length we have spaces in many a town, and most distinctly in our own [Edinburgh], comprehensive of whole streets, nay, of whole parishes, in a general state of paganism.'[33]

The discourse which Chalmers intellectualised on the 'heathen' and 'pagan' city became a central tenet of the British churches in the nineteenth and twentieth centuries. It also became one of the enduring principles of social science itself. His fame came to rest on his vision of religion in the troubled industrial city, and he became the darling of the evolving British evangelical circuit. Mobbed on a visit to London in 1817, Wilberforce wrote of him 'All the world wild about Dr. Chalmers'.[34] His volume of *Commercial Sermons* sold widely in England, attracting attention for their guidance on how evangelical Christianity was to be located in business and commercial lives; *The Methodist Magazine* recommended it strongly, and devoted an unprecedented seventeen pages to extracts.[35] *The Times* dubbed him a 'distinguished man', and in 1827 he was offered the Chair of Moral Philosophy at London University but chose to stay in Scotland. His fame ensured that from the 1820s until the 1880s he was the most widely quoted authority on urban religion. He provided a concept of Christianity as an 'economy' which could be conceived as a parallel to the wider 'civic economy' embracing industry, social relations and the political process. He invented 'ecclesiastical economics', rendering the social study of religion a 'science' as much as Adam Smith and the political economists had done for commerce and demography. He offered both analysis of the problems and – most importantly – solutions.[36] But critical to his conception of the task of the committed Christian church was an appreciation of both its magnitude and the priority. Chalmers supported the mission to foreign heathens, but, he wrote, 'We must do with the near, what we are doing with the distant world. We do not expect to Christianise the latter, by messages of entreaty, from the regions of paganism. But we send our messages to them.'[37]

Along with the discourse on the unholy city, Chalmers injected social-scientific method into church life (such as the widespread use of religious censuses as an inherent part of the home mission). His 'principle of locality' and the 'aggressive system' remained as tenets of home evangelisation. In 1835 the English Methodist paper *The Watchman* quoted him on the 'fearful remainder of irreligion and practical heathenism' in cities which could be 'broken up in no other way than by the subdivision of the mighty aggregate into manageable parishes'.[38] Anglicans felt just as drawn to his ideas as nonconformists. Whenever censuses of churchgoing were analysed, Chalmers was almost universally quoted. 'A population like this,' wrote one Anglican cleric of London's unchurched in 1835, 'as Dr. Chalmers has justly argued, can never be reached but by a series of aggressive efforts.'[39] The heathen city became an official discourse of the British state. When in 1854, Horace Mann presented the results of the 1851 Census of Religious Worship to parliament, his commentary was wholly reliant on Chalmerian interpretation. Of 'the alarming number of non-attendants' at church, Mann wrote of large towns: 'What Dr. Chalmers calls "the influence of locality", is powerless here: the area is too extensive and the multitude too vast.' Whilst the middle classes had become more religiously devotional, he wrote that 'in cities and large towns it is observable how absolutely insignificant a portion of the congregations is composed of artizans' – a class so 'utter strangers to religious ordinances as the people of a heathen country.' The solution, asserted Mann, was the aggressive evangelising system.[40] After Chalmers, the language of class placed religiosity and its absence as the centre of the conception of society, its ordering and its problems. Chalmerian terms like 'masses of ignorance and irreligion'[41] and 'heathen-ism' became the vocabulary of ecclesiastical and civil rhetoric.

Despite a few who expressed more optimistic views of urban religion,[42] the discourse on the unholy city was by 1850 established as a cornerstone of British ecclesiastical and social policy, driving forward appeals to church members for 'Christian liberality' for church-building, evangelisation and educational schemes. Social-science methods were deployed in mid-century to educate and inspire the laity. In the 1840s and 1850s, churches were infected as much as other branches of the nation's life by the mania for statistics. Statistics of church membership, churchgoing and Sunday school attendance took pride of place beside vast reams of statistics on crime, pros-titution, drink and gambling as what were called 'moral statistics' of the nation and of the larger cities in particular.[43] By the 1850s popular maga-zines were routinely publishing data on crime, 'morals', church members and Sunday school scholars side-by-side. In 1853 *Chamber's Journal* pub-lished a study of the ratio of population to the numbers of drunk and disorderly persons picked up in the streets of major cities, with London in 1851 achieving a ratio of 1:106, whilst the worst recorded places in Britain were Edinburgh with 1:60 and Glasgow with 1:22.[44] Statistics were manu-factured by ways now lost which calculated that there were in Britain in 1860, 25,000 persons of 'disreputable character' living in 'dens from which no fewer than 134,922 persons of both sexes daily proceed on missions of vice and immorality'.[45] The discourse on the unholy city placed 'scientific' evidence in the form of statistics at the heart of analysis, providing a powerful objectification of 'the problem'.

Whatever the statistics showed of irreligion in provincial cities, London had a reserved and, indeed, revered place in evangelical thinking. It repre-sented the ultimate test of evangelicalism, for its sheer scale and density was the antithesis of the Christian rural parish of the pre-industrial age. It was in the 1880s that London reached its nadir as the city of moral nightmare, Jack the Ripper and 'Darkest England'. The tone was set in 1880 by James Thomson's narrative poem *The City of Dreadful Night* in which an unearthly preacher in an anti-sermon informs the 'spectral wanderers of unholy Night' that 'There is no God; no Fiend with names divine'.[46] The 1880s was the decade of moral panics, promoted in part by the anonymous pamphlet of the Congregationalist minister the Revd Andrew Mearns, *The Bitter Cry of Outcast London*, and in part by the revelations of Stead's articles in the *Pall Mall Gazette* about, and subsequent prosecution for, obtaining a young girl for immoral purposes.[47] When in 1886 the *British Weekly* was founded as the main religious newspaper of the British evangelical community, its prime concern was the irreligious nature of London. A pre-launch census of London churchgoing gripped the attention of church leaders (especially the clergy) as its results appeared over several months, showing that 12.6 per cent of the population attended morning services of Protestant parish churches and 13 per cent at evening services.[48] Two years later, William Booth's *In Darkest England and the Way Out*[49] not only intensified evangelical sensitivity to London but provided an enduring image of London as an impenetrable continent of social danger. Charles Booth's and Seebohm Rowntree's studies of poverty provided further grist to the mill of the mythology of cities in secularising danger, causing one Liberal politician to conclude that 'present belief in religion ... is slowly but steadily fading from the modern city race.'[50]

Pessimism propelled the evangelising cause. For the Scot Henry Drummond, the city was 'the antipodes of Heaven' and a problem for mankind and for the Christian: 'To make Cities – that is what we are here for. To make good Cities – that is for the present hour the main work of Christianity. For the City is strategic ... He who makes the City makes the world.'[51] Clergy drew on a variety of ideologies and social movements to reconstruct the city: civic gospels in industrial cities like Birmingham and Glasgow between the 1850s and 1870s,[52] municipal socialism in the 1890s,[53] and the garden-city movement in the 1900s. 'Let us notice', wrote one clergyman in 1910, 'how the Garden City ideal possesses some of the features which belong to the ideal city of God described in the end of the Apocalypse.'[54] But the emergence of these ideals was dependent on the city remaining a perpetual social and religious problem. Objectified by statistics and surveys, and by botanical-style expeditions into the slums to collect specimens of the irreligious and depraved, idealism depended on the embedded idea of the urban crisis of religion.

The myth of the unholy city remained largely untarnished at the heart of British ecclesiastical thinking throughout the twentieth century. But it only started to seriously invade the academy of historians after 1950. E.R. Wickham established a very firm principle at the start of his pioneering study of the history of urban religion in Sheffield:

From the emergence of the industrial towns in the eighteenth century, the working class, the labouring poor, the common people, as a class, substantially, as adults, have been outside the churches. The industrial working class culture pattern has evolved lacking a tradition of practice of religion.[55]

With Wickham, the theory of secularisation turned Thomas Chalmers' fears, his statistical methodology and his discourses into an entire academic discipline relying on Chalmers and his clerical ilk as the 'sources' to 'prove' the theory. Wickham, like many who followed him, relied on church sermons and clergy's social commentary to identify the working-class haemorrhage from the nineteenth-century churches:

Hitherto [before 1830] the general alienation of this class from the churches has been a matter of deduction from circumstantial evidence, but in the 'thirties and 'forties there is forthright evidence to support the desertion; it is middle-class comment, literate comment, but its objective accuracy need not be questioned.[56]

This reliance on 'middle-class comment' became a hallmark of much scholarship on secularisation theory in the 1960s and 1970s. K.S. Inglis in 1963 rejected *a priori* that 'the typical late-Victorian working man went to public worship for part of his life and then stopped', and equally rejected the notion of 'his early-Victorian father or Georgian grandfather worshipping for a time and then staying away'. Instead, Inglis returned to a purist Chalmerian view of modern British religiosity, arguing that 'the social historian of religion in modern England could find a worse guide than the clergyman who remarked in 1896: "It is not that the Church of God has lost the great towns; it has never had them."'[57] Completing the circularity, the man Inglis was quoting, A.F. Winnington-Ingram, cited Chalmers as a prominent source.[58]

From this point, the clerical myth of the unholy city, and of the irreligious working classes in particular, was cemented into modern scholarship. It more especially re-entered general history books as historians used Victorian clerics as sources. G. Kitson Clark in 1962 discussed how evangelists sought 'to penetrate to the savagery and ignorance of the neglected and indifferent'. In 1973 John Kent wrote that 'in the years 1815–48, when the new cities were at their most chaotic, it had looked as though working-class Christianity would vanish', whilst David Mole wrote that the majority of the Birmingham working classes were 'lost to organized religion, and were scarcely or never seen in the churches or chapels, for whom they formed a vast and increasing mission field'.[59] John Kent repeatedly returned to the theme of an alienated working class, arguing in 1978 that revivalism left them largely untouched.[60] Many historians from the 1950s to the 1980s came to uncritically *believe* Victorian church sources on the alienated condition of the working classes, and moreover to describe them, without inverted commas, as the masses, the ignorant, the unchurched, the lapsed and the pagan.[61] This was especially true of church historians who were then widely cited in general social histories by academics who, by the 1990s, should have known better.[62]

Some social historians of the later 1960s and 1970s arrived at a compromise position. They acknowledged the popularity of Methodism and new dissent amongst the common people between the 1770s and 1830s, but, at a time of widespread secularist cynicism amongst social historians, a functionalist gloss was liberally applied to working-class religiosity. Some on the left regarded it as 'the chiliasm of despair' of the working class emerging within exploitative industrial capitalism and being subjected to evangelicalism as a bourgeois social control which turned the worker into 'his own slave driver'.[63] A more widely accepted anti-Marxist version interpreted religion during these years as 'the midwife of class', the gateway through which the working classes passed into secularism or religious indifference – 'the ultimate spiritual state of the majority in the great towns of the industrial age'.[64] This view of working-class religiosity as a *temporary* phenomenon of 1770–1830 became so highly regarded that it has had a strong influence on subsequent research. Some Marxist historians associated the emergence of a new middle class in the 1830s and 1840s with the exclusion *en bloc* of the working classes from the churches,[65] whilst others associated a schism in the 1830s and 1840s between upper and lower working classes (between the 'labour aristocracy' and the lumpen proletariat) with a schism between the churched minority and unchurched majority of working people.[66] Meanwhile, specialist social historians of religion were pushing back the critical period of decline to the years between 1870 and 1914, and were adopting short-period case studies of London (or parts of it) and individual towns.[67] The only historian to move significantly away from the local study was Alan Gilbert, whose work on national church statistics formed the basis for three critical volumes of the 1970s.[68] These books deployed statistics to ostensibly prove the theory of secularisation – the inevitable decline of religion in industrial society.

In these ways, scholarship in the 1970s and 1980s tempered secularisation theory's most excessive claims, but tended to affirm the theory itself by qualifying it rather than refuting it. Secularisation theory was being judged on its own terms. This remained the case even with the most 'optimist' revisionism of the 1980s and 1990s. The theory has been condemned for its unfalsifiability in claiming religious decline as an irreversible progress of history. Its social-scientific narrative was rejected by quantitative and qualitative rebuttal of its account of religion's nineteenth-century collapse (especially amongst the working classes); and the reputed relationship between urbanism and religious decline was assailed by new techniques.[69] The rise of experiential historiography, of 'history from the bottom up', brought reassessments based on oral and autobiographical sources, showing how strong were the continuities in popular religious experience between the mid-nineteenth and mid-twentieth centuries.[70] But even the most active, and in many ways most innovative, historian in the field, Hugh McLeod, has continued to perceive secularisation as centrally located in social changes between the 1880s and 1914. He recently wrote that it was from those decades that English society became one in which 'religion has become to a considerable degree privatised'. From those years, he says, it affects 'the thinking and behaviour of the individual believer, but no longer to any great degree shapes the taken-for-granted assumptions of the majority of the population', whilst religious institutions cease to dominate 'non-religious' areas of life.[71]

There have been hints since the late 1980s of radical change in the way the subject is conceived and studied. Women's historians have started to analyse the discourses of religiosity for women. This was most notably and ably pioneered in the late modern period by Davidoff and Hall in a book which made great methodological strides in analysis of religious identity in the middle classes, but which adhered rather too resolutely to notions of working-class irreligion.[72] David Hempton, in a perceptive and tantalising chapter, started to gnaw at the terminology of our subject, and to hesitate over past dismissals of informal religion.[73] Most tantalising of all, Sarah Williams argued that historians need to fundamentally reconceive the issue of working-class religion, moving out from official and formal perceptions towards informal, folk or 'superstitious' religion and rites which constitute a hitherto ignored world of popular religiosity in late-modern society.[74] It is Williams' work, more than any other, that comes closest to redefining the study of religion in industrial society.

Yet, secularisation theory and the myth of the unholy city remain at the heart of the social historian's conception of late modern Britain. Behind this conception lies an intellectual and methodological continuity stretching from 1800 to the present, in which the theory was sustained by those who found it convenient (and in some cases essential) to project an image of religion in perpetual crisis in urban–industrial society. It is actually extremely hard to think of one group of people for whom the existence of a *concept* of religious growth would have been an intellectual or professional benefit, and how anybody was significantly disadvantaged by its absence. Perhaps it was only in a truly religious society like Victorian Britain, where it mattered whether religion was perceived to be growing or declining, that such a vast range of interested parties – from clergyman to Marxist, politician to trade unionist, feminist to temperance reformer – felt an investment in the concept. If religion had been weak, it would have been only the clergy who would have cared one way or the other. It was not until the 1970s, 1980s and 1990s, when everybody affirmed secularisation was happening, that few but the clergy cared.

The myth of the unholy city is now two centuries old, kept alive by historians and sociologists quoting the 'evidence' of its originators: Thomas Chalmers, Horace Mann, and every statistic and clerical exclamation of irreligious slums. The story told by academics in the second half of the twentieth century has been the same story as that told by clergymen in the 1810s and 1820s. The present becomes blurred with the industrial past in a way which leaves understanding of contemporary religious decline entangled with understanding of past religious decline. Secularisation theory removes any need to ask *why* religion is declining now – at the start of the third millennium – because it all started so long ago in the milltowns of industrial Lancashire and Lanarkshire. Our secularisation in the 2000s is the same secularisation of the 1920s or the 1880s or the 1810s – declining churches, alienated working classes, residual religiosity amongst the respectable middle classes. The textbooks and research papers are empty of reasons, only seeking to decipher *what* has been happening. Secularisation theory demands no new reasons for the halving of church affiliation in the last forty years, and sociologists and contemporary historians will not offer you anything fundamentally new.[75] Our modernisation is the same modernisation as of old – increasing technology, urban anomie and privatisation of the individual, decreasing shared values, communality and community. The world we have lost, the pre-industrial world, was the last truly religious age. The world we have today is the same as that found by Thomas Chalmers in the slums of central Glasgow in 1815.

ENVISIONING RELIGION

This book argues that the world of 2000 is not the world of 1815. Even the world of 1950 is not the same as now. What has happened to popular religiosity since 1950 has been very different to what happened in the previous century and a half. It is in my lifetime that the people have forsaken formal Christian religion, and the churches have entered seemingly terminal decline. It matters that we understand why.

Secularisation theory is now a narrative in crisis.[76] It is in crisis partly because it professes to be a 'scientific' or 'social-scientific' account of the decline of religion, gauged by 'objective measures' which it itself has set. It defines 'the rules of its own game', and they must be challenged. At the heart of the game are its rules about what religion is. These rules were drawn up in the nineteenth century by society itself, the rules which defined what it was to be 'religious' and what it was to be 'irreligious'. Those rules were not 'neutral'; they were loaded, 'social-scientific' definitions. They were rules developed by men (sometimes women) who counted themselves part of the birth of social science itself. Men like Thomas Chalmers developed a social science in the conscious wake of those Enlightenment thinkers who were developing classical economics: Adam Smith, David Ricardo and Thomas Malthus. To bend religion to economistic principles, they had to draw up the laws, the rules, by which religion could be defined like any economy: what it was to be religiously 'rich' and what it was to be religiously 'poor'.[77] Supposedly 'objective' tests of religiosity were developed, tests which, with remarkable little change, have survived within the Christian community until the end of the twentieth century. They were tests which, from time to time, were challenged by radical Christians, but they retained a hold on not just the ecclesiastical mind but the 'common' mind as well: society accepted these 'objective' tests of religiosity. It constructed its vision of popular culture upon those tests. If you understand the origins and non-universal nature of those tests, you undermine the foundations of secularisation theory.[78]

In the previous section, the evolution of secularisation theory was summarised. Foucault's description of how a field of academic knowledge operates may be usefully applied to this. The 'knowledge' of secularisation theory, its very 'evidence' of statistics and contemporary reports on religiosity, is located within a group of related discourses – what Foucault calls the 'discursive practice' of an academic subject – with the rules of that discursive practice determining the collection, editing and deployment of evidence such as quantitative data. Conversely, as he states, the discursive practice 'may be defined by the knowledge that it forms' – a phenomenon especially characteristic of Enlightenment positivism.[79] Certain relations (or linkages) are established between discourses 'interior' to the subject (such as on the unholy city, the 'religious' middle classes, and the 'irreligious' working classes) and 'exterior' objects (such as the cities and different social classes themselves, their habits and behaviour) which must be named, classified, analysed and explained.[80] Secularisation theory first emerged as a 'field of discourse' between the 1790s and the 1820s when a set of relations or conditions came into being which linked discoursers (principally clergy), techniques of observation (statistical and other systems of recording religiosity) and sites of discourse (Sunday schools, home missions and religious publications), and simultaneously permitted the clergy a discursive power in a 'space of exteriority' beyond their own domain (in sites such as town halls, official censuses, parliament, press and academe).[81] By this dispersal, a field of discourse like secularisation theory is distinguished and given power across a wide range of disciplines (church history, social history, sociology, town planning), across ideologies (Marxism, conservatism, liberalism), and across institutions (churches, charities, voluntary organisations, municipal authorities, the labour movement and central government).

As Lyotard contended in the 1970s, the 'metanarratives' of scientific and, one might add, social-scientific disciplines are in crisis because they are self-legitimating. In his terms, secularisation theory is a self-referential (and self-reverential) metanarrative, whose phalanx of adherents – clergymen, Marxists, sociologists, social historians, liberal politicians and others – form a unanimity of rational minds telling an irrefutable 'normative' story, thereby establishing a myth which becomes seemingly normal, unquestionable, eternal. Secularisation is the rationalising accompaniment of modernisation, the great Enlightenment project which has been making the modern world one in which the mind is liberalised, the people urbanised and urbane, literate and educated, devoid of irrationality, and scientific in their understanding of this new world of machines. Secularisation is a salute to reason, the intellect and to progress. In this it is both threat and promise. Welcomed by Marx and Engels,[82] abhorred by Thomas Chalmers and other clergy, it nonetheless united these adherents in legitimation of the Enlightenment narrative which they inhabit as the heroes of knowledge. The Enlightenment hierarchy of knowledge and power reduces religion to a 'rational' object to be 'rationally' understood, 'rationally' promoted or 'rationally' undermined. Secularisation is a revelatory experience, revealing reason in a 'modern' society.

Secularisation theory as a field of discourse had an enormous influence in British society between 1800 and 1950. The next four chapters analyse the enormity of its influence through media (Chapter 3), which promoted gendered discourses on how to be 'religious' (and conversely how to fall into irreligion) in industrial and urban society (Chapters 4 and 5). The discourses promulgated 'tests' of religiosity which were broadcast within the society, suffusing the written, legal and governmental world of the day and defining the moral dialectics of popular culture – of 'rough' and 'respectable'. Those tests divided the nation's economic and recreational habits; the useful and the useless, the rational and the irrational, the religious and the heathen. Popular culture became conceived as a polarity, a binary on/off, religious/non-religious. These were the tests of religiosity which were both personal and social, confronting the individual in a jarring, intrusive way. The Victorian home missionary and district visitor knocked on the door and asked about the 'religious condition' of those inside. The answers were written down in notebooks: 'they have found Christ', 'man a drunk', 'wife struggling', 'man a specious fellow', 'children in danger'. The entries in the notebook were counted, the numbers from the notebook added together, the district totals added to the city totals, the city totals added to the national totals, the religiosity of the nation totted up to produce a percentage figure. City Missions counted doors knocked on, doors opened, the numbers inside who were clean or dirty, drunk or sober, in sickness or in health, those willing to pray or sing a psalm, and those not. Tract distributors counted the numbers of tracts handed out at street preaching stalls, public hangings, in public houses and at army garrisons. Congregational penny banks counted the numbers of transactions, and the amounts saved and withdrawn. Preachers wrote diaries where they counted and named those who were 'struggling', 'anxious' and those who 'found liberty'. Churches counted members, communicants, the baptised, the Sunday scholars, the tracts distributed, the numbers at mission services. Sunday school superintendents counted enrollees, attenders, those who could read the New Testament, and those who qualified by good attendance for the summer outing. It seems irrefutable that more statistics were counted on religion than on any other single subject in Victorian and Edwardian Britain.

This mass of 'evidence' gave secularisation theory its discursive power in the age of Enlightenment 'rationality'. As one of the cornerstones of social science, secularisation theory is a social construction which is *inherently* disabled from allowing that religion is a discursive power because, to do so, it would have to admit that *it also* is an adjunct to that discursive power. Secularisation theory judges the people of the past (and of the present) by social-scientific measures derived from nineteenth-century discourses on what it meant to be religious (such as to be teetotal, thrifty, churchgoing, respectable, 'saved' or a believer in God) and what it meant to be irreligious (drunk, spendthrift, unchurched, 'rough', unconverted or a non-believer). These discourses were, and are, laced with a medley of prejudices about poverty and prosperity, social class and ethnicity, religious bigotry, and the nature of belief or unbelief. 'Religious decline' is at its root a moral judgement, whether brandished by Christians, atheists, social scientists or philosophers. Early psychologists of religion like William James infused their spurious 'empirical Science of Religion' with explicit evangelical precepts and moral judgement on religious worth.[83] Even the recent 'philosophical anthropology' of Charles Taylor, whilst legitimately seeking to reject 'the ambition to model the study of man on the natural sciences' (notably behaviourism), extends discursive secularisation theory from social science to linguistics. He identifies the rising study of language in the twentieth century as evidence of a 'a largely inarticulate sense of ourselves' which is affecting the 'reflexive awareness of the standards one is living by (or failing to live by)' through which 'moral agency' creates 'a fully competent human agent'.[84] This is perpetuating secularisation theory as discourse by translating it from the terms of the social scientist to that of the linguistic philosopher – an ironic translation given the role of the 'linguistic turn' in challenging social science.

Christian secularisation theory is thus very powerful. It is deeply ingrained as discourse in ways of conceiving history, progress and the human condition. To break its power does not mean new research need, or should, claim a better 'neutrality'. On the contrary, this book acknowledges the presence of the 'personal' in research, and the methodological virtue of this to academic scholarship.[85] The 'reading' here is not 'neutral' but in itself highly subjectified, the product of personal experience of the discourse change explored in Chapter 8. The power of traditional religious discourse collapsed in my lifetime, its ubiquitous circulation and widespread subjectification spent. There is a dissonance between the traditional theory of secularisation and my personal experience of secularisation, and this book is its product.

CHAPTER THREE

THE SALVATION ECONOMY

—— ·◆· ——

THE PRIVATISATION OF FAITH

In 1844 Albert Bradwell, a small businessman in Sheffield, published his *Autobiography of a Converted Infidel*. In this publication he described weeks of nightly attendance at Methodist services and prayer meetings, and the harrowing spiritual anguish resulting from his failure to experience evangelical rebirth or salvation. Following one of many sermons which failed to bring him to conversion, he recalled: 'I went and knelt down among the penitents, but could not obtain a blessing, for my mind was opposed to the doctrines involved in the salvation economy'. After several days and nights of physical and mental distress, a Wesleyan Methodist preacher spotted Bradwell resisting the call for sinners in the congregation to come forward; the preacher shouted at him across the crowded chapel: 'Come out, man! and save your soul now.' 'So,' Bradwell relates, 'the poor self-condemned sinner went to seek the face of God.' Coming to the front of the chapel, he knelt down:

> I began to reflect on the economy of salvation, and concluded that ecstacy, or feeling of any character, was not salvation, but only an evidence of it; and so again I threw myself upon Christ, and said, 'I know my sins *are forgiven*,' and that moment such a flood of joy rushed in my heart, that every vein in my body tingled, and my tongue found utterance, and shouted – 'Glory! Glory! Glory be to God!' My Lord has smiled upon me; I was indeed a sinner saved by grace, and I lifted up my heart, and said, 'ABBA, FATHER! MY LORD, AND MY GOD.'[1]

This was a conversion, the point of salvation, or 'my spiritual birthday' as Bradwell put it. From the beginning of the nineteenth century, the objective of Christian evangelicalism was to lead every individual on earth to this point.

Describing Christian 'new birth' as 'the salvation economy', Bradwell was reflecting a common parallel drawn in nineteenth-century industrial Britain between the capitalist economy and evangelical renewal. Two 'economies' existed back-to-back to each other, like the two sides of a coin. An 'economy' was not merely an abstract entity of production, distribution and exchange, but was the divine government of the world, a moral entity in which the individual was placed by receiving God's grace. Conversion represented consanguineous values to capitalism: self-help, self-reliance, taking responsibility. Similarly, the 'Christian economy' was not merely to be conceived of as the church and attendance upon its rituals, but as the enveloping of life within an evangelical framework. Evangelicalism's scheme of salvation, as Boyd Hilton has said, had as its centrepiece 'an "economy of redemption" in which souls were bought in the cheapest market and sold in the dearest'.[2] The scheme was a 'rational' one, elevating the economy of business and commerce into 'an arena of great spiritual trial and suspense'.[3] Evangelical theologians of the late eighteenth and early nineteenth century admitted a scientific conception of causation in which God's works had mechanically harmonious consequences, most observable in William Wilberforce's mathematical chart of his state of salvation.[4]

This economy was not measurable merely by counting churchgoers or Sunday scholars, rates of church membership growth or numbers of religious marriages. It has to be gauged by the discursive environment within which such high rates of church affiliation and worship occurred. Evangelicalism held up discursive mirrors against which the individual negotiated his/her self. While the next two chapters examine the discursive strength of evangelical culture, the present chapter focuses upon the 'salvation economy' – the machinery of ideas and agencies by which the discursivity of evangelical piety dominated public culture.

Conversionist evangelicalism broke the mental chains of the *ancien régime* in Britain. If pre-industrial religiosity stressed individual faith within the context of obedience to church and state, modern evangelicalism laid stress on faith in the context of the individual as a 'free moral agent'. Faith was disjoined from the state by reconceiving religion outwith the ecclesiastical monopoly of the established churches. John Wesley started to explore the ambiguities and contradictions in the faith–state relationship in the mid-eighteenth century,[5] but it was in the two decades between 1790 and 1810 that the full theological and personal implications of modern evangelicalism emerged into popular religiosity and popular culture. The key was the Enlightenment, for, as several scholars have shown, evangelicalism became intrinsically shackled to it, deriving rationality for religious experience.[6] The result was that a person's religious experience attained a new validity which called that individual to evangelical action. Instead of implying obedience to church discipline and ecclesiastical courts, the religious test became one for the individual to impose upon his/her self.

It was during the Revolutionary and Napoleonic Wars, when 'democratical' dissent was put to the test by the Establishment, that Methodism, New Dissent and Scottish dissenting presbyterianism restructured popular piety as no longer subservient, secondary or, as so often in the past, oppositional to the public order, but as the new and dominant Christian economy. From 1800, evangelicalism arrived as the new moral order of British society.

The transition that occurred in the 1790s and 1800s constituted a recrafting of what religion and 'being religious' consisted. The transition in the ecclesiastical system was the transition from one dominated by established churches which represented the state in matters spiritual and which held real, if not complete, moral and religious authority over the whole population, to a system in which there was a plurality of churches operating *de facto* in competition with each other for the religious affiliation of the people. This translated into a wider and more troublesome transition in the nature of religiosity, from an early-modern (and indeed mediaeval) conception of it as 'conformity' and allegiance to the state and submission to moral and civil authority, to an essentially 'modern' conception of religion as a personal choice – a decision, or a series of decisions.[7] The first decision was whether to be an active church adherent (in itself a modern idea) or not (now a choice, where before it tempted ecclesiastical censure); the second decision was which church to join. The implication of making this last choice rapidly developed away from making a decision of which church to join and toward 'making a decision for Christ' accompanied by a series of decisive moral choices regarding personal and family behaviour. With God's grace, this became a conversion, denoted by many evangelicals as 'finding liberty' in a deliberate linguistic evocation of democracy.

The private conversion, the individual's struggle with sin and personal relationship with God, had been central to mediaeval and early-modern Christianity. But the cultural implication of the conversion had changed by the end of the eighteenth century. It was no longer something mediated by established churches within a framework of obedience to the state. It became, notably with John Wesley, the emblem of freedom from the unspiritual state church, but it was also an emblem of renewal within that church. The conversion came to be the most powerful and widely understood symbol of individual freedom in late eighteenth- and nineteenth-century Britain. In a society where equality in political democracy had still a century to run, the equality of the conversion was a powerful notion. It mobilised those most affected by economic and social change, and evangelicalism became associated with 'improvement', 'the coming of industry', independent craftsmen, merchants, entrepreneurs, quarry workers, miners, weavers, new breeds of tenant farmers, the dispossessed, migrants and emigrants. It was the religion of the new frontiers: of the American colonies, of the agricultural revolution, of textile development. Evangelicalism came to represent a people on the move spatially and socially. Evangelicalism in the eighteenth century 'came out of the closet' as an expansive force, a partner to economic individualism, and the spiritual manifestation of a new economic order.

Evangelicalism's link with the Enlightenment was very important. For one thing, it made religion a 'rational' matter of study – not merely Bible studies and theology, but conversionism itself. The Enlightenment made the conversion and the religious revival objects for study. Instances of revival became studied; cases were recorded, written down, the age, sex and occupation of the converted registered, the economic, social and even meteorological circumstances of the revival recorded. Preachers and clergy started writing diaries which detailed the religious experiences of their flocks. These were like laboratory reports recording times, dates and observable physical symptoms. They were written up into learned articles and books which amounted to a pathology of the conversion experience.[8]

This made the study of religion a social science with clergy and preachers themselves the social scientists. It was now a measurable phenomenon, with numbers of 'the saved' of immense interest. The Methodists were the first to produce, from 1767, reliable annual statistics of members in each of the constituent countries of the British Isles.[9] Other denominations were much slower – between 80 and 120 years slower – in reaching the same standard, but other forms of religious statistics started to become collected with increasing mania from the 1790s: parish membership data, numbers of people without church seats, numbers of pews per head of population, numbers of Sunday school attenders, and so on. Numbers started to represent a new power for the churches, especially for the dissenters and for the evangelicals who promoted voluntary organisations committed to evangelisation at home and abroad.[10] Evangelicalism exerted its power by broadcasting rising statistics of 'the saved' which, in a context of rapid population growth, was almost inevitable. But in the simple statistical methods of the time, evangelicalism entered almost a century of continuous euphoria with rising numbers.

The power being exerted by evangelical numbers was a discursive power. Religious statistics divided people: into church members and non-church members, churchgoers and non-churchgoers, those with a church pew and those without. This challenged established religion. Its condoning of personal conversion challenged the established definition of religiosity as conformity, as submission to authority. It was, to use a modern word, 'democratic'. It was a leveller, tearing the formal expression of religiosity from the serried ranks of churchgoers in the landlord's parish church, and ceding it to the personal experience of high and low wherever they might feel it. It moved religion out of the control of civil–ecclesiastical power. It deregulated religion, in the economic-speak of the late twentieth century, 'privatising' it, opening up the saving of souls to any passing evangelist or preacher, and denying the authority and control of ecclesiastical regulation.

In this, evangelicalism made religion potentially dangerous, and was resisted strongly by many clergy of the established churches. In the context of the Revolutionary Wars of the 1790s, evangelical preachers of many denominations and none became harried by civil and ecclesiastical power, and their methods – open-air preaching, tract distribution and 'unregulated' Sunday schools – became seen as 'democratical'. Some Establishment clergy who had initially welcomed evangelicalism either turned on it (sometimes by becoming informants for the government), or were scared off from it. In Scotland, the agitation of one former evangelical minister caused all but one of the Established Church clergy to resign from the Glasgow Missionary Society in 1798, and instigated the Church of Scotland in 1799 to issue a 'pastoral admonition' prohibiting clergy and people from supporting Sunday schools.[11] Though Scotland in the 1790s represented an extreme established-church reaction to evangelicalism, such hostility was evident throughout Britain, and especially in the Anglican attitude to Methodism. An immediate consequence was the direction of initial evangelical energies into the patriotic and 'safe' foreign mission rather than the politically dangerous home mission. It was in the mission to foreign lands where a key characteristic of evangelicalism – the voluntary organisation – was developed. From the Ladies Auxiliary of the foreign mission organisations of Britain's cities in the late 1790s, evangelicalism emerged not merely as a personal conversion experience but as a 'doing' – as an active work as Sunday school teacher, tract distributor or fund-raiser. And the activity had one aim: to bring everyone to conversion.

THE SALVATION REVOLUTION

Despite its important doctrinal emphases, it was the *route* to salvation which was the distinctive feature of evangelicalism; as Ian Bradley has said, 'Evangelicalism was never really a theological system so much as a way of life.'[12] If salvation was a personal experience, to engineer it on a grand scale was a social issue. Millions had to be 'called', and this required a cultural environment in which it would be widely received. It required machinery in the form of propagandisation and outreach agencies to foment a modern puritan revolution – a call to the individual to self-contemplation and conversion, to congregational participation, and to evangelical action in society at large. From 1796 to 1914, Britain was immersed in the greatest exercise in Christian proselytism this country has ever seen. It focused the individual on personal salvation and ideals of moral behaviour and manifestations of outward piety. It reconstructed the local church in its modern form – not a parish state of regulatory courts, church discipline and landowner power, but the congregation as a private club and a parliament of believers. And it spawned the 'associational ideal' by which true believers could express their conversion in the assurance shown through commitment to evangelising work in voluntary organisations.[13]

From 1800 Britain was puritanised by evangelicalism. Through the influence of secularisation theory and the Marxist-derived agenda of class politics, this process has been most commonly understood by historians as a predominantly middle-class class development.[14] Certainly the middle classes of non-metropolitan Britain experienced savage change to their lifestyle with the rise of evangelical culture. The temperance pioneer John Dunlop recalled lodging as a student at Glasgow University in 1801 with the Revd Stevenson Macgill, a pioneer 'modern' evangelical in the Church of Scotland: 'In vain D[r] MacGill reprobated excess; in vain he & his brothers Thomas and Francis exhibited specimens in themselves of almost continental temperance.' Dunlop remembered that the social and business life of the patrician middle classes, clergy and students was infused with drinking to excess, hunting parties, and attendance 'at an infinity of voluptuous parties' thrown by parishioners for their minister. 'Purity of thought & morals were at a low ebb ... Everyone of a serious cast in the middle class (male or female) was insulted & spoken against.' However, by the following decade the struggle to puritanise was starting to win over Glasgow society, especially with the arrival of Thomas Chalmers. By 1860, Dunlop recalled, Glasgow had been 'advanced & improved in science, literature, morals and piety'.[15]

Evangelicals like Dunlop were by the 1830s active in developing new elements of piety. One essential ingredient in this process was rewriting the history of the recent past – writing a 'moral history' of Britain. Some saw this as resurrecting the puritan divines of the seventeenth century and the early evangelicals of the eighteenth century (such as Jonathan Edwards), but more urgent was rewriting the moral history of the most recent past. Evangelicals were conscious that every age was distinguished by different moral tones, by what the *Chamber's Journal* in 1836 called 'tendencies'. This was evident in literature where in the 1790s and 1800s 'poets and versifiers' had been dedicated 'to the production of pieces directly calculated to injure the morals of the people':

> Take up the works of these authors, and see how many songs they have written descriptive of the delights of an indulgence in intoxicating liquors, or commemorative of the wild enjoyments of a drunken brawl. . . . According to their definition of moral qualities, no one is to be considered honest, good-hearted, generous, cheerful, or merry, unless he can take his glass freely; that is, unless he be a drunkard.[16]

'Fortunately,' the *Journal* claimed, 'the race of drunken poets is now pretty nearly extinct', replaced with a 'new order of men ... in correspondence with the tendency of the age' who were promoting 'the practice of sobriety in connection with a sound moral state of feeling'.

The puritanisation of society reached its key moment in the early 1830s with the advent of the temperance movement. Dunlop was a pioneer, starting work as so many others did in the Sunday school movement, and then seeing Britain's first North American-influenced temperance societies in Maryhill in Glasgow and in his native Greenock. He was finally persuaded of the temperance ideal on a European tour in 1830, and then started campaigning nationwide, producing pamphlets and undertaking lecture tours. This produced significant, immediate and permanent changes in the definition of piety. Equally, the identification of drinking as a moral and religious evil to be countered by pledge-taking heightened the maleness of impiety. It amended the nature of religiosity, including the piety of the existing Christian community: 'The irreligion of the religious must be subdued,' wrote one correspondent in the Baptist New Connexion journal in 1834, 'their affinity to the world destroyed, and their lust for vanity and sensuality be crucified. The manners and habits of the professing community are decidedly intemperate.'[17] It was a considerable struggle to convince each denomination. By 1834, it was reported that in the cities of Leicester, Nottingham and Loughborough only two dissenting clergy had become members of temperance societies.[18] With the rise of teetotalism in 1836, the evangelical moral agenda became closely linked with self-improvement ideology in working-class communities, notably in the Chartist movement from 1837. The whole of society was being reassessed by a new moral barometer in which the alcohol test was supreme.

The salvation revolution coincided in the 1790s and 1800s with the industrial revolution and its accompanying rapid urbanisation. These created new 'social problems': the breakdown of traditional social relationships;[19] working men in expanding or new trades with an increasingly machismo culture which redefined gender roles and fomented domestic violence;[20] uneducated child workers working long hours six days a week but roaming the streets and fields on Sundays; and prostitution, drunkenness and the expanding cultural dissipation of traditional forms of popular culture (including unregulated folk sports, brutal sports, fairs and gambling).[21] Three things followed immediately: first, there was heightened sensitivity amongst the social elites – the landed classes, patricians and middle classes – to the adverse social consequences of industrial and town growth. The 'rough culture' of the predominantly urban new working classes became a 'problem' which required solutions. Evangelicalism provided a 'moral package' of admirable social values and agencies suited to the regulation of lower orders who were now out of the reach of traditional forms of institutional control.[22] Second, evangelicalism became immediately popular amongst the new working classes. This was most obviously seen in the development of churches in new textile, metallurgical and mining villages where, in the 1780s and 1790s especially, they became hotbeds of fervent Methodism and Protestant dissent in which groups of men came together to organise chapel committees, start savings schemes, rent a room for worship, build a church, and acquire a minister or join a Methodist circuit.[23] Evangelical religion conferred the identity of a self-managed organisation for the men of the new industrial working classes 'who had very little to do with the government of anything else'.[24] Third, as Anna Clark has cogently argued, evangelical religion imbued women as well as men 'with a sense of spiritual equality'. Working people created their own systems of moral authority in plebeian chapels, and members submitted to them to regulate moral offences such as fornication, drunkenness, and Sabbath-breaking. Though this could involve middle-class congregational leaders disciplining working-class members (especially in churches of the larger denominations in the larger cities),[25] it also involved congregations composed of those from the same social background (and indeed occupations) operating a collective moral code upon each other. As Clark stunningly reveals, sin and salvation were highly gendered issues for the individual sinner, with women submitting to the patriarchal authority of male church leaders but, at the same time, exploiting the system as the only one which really addressed familial issues and which could enforce redress (marriage or child support) upon the men who had abused or deserted them or made them pregnant.[26]

Evangelical religion, especially in its more radical form, thus became an enforcer of domestic ideology for an evolving, though troubled, masculinity of the artisan chapel-goer, and a community venue for the exploration of women's roles, ideals and protests. In short, if the gender division of work created the separate spheres for men and women of the new working classes between 1780 and 1850, it was evangelicalism which provided the community location for the elaboration and affirmation of those separate spheres as domestic ideology. Faith was being privatised as an individual choice, but one which had the potential to privilege female piety and institute anxiety about masculinity.

These developments were widespread phenomena within British Christianity of the nineteenth century, and by no means limited to Protestantism. Changes in the English Roman Catholic Church between 1850 and 1914, as Mary Heimann has persuasively demonstrated, had less to do with Irish, Roman or ultramontane influences than with native Christian sensibilities. Catholic devotion in Victorian and Edwardian England, she shows, had a great deal in common with Protestant spirituality, including the inducement of anxiety, the conversion experience and moral earnestness, whilst the rise of late-Victorian Marian devotion seemed to owe more to the emergence of English feminine and domestic piety than to the French growth of apparitions of the Blessed Virgin. Heimann concludes: 'Indeed, some aspects of English piety in the period, Catholic and Protestant, were so alike as to seem virtually indistinguishable.'[27] In this way, both Protestant and Catholic had stakes in the salvation economy.

Nonetheless, in 'the Evangelical century' it was Protestant evangelicals of Nonconformity who were critical, exerting an influence well beyond their numbers.[28] Evangelicalism was the crucible for both personal redemption and for social policy to solve urban–industrial problems. As Bebbington has rightly stated, 'it called for souls to be saved one by one, and yet held up standards of a just society that could often be imposed only at the expense of individual freedom'.[29] Evangelicalism provided a complex model for a democratic and harmonious society. As such, the salvation revolution was no middle-class monopoly as too many historians have portrayed it. From its very inception in the 1790s and 1800s, it was interacting with the formation of bourgeois and plebeian identities in equal measure. And the means by which it did this was the salvation industry.

THE SALVATION INDUSTRY

Whatever arguments continued after 1800 about the role of the state in the nation's religious life, evangelicalism placed the responsibility for collective moral action at the door of the free moral agents of a 'democratic', individualistic society. It was to them that the construction of the salvation industry devolved.

The starting point was the congregation. The congregation became characterised not merely as a body of people who met on a Sunday for worship, but as a centre of social faith. The congregation was composed of voluntary organisations which emerged from the 1780s and 1790s with the dedicated aim of rescuing for Christ the adult 'lapsed masses', the young, and the native peoples of Britain's emerging empire. The individual did this firstly through giving money and secondly through giving time to work as Sunday school teachers, tract distributors, collectors, penny-bank organisers, and supporters of literally hundreds of other religious voluntary organisations. The bulk of these organisations became congregationally based though others were interdenominational local organisations for a given city or town. The voluntary organisation became the hallmark of modern religion.[30] It defined belonging, and it defined exclusion. A vast new territory was formed to which were entrusted the meanings of 'being religious' and 'being irreligious'.

The congregation was a club. Getting into it defined one state of 'being religious'; being excluded or, worse, ejected from it defined one state of 'being irreligious'. Being a member of another 'club' met with varying degrees of approval depending on whether it was doctrinally and socially in close affinity; some clubs were beyond the pale for being distant in belief and practice and some for being too close, especially when they were splinter clubs from the original. Congregations were linked in denominations – the Wesleyan Methodists, the General Baptists, the Congregationalists, the United Secession Church – which formed assemblies or synods to act as regional and national (and indeed international) parliaments, exercising control over congregational behaviour and organising the bigger schemes of evangelisation and church growth. So the member of one club could enjoy reciprocal rights of membership wherever he or she might go in the country, finding a welcome for Sunday worship and like-minded people with whom to socialise and make contacts.

The congregational clubs of Victorian Britain recreated the nature of organised Christianity as an expanding, evangelising territory. Almost every club had territorial dimensions, a 'parish' defined by its denomination, but it overlapped with parishes or clubs of other denominations, and in any event usually had only notional significance. Members of the club might come from long distances, and new members were rarely rejected because they lived outwith the parish. The congregational club differed from the parish state of the pre-industrial period in creating an abstract territoriality, a claim on social space. In one particular, though, there was an important literal territoriality: the home-mission district. By the 1840s and 1850s, urban dissenting congregations drew up parts of cities, often quite small ones of a few streets, inhabited by what were deemed alienated working-class families which became targeted for intensive evangelisation on a permanent basis. Here the agencies of the congregation were deployed in integrated work: Sunday schools, millgirl prayer meetings, young men's societies, bible classes, medical missions, gospel temperance societies and tract distributors. The home-mission district was a defining function of the congregation. It gave the members a sense of religious and social 'otherness', a group of people in more straitened financial conditions who required Christian charity of a 'useful' and 'improving' kind. This work was not the giving of dole, but the offering of means to social and moral rescue: the Christian gospel, the temperance gospel, the thrift gospel and so on. The congregation deployed these 'agencies' as different but integrated means for social reform.

This work made the church, and especially the dissenting church of the nineteenth century, a hive of activity.[31] In physical terms, the congregational church grew from being in 1800 a mere meeting house to being by 1900 a centre with many different halls for various meeting groups, and usually also with a satellite church or station in the mission district. Dissenters were ebullient with their success. They did this work themselves, they donated vast amounts of money, organised committees and collecting systems, got building loans, and managed themselves into a religious entity. But they were always aware of the 'problem' – the non-churchgoers of the slums and industrial districts. Indeed, it was this awareness that drove them in their evangelisation work. The existence of the 'religious other' was central to their perception of their own success, and for this reason religious 'decline' was the perennial fear of the evangelical. In a practical sense, the fear of the 'lapsed' multitude was the primary propaganda used by evangelicals amongst themselves to cajole each other into giving money and time to the cause.

In a sermon entitled 'The Contemplation of Heathen Idolatry an Excitement to Missionary Zeal', the Congregationalist Revd Ralph Wardlaw told the London Missionary Society in 1818:

> The reproach of many centuries has of late been rolling away. An unprecedented impulse of benevolent zeal has been given to the whole Christian world. All is life, and energy and action. By Bible Societies, and Missionary Societies, and Tract and School Societies, efforts are now making, the most extensive, the most prosperous, and the most promising, for enlightening and evangelizing the entire population of the globe.[32]

The great invention of evangelicalism was the voluntary organisation. It turned the elite organisation of eighteenth-century charity into the backbone of urban-industrial society, providing spiritual, educational, recreational, evangelising and moralising opportunities for the whole population. From the first true product of the evangelical movement, Robert Raikes' Sunday school in Gloucester in 1780, literally hundreds of types of organisation were spawned within the evangelical community. These were the 'agencies' of mission, using differing techniques and evolving agendas to impart elements of the overall evangelical message. The voluntary organisation took over the regulation of the people's habits from the established-church parish-state of the early modern period.

It started with the Sunday school in 1780, progressed by 1800 to the tract distribution society, and from 1826 emerged as the mission-district visiting system – the 'aggressive system' popularised by Thomas Chalmers, spread by the City Mission movement from the mid-1820s, and taken up almost universally by the 1850s amongst British Protestant churches. There were three core agencies of discourse dissemination: Sunday school, tract and visitation. But to them were added other specific agencies: the Penny Bank movement from the 1840s; the myriad of organisations for older youths which developed from the 1840s (the YMCA, the YWCA, bible classes, Christian Endeavour, millgirl meetings); and organisations for adults (mothers' meetings, and missions to specific occupational groups).[33] The density of these organisations within urban society increased as the nineteenth century progressed. They became a mania of the committed evangelical, designed to provide a wall-to-wall bombardment of citizens. It was in the 1810s that the integration of evangelical agencies started, initially in the experimental scheme at the Tron parish of the Church of Scotland in Glasgow where Thomas Chalmers attracted to his side many who were to be key innovators in evangelical agency: William Collins (whose publishing empire was to be founded on Christian and temperance work), David Stow (the innovator of infant schools), and David Nasmyth (who in 1826 founded the Glasgow City Mission upon the aggressive system of evangelisation, and who later inspired the formation of city missions in Dublin, Liverpool, London and New York). So much innovation occurred in Glasgow that by the 1830s one evangelical dubbed it 'Gospel City'.[34] The core of the Chalmerian system had three elements: locality, the 'aggressive system', and entry to the home. Chalmers argued in 1821 for 'an actual search and entry upon the territory of wickedness': 'go out to the streets and the highways,' he urged, 'and, by every fair measure of moral, and personal, and friendly application, compel the multitude to come in.' To win cities to Christianity, the passive building of churches and even distribution of tracts in the street was insufficient: 'we most assuredly need not expect to Christianise any city of nominal Christendom, by waiting the demand of its various districts, for religious instruction, and acting upon the demands, as they arrive. There must be as aggressive a movement in the one case as in the other.'[35] Action in the streets was not enough. 'The readiest way of finding access to a man's heart,' wrote Chalmers, 'is to go into his house, and there to perform the deed of kindness, or to acquit ourselves of the wonted and the looked for acknowledgement.'[36]

Taken together, locality, aggression and entry to the home delineated the system of the home mission which started to take shape in the 1820s and which was spread by the 1850s to virtually every Protestant denomination of Britain, North America and the Empire. It involved the creation of a massive system of evangelisation, involving a variety of agencies, techniques and personnel with different skills. In 1863, the London City Mission was reported as having 380 paid agents who closed 203 shops on Sundays. They made 2,012,169 home visits during the year at which the Scriptures were read 579,391 times. They distributed 9,771 copies of the Bible and 2,970,527 tracts, and held 46,126 indoor meetings. They 'induced' 1,483 persons to become communicants of Christian churches, 619 families to begin family worship, and 360 cohabiting couples to marry; and 'saved from ruin' some 619 'fallen ones', presumably women. Nine of the Mission's agents were dedicated to visiting public houses, one of whom alone made 26,564 visits during the year.[37] This was typical. Evangelising work involved multi-targeting: of individuals by age, sex and occupation; of sites of 'sin' such as public houses, betting houses and Sunday traders; and of town councils and parliament who were lobbied for restrictive byelaws and legislation. Moral suasion and moral force were combined to create a moral nation.

One of the most remarkable features of the aggressive system was its opening-up of the British working-class home. District visitation called not just for door-knocking and conversation at the doorstep, but entry to the family home, inquiry into the 'religious condition' of each of the occupants, and, if possible, reading of Scripture, handing over of tracts, recruitment of adults and children to appropriate religious organisations or mission churches, accompanied by prayer and sometimes the singing of hymns or psalms. This work was 'scientifically' organised, with both professional missionaries and volunteer visitors assigned streets and houses, and a duty to compile notebooks of visits and progress with individual families. One woman, Miss M.S.S. Herdman, established a small organisation specialising in the evangelisation of soldiers which in 1878 became the Soldier's Bible (later Scripture) Union. Much of her own work was at Aldershot, where 'visiting in married quarters is similar to ordinary district visiting. In a general way commonplace and disheartening, occasionally a gleam of sunshine and hope breaks the clouds.' Here are samples of her visiting notes:

> No. 4 we found to be a dirty hovel. Private —, minus his tunic, was nursing a squalling child, while another lay asleep in a basket cradle. His wife came in from the public-house secreting a bottle of gin under her shawl. Drink was here the bane of happiness.
> Visited No. 1, E lines. – Corporal —, a steady, well-educated, Christian man. His wife tidy, clean, respectable, the room a model of neatness, quite a pleasure to hold a little service in.[38]

Refusal of entry must have been common though it was rarely openly reported in evangelical publications. In 1871 a minister reported how he knocked at a seventy-five-year-old woman's door asking if he might read the Scriptures and pray in her house. With 'a scowling look, a muttered curse, and a closed door,' he was rebuffed 'as every minister must have had in indiscriminate visiting'.[39] But what is most astounding to the modern reader is how readily entry to the home was gained, despite the apparent gulf in attitudes between visiting evangelist and the occupier. The Anglican parish missionary in Islington in the 1890s held quite profound and personal conversations with householders, and was able to make notes – like that concerning Mr Duncan at 34 Pickering Street: 'really an infidel and ridicules many of the truths of the Bible such as the Fall of Adam and Eve and the Resurrection of Christ and called it "a beautiful hallucination".'[40] This was intrusive work, and it is remarkable to the early twenty-first-century eye the extent to which evangelical visitors were admitted to the homes of the poor and the working classes.

Evangelism, and especially the aggressive system, had a profound impact on its practitioners as well. David Stow, founder of infant schools, noted the impact upon Chalmers' lay elders at the Tron Church in Glasgow in 1815–19:

> Till Dr. Chalmers came to Glasgow, parochial Christian influence was a mere name – it was not systematic, it was not understood – there

was not the machinery for the moral elevation of a town population. The people were let alone. Some of the elders of the Tron Church were excellent men, but their chief duty was to stand at the plate, receive the free-will offerings of the congregation as they entered, and distribute them to the poor by a monthly allowance. Their spiritual duties and exertions were but small.[41]

The aggressive system changed this, leading evangelicals to self-sacrifice. In the age of refined sensibilities, good taste and decorum, it called for doing things and going places that could be repellant or deeply embarrassing. In 1853, a minister in Belfast recalled his resistance to the congregation's expectation that he would preach in the streets of the city: 'It appeared a lowering of the gospel to proclaim it in the street – an act of personal degradation to stand in the open air and preach to any who might stop to hear'. But he agreed to do it: 'Looking at it more closely, however, I felt that Christianity is essentially aggressive, that its command is, "Go out into the streets and lanes, and highways, and hedges".' He recalled his first attempt:

> I shall never forget my first effort, when I stood on a chair in the street surrounded by two or three dozen persons, and took off my hat to commence worship. I felt, for the first time, what it was to be ashamed of the gospel. Some passers by looked to laugh, others to pity; others looked to condemn as utterly demeaning to the preacher and hearer; but others, thank God, looked to listen, and, I believe, went away to love and pray. The first laugh I heard I wished myself at home, and my courage well nigh gave way; but when I finished the singing, had closed my eyes, and had poured out my soul in prayer to God for the outpouring of his Spirit and the assistance of his grace, I did not ask in vain, – all fear fled, all shame vanished, and I never preached the glories of the gospel with greater pleasure to any people or in any place.[42]

Open-air preaching became a fixed feature of the mid- and late nineteenth-century city. The site of the Great Exhibition in Kensington in 1862 was described as having 'a moral grandeur thrown around it' because two preachers (one a former navvy and 'admirably adapted for the work') preached to the building workers every lunchtime and distributed tracts.[43]

The work of evangelising the very poor in British slums often lacked the lustre of other Christian activities – notably, for the adventurous, the overseas mission. A poem challenged why an evangelical should be idle:

> Ah, why indeed? It maybe, thou art seeking
> For something great to do, beyond thy sphere;
> To preach, perhaps, in some remoter region:
> And yet thou carest not for sinners near.[44]

Indeed, self-criticism of motives was frequently to be found in religious magazines. 'Some persons are for ever running around for revivals,' commented the *British Messenger* in 1862, 'careless of home, neglectful of children, and seeking their own pleasurable excitement frequently in a kind of religious carnival.'[45] It was, nevertheless, ultimately necessary work and essential to the personal development of the converted Christian. Michael Connal, an evangelising merchant in Glasgow, kept typical notes in his diary:

> 1838, November 6th: Visited two poor women, as a member of the Stirlingshire Charitable Society; one a Mrs Buchanan, a poor object, five children, just out of scarlet fever, three stairs up in a back land in the High Street; dreadful poverty, suffocating smell, rags, filth; these sights should make me more and more active doing good.
> June 29th, 1847: It is good to go the houses of the poor and see how they struggle through with their difficulties. It puts to flight every shadow that may have hung upon one's spirits. Visited an Irishman – a very specious fellow; I shall keep my eye on him.[46]

An essential part of the salvation industry was tract publishing. The tract was a flyer, commonly one piece of paper with between one and four pages of text, comprising exhortation, a short sermon, a didactic attack on the recipient sinner, or a short 'true' story of how a sinner was reborn. Some tracts could get longer, with eight or sixteen pages, but these tended to be tracts which were used sparingly. Tracts were characteristically distributed free of charge to the end-user, but the distributor or the distributing organisation usually had to buy them from a tract publisher or wholesaler. They were bought by the hundred or the gross, bundled in paper wrappers, sometimes in special 'mixer' packs of six or twelve different titles. In its first year 1799–1800, the London Religious Tract Society sold 200,000 tracts and 800,000 in its second year.[47] Regional societies emerged with their own tract-publishing and distribution agents, providing along with Sunday schools the main avenue for lay evangelisation between 1800 and 1820. The growth of religious literature for a popular market really started in the 1830s, with 'improving' and religious magazines from private publishers and evangelical organisations. In 1837 the London Religious Tract Society started its *Monthly Volume* series of 192-page books on religion, nature, religious heroes and biblical stores, 'fully adapted to the educated families of our land, to day and Sunday schools and the libraries of mechanics and others'.[48]

Tract publishing was by the 1850s and 1860s a vast enterprise, with publishers – or 'tract depots' as they were characteristically called – in many different towns of Britain. Probably the largest and one of the longest-surviving was the Drummond Tract Enterprise in Stirling. Started by Peter Drummond, a seedsman, after he launched a pamphlet war in 1848 against the 'evil' of breaking the Sabbath and the Stirling races (which were closed down as a result in 1853), the depot had printed over 200 publications and eight million copies within ten years. Between the 1860s and 1914, the depot supplied evangelicals all over Britain and the Empire, running five evangelical magazines, holding over 300 different tracts at a time (constantly replacing and updating them on a cyclical pattern), and also published short stories, religious poems and novels. Novels and fiction became an increasingly important part of the output; by the 1930s, there were still over 2,000 titles in the Drummond catalogue, a third of them novels, each with print runs of between 10,000 and 50,000 copies. The rest were tracts and children's books varying from two to sixteen pages, many with print runs totalling over 100,000 copies, and monthly religious journals for different age groups. The Enterprise was by 1900 specialising in evangelical fiction, published in a wide variety of formats and lengths, from the 'Stirling Penny Stories – Intensely Interesting and Thoroughly Evangelical' to the full-length novel. It survived longer than most, absorbing in the 1950s most of Britain's remaining tract and religious magazines.[49]

Many different forms of tract came into being. The buyers of tracts, ranging from large missionary organisations to congregations and individuals, demanded effective material which had to be 'of an interesting character, principally narrative – plain and pointed. People here will not read anything "dry".'[50] New ideas were constantly emerging. Drummond started the 'Stirling Tracts for Letters' series in 1862 in which small tracts could be bought (at 6d.–8d. per dozen) for insertion in postal letters.[51] Miss V.M. Skinner in Cambridgeshire started the Friendly Letter Mission as a small private undertaking in 1877, visiting public houses to hang Scriptural texts such as 'This is a faithful saying, and worthy of all acceptation, that Christ Jesus came into the world to save sinners'. Initially centred around Huntingdon she had personally claimed within months to have hung texts in 236 tap-rooms and hotels. A publican wrote to her:

> Thank you for so kindly sending me the text and those other things, which I know you must be doing for a good cause, and I hope precious souls. I have hung up those texts in my tap-rooms, and hope they will be the means of bringing some souls to the Saviour: then brighter will be your crown, and although I know you not here, I hope I shall meet you in heaven.[52]

After publicity in *The Christian* magazine in the next two years, she started a mail-order system to other evangelical women, extending the work around England. In two years it was claimed that 2,673 pubs stretching from Cornwall to Brighton had texts, plus police stations across much of England. This led in the 1880s to the development of a 'Friendly Letter' industry at the Samuel Jarrold Tract Depot in Norwich, which produced specialist tracts and text posters for twenty-nine different occupations and in seven foreign languages for distribution in western Europe and Scandinavia.

Tract distribution was work not merely for organisations but for the individual evangelical. 'A tract is a vicarious witness that can go where a humble minister of the Gospel would be debarred from entry.'[53] Predicting the impact of tracts was almost impossible: 'Why should some tracts carry with them blessing resulting in abundant fruit, and others be apparently worthless paper?' The answer, most tract organisations recommended, was 'praying always when giving them'.[54] Of all forms of missionary work, it required the least resources: 'The outfit of the tract distributor is modest enough. It consists in the acquisition of one or more suitable tracts, a gracious manner, a humble heart willing to be guided, and a prayerful spirit. Let your behaviour, before and after offering the tract, be Christ-like and gracious.' Careful advice was given:

> Cultivate an attractive manner of offering a tract. You see a gentleman sitting quietly on a seat, resting; do not bustle up to him, thrust a tract upon him with a hasty word and be gone ... If you can spare the time, sit down for a moment, take a booklet from your pocket, and begin reading it. Then in a minute or two say, perhaps, 'I wonder whether I might offer you a copy of this booklet.' He takes it with a smile and a word of thanks, while you add, it may be, 'I have read and re-read it many times; I feel sure you will enjoy it.' A moment or two later you leave with a bright 'Good morning', which he, engrossed in his reading, looks up to acknowledge and returns to the tract. Even if you have not time to sit down, spare a moment to slow up, offer a booklet with a bright smile and a courteous word, and leave him with the realisation that you are a messenger of God, interested in his eternal welfare.[55]

If offering a tract to a member of the opposite sex, 'wisdom and discretion' were required: 'Let dignity be added to courtesy, and to both a gravity that consorts with the holy business at hand.' Every opportunity was to be taken: 'You get into a lift and find yourself alone with the lift-man. "Fourth floor, please; slip this in your pocket and read it when you get a chance."' Taxi drivers, the novice was advised, 'rarely refuse a courteously offered booklet.'[56]

There were almost endless variations on the religious publication. Charles Cook specialised in visiting prisoners in London prisons and using the stories he heard there to write tracts on 'sad ends'.[57] Tracts contained a fairly limited style of content: didactic exhortation to keep the Sabbath, acknowledge sin, and come to Christ without delay. After the mid-1850s, the several hundred Drummond Tracts showed a noticeable shift towards the narrative story, dramatic and sometimes melodramatic in form, and invariably claimed as true. There is little way to assess the authenticity of these stories, some of which give authors' names (often clergy) and others merely attributed to 'a close friend'. Peter Drummond in Stirling wrote many tracts himself (notably on the evils of horse-racing, dance halls, theatres and ballrooms, and on Sabbath sanctity), and selected items to use as tracts. He would cut-and-paste items from his in-house journals like the *British Messenger* and *Good News* to use as tracts; an article in the *Messenger* in October 1862 he marked up to be a four-page tract, providing instructions to the typesetter to alter and abbreviate dialogue quite freely, altering tenses, but in general keeping faith with the sense of the original.[58]

The volume of material published between the late eighteenth and early twentieth centuries was enormous. It is virtually impossible to gauge the full magnitude of the publications, or their print runs and distribution, but it was a literature that enveloped Britain and the Empire. By the 1830s, evangelising publications were joined by mass circulation popular 'improving' magazines whose whole tenor was implicitly religious, teetotal-supporting and often openly evangelical. Mass publication magazines were pervaded with evangelical morality. *Chamber's Journal*, established in 1832 for a Scottish readership, had a circulation of almost 60,000 within three years throughout Britain, and by 1860 had moved the focus of its material overwhelmingly to London and the south of England. It was founded with a keen eye to its market, aiming at young and old, men and women alike. It was to be a journal of knowledge and stories, but with moral effect:

> Every Saturday, when the poorest labourer in the country draws his humble earnings, he shall have it in his power to purchase, with an insignificant portion of even that humble sum, a meal of healthful, useful, and agreeable mental instruction: nay, every schoolboy shall be able to purchase with his pocket-money something permanently useful – something calculated to influence his fate through life – instead of the trash upon which the grown children of the present day were wont to expend it.[59]

The *Chamber's Journal* was aimed at 'diffusing knowledge ... under its most cheering and captivating aspect', and 'on respectable principles'.

> For the benefit of poor old men and women who live in cottages among the hills, and who cannot sometimes come to church, because the roads are miry, or because the snow lies deep on the ground, I shall give excellent pithy passages from the works of the great British moralists, the names of which they hardly heard of.... With the ladies of the 'new school', and all my fair young countrywomen in their teens, I hope to be on agreeable terms; and I have no doubt but that in the end I shall turn out a great favourite.

The 'new women' were to be given in every issue 'a nice amusing tale ... no ordinary trash about Italian castles ... but something really good', along with household tips 'calculated to make them capital wives'. Boys were to get 'lots of nice stories' about travellers in Asia and Africa, and aspirational tales:

> I shall give them accounts of men who were at one time poor little boys like themselves, but who, on paying a daily attention to their studies, and being always honest, and having a great desire to become eminent, and not be mere drudges all their days, gradually rose to be great statesmen, and generals, and members of learned professions, and distinguished authors, and to have fine houses and parks; and that at last they even came to be made kings or presidents of powerful nations.

After four years and rising circulation, *Chamber's Journal* claimed to have been addressed 'to the whole moral and intellectual nature of its readers', impressing 'sound moral lessons, and elevating human character as far as possible above its grosser elements'.[60]

The magazine, the pamphlet and the tract were, after the Bible, the most common form of personally-purchased reading in Britain before the 1870s. The novel was characteristically serialised in magazines, including religious ones: 'Novels are read right and left,' wrote Anthony Trollope in the mid-1870s, 'above stairs and below, in town houses and in country parsonages, by young countesses and by farmer's daughters, by old lawyers and by young students.' So pervasive were they, says Trollope, that 'a special provision of them has to be made for the godly'.[61] From the 1820s to the 1890s, the 'serious' novel was characteristically a three-volume and massive purchase of 31s. 6d., far too expensive for most readers, and usually issued in relatively small print runs at high cost sold to circulating libraries – a system kept alive by a cartel of publishers and circulating libraries (including W.H. Smith's). It was only in the 1880s that the single-volume novel of 4s. became the standard format.[62] In that context, the fictional novel was only made popular between the 1830s and 1880s by the improving magazine. When the modernist novel appeared between the 1890s and the 1920s, it deposed the evangelical narrative from its unchallenged position in British fiction. Though religion still sold novels, especially a skilful combination or religion and romance,[63] a disjunction started to emerge between 'high' literary novels read by small sections of the middle classes and the reissue in the 1890s and 1900s of republished Victorian masterpieces: notably the *Everyman's Library* and similar series.[64] As a result, it was in the 1890s and 1900s that the British working classes really became familiar with 'high' Victorian moral fiction, published as cheap reissues, and at the same time drank at the well of the still-rising evangelical output of popular magazines. Popular access to new novels tended to be very narrow and selective, limited to a few celebrated authors like H.G. Wells and Arthur Conan Doyle. Improving magazines, many of them published by the Religious

Tract Society, continued to proliferate and dominate: *Household Words* (and its 1870s' successor *All The Year Round*), the *Girl's Own Paper*, the *Boy's Own Paper*, *The Strand Magazine*, *The Leisure Hour*, *Cassell's Family Magazine Illustrated*, *Chatterbox*, and *The Sunday at Home Illustrated*. For news, Christians could turn to the *British Weekly*, the *Christian Herald* and others. Though less-improving magazines grew in number, especially from the 1890s, the bulk of the domestic literature of the British family remained strongly evangelical in origin until at least the 1910s.

The salvation industry was by no means confined to mere associational and literary endeavour. It deployed a panoply of techniques to spread symbols and signs of evangelical discourses in everyday life in Britain. One of the most notable of these was music which in the nineteenth century changed from being merely church music to being a music of popular culture. Though the Wesleys had introduced popular hymns in the eighteenth century, it was in the next century when the hymn became the basis of a widespread diffusive Christianity, spreading out from the church to the fair, the workplace, the street and the home. The development of the church choir as a feature of not just the major Anglican but also the Nonconformist churches really took off in the 1780s with psalmody classes in Sunday schools, but spread even more in the 1840s with Nonconformist congregations developing weekday practice sessions and semi-professional choirs. Evangelicals of the Victorian period introduced a new energy, enterprise and enthusiasm for religious music, exemplified in the vigorous melodic construction of the hymn as an exemplification of the evangelical call to action: 'Let us sing, never mind what we sing.'[65] Most Scottish presbyterian churches adopted hymns in mid-century and organ music in the 1870s, symbolising the growing popular demand amongst evangelical people, against the wishes of many 'traditionalist' puritans, to enliven and enrich formal religion with new forms of praise. In the 1840s choral societies and unions spread across Britain, the first of many specialist magazines, *The Musical Times*, appeared, and the culture of romantic Christmas – marked diversely by Dickens's *A Christmas Carol* (1843), the Christmas tree and the Christmas card – created the setting for the developing popularity of the Christmas carol.[66] State recognition for music developed from this decade, for, as J.P. Kay, a government commissioner, noted: 'The songs of any people may be regarded as an important means of forming an industrious, brave, loyal and religious working class.'[67]

This was extended further by the musical revolution wrought by the revivalist Ira Sankey from 1874. Sankey introduced hymns which retained a popularity in working-class congregations until the 1930s and even later (notably amongst stricter Protestants like the Brethren), and the harmonium which he played on his revival tours with Dwight Moody, leading to a mass market for the domestic harmonium imported from the United States. The availability of musical instruments, and especially the piano, brought the making of music within the reach of not only middle-class families but, by the 1850s and 1860s, many working-class communities as well.[68] From the 1850s, and more especially the 1870s, came the dramatic rise of the brass band, the vast bulk of which used predominantly religious and temperance music. Brass and silver bands were initially associated with temperance organisations, but by the 1880s many congregations, especially Nonconformist ones, had bands playing as part of worship. These bands together with the bands of the Salvation Army, factories and town councils took their music to the streets, public parks and festive occasions, especially on Saturdays and weekday evenings. Bands toured working-class areas, standing on street corners, as a symbolic evangelisation, playing overwhelmingly religious and temperance tunes which remained from the 1880s to the 1920s a prominent feature of the popular culture of working-class communities.[69]

Religious music was a vital part of the growing popularity of music in Victorian and Edwardian popular culture. Music symbolised so much of the character of the evangelical discursive culture. It was loud, powerful (and, as we shall see in a later chapter, masculine), uncompromising in its auditory symbolism of battle with evil (especially drink), richly militaristic, and at the same time resolutely communal in its role in streets and bandstands of public parks. It was a clarion call which reminded the hearer unequivocally of the complex discourses on religiosity which we explore in the next two chapters. And above all it bred *esprit de corps* in the evangelical ranks.

Music also symbolised something greater about the salvation industry: its optimism. The religious magazines of the nineteenth century held profoundly optimistic general views of 'progress'. Optimism was doctrine: 'How rapid is the progress of time! How fast eternity approaches! How soon will the period arrive when our opportunities for religious improvement in this state will be for ever gone! . . . During the past year, it has pleased the Sovereign Disposer of all events, to continue to us the outward means of grace.'[70] In 1835, the Congregationalist minister in Pentonville, John Blackburn, told the London Missionary Society that moral evils had declined over the previous hundred years and that 'a national reformation' was being achieved by evangelical action. Violence and venality had decreased, sales of Bibles were booming, and 'The social vices of profane swearing – Sabbath breaking – drunkenness – and of brutality, as once displayed in popular sports and pastimes; are, in my judgement, greatly decreased.'[71] In 1867, the Wesleyan *Christian Miscellany* summed up the previous thirty years:

> Drunkenness has decidedly decreased, and habits of sobriety and moderation have become much more general among all classes. Duelling is abolished. There is far less of horrid profanity and blasphemy. There are few open exhibitions of brutal passion and disgusting vice.

Society has gradually risen in intelligence and general good feeling. The Bible has become an honoured book. Christianity has secured public sentiment in its favour. The house of God was never attended as it is at present . . . Never was there so much true piety among all classes, the rich as well as the poor.[72]

In its first edition in 1886, the *British Weekly* (subtitled *A Journal of Social and Christian Progress*) wrote: 'To His appearing, and to the work He planned and did, we trace all that marks the superiority of the new world to the old, and all that is pregnant with growth and improvement yet to come.' The extension of the franchise, 'the hour of the emancipation of the people', it linked to moral revolution: 'the movements for temperance and chastity are not temporary crazes, but great uprisings'.[73] This was a profoundly Whig view of the upward progress of man, based on the evangelisation of the world. It was a message of equality and of progress: 'Salvation is offered to you: it is offered to all without distinction; it is for the poor as well as the rich; the beggar as well as the king; for men of all climes, and all complexions, and all ages.'[74] For the true evangelical, the work of mission as much as of family life was upward preparation for the second coming. For all the moral and ecclesiastical panic created (and intended) by the discourse on unholy cities, the evangelical's ultimate view was that the salvation industry was working, and that Britain was becoming ever better prepared to be in a state of collective grace to receive the millennium of Christ's kingdom.

The salvation industry was a vast and inescapable facet of nineteenth- and early twentieth-century Britain. Its perfection (and indeed innovation) of multi-media propagandisation propelled its ideas into the public domain to transcend political, regional, ideological, gender, social and class boundaries. Most importantly, it also transcended denominational boundaries. Whilst Methodist, dissenting and presbyterian churches were undoubtedly the leading edge of evangelical endeavour, the apparatus of discursive Christianity developed also in the Anglican and Catholic churches. Though the divide between church and chapel, high and low church, and between Catholic and Protestant, were important facets of the religious landscape in nineteenth-century Britain, the historian must not exaggerate this and overlook the Christian common ground.[75] This was nowhere more observable than in the post-1850 development of Catholic devotion and mission in Britain on a parallel basis to Protestantism, incorporating voluntary organisations promoting devotion and moral coda in equal measure, and a responsiveness to revivalist impulses (including from Moody and Sankey).[76] For the Protestant evangelical, to be in the 'State of Grace' was the goal. All humankind was to be encouraged that it was their goal too, and it was this that gave rise to the greatest evangelisation effort the world has ever seen. It was a levelling doctrine:

Every man and woman, also every child who has reached the age of responsibility, stands before God either condemned or acquitted. This condition does not depend upon social status, nor upon educational attainments or otherwise, not even upon religious profession, or lack of religious pretensions. But it depends solely upon their attitude toward God, and toward the Son of His love.[77]

This reflected how there was a unifying Christian environment which commandeered the vehicles of public discourse, penetrating home and office, school and hospital, street and pub, parliament and town hall. The agents of evangelism were literally everywhere, constantly challenging individuals about their own religious state. There was no escape. The individual might reject the terms of the evangelists' offer, but could not avoid the message. Through this vast machinery of Christian 'agency', the discourses on personal religiosity were circulated.

ANGELS: WOMEN IN DISCOURSE AND NARRATIVE 1800–1950

—— .◆. ——

THE FEMINISATION OF PIETY

One of the great mythic transformations of the early nineteenth century was the feminisation of angels. Until the 1790s, British art and prose portrayed the angel as masculine or, at most, bisexual – characteristically muscular, strong and even displaying male genitalia, and a free divine spirit inhabiting the chasms of sky and space. But by the early Victorian period angels were virtuously feminine in form and increasingly shown in domestic confinement, no longer free to fly.[1] Woman had become divine, but an angel now confined to the house.

This transformation was an important transition in the representation of female piety. In the Middle Ages and much of the early modern period, female piety had been conceived in terms of the woman 'becoming male'. Icons of female piety, such as martyrs and ascetics, had been represented as 'masculine', whilst femininity, menstruation and childbirth were regarded as dangerous and polluting to piety.[2] Though the early-modern woman was able to use religiosity more freely under Protestantism to express her identity, her freedom to do so was severely restricted within formal religion. Between the sixteenth and the eighteenth centuries, the Protestant churches in England (and without a doubt in Scotland also) made abandonment of many traditional 'popish' rituals a test of faith. The most critical of these customs (such as those surrounding childbirth and churching) were women's domain, and their suppression drove their observance into secrecy and female piety into the closet.[3] Continued recourse to folk religion or 'superstition' aroused intense discursive and institutional condemnation most visible in the witch-hunt.[4] Until 1800, masculinity lay at the core of representations of piety, whilst femininity lacked exemplars and was constructed as a religious problematic.[5]

But around 1800, these polarities were dramatically reversed. This was a gender shift in the centre of religiosity which laid the cornerstone for the discursive power of Christian religion in Britain (as well as in Western Europe and North America) for 150 years.[6] The feminisation of piety in late eighteenth- and nineteenth-century Britain and America is now a key concept in feminist historiography. In the context of the Enlightenment, urban-industrialisation and the formation of a class society, 'separate spheres' for men and women emerged to impose domestic ideology as a heavily religious and moral discourse on angelic confinement from the public sphere. Historians have placed religion as central to the lives of middle-class women of the nineteenth century as they developed identity and a moral agency over their own destinies, as well as developing a 'space' in religious, temperance and philanthropic organisations within which they cultivated a worldly role. Further, such space and functions within the 'religious sphere' provided a seedbed for feminism through a collaborative tension between women's purity and suffrage movements and their notionally oppositional discourses.[7] From the standpoint of women's history, British religiosity became highly feminised, and evangelicalism created a vital site for the discourse on women's identity and role.

For the student of religion's social history, the implications of this work are very great. Christianity remained an ecclesiastical system in which women's role was institutionally marginalised. Yet really quite suddenly around 1800, women's religiosity became privileged. This was to be an enduring and extremely important discourse change which established the place of religiosity in popular culture on a new foundation. As well as feminising piety, evangelicalism pietised femininity. Femininity became sacred *and nothing but sacred*. The two became inextricably intertwined, creating a mutual enslavement in which each was the discursive 'space of exteriority'[8] for the other. Each would endure for as long as the other did.

EVANGELICAL SOURCES FOR DISCOURSES ON FEMALE PIETY

The journal of the Baptist New Connexion said in 1848:

> It is our mothers and our sisters that mould nations and impress communities. It is the nursery song, the impression of infantile years, the instructions of the fireside, that are to guide and influence. We hear little, very little of the fathers of great men. It is the mother and sister of Moses that interest us. We almost forget that such a man as the father of Moses lived.[9]

After 1800, the religiosity of women was paramount to the evangelical scheme for moral revolution. They were regarded as having special qualities which placed them at the fulcrum of family sanctity. In addition the very same qualities which made them special in the home rendered them extra special in the wider reformation of communities and the nation as a whole. Theirs was a privileged and pivotal religiosity.

Women's importance in the evangelical design was nowhere so apparent as in the obituary columns of religious magazines. From the outset of the London Religious Tract Society in 1799, biographical obituaries – 'the writings, the experience, the devoted lives, and the triumphant deaths, of eminent and exemplary servants of Jesus Christ' – were vital to the diffusion of 'religious knowledge and moral instruction'.[10] The Wesleyan *Methodist Magazine* in 1811 sought to perpetuate 'the recollection of exemplary and uniform piety': 'In Biographical accounts', it went on, '*three* things are peculiarly interesting; the *commencement* – the *progress* – and the *conclusion* of a Christian's course', and it was most vital to 'learn the manner and circumstances of his conversion'.[11] Obituaries dominated denominational magazines of many churches in the early nineteenth century, and still remained a vital feature in the second half. Throughout this period obituaries of women vastly outnumbered those of men. In many evangelical journals, obituaries were written by the closest relatives – husband or daughter was common – and full of details on the deathbed piety and 'signs' of holy entry to heaven. In *The Methodist Magazine*, the obituary was the privileged genre by the early nineteenth century, always led with a ten- to fifteen-page 'star' male obituary, but followed by shorter obituaries predominantly of women written by husbands or brothers. Thomas Bartholomew from Blackburn in 1811 wrote of his wife's death: 'I found her magnifying and praising God. "Now," said she, "I can die happy." ... In the second agony, in a holy rapture, she twice cried out, "Glory! Glory!" ... Thus left this vale of tears my dear companion in the wilderness, triumphing in joyful hope of eternal glory.'[12] Twenty years later, this journal was giving over half its space to obituaries of which 64 per cent were of women.[13] Similarly, *The Primitive Methodist Magazine* in the 1820s was filled with women's obituaries, all with detailed descriptions of deathbed scenes and expressions of piety, and sometimes with deathbed conversions.[14] In *The General Baptist Repository and Missionary Observer* between the 1820s and 1850s, the wives of New Connexion ministers were extremely numerous and prominent. A minister's wife exemplified everything that an evangelical dissenter could wish for. Mrs Frances Goadby, wife of the New Connexion minister at Ashby de la Zouch, had had to maintain the manse as the fulcrum of the Connexion's community on a mere £20 a year:

> what a demand must have been made on the piety, patience, frugality and industry of the mistress of a small family. Yet this, for some time, was her position. But her ardent and unceasing flow of spirits, her extreme activity and diligence, her punctuality, uprightness, and remarkable frugality, combined with a firm reliance on providence carried her through the severest of pressure, both with credit and respectability ... her range of opinion and remark even extended

beyond the sphere usually allotted to the female sex. In matters political and ecclesiastical she cherished the most decided opinions. She was a dissenter of the firmest order, intelligent and well principled. The ardor [*sic*] of her piety was not less remarkable than the general activity of her habits ... she was given to secret prayer, being accustomed to retire daily, unto the close of life, to pour out her soul to God.

Her vital role in the Connexion was plain: two of her four daughters married New Connexion ministers, and one of her three sons became a missionary and another a minister.[15] But women outside the manse were equally privileged. In the New Connexion's magazine of 1848, there were forty-eight obituaries of which thirty were of women.[16] In addition in that year, each month's edition carried a lead story which eulogised women as mothers, sisters and wives.

Though some evangelical papers gave prominence to male preachers, women's obituaries were not only more numerous but more socially varied. There was conscious unprivileging of the wealthy. Martha Buckley died in 1823, having been baptised in the dam of a Stayley Bridge cotton mill at the age of 59, and was noted as 'in narrow circumstances; and passed the last year of her life in the workhouse' where Methodist visitors gave her religious exercises and saw her 'patient, calm resignation to the will of God, and her pious composure under trying afflictions and heavy sufferings'.[17] Conversion was socially democratic, the pains of the poor in coming to Christ being more exemplary than that of the rich. 'It has pleased the all wise Governor of the Universe recently to call home several of his aged servants; and though some of them moved in the lower circles of society, yet their respectable and long tried characters as christians demand a short memorial.'[18] And within that coda of suffering conversion, women were far more important then men. The intensity of the privileging of women's piety in religious magazines from 1800 to 1950 is quite extraordinary. It was an overpowering discourse that women were central to the life of not just the churches but of the nation.

Female religiosity was for evangelicals relatively unproblematic. A woman's very essence was pious, conferring 'natural' piety which merely required judicious guidance and self-deliverance – a deliverance easily attained if women kept out of 'the world'. The author of a series of published addresses for the young in 1911 was able to specify the 'weaknesses' of boys and men (ranging from drink to blasphemy), but for girls sin was merely 'choosing the world':

> She has chosen the world,
> And its paltry crowd;
> She has chosen the world,

And an endless shroud!
She has chosen the world
And its mis-named pleasures;
She has chosen the world
Before heaven's own treasures.[19]

The 'world' meant the public sphere. It was a plea to domestic ideology for girls and young women. 'We women,' wrote Margot Arundell, the columnist of the *British Messenger* for nearly thirty years, 'are called to be saints here and now, during our earthly pilgrimage, amidst all the petty annoyances and disappointments of home or business life. Do you ask how? By our holy lives. And "holy" is simply another word for separation from the world.'[20] If out of 'the world', women's nature made them easy converts to a suitable 'religious condition'.

Once separated from the world, women were the moral heart of a family constantly endangered by unpious men. *The Edinburgh Christian Magazine* said of one woman in 1851: 'The all-engrossing occupations of a wife and a mother seemed soon to absorb her whole being; – only one theme occupied her, – the training of her children; ... the midnight hours, which she past in watching and labouring for him and his children, were spent by her husband in scenes of folly and of vice.'[21] Articles on 'Good Wives' and 'Good Mothers' abounded, using examples from 'real life', from Scripture, or idealised models. 'The best qualities to look for in a wife,' advised *The Day-Star* in 1855, 'are industry, humility, neatness, gentleness, benevolence, and piety.' It went on: 'When you hear a lady say, "I shall attend church, and wear my old bonnet and every-day gown, for I fear we shall have a rain-storm," depend upon it she will make a good wife.'[22] Woman was the moral linchpin of society:

> The character of the young men of a community depends much on that of the young women. If the latter are cultivated, intelligent, accomplished, the young men will feel the requirement that they themselves should be upright, and gentlemanly, and refined; but if their female friends are frivolous and silly, the young men will be found dissipated and worthless. But remember, always, that a sister is but the guardian of a brother's integrity. She is the surest inculcator of faith in female purity and worth.[23]

From the 1840s, mothers were ascribed a special role in discourse in combating the evils of drink:

> If then, O mothers of Britain, you will only sweep your own hearthstones, and each one cleanse their own from this insidious foe, and firmly resolve it shall never cross your threshold more, the homes of Britain will blossom as the rose. The mother and child will sing songs

of joy and gladness. The father will go forth in the morning strong, well fed, and well clad to his daily toil, and will return in the evening with pleasure and gratitude, to his now happy home.[24]

Working-class girls were particularly targeted by evangelicals. A woman who advocated girls' clubs wrote in 1889: 'if we raise the work-girl, if we can make her conscious of her own great responsibilities both towards God and man, ... we shall give her an influence over her sweetheart, her husband and her sons which will sensibly improve her generation'.[25] Unless mothers did their duty, *The General Baptist Repository* said in 1848, our children 'will be morally, and intellectually weak'. It went on: 'As women, it does not become us to stand upon platforms, or to fill pulpits. No, we are entrusted with a more important mission. We have to mould and cultivate the minds of those who will be called upon to stand in such positions. ... We are accountable to our children – our country – and to God.'[26] The discursive injunctions on the mother were by the late 1840s unremitting:

> She is responsible for the nursing and rearing of her progeny; for their physical constitution and growth; their exercise and proper sustenance in early life. A child left to grow deformed or meagre, is an object of maternal negligence. She is responsible for a child's habits, including cleanliness, order, conversation, eating, sleeping, and general propriety of behaviour. ... She is responsible for the principles which her children entertain in early life. For her it is to say, whether those who go forth from her fire side shall be imbued with sentiments of virtue, truth, honour, honesty, temperance, industry, benevolence and morality, or those of a contrary character – vice, fraud, drunkenness, idleness, covetousness.[27]

Mothers had to sacrifice their sons and daughters to the dangers and loss of overseas mission work: 'To send a son to heathen shores is like burying him alive. ... The record of such mothers is on high; to the end of time, the church shall call them blessed.'[28] Wives of missionaries, as with one Mrs Cargill of the Wesleyan Methodists in 1832, had to be 'literally torn from her mother's arms' at the dockside before sailing to Tonga and Fiji where she died in 'exalted heroism'.[29]

Whilst such accounts in the religious press established women as heroic sources of piety, female piety was centrally located in the home. A temperance tract from Preston in 1837 described the ideal woman: 'The care of her family is her whole delight; to that alone she applieth her study; and elegance with frugality is seen in her mansions.'[30] In 1890, *The Christian Miscellany and Family Visitor* wrote in its regular 'Hints for Home Life' column: 'She is the architect of home, and it depends upon her skill, her foresight, her soft arranging touches whether it shall be the "loadstar to all hearts," or whether it shall be a house from which husband and children are glad to escape either to the street, the theatre, or the tavern.'[31] Female vices would undermine the home: 'Gossiping often leads to disorder. A woman who "looks well to the ways of her household" never has leisure to stand for an hour or two during the day in a self-constituted court of busybodies to discuss the character of her neighbours.'[32] Gossip, the woman's column in the *British Messenger* reported in 1930, is always to be found amongst women having tea together, but warned that 'when we are retailing tit-bits of gossip, even should it be true, it is neither more nor less than evil speaking'.[33] Bad temper was a particular vice; one moral tale was told of a Mrs Bryson who had 'marred her son's character for life by her variable, uncertain treatment of him in childhood'.[34] The *Girl's Own Paper* in 1883 advised the teenager that 'no trait of character is more valuable to a woman than a sweet temper. Let a man go home weary and worn by the toils of day ... [and] it is sunshine on his heart.'[35] Obstinacy in curmudgeonly old women was frequently harangued: a minister rebuffed on district visiting at a door grieved that 'a woman of seventy-five, so soon to take her trial before the judgement seat of God, should have so little concern for her soul'.[36] The codes of female respectability were many and varied. Yet, obsessive regard for some codes was unhealthy: in 1890 'a respectable maid' thought it improper to take all her clothes off for a bath, even when alone, and as a result had not washed her chest and back for sixteen years, giving her 'blocked sweat glands and pimples'.[37] In these ways, piety *and* femininity were explored and discursively constructed by mutual cross-reference.

Meanwhile, other's virtues were endangered by female faults. 'Our light words, our frivolous treatment of sacred things, may often have helped to lower another's standard of goodness.'[38] Mothers could also do harm by their innate goodness. In a tract of the 1870s, a mother was criticised for not being honest with her dying seventeen-year-old son, whom she had 'always comforted, telling him that the Lord will never suffer such a poor suffering creature to perish, but will take him to heaven'. This was 'a fearful mistake' by 'the affectionate mother', an 'unscriptural and most dangerous' lie, leaving the son 'at death's door, I fear, unprepared, and needing to be warned to seek mercy where alone it could be found, and to cry, "Lord, save me; I perish." '[39] Evangelical magazines carried long and detailed articles for young men on how to detect the flawed future wife and mother. *The Christian Miscellany* advised in 1867 to 'get to know ... the stock' from which a bride-to-be came: 'Moral as well as physical qualities must be considered. Dirty, slatternly, brawling mothers have sometimes clean, tidy, gentle daughters; but, I am afraid, not often. In most cases the scold and the slattern are reproduced.'[40]

If the godly mother was the ideal of pious womanhood, the young girl had detailed injunctions for every step of the way to that condition.

Children in the first sixty years of the nineteenth century were subjected to shock treatment in the evangelical press by being bombarded with the issue of death. Obituaries made up as much as half of the pages of the early magazines for children. Typical from 1827 was *The Primitive Methodist Children's Magazine*'s account of Hannah Rorhs who died in Paris two years before at the age of eight years. Her grandmother had met John Wesley and she was 'blest with pious parents'. 'Little Hannah had the fear of God before her eyes: she was never known to tell a lie in all her life'. But on a trip to Paris, she caught a fever which lasted three weeks and took Hannah to her deathbed.

> During this time she frequently requested her brother John to read the Bible to her ... In general she was perfectly sensible, and especially so towards the close of her earthly career. She lifted herself up in bed twice, as if she saw some object, and said, 'Let me come to your lap.' She often raised her hands as if in prayer, and seemed lost to those around her. When Death struck the last blow, and her spirit was about to take its flight, Hannah, with an audible voice, repeated the following lines:– 'How kind is that inviting voice/Which bids me seek immortal joys;/ ...' Her voice was lost, and she expired as she uttered the last word, not being able to finish the verse.[41]

The obituary was not a passive recording of a holy little life, but was a didactic challenge to the very young reader. One obituary of 1843 in the same children's magazine ended:

> Little reader, do not put off repentance in hope of being saved on your death-bed; for you do not know that you will die on a bed. You may be taken ill suddenly, and die at school, or when you are playing. If this were to be the case, whither would your souls go? Would they not go to the place of darkness and fire, such as you never felt? Many children die unexpectedly.... Lay aside your Magazine, and fall on your knees before the lord, and cry to him for mercy; then he will save you, and make you happy.[42]

This was powerful, intense material with which the generations born before 1850 were raised. At the same time, young girls were made aware of their transformative power over men's natural weakness. One story of the early 1870s told of the heroism of an eight-year-old girl sent by her mother ('we hope, truly converted to God') on an errand to 'a family notorious for wickedness, and especially swearing'. In their house, she was trapped by an older lad who pointed a shotgun at her, who demanded: 'You must swear or die.' She replied: 'Fire, then, for I'll rather die than swear!'[43] Such 'martyr-courage' gave female piety an heroic edge that remained a key element of the construction of the adult woman's piety.

By teenage years, religiosity was drawn in an intensely romantic context. Magazines soaked the young female in poetised and illustrative visions of the ideal woman. Wordsworth was frequently quoted in religious magazines throughout the nineteenth century:

> I saw her upon nearer view,
> A spirit, yet a woman too!
> Her household motions light and free,
> And steps of virgin liberty;
> A countenance in which did meet
> Sweet records, promises as sweet;
> A creature not too bright or good
> For human nature's daily food;
> For transient sorrows, simple wiles,
> Praise, blame, love, kisses, tears and smiles.[44]

The teenage years were the woman's most morally vulnerable period of life. In the 1840s and 1850s evangelicals counselled parents about letting their daughters near ballrooms or even private dancing parties. 'Ah! how many a cruel wound may have been inflicted on the yet tender conscience of your child as she has threaded her way through the mazes of the dance, while with throbbing breast she has drank in the soft flattering words of the heartless trifler by her side.' Through the dance, 'circumstances so full of peril to their purity and peace' could arise which could irredeemably lose female piety: 'The grass hath withered, the flower thereof hath faded, and the chiefest of the many charms of her sex and age, in the grace and fashion of it, hath perished for ever.'[45] Parental prevention of that loss was critical. The dance halls, ballrooms and theatres were, for most evangelicals of the mid-nineteenth century, strictly off-limits to the moral and pious woman. Equally, sporting events were much too 'rough'. Horse racing events were corrupted by 'the bearded, bestial-looking nondescript which issue from their dens in every corner of the land', but evangelicals had to acknowledge the moral negotiation – the 'dialogue', as one tract of 1852 put it – that had to be entered into: 'Respectable people, in large numbers, attend on such occasions – the Queen herself attends, and she is held to be a pattern of all that is correct and becoming, even in the female portion of the community of our religious land.'[46] The development of music hall, variety theatre and the cinema from the 1880s to the 1920s created a particularly tricky time for evangelical negotiation of 'fashion'. Film was much used by evangelical organisations between 1905 and 1914, but by the 1920s most spurned it and advised young women against cinema-going for, as the woman's columnist in the *British Messenger* put it, 'by the very fact of your being there at all, however good a moral a few pictures may illustrate, you are in a certain way sanctioning the whole vaudeville show,

which is of the world – worldly'.[47] Reading habits also constituted a problematic for the pious woman to negotiate. Whilst it was folly 'to refuse to
the overtasked mind an innocent or rational recreation', reading needed to
be taken in moderation: 'I knew a lady', reported a tract of 1853, 'who
completely used up her stock of sensibility, by devouring novels at the rate
of fifty or a hundred a-year; and when she came to a dying bed (an awful
one), her complaint was that *she could not feel.*'[48] The pious were warned
off even the most popular novelists. The *Christian Treasury* analysed *David
Copperfield* in detail, and found 'all the characters in the story [that] are
so painted as to awaken the abhorrence of the reader, are described as
professors of religion'.[49] Even Walter Scott's *Rob Roy* and *Kenilworth*
tended to associate reformed evangelical religion with 'repulsive and forbid-
ding sternness, with avarice and meanness', and as such were adjudged to
have done more to undermine true Christian faith and reverence for the
Bible than Tom Paine's *Age of Reason*.

However, the evangelical press was far from purely negative in its
discourse on the femininity of the young woman. Evangelical magazines
and books lingered long on feminine fashions, especially for young teenage
girls, with illustrations of heroines in the latest clothes. By the 1890s and
1900s, religious papers like the *British Weekly* were full of advertisements
not merely for women's fashions but for sanitary towels (which were explicitly described in their operation and fastenings), corsets (including electrical
corsets for curing all manner of ailments), stockings and other products to
save women from biliousness and other discomforts.[50] Such advertisements
– pages of them and heavily illustrated – signified how women's bodies,
and especially younger women's bodies, had become a major focus of attention in religious, improving and domestic magazines.

Meanwhile, denominational magazines debated women's role in society
from a strategic and scriptural standpoint. In 1824, the Baptist New
Connexion queried: 'In what way may females be most usefully employed
in a Christian church consistently with the apostolic decision, 1 Tim. ii.
12?',[51] to which respondents agreed that women could teach children in
Sunday schools if a man was absent unavoidably, but it was really a job
'incumbent on male teachers'. When women visit ill women, said one writer,
'they can pray with them with affection and holy fervour; when they meet
together for the express purpose of prayer, they can pour out their souls
before God, with earnestness, feeling, fluency and correctness'; women
should not be 'limited within their own circle of acquaintance, or be with-
held in such cases of emergency'.[52] In 1844, the *Free Church Magazine*
discussed 'Female Methods of Usefulness', describing women as 'benevolent from natural sensibility, active from constitutional inclination, amiable
from temper'. Yet, such 'respectable, and in many ways highly useful
persons' could not be thought of as automatically 'renewed characters';
women had to be called forth in Christian action with a 'becoming spirit':

Zeal and activity are, in their own places, excellent and essential qualities; but Christian women require to be very cautious, lest, even in the midst of praiseworthy exertions, they sacrifice those meek and lowly tempers which are so calculated to adorn and promote the cause they love and advocate. Female influence should shed its rays on every circle, but these ought to be felt, rather in their softening effects, than seen by their brilliancy. There are certain duties which sometimes call Christian women out of their quiet domestic circle, where both taste and feeling conspire to make them love to linger; such duties will, we humbly think, be best performed by those who enter this enlarged field, not from any desire of a more public sphere, but because, in obedience to the precepts of their divine Lord, the hungry are to be fed, the sick comforted, the prisoners visited.[53]

Each denomination negotiated, often very slowly, the extension of female roles. Whilst small numbers of women preachers were known by mid-century, usually in the smaller English evangelical churches, many mainstream denominations experimented from the 1850s with the formal role of women in nursing and parochial work. But the years 1887–91 were critical, with the Church Missionary Society admitting single women as foreign missionaries, the Church of England solemnising deaconesses, and the Church of Scotland appointing deaconesses and forming the Woman's Guild.[54] By 1900, women were an accepted part of the professional mission scene, and female missionaries became role models in the popular magazines.[55] Their part in converting men of industrial towns of the north of England – the archetypal 'home heathens' – was especially prominent.[56]

What is important in all of this was not just the *content* of the discursive injunctions that were being circulated in the religious press, but the intensity of the link that was being established between the social construction of female piety and the social construction of femininity as a whole. From the 1840s these two were envisioned in discourse as being inseparable. Piety and femininity were mutually enslaved discursive constructions, each providing the primary exterior site (or exteriority) for the other. Just as piety was constructed as an intrinsically feminine quality to be expressed in female duty, biology, dress and recreation, and femininity was enshrouded in a pious respectability, so the woman's magazine emerged as a shared religious-secular 'site' for discourse. The religious press pioneered the format of the girl's and woman's magazines. It was in magazines like the *Girl's Own*, *The Leisure Hour* and *Chatterbox* that the very format of the woman's magazine emerged: the agony aunt, the columns on cookery, gardening and thrifty hints, and the fashion pages. The agony aunt's column in the *British Weekly* of 1886 gave detailed advice to a reader's earnest inquiry:

I hope your winter costume is of the ever-fashionable navy blue, for there's nothing so becoming to a complexion as fair as yours. You look well in bronze; but any of the dead-leaf shades are too staid and sombre for a girl in her teens. Girlhood lasts such a little while that we ought to do our utmost to set off its early bloom. For an evening gown I like to see you in pale blue . . .[57]

From 1900 the reader-to-reader advice column became a primary location for moral advice:

What to Do. Problems of Conduct No. 689.
Miss Lily Alexander has worked in a soldier's canteen for nine months. She is leaving to go to similar work in France. Unknown to her the other workers subscribe for a present. She does not approve of presentations in war time . . . What should Lily do?[58]

Equally, the religious woman's magazine was by the 1880s and 1890s a major site for manufacturers' advertisements for ladies' products. Every advertisement and article format delivered the same message: women's piety was not a struggle but a negotiation. Most enduring, penetrative and influential of all the types of article in magazines was the fictional story.

TELLING STORIES ABOUT WOMEN

From the late eighteenth until the mid-twentieth centuries, the British developed a passion for stories. Whether in the full-length novel, the magazine-serialised novel, the novella or the short story, the nineteenth-century mind was brought up and regularly fed on grand, sweeping narratives focusing invariably on the life history of one central character. 'The dominant artistic form', as the modern novelist Ian McEwan has recently written of the nineteenth century, 'was the novel, great sprawling narratives which not only charted private fates, but made whole societies in mirror image and addressed the public issues of the day.'[59] The characteristic form of the nineteenth-century novel was a vast landscape of personal time – invariably great chunks of an individual's life (and critically the period from puberty to young adulthood) – in which a medley of characters come and go whilst the hero/ine navigates the self to a 'higher' plain. With the take-off in popular publishing in the 1840s, such life narratives formed the almost daily diet of most literate Britons. They were reared on stories, fictional and non-fictional. Indeed, the non-fictional story was invariably told in the same format as the novel, charting the individual's life through critical years in a highly descriptive and dramatic story-form. As McEwen says: 'Storytelling was deep in the nineteenth-century soul.'[60]

The study of narrative structures is a growing and productive area of historical research. It reveals how societies imagine their own configurations, how they typecast and stereotype the individuals in social dramas.

Two historians of narrative have written that scholars of narrative are showing that 'stories guide action; that people construct identities (however multiple and changing) by locating themselves or being located within a repertoire of emplotted stories; that "experience" is constituted through narratives ... and that people are guided to act in certain ways, and not others, on the basis of the projections, expectations, and memories derived from a multiple but ultimately limited repertoire of available social, public and cultural narratives.'[61] Of critical literary significance in the nineteenth century was the melodrama which, as Patrick Joyce has persuasively argued, was a narrative form which began as 'populist' in the early decades but which was adopted for the mass-circulation 'improving' magazines of the 1840s, 1850s and 1860s. In these, an audience, already accustomed to the melodramatic form, were invited to identify with the virtues of social improvement – teetotalism, churchianity, hard work, thrift, rational recreation, imperial patriotism, and so on – through the narrative tales of individual lives and social commentaries. Stories of heroes and heroines overcoming insuperable odds – poverty, crime, drunken husbands – were allegories of social redistribution and social reconciliation, a 'probing of the moral drama of an unequal society'.[62] Judith Walkowitz has shown the centrality of the melodrama for sexual narratives in late Victorian London, narratives which in newspapers, court cases, learned journals and elsewhere imagined women almost exclusively as victims.[63] This melodramatic literature of 'improvement' laid out the burning questions of moral relations in a society of manifest inequalities of income, wealth, opportunity and gender. It turned over these questions, investigated them, and postulated through narrative example (supported by straight exhortation) the triumph of morality over inequality. As Elizabeth Ermarth has written: 'Social order in nineteenth-century narratives ... is not a reality to be reflected but a problem to be solved.'[64]

The stories of the popular, as well as religious, magazines of the Victorian period were invariably founded on implicit Christian interpretations of 'improvement' and of life 'dramas' as obstacles to that improvement. In essence, moral 'improvement' became synonymous with Christian 'salvation', and the journey, often melodramatic, to that state of grace acquired exemplars. These exemplars were used to express the nature of male and female irreligion and religiosity and the means of progress from the first condition to the second. There was a strong inheritance of religious life narratives to draw upon. First and foremost amongst these was John Bunyan's *Pilgrim's Progress* (1678–84) which is frequently cited alongside Dickens, Scott and Thackeray in autobiographies and oral testimony of those born in humble homes in the nineteenth century. The *Progress* in both its title and its narrative was a literary template for the nineteenth-century novel, religious and secular, and in the late eighteenth century the dramatic autobiography of the 'religious life' became well established.[65]

When the novel boom began in the 1830s, evangelicalism almost instantly captured the genre and popularised it.[66] If Dickens, Scott and Thackeray were the most widely read individual storytellers, evangelical stories were more widely disseminated. The religious magazine adapted the life-story to the fiction format with ease. In fictional or 'real-life' stories, the life-story was an odyssey between polarities: from youth to age, puberty to maturity, poverty to prosperity, sadness to happiness, spiritual death to spiritual life.[67] There was adventure in the form of heroic deeds and far-flung travels in dangerous places, especially, as we shall see, in stories for older boys and men, but the inner adventure of the individual was far more prominent. It was the personal adventure, the negotiation of the polarities of good and evil, right and wrong, morality and immorality, which dominated the long discursive passages of the Victorian and Edwardian story.

If melodrama provided a familiar scheme for tales of personal advance and negotiation, romance was equally critical for representation of the conversion. 'What story can you find for romance like His?', wrote a major-general in the British Army. 'It is the reality of romance, as well as the romance of reality. It is indeed His story, and it is history.'[68] By the 1870s and 1880s the story was conceived widely in evangelical terms, becoming sacrelised by the conversion which became the emblem of not just spiritual but also social salvation of the individual. The story of conversion was told and retold endlessly in the form of a fictional short story (usually complete in one magazine edition, though sometimes serialised or in separate longer-novel form). Starting in the early 1830s, improving magazines pioneered the serialisation of novels, and from the 1860s these stories were usually accompanied by at least one lithograph illustration of a scene from the story which, by 1900, was customarily on the front cover of the magazine with the story immediately following. The format was regular, familiar and repetitive.

So too was the structure of the life-story narrative. Such qualities in the construction of narrative have attracted scholars' attention in recent decades, but at different levels. Northrop Frye was struck as a child by the regularity of Walter Scott's 'formulaic techniques', and came later to locate the structure of all romance in 'four primary narrative movements in literature' which constituted a 'secular scripture'.[69] He subsequently postulated that the Bible offered 'the Great Code' of seven main phases of 'dialectical progression', providing the recurrent shape of all literature in U-shaped narrative structures of apostasy followed by descent, repentance and rise.[70] Umberto Eco explored similar terrain in his analysis of Ian Fleming's James Bond novels as 'a narrative machine', in which he compared the rules of the narrative to 'a machine that functions basically on a set of precise units governed by rigorous combinational rules. The presence of those rules explains and determines the success.'[71] Essentially constructed on Saussure's pioneering study of linguistics and Lévi-Strauss's structural anthropology, the narrative is studied in terms of a series of oppositions which are, in Eco's words, 'immediate and universal'. The oppositions can be permutated, the interactions varied from story to story, but they form an invariant structure of oppositions which breed a familiarity in the reader. In the Bond novels, the oppositions are between Bond and the villain or the woman, between the ideologies of democracy and totalitarianism or communism, and a large number of relations between value-types such as perversion–innocence, loyalty–disloyalty, chance–planning. These bipolarities form in succession the narrative's progress from its start point of 'danger' to its conclusion of 'victory' (Bond over villain, Bond with the woman, the free world over communism/totalitarianism). These oppositions in succession form the sequential structure of the story, what Eco calls a succession of 'play situations' in which each move gives rise to a countermove, propelling the story forward.[72] Eco identifies within the story a series of oppositions which correspond closely to Foucault's notions of discourse in which ideal and anti-ideal exist in necessary conjunction. These oppositional discourses emerge within the story in succession, forming its episodes or narrative structure.

Eco's methodology is highly relevant to the evangelical narrative. Indeed, it is entirely possible to read the evangelical narrative structure as a common thread linking popular religious and secular fiction of the nineteenth and twentieth centuries. Though it may have earlier origins (and was most certainly popularised in *Pilgrim's Progress*), it only became thoroughly regular and repetitive in the nineteenth century and – most importantly – assumed a dominant discursive role in popular culture. Whilst Frye may be right in identifying the Bible as 'the Great Code' for narrative romance, religious literature of the nineteenth century familiarised English-speaking people (and very probably others) to the specifically *'evangelical* code'. It was this code that established the appetite for the literary boom of the late nineteenth and early twentieth centuries which almost universally used that code, providing Britons with the primary format in which they learned, explored and negotiated their own individual life destinies. The published story was no mere invitation to self-conception; it was an injunction to do so. The life-story, including the obituary, was a guide to behaviour: 'What a hint is this', said one magazine in 1848 at the end of a story, 'to pious young women, whose husbands are not religious!'[73] Within the life-story were located the issues of life destiny which each person was compelled to negotiate, placing piety within personal narrative. Stories were consequently vital to the conception of religiosity in Britain in the nineteenth and twentieth centuries.

The stories contained vital variations in how religiosity was conceived. The vital, primary variation was that between women and men. Just as discourses on male and female piety varied, so the evangelical narrative in which they were located varied. Both the female discourse and the female narrative structure constituted the benchmarks of piety, the discursive 'good' against which the discursive 'bad' of male piety was to be measured. Men had lower religious credentials than women, and the life narrative of each was structured around this discursive understanding. While men were the religious problem, women were the religious solution.

In the inter-war period, Grace Pettman was a prolific evangelical novelist. One of her short stories in the late 1930s was *The Unequal Yoke*.[74] The story was told in the first person by Peggy, and started:

> Had not Guy Wilbraham come into my life – never, never to go out of it again? An elder brother of my old school chum, Guy had gone to Northern India tea-planting some years before. But Mollie had chattered incessantly of her absent brother, so I was quite ready to join her in her hero-worship, even before he came home on furlough. And then? – Well, the first meeting changed everything. What he saw in me to love I can't imagine, but as for Guy – well, every girl in the place was ready to lose her heart to him, and no wonder. Before I realised it, I had given all the heart I possessed into his keeping, with all the freshness and pureness of a first great love, unspoiled by any senseless flirtations to take the bloom off the gift.

From the outset, widely appreciated evangelical codes were deployed to establish binary oppositions: empire and home, worldliness and innocence, experienced man meets young woman with no 'bloom off the gift'. The couple became engaged, and Guy returned to India waiting for Peggy to join him. Meanwhile, Peggy was asked by a Sunday school superintendent to take a difficult Bible class of 'one or two clever high-school girls, and three or four young women who were engaged to be married'. There she tells Solomon's warning of taking 'a heathen wife', frightening one woman in the class whose fiancé was far from godly. This in turn frightens Peggy: 'I had all along known quite well that Guy and I could never walk together in the ways of God, and marriage between us would be an unequal yoke indeed.' Guy wrote from India urging her to give up Sunday school teaching, saying: 'The Sunday School type doesn't work among the set I'm in here ... I have got more sick than ever of the whole religious show.' Guy was, Peggy says, a 'free-thinking sort'. She then broke off the engagement, Guy got married (in a registry office, not a church) to 'Fanny Farne, of the Frivolity Theatre, London', and Peggy heard no more of him. She took to doing mission work in a small rural village, finally moving to Cornwall where her mission work had great resonance:

> ...a great work commenced. Men and women who could remember the Cornish revivals in the days of old, said that the former times had come back again. Night after night rough lads and young girls,

older men and care-worn women, crowded the after meetings, and there were many decisions for Christ.

One night there was a fierce storm and a shipwreck on the shore. Peggy assisted the survivors, and Guy was washed up, near death. Peggy heard that he had been preaching to the sailors on the boat as it made its way from India, and as he recovered Peggy heard his story. Guy's wife had died after a year of hateful marriage: 'He had hardened his heart, and lived a life of forgetting God until a year before. Then slowly the hard heart was broken, and at length Guy was surely led from infidelity to Christ. God at last claimed him for his own.' Coming round on the beach, Guy was repentant:

> 'I know I am not worthy, Peggy,' he said, 'but I love you. Can you after all the past, trust yourself to me?'
>
> And so, instead of spending my life alone, henceforth the two of us will go together, the glad work of telling the Gospel story will not be ended – rather – rather, since two are better than one, the best work lies before.

The structure of this story depends on a series of binary oppositions, culminating in the conversion of the 'villain' to God and to woman:

A. Godly young woman falls in love with ungodly man
B. Wickedness of ungodly young man destroys plans of godly young woman
C. Godly young woman works hard and unselfishly
D. Ungodly man pays price for his ungodliness
E. Ungodly man is converted
F. Chance event
G. Man and woman make godly union

This scheme of narrative episodes was the template of the evangelical narrative, usually composed of around eight segments. The narrative episodes each contained, with the exception of the chance event, an opposition between *two* things: 'godliness' and 'ungodliness', man and woman, and so on, the number *two* becoming, in its repetitive usage, what narratologists refer to as a 'pattern number' of storytelling to which the reader becomes accustomed.[75] If the pattern number remains a constant, the order of moves between narrative segments could vary between stories. Moves could be varied first, as with Eco's analysis of Bond novels, by changing their order (by moving the chance event to a different narrative spot, for instance) or the nature of the agency for converting the ungodly man. Second, this narrative with an 'ideal' outcome could be inverted into a 'tragic' outcome; instead of happy temporal results from Christian rebirth, there could be an unhappy or even horrific end, despite rebirth in woman, because of the power of evil and of Satan within ungodly man.

One important and common variation is that the godly woman herself may be the agency, or part of the agency, for the conversion of the ungodly man. In a story from 1903, 'Won by his wife', a 'good woman' Carrie Foster 'made a bad match' in Tom Grant, a London cabman, who with his drinking kept the family income low for twelve years and left the home threadbare: 'So clean and tidy it was, but, oh – so bare! Sitting there I soon heard the story of the blighted hopes, the shadowed home, the saddened heart; and all through drink.' Then Tom had an accident falling off his cab, and through this accident and Carrie's attentive Christian nursing, he was converted: 'So it's true enough that Tom Grant is converted, and if anybody asks you how it came about, you can just tell them that it was no parson and no preaching, but it was his wife's life.'[76] In this variation, the narrative order changes with the conversion and the chance event being inverted so that the latter becomes the instigator of the former. This was a very common narrative structure, its theme replicated many times. In 'Fanny's Mistake and Its Sequel' (1924), orphan girl Fanny Irwin worked as a domestic servant and was 'a joy' to her employer until she took up with dissolute youth, Jim Pollock, who was 'handsome and attractive, constantly in bad company, [and] he was known to bet and drink'. Fanny married him but could not reform him: 'he soon plunged into drink more than ever to make him forget his betting losses'. A baby came along, Jim lost his job, and Fanny had to go out to work. Then, Jim was run over by a motor lorry (the chance event, shown in illustration) and told by the doctor that he would only survive his injuries if he gave up drink. Through this 'miracle', Fanny is able to turn him to God: 'Jim Pollock knows from blessed experience that there is power in the blood of Christ to break the chains of evil habit and to set the captive free.'[77]

In this way, women's religiosity was critical to moral change in men. Indeed, it is hard to find a fictional evangelical narrative in which a man's conversion did not involve a godly woman. In a serialised novel in the *British Weekly* in the late 1880s, Annie Swan's *Doris Cheyne*, the young heroine discovered that Mr Hardwicke in the manor house had lent money to her mother for the purchase of a school on the 'understanding' that Doris would wed him. Learning of this, Doris refused Hardwicke marriage and asked him to pass the debt to her. Overwhelmed by her nobility, Hardwicke in an instant cancelled the debt and became 'a better man': 'You've shown me that there are things better than money in this world. I'm in your debt, my dear, deeper than ever I'll be able to pay. You don't know what you've taught me. I've watched you, and I've been a better man since a thought of you filled my heart.'[78]

In fictional evangelical narratives, the chance event was usually of a dramatic kind, appealing to the melodramatic appetite of Victorian and Edwardian readers. But in true-life stories, the chance event is often portrayed as duty. In 'The Wife's Six Mile Walk', a story from 1862, a woman has married a bad man: 'In N. H— lived Mr. and Mrs. B—. The husband was a rough, profane, wicked man, a despiser of the Gospel of Christ, caring only for the things of this life. His wife was awakened to an interest in spiritual things, and at length, as she hoped, became a new creature in Christ.' She walked six miles to church to profess herself as a sinner and be reborn in Christ, while her husband despised her effort. Her regular attendance at church and her new religious state introduced severe tension in their relationship: 'The conflict was severe, but not long. He felt himself to be the chief of sinners and was enabled soon to surrender all to Christ. His wife's strict and patient performance of duty, and her simple loving prayers were the means which God blessed to his conversion.'[79]

The evangelical narrative had the ability to be inverted from romance to horror. In the full-length 1894 novel, *The Sacrifice of Catherine Ballard*, the story began at an auction in London with a man buying the forty-year-old diary of a young woman. The reader gradually realises that the purchaser, Oliver, had sought the hand of the diarist, Catherine, in marriage in the 1830s, but Catherine's father had blocked it. What Oliver discovered from the diary was that Catherine's father had given her in marriage to Gideon, the planter son of a business partner, because of business debts. Oliver learns, many decades on, that Catherine was an unwilling bride, marrying to please her father and save his business:

> We pass over the wedding. The awful lie was consummated. God's name was outraged, as it too often is at the marriage service. And all the fearful enormity of Catherine's sacrifice and her sin came so over-poweringly to her soul, as that service closed, that, with white face and listless, nerveless frame, she sank fainting at the communion rails.[80]

Oliver learns from the diary that things went from bad to worse for Catherine. She joined her husband Gideon on his Jamaican plantation and bore him a daughter in 1832. The year following, slavery was abolished, a development Catherine not only welcomed but which set her to teaching the Bible to her husband's slaves, encouraging them to seek their own dignity in the Lord. On hearing this, Gideon had become a monster, telling her:

> 'I hate you, loathe you, would like to shoot you down as I would a nigger – only that would be too quick, too easy a death for you. . . . I bought you on purpose to kill you, but to kill you slowly. I found out from your father that some one else, some canting religious sneak, wanted you, and you wanted him, I believe; so I bought you right out to take you down . . . Yes, madam!' he hissed; 'my slave. Bought with gold, as I bought all my field hands. Aha! Madame Sancti-monious, that has found out your temper, has it?'[81]

Gideon overpowered and whipped her unconscious with his riding crop, and she fell seriously ill. Meanwhile Oliver, broken-hearted, had buried himself in colonial service, but he heard of Catherine's illness and rushed to Jamaica just as she died. He rescued the baby daughter and her black nurse, bringing them back to London where he raised the girl, only to discover the full story in the diary many years later.

Catherine Ballard is a novel of considerable social as well as spiritual seriousness. It makes horror of parental selfishness, black slavery and male brutality, gelling these issues of human dignity in a single Christian perspective. Most powerfully, it presents women as the victim of male exploitation – of fathers who corrupt their daughters and destroy their lives for commercial gain, and of husbands drunk on power and an insecure masculinity expressed in racist denigration and extreme domestic violence. It is also about women's secret sacrifices, which may be hidden from good men, and known only to God and the personal diaries of 'His dealings with me'. In tackling these themes, it varies the nature of the evangelical narrative, bringing in the spectre of the unreformable man, premature death, and the ruined domestic partnership of a godly couple. It is a tale which provides negotiation between a woman's duty and a woman's Christian rights. She is not a piece of property to be bought and sold, even by her parents. Her duties should not force her to lie before God (as in the marriage ceremony), and should not force her to forsake a godly union with another professing Christian. The professing Christian woman must profess in matters of love as well as in matters of religion.

Though the female evangelical narrative structure might vary in these ways, there were uniform characteristics. First, women's conversions were usually taken for granted; the issue was their ability to choose a godly husband or to reform an ungodly one. Second, women's spiritual destiny was virtually never portrayed as a battle with temptation or real sin; fallen women did not appear as central characters, and none of the usual temptations like drink or gambling ever seemed to be an issue with them. The problem is the man, sometimes the father, but more commonly the boyfriend, fiancé or husband, who is a drinker, gambler, keeps the 'bad company' of 'rough lads', and is commonly also a womaniser. The man is the agency of the virtuous woman's downfall; he does not make her bad, but does make her suffer and poor. She is not always portrayed as having undergone a major conversion experience, but to have emerged from childhood into a disciplined and natural 'goodness'. Those virtues are ordinarily unalterable, only open to mild subjugation through the influence of men or frivolity. In 'Saved from Drifting' of 1922, a twenty-two-year-old well-to-do orphan with time on her hands dabbles with spiritualism to contact her parents. An aunt exhorts: 'Like too many today, Lucia you are, I fear, drifting and clutching at any fragment of new thought.'[82] Here the temptation is drawn from natural grief in bereavement; the temptation is a fad or frivolous. The totally depraved woman was hardly ever portrayed in detail in the evangelical narrative, and certainly not as the heroine, though she might appear as an off-stage character as with Guy's theatrical wife in *The Unequal Yoke*, whose sinfulness is also mediated by being described as 'of the Frivolity Theatre, London'. The depraved woman is a freak, and seemingly very rare: arty, 'free-thinking', and invariably from London. Interestingly, prostitutes rarely feature and hardly ever as named characters; they are beyond the pale for a 'women's narrative', being reserved as a 'temptation' for men's stories.

In featuring women's relationships with men, the evangelical narrative was invariably drawn into romance. In the 1850s and 1860s some improving magazines negotiated a fine line between criticising it and adopting it. 'Dear reader,' the *British Messenger* quizzed in 1865, 'is your heart broken, completely broken? If so, it is about the happiest heart out of heaven. True, a breaking heart is not a happy heart, but then it is unhappy, not because there is so much of it broken, but because there is so much of it whole.'[83] Romance was a test for all manner of virtues. In 1867, *The Christian Miscellany* warned against marriages that were 'imprudently early' because of the 'dread', the 'utter horror', of debt: 'It deadens conscience; it is the parent of all kinds of evasion, and trickery, and falsehood; it oppresses the spirit; it mars domestic peace; and, sooner or later, in most cases, it presses the subjects of it down to the earth in humiliation and tears.'[84] Finding the right Christian man was the uppermost consideration rather than the age of engagement. The ending, as in all evangelical stories, was always happy – as in *Love's Healing* in the 1920s which concludes with the heroine marrying 'a splendid Christian man. She is fortunate indeed and will be a happy wife.'[85] By the 1930s and 1940s, scores of paperback religious novels appeared, aimed almost exclusively at teenage girls and young women. Love was the dominant theme, following a format familiar to Mills & Boon readers, but with a Christian 'spin', ending with lines like: 'What are you thinking of, darling?' whispered her husband. 'I was thinking how good God is. I've never been so happy in my life.'[86] Romance was set within a tough system of moral values, but it was invariably the *man's* moral values that were the criteria, making the women's issue the arrival at the right judgement on the man's worthiness.

The discourse on women's piety involved change during the period. Women's economic role was expanded in evangelical narrative with, by the 1920s and 1930s, ever-increasing representations of the professional woman. This resulted in many stories excluding men. *The Doctor's Story* of around 1930 was set in London, and began: 'Yes, it was over at last – all the waiting time, training time, and learning time, in Hospital and Medical School. I was a fully fledged doctor at last, able to write the coveted letters after my name, "Lucy Larkin, M.D.," to put up my brass nameplate – and to wait for patients.'[87] Lucy met a down-and-out woman in need of medical assistance who led her to a City Mission run by Sister Faith who persuaded Lucy that her skills as a doctor should be combined with mission work 'in the East'. Lucy hesitated for long, but was convinced when Sister Faith told her on her deathbed: 'Ask them – those women over there – to accept the Lord Jesus Christ as their own personal Saviour. Tell them – how much He means, especially to us women.'[88] It was not merely new jobs for women to which the evangelical discourse on female religiosity had to adapt. In 'Red Emily and Her Changed Creed' of 1937, Emily was described as 'an incorrigible rebel' at the age of fourteen, and at sixteen was sent to be trained as a domestic servant on a farm where she stole and was forced to leave. 'That was the beginning of her career as a revolutionary', and Emily joined a band of disaffected young communists in the Midlands, reading Marx on economics and urging violent overthrow of capitalism, and becoming a street-corner orator. But she happened upon a late-night gospel meeting, attracted by the oratory, and heard the message within it and came forward to be saved, whereupon she became a happy and contented domestic servant.[89]

In these and other ways, the evangelical narrative responded to changes in the wider discourse on women's economic and social lives, and thereby sustained core characteristics of female piety and femininity. This could be seen in stories for the very young girl. *The Good Way* and *Daybreak* of the Edwardian period (both priced at a penny-ha'penny) contained stories and homilies with simple messages imparting a notion of good behaviour in young children: 'Mamma, I wish I might always dress in white … Because, Mamma, the angels dress in white, and I want to be like them.' Mamma: 'white is the emblem of purity, and that is the reason it is spoken of as the raiment of heaven.'[90] Stories for young girls tended to be less melodramatic than for teenage females, but they utilised a whole range of 'feminine' contexts to explore simple moral issues of goodness, meekness, obedience and self-discipline: contexts like gardening, pretty clothes and household duties.[91] The almost constant concern with girls' clothes, with the prettiness of 'Sunday best' dresses especially, symbolised the way in which female religiosity and femininity were closely allied in discourse. As the next section contends, the sites for these discourses were also closely allied.

EVANGELICAL NARRATIVES IN THE SECULAR WOMEN'S PRESS

From the 1830s, the massive popular press of weekly and monthly magazines absorbed the evangelical narrative structure into a 'secular' context. The connection was so close that it is almost inappropriate to speak of separate 'religious' and 'secular' popular magazines until at least the last decade of the century. Some magazines avoided obviously 'religious material', such as the *Englishwoman's Domestic Magazine*, launched in 1852 by Samuel Beeton, whose empire of improving publications went on to include the *Boy's Own Magazine*, *Queen*, and his wife's *Beeton's Book of Household Management*. But when not explicit, piety was embedded in discourses on femininity in articles on clothes, cleanliness and above all romance.[92] From the 1860s, the romantic genre expanded massively into popular papers for girls, cheap novels and short stories. The religious and secular women's press formed a continuum; the immensely popular romantic fiction writer Annie S. Swan wrote serialised novels for the religious paper the *British Weekly* and started her own 'secular' *Woman at Home* in 1893. With more downmarket varieties like *Home Chat*, romantic fiction had by the 1890s a fixed and prominent position beside needlework, the agony aunt and domestic advice in the woman's and domestic magazine.[93] The market for romantic fiction then grew with the arrival of the cheap novel, reaching a mythic quality in the output of Mills & Boon from 1909.

In the early decades of the improving magazine, exhortation was more common than fiction for circulating moral discourses. This was particularly the case with the temperance message, which was inherent to all improving literature.

> See the temperate man entering his house to spend his evening with his family. How delighted they are by his presence! Some of the pence he has saved from the liquor vault have purchased a copy of some cheap and useful publications ... Let it not be said, then, that man wants artificial excitements. He will have excitement and pleasure enough in his evenings at home, and, in his frequent walks abroad with his wife and children, pointing at the beauties of the heavens and the earth, and discoursing with his family on the nature and design, so far as yet discovered, of the works of the Almighty.[94]

But from the early 1830s, improving fiction was developing as a genre particularly aimed at women. With women rarely depicted as managing economically without a man, picking the right husband was a prioritisation drawn straight from evangelical discourse.[95] 'The Runaway' by Miss Mitford, published in *Chamber's Journal* in 1832, was set in a small English village in which the heroine Mary Walker was an heiress to a small inheritance who attracted so much male attention that she rarely went to the inn for 'dread of encountering some of her many lovers'. She became engaged to William, a humble but likeable fellow, but on the day before their wedding she accepted a present of two live pheasants from George, the gamekeeper, 'a good-natured a fellow as ever lived, and a constant visitor at the sign of the Foaming Tankard'. On the wedding day, William heard of the gift and became jealous, telling Mary: 'George Bailey is the beau of the parish, as you are the belle'. With that he stomped away from the village, to return four years' later 'a poor ragged famished wretch' at death's door. Mary came to his side:

> ... and the poor runaway grasped her hand between his trembling ones (Neptune fondling them all the time,) and life, and health, and love were in the pressure; and the toils, the wanderings, the miseries of his four years' absence, were all forgotten in that moment of bliss.[96]

In 'Miles Atherton', a short story of 1832, Mary was married to a lazy man who gave his son to a chimney sweep in return for cash, but the boy was returned to his mother by a passing soldier. So taken with the guilt of neglect, Mary was immediately converted:

> 'Not yet gone to bed!' said Miles Atherton, with a harsh voice, as he entered the room in that reckless and violent manner habitual to the profligate. His wife was now above the power of fear – no beating at her heart – no trembling in her limbs; for the comforter had been with her, and there was such an expression of blessedness on her countenance, as moonlight shewed it pale, wan, sunken, but rejoicing, that the wretched intruder was fixed in amazement.[97]

At which point Miles was also converted, and both Miles and Mary fell to their knees in prayer. 'Evil found now no abiding place in his spirit', and both then went to church every Sunday.

The theme of spiritual journey was central to Victorian and Edwardian novels. The plots were 'often episodic and based on the journey trope: the idea that life is a road with a moral destination, a pilgrim's progress'.[98] Ermarth comments that evangelical self-examination 'literally provided a narrative structure' for Victorian fiction: 'The history of "turning" or conversion from one way of life to another moved from the diaries of Methodists straight into the autobiographies and novels of the nineteenth century'.[99] The 1840s was a decade when the evangelical narrative structure emerged in the 'secular' novels of the Brontes, Thackeray and the early Dickens novels.[100] The quest for salvation, even when none appears, informs the narrative pattern of even *Vanity Fair*, a novel consumed with the profound arbitrariness of life.[101] Bunyan's *Pilgrim's Progress* of 1678 was a model for so much of the romantic and religious fiction of the nineteenth and early twentieth century – for Thackeray and Charlotte Bronte[102] – and many other novels were infused with religious structuring or motifs (including the use of Anglican references to the Book of Common Prayer in *Dombey and Son* of 1846–80), whilst the genre was utilised by churchmen like Cardinals Newman and Wiseman.[103]

What Ermarth calls the evangelical 'experimental narrative structure of error, crisis and conversion' gave way in the later Victorian period, with the impact of Darwinism, higher criticism and scientific 'doubt', to a new style of 'high' fiction in which negative conversion narratives were characterised by unresolved doubt. In these, characters despaired of salvation, culminating in Joseph Conrad's reversal of the salvation story in *Heart of Darkness* (1902).[104] However, the experimental novel with an inverted salvation narrative could not compete with the mass popularity of other genres which depended upon the evangelical structure. Foremost among these was the romantic novel, the most popular British novel form, which owed its origins to evangelicalism. Walter Bagehot opined in 1858 that romantic fiction was an 'addiction' of young readers, and 'a kind of novel has become so familiar to us as almost to engross the name, which deals solely with the passion of love'.[105] For Victorian women writers, fiction was almost inconceivable without romantic relationships between men and women, even when exploring their anxieties, anger and ambivalence concerning women's subordinate position in British society.[106] Its secular pinnacle was attained in the output of the Mills & Boon publishing house which started in 1909, whose novels followed the evangelical narrative in mixing the male public sphere and the female private sphere – not, as jay Dixon argues, to subordinate and imprison women in inferior roles, but by conflating them 'to reaffirm the heroine's world – her values and expectations, her needs and way of life'. The shared characteristics include the periods of tribulation and physical crisis which the man undergoes. Mills & Boon novels employed notions of a journey, describing the emotional and sometimes moral journey a hero must endure before 'finding' his heroine. By validating her world of home, romance and family, and by the fusion of the hero and heroine in marriage as the final resolution, the romantic novel is emphasising that the female sphere is necessary to the public sphere.[107] This argument can be taken a little further. In the romantic narrative the home becomes the place of feminine power to which men become subordinate as the source – discursively the only source – of their moral authority. Indeed, in Mills & Boon's pre-1918 novels, religion is an explicit element in the heroine's romantic odyssey, and even after 1918 when explicit references to religion waned, love continues to be described in terms of religious salvation: evangelical terminology continues to be used, such as 'cleansing', 'fallen so low' and finding love as 'the Promised land'.[108] Most fundamental of all, the Mills & Boon novel shares with the evangelical narrative structure the absolute certainty of marriage as the final act of the story.

One curious omission from secular fiction of the 1840–1940 period, unlike evangelical literature, is the mother. Ermarth comments that in historical and social novels they are 'an especially endangered species', appearing as dead or 'ghostly women', often off-stage or characters previous to the plot.[109] But this divergence was perhaps not surprising. The time between puberty and marriage was the critical evangelical space for a woman to be saved and find a 'good man'.[110] Even in the evangelical narrative, engagement and the wedding become the displaced conversionist experience for a woman, with the marriage the arena for the contest to ensure the training and conversion of children and, if necessary, of her husband. The period of marriage is then, in narrative terms, not about the woman as the central character of the plot but about her husband or children. The woman in marriage is the facilitator, the moral foil, for the endangered moral state of others.

Thus, a subtle change came upon the domestic setting of the evangelical narrative within 'secular' literature between the 1920s and 1950s. The home was no longer discursively the arena for tense and anxious maintenance of the moral being, but became the venue for the depiction of unalloyed happiness. The foundation of the married home was no longer the restart of the 'moral cycle' of conversion. This reflected how in these decades the moral campaigns of evangelicalism against sites of male temptation finally ground to a halt. The prohibition cause died in England in World War I, and in Scotland and Wales in the 1920s, while the anti-gambling campaign lost its argument when the 1934 Betting Act signalled the commencement of legalisation through government participation and taxation of revenue.[111] A poised ambivalence and hypocrisy reigned over the governance of British moral law between the mid-1930s and the late 1960s. Most forms of gambling remained illegal, but they were virtually rampant in British life until the final legalisation of off-course betting in 1961. Whilst prohibition was almost government policy in the 1914–18 war, drinking and 'playing hard' were actively condoned in the 1939–45 war. By the early 1940s, the pub was shown in many wartime films as not only 'moral' but as the centre of the British man's firm resolve to beat the Nazis.

This reduced pressure upon the woman in the moral sanctuary of home, and was reflected in the emergence of the married woman in the 1930s and 1940s as a revered figure in British secular fiction. A classic representation is *Mrs Miniver*, which first appeared as a fictional serialised diary in *The Times* in 1937–9, then as a novel, and subsequently as an MGM film of 1942 starring Greer Garson, and celebrated as 'one of the most effective pieces of propaganda for Great Britain' during the war.[112] In both literary and film versions, *Mrs Miniver* was striking for its portrayal of the happy home-loving domestic wife to whom nothing much happens. Domestic peace and orderliness is her joy: 'Her normal life pleased her so well that she was half afraid to step out of its frame in case one day she should find herself unable to get back.'[113] The ability to negotiate relations with servants and the working classes, to be the social peacemaker and the anti-snob, reveals a new egalitarian agenda – one noticeably developed in the Americanised film version which deployed Mrs Miniver (the character) as the model of how World War II's corrosion of class division should be accomplished. She is a woman of capability and good works, freer (as Alison Light points out) from the constraints of aspiring to be 'an angel in the house' than the Victorian middle-class woman, and ironically freer from the greater domestic confinement of the 1950s servantless middle class.[114] In this way, whilst Mrs Miniver still acted as a cipher for Victorian domestic ideology, yet she had greater freedoms and more democratic inclinations. Marriage sustained romance and her sexually attractive qualities; for her 'the most important thing about marriage was not a home or children or a remedy against sin, but simply there being always an eye to catch'.[115] Nonetheless, Mrs Miniver was not secularised. In the film especially, churchianity has a central moral and community place in the social fabric, with Sunday worship in the Anglican parish church displaying the social hierarchy (of boxed pew for the aristocracy, front seats for the middle-class Minivers, and rear pews for the servant class), and the venue for romantic liaison between the Miniver boy and the aristocrat's daughter. News of the declaration of war comes – as it did for many of Britain's churchgoers on Sunday, 3 September 1939 – in mid-worship. As Alison Light observes, the novel is 'a fantastic, fictional resolution of anxiety' for the English middle-class woman of the 1930s,[116] but the film unites this fable of domestic romance with Mrs Miniver's quiet heroism in capturing a crashed German pilot. Perhaps unrealistically, Mrs Miniver in the film has no apparent wartime duties, so her incursion into 'manly' bravery is transitory and not a transformation of woman's role away from domesticity.

Mrs Miniver's diary in *The Times* was matched by Patience Strong's 'Quiet Corner' in the *Daily Mirror* for expounding the role of home life as central to personal and spiritual well-being. The fad for domestic self-satisfaction was even the object of satire in a 'Contentment Column' in a Graham Greene-inspired weekly magazine in which the British home was caricatured as 'full of sanctity and lethargy'.[117] Though a consciously class-based depiction of British life, this literature and film of the 1930s and early 1940s took an evangelical narrative shorn of sin – its threat, let alone its contemplation – and placed the angel in a house of serenity and goodness. The central moral coda of the evangelical narrative not only remained untouched, but was reinvigorated by the loss of 'sin' and depiction of manly temptation. The secular variant of the evangelical story was shutting its eyes to sin; with the prohibition and anti-gambling campaigns losing their arguments in the 1930s, the domestic story left the woman presiding over a house where moderation in drink, wagering and enjoyment was entirely consonant with domestic bliss.

By the 1930s and 1940s, a rift had developed in the portrayal of women between the evangelical narrative of traditional religious literature and the secular narrative of popular literature for girls and women The secular narrative was showing less and less interest in overt religion, and notably conversionism which all but disappeared. This may be explained in large part by the decline of specifically evangelical Protestantism, marked by the fading fortunes of the Nonconformist and dissenting presbyterian churches, the decline of evangelical campaigns for temperance and abolition of gambling, and decline in the religious press. On the surface, it appeared that religion was disappearing as an issue in the discursive portrayal of British womanhood. However, the change was less radical and more subtle than this. The religiosity of woman was being shorn of its *literal* religious conversionist character, but was left in an intensified metaphorical character. Women were being shown not as striving to create an anxiety-driven climate of Christian rebirth in the home, but as effortlessly attaining a state of moral domestic contentment.

The decay of conversionism and the rise of the cult of contentment was most discernible in literature for teenage girls and young women. Between the 1880s and the 1920s, the *Girl's Own Paper* was dominated with stories of 'waiting for the right man': a man of good morals, sensitivity and interest. In the main serial of 1886, the heroine weighed up her leading man: 'He had his taint of worldliness; he was by no means perfect – kind-hearted, frank, and generous as he was. He had a high regard for the world's standard of gentlemanly decorum, and would have felt as much ashamed of failing in a point of etiquette as of committing a far graver error.'[118] The heroine waited on him day and night: 'There were days when he did not come to the house, mornings when I lingered till the last moment in the garden without seeing him'. The *Girl's Own Paper* urged women to train to please men; the ultimate danger was not a 'moral fall', but spinsterhood. One article provided the precise demographic data of women's problem: in London in the mid-1880s there were 1,123 women to every 1,000 men, with the clear message that moving to London in search of 'a position' reduced the odds in the lottery of man-hunting.[119] Women's role remained unremittingly domestic. On the problem page, a male inquirer worried about finding a woman to teach geometry to his future sons, and was told: 'it is more essential for her to study the art of nursing the sick and the care and rearing of young children; the arts also of teaching needlework in all its branches, of housekeeping and cookery, and of guiding and directing a household, and the work of each servant, as well as the etiquette, under all circumstances to be observed by the mistress of the house who receives and goes into society.'[120] In 'Between School and Marriage' (by the much published author of *How to be Happy Though Married*), a woman's years between the ages of 18 and 21 were delineated as 'golden girlhood' when boys might go to university or training, and girls must guard against 'uselessness'.[121] Jobs for women remained before World War I not vocations, but moral interludes: women should select positions in 'thrift', not finance, as church organists, or sanitary inspectors.[122] Prize essays for readers were on 'My Daily Round', calling for and getting lists of domestic or work duties placed in a moral framework, ending with homilies from hymns: 'Labour is sweet, for thou hast toiled,/And care is light, for thou hast cared.'[123] Evangelical religion remained dominant. In the 1880s and 1890s, the paper had its own branch of the YWCA for readers and the 'Girl's Own Guild of Scripture Reading and Study', each with their own weekly columns.[124] As late as the 1910s and 1920s, the *Girl's Own Paper* had the familiar symbols and signs of the evangelical discourse on femininity. The magazine had an unrestrained piety, including weekly 'Prayers of Unfolding Womanhood' contributed by a clergyman ('consecrate to Thy service my womanhood's strength and grace'[125]), and editor's lead articles entitled, 'The Joy that Remains: One of the Miracles of the Spiritual Life', and 'Our religion will bring us no real joy until Jesus Christ becomes the Personal reason for all our actions.'[126]

But in the mid-1920s the *Girl's Own Paper* entered a period of extraordinary transition, in large part because it faced competition from a plethora of more populist magazines for elementary, secondary, and working girls, though many did not survive the slump.[127] Romantic and 'schoolgirl-gang' fiction predominated in these competitors, and started to lead teenage girls away from preoccupation with marriage. The *Girl's Own Paper* responded, largely in the 1930s. In 1926 it still had stories like 'The Adventures of a Homely Woman' and 'The Better Man: It's not always a Misfortune to be Jilted' (which compared closely to a 1917 story on 'The Barrier to Intimacy: The Joy that Followed a Broken Engagement'), and contained items on the Women's Institute, prayers, 'Facts and hints for the Reading Girl' and 'The Verse Book of a Homely Woman'. But it also had features on 'Things for the Bachelor Girl' (primarily furniture for the bachelor-girl flat).[128] The discourse on spinsterhood was beginning to disappear. By the late 1930s, the transition was in full swing, with remnants of evangelical discourse heavily muted by a new editor who gave the magazine a revised subtitle: 'Stories of adventure, mystery and school: articles on careers, handicrafts, hobbies, sport and travel.' The lead fictional stories were now school japes, led by 'The Jays', a group of fourth-formers, their silly dormitory activities and their amazing adventures. Sports were now a central item, with every issue carrying photograph strips on how to play games: netball, skipping, rounders, lacrosse. Career opportunities as barristers and photographers now provided a thoroughly modern image, enhanced by colour plates of fictitious historical heroines in modern clothes and make-up. One colour painting was of an attractive blonde girl on the beach, dressed in loose and sleeveless beach blouse, a ball in one arm and her other hand on her hip in a muscular, brash and sexy pose. This is nothing short of a pin-up, but it is of a girl not a boy; indeed there were virtually no pictures of men in the magazine of the late 1930s. The image is that of a cheerleader.[129] Teenage girlhood was no longer an interlude between school and marriage, a period of mere preparation for the domestic role. It was now a period for expressing independence and developing contentment with the physicality of the female body. With religion now relegated to a few lines of holy poetry, a 'muscular girlhood' had apparently superseded evangelical discourse.

However, contented marriage and home, though decreasingly discussed in 1930s girls' magazines, was still an imbedded meaning, especially evident in what Tinkler classifies as mother–daughter magazines.[130] This reflected greatly what was happening to the depiction of the mother as symbolised by Mrs Miniver. What changed in the 1930s and 1940s was that contentment displaced anxiety in moral discourse. The artefacts of male temptation – drink, betting and pre-marital sex – were no longer the problem; it was *discontented* rather than *immoral* manhood which the woman had to combat in the home, and to do this she had to make the home an unremittingly happy place. This necessitated a broadening of girlhood from the pursuit of goodness to the achievement of personal happiness upon which a contented home could follow. The happily married woman was turned, in discourse, from an anxiety-inducer into a cheerleader.

In this, there was more troublesome internal contradiction. It called for a cheerfulness and contentment which still demanded absolute moral virtues of thrift, sobriety, self-discipline, chastity before marriage and suffering of others' faults. Men were being discursively 'freed' from the moral constraints of anxious pious women; instead, their morality was to be achieved by women's achievement of a contented household. But embedded meanings remained for women. They were still expected to seek their femininity from a religious-based coda which, however liberated from conversionism, was still tied to an evangelical vision of the 'good woman'. However, to some, this linkage appeared fragile by the late 1930s. As David Kyles, a prolific tract writer, told women in 1938, 'we have seen a moral paralysis creeping over our people'. The Great War, he wrote, 'unleashed a pagan flood which swept away many a sacred sanction' and drove the nation into 'a remarkable surge of pleasure-seeking, heightened by a not disinterested devil's brew of press, cinema, wireless, tobacco and drink combines, gambling and other vice industries'. As a result, said Kyles, 'women ceased to prize their womanhood'.[131] On the eve of World War II, pious femininity and feminine piety both seemed endangered, and the ties between them threatened.

HEATHENS: MEN IN DISCOURSE AND NARRATIVE 1800–1950

——— •✦• ———

THE PROBLEM OF MALE RELIGIOSITY

As femininity and piety became conjoined in discourse after 1800, the spectre arose of masculinity as the antithesis of religiosity. From the sixteenth to the eighteenth centuries, a wife's femininity was perceived as a threat to piety and household, and a husband established his moral status by controlling her. From 1800 to 1950, by contrast, it was a husband's susceptibility to masculine temptations that was perceived as a threat to piety and household, and the wife established a family's respectability by curbing him.[1] Exemplars of piety changed sex, from being overwhelmingly male to being overwhelmingly female, and the route to family harmony no longer lay in the taming of the Elizabethan shrew but in the bridling of the Victorian rake, drunkard, gambler and abuser.[2]

For men as for women, the discourse change around 1800 was dramatic. As domestic ideology and separate spheres caused gender roles within the home to become increasingly segregated, men were expected to submit to the pious domain of the feminine hearth and home. Though the reality of the Victorian man's attitude to piety and domesticity was far from universally hostile (certainly in the middle-class world),[3] this submission was depicted as a sacrifice of innate masculinity. If women's piety became depicted as intrinsically contented, and remained remarkably stable in this condition during the nineteenth and early twentieth centuries, men's piety was perceived as in constant inner turbulence and its depiction subject to increasing discursive instability. As a result, there was extensive experimentation in the construction of moral masculinity: in the rise of muscular Christianity from the 1840s and 1850s, and its role in sport; in the advance of militarism as exemplified in the Volunteers after 1860 and militarised youth movements (like the Boys' Brigade) from the 1880s; and in the attempts of some religious organisations like the Salvation Army to utilise a curbing of manhood as an evangelising strategy.[4] This chapter argues that these were not changes to masculinity as such, but rather 'sub-discursive' struggles going on in the shadow of an overarching opposition between the conceptions of piety and masculinity. The problem for religion after 1800 was the need to corral masculinity within the newly constructed and feminine-prioritised piety, to attempt resolution of men's exclusion from the domain of piety.

During 1887 and 1888 the religious newspaper the *British Weekly* published some forty articles on 'Tempted London', a series concerned with the moral condition of men and women in the capital. Men and women were dealt with separately – men during the first thirty articles, women in the last ten. The nature of moral weakness in the two sexes was conceptualised very differently. The articles on women were organised on the principle that occupational exploitation corrupted women. 'We intend to arrange them in classes,' the first article on women stated. 'We shall begin with the lowest class – namely, flower-girls, watercress-sellers and street hawkers. From this class we shall pass on to factory hands, girls in trades, servants, milliners, dressmakers. . . .'[5] The iniquities of the trades in which the women worked were studied in detail, focusing on low wages, home working, long hours and the exploitation of employers and merchants. Home workers and street sellers were the main object of attention, from the palm-weavers and necklace-makers of Tower Hamlets to the fraudulent servants' registries which ripped-off poor migrant girls.[6] The women themselves were not deemed 'immoral', either explicitly or implicitly, but as victims of casual work, street work and home working. Women were regarded as degraded rather than demoralised or immoral, and interestingly there was no mention of prostitution.

The *British Weekly* spent only four months studying women, but seven months on men. The organising principle here was different, with the focus not being on work but on sites of male temptation. The men's articles were organised around three headings: drink, betting and gambling, and impurity. The venues for each temptation were studied in detail through the personal visits of the newspaper's 'commissioners' to business houses, pubs, clubs, betting houses of various kinds, gambling clubs, music halls, dance halls and so on. 'The danger of the quiet, orderly club', a typical article on the 'respectable' gaming club ran, 'is more invidious and its influence more unconscious to the youth who chances to be introduced there. He has been taken, say, by some one who does not appear a special blackguard, but simply a man who "knows the town".'[7] Gambling clubs, by contrast, were visibly dangerous: 'If you go into Soho you may get your head broken, in others one is as safe physically as in one's own dwelling. But in all the atmosphere is unhealthy and vitiated; the myriad microbes of moral disease abound in the very air.'[8] The pubs were the key, being invariably the first stop on a man's route to other venues of temptation: 'Having a drink may almost be called the latch-key to everything that is vicious'.[9] Music halls 'engender looseness of behaviour and laxity of morals', especially through familiarising young men to banter with girls: 'Lads who would probably not think of accosting girls out of doors, see every one exchanging chaff with the opposite sex, and therefore do likewise, in fear of being deemed soft: and when nicely-dressed young women knock against them in the crowd, ... find it quite an ordinary thing to have drinks with them.'[10] After much advance publicising, the articles on male 'Impurity' turned out less than a voyeur's fantasy. The editor of the *British Weekly* backed off, saying that 'our business is not to furnish unclean details'.[11] He attacked 'loose reading' in the form of translated French novels, pornographic pictures and copies of *Maria Monk*[12] available in the streets around the Strand. He added one paragraph on 'secret vice', the code for masturbation, 'generally learnt early at school, and when it gets a hold is rarely shaken off', which resulted 'in many cases [in] complete collapse of body and mind', 'premature break-downs among young men', full lunatic asylums and suicide. 'It is necessary,' the paper wrote, 'for parents and teachers to warn their sons against this ruinous practice and its consequences.'[13]

The *British Weekly* series reflected the view that at the heart of urban society, the problems of social order, crime, immorality and irreligion were interconnected products of male weakness. This weakness was intrinsically rooted in maleness, a heathen 'other' located at sites of temptation:

> O lift the workman's heart and mind
>   Above low sensual sin!
> Give him a home! the home of taste!
>   Outbid the house of gin![14]

Victorian tags blended discourses on men's moral and religious condition with discourses on their economic, sanitary and cultural condition: the 'loose', the 'fast', the 'pagan', 'the lapsed masses', 'the sunken portion', 'the submerged tenth', 'the rough', 'the residuum' and 'the great unwashed'. These were moral pejoratives of great currency in Victorian and Edwardian Britain, terms which instantly resonated with the central problems of indus-trial and urban society – a language which simultaneously identified problems and solutions.[15] Clergyman used this language as the basis of religious rhetoric. This was especially the case amongst those providing 'social-science' analysis of the religious problem; a church census of 1904 stated that the 'immense battalions of non-churchgoers' were 'degenerating into materialism on the one hand and paganism on the other'.[16] The home heathen was characteristically a member of the working classes, but the subject of discourse was not confined to him. 'Nothing retards the progress of the Gospel in any neighbourhood,' wrote one evangelical journal in 1867, 'and hinders the conversion of the ungodly, so much as the misconduct of the men who profess to live a Christian life. When such men are lax in their morals, of dubious honesty, untruthful, and guilty of occasional acts of intemperance, they harden sinners in their impenitence, and weaken the hands of the real friends of Christ.'[17] This was the 'Bill Banks' factor: a man being never wholly 'rough' and never wholly 'respectable'.[18]

After 1800, one of the first manifestations of men's exclusion from feminised piety was the evangelical obituary. 'This blessed revelation of the happiness of the pious dead', wrote an evangelical obituarist in 1840, 'is designed not only to comfort but to stimulate surviving Christian relatives in their faith and hope to press forward, till they also shall be called to put off their armour, and enter upon the same state of a blessed immortality.'[19] Obituaries of men tended to display a degree of honesty about men's religious conversion that was not apparent with women. In 1867, Henry Currie was noted as having been 'brought to God in a prayer-meeting' four years before his death, and as 'a prayer-leader and the head of a household he was faithful in the discharge of all his duties, never missing family worship, morning and evening, no matter what the pressure of business might be'. He died a 'happy death', but yet his obituary acknowledged that 'He had a severe struggle in obtaining mercy'.[20] Obituaries giving unqualified praise to women for providing husbands and sons the correct environment for their salvation rested side-by-side with men's obituaries about 'long and painful application' before attaining salvation.[21] Joseph Knight, a divinity student who died at the age of 26, made 'fervent and numerous supplications' for an 'early piety', but despite intense 'conversation' from others 'respecting the necessity of his fearing and loving God supremely', and though the 'depravity and sinfulness of his nature was pointed out to him', his obituary left a noticeable blank concerning his conversion.[22] Some obituaries went further and detailed the sins of men before their conversion. Thomas Gray from Lincolnshire was taken regularly as a child by his parents to the Church of England, but 'being destitute of the power of religion, he addicted himself to cock-fighting, card-playing and similar dissipations'.[23] Most common of all was exploration of the deceased's spiritual struggles, notably amongst clergymen. Obituarists were spiritual commentators: in one Methodist preacher's struggles, it was explained in 1811, 'we may perceive a good foundation was laid, in a sound conversion, on which a superstructure of holiness was erected; – and ... by the *hell* and *heaven* which Mr. L. had experienced in his own mind, he was prepared for usefulness in future life'.[24]

The evangelical challenge from 1800 was to develop strategies within the overarching discourse of the 'home heathen'. Feminising men was undoubtedly the most important of these strategies. This started with young boys who had to be 'feminised' by maternal influence. The evangelical press illustrated stories with drawings of boys and young men with their mothers, often sitting on the floor by their mother's chair. Fathers were rarely pictorially depicted. A leading woman of the Baptist New Connexion in the 1840s advised fellow mothers:

As to drums and flags, we should never think of encouraging these as toys for our children lest we should excite in their minds a warlike, and consequently a wicked spirit. . . . We will try to prepare them, not to be generals in the field, but heroes in the moral world.[25]

Boys had to suppress their masculinity to be good Christians: 'Now, why is it you boys are always ashamed of your best side – anxious to be thought gruff and hard-hearted? I fancy it is because you dread all things to be called unmanly – "soft".' Their mothers were the source of, and should remain the constant inspiration for, their true religion:

You will stand by her open grave in the churchyard, and you will weep – for men and boys shed tears – ay! – *hot* tears over their mothers' graves, and there will come back to your memory all the kindly things she did for you, and all the good words she said to you, and all the tears she shed for you, and the sacrifices of pleasure she made for you, until the thought of it all swells your heart to bursting. Yes, *one* day you will remember! . . . Never get too big, or too busy, or too manly for mother's love and mother's counsel.[26]

Adult men were constantly challenged in religious discourse about their masculinity. In 1878, the *British Messenger* mounted a series on 'Are you a man?'

My friend, are men – real, downright, genuine men – men that would meet God's high purpose, plentiful now? Has our boasted civilization largely produced them? Do they congregate in our towns and great commercial cities? Have our political schemes and parties, even our numerous churches and chapels, evoked them? Is the crop really good?[27]

Even the men of 'so-called Christian nations' did not supply 'what in God's sight would be accounted a man'. Heaven's definition was at variance with earth's: 'We are fully aware that according to men's own ideas of themselves there are plenty of men, that they are to be numbered by the million, and no bad specimens of the race either'. But men defined manly qualities in physical terms: courage, muscular strength, brains, independence. These were not God's definitions: 'to be a man, a true and real man, we must keep the "body in subjection," put a rein upon the appetites, and a bridle on the passions. So far as anyone fails in this, he ceases to be a man, and takes level with the brutes.' The 'unclean person', anyone who 'lives after the flesh', is not a man. Even intellect is not enough: 'Is the drunkard, with brain soddened in strong drink, a man?'[28] A true man has feminine qualities; he has sympathy and compassion for other men, is righteous, 'has mastery over his lower self', and has 'the courage of the truth'. True men have been 'a moral and spiritual power in the world': Abraham, Paul,

Luther, Knox, Chalmers, Wycliffe, Cromwell, Wesley, and Christ, 'the perfect man'.[29]

The masculinity of soldiers and sailors was seen by evangelicals as the severest of tests. One woman who specialised in evangelising at Aldershot found soldiers were hindered in coming to Christ: 'They tremble, but they do not decide; they come a certain length, but no farther.' Religious meetings were well attended at the garrisons, but at after-meetings only small numbers fell under 'great contrition' and wept on account of their sins. Lack of emotionalism was a key stumbling block. But the two distinctive problems with soldiers was fear of ridicule and love of sin: 'Many a man would rather encounter the enemy's fire in open line, "than be laughed at in the barrack-room." He would "die for the colours," but he cannot live for Christ.' This was intensely frustrating to the true evangelist. Tracts were taken and ridiculed in the barrack-room, and all the vices of the male world reigned: lust, the 'fast life', 'sowing wild oats', and above all drink. This gave rise to two big moral problems in the army: desertion and suicide, each the product of absence of true religion. Soldiers would not kneel for appearing foolish: 'I'm quite converted, thank you,' one soldier was quoted as saying, 'but there's no occasion to kneel down; I can praise the Lord in my heart.' Pride would not take the soldier further, even on his deathbed. This type of converted soldier was reported as common, displaying an 'outward reformation' or a mere 'turning over a new leaf'. The lady evangelist reported: 'It goes by the name of "Ladies' Religion".'[30]

As a result, the way in which the strategy of feminising male piety was constructed in discourse *to men* was very important. To attract a man's attention to feminine piety, the language of discourse had to be 'manly'. This was evident in the masculinity in which the evangelical 'spoke' to his unreformed brothers in tracts. Religious tracts were particularly targeted at men, and adopted a virile, 'fellow-sinner' tone and a bold presentation. The voice of the tract was male, a man of the world who had known the sins of drink, the flesh and moral corruption, and was no wilting violet. This is especially true of the plain didactic tract, usually of one, two or four pages, which tended to be based on straight exhortation. These were characteristically on the themes of drinking, Sabbath profanation, swearing, prayer, and failure to come to a decision for Christ. Tracts were forthright and challenging, using large letters and block printing in forceful text. They presented opposites in clear form:

> Reader! – There are two ways of beginning the day:– with prayer or without it. *You* begin the day in one of these two ways. WHICH?
>
> There are two classes of people in the world: – the righteous and the wicked. *You* belong to one of these two classes. WHICH?
>
> There are two places to which people go:– *Heaven and Hell. You* will go to one of these two places. WHICH?[31]

Short tracts were undemanding literature. They used simple metaphors of life to convey notions of bipolar opposites. In *What is Lost by Strong Drink?*, the losses were listed:

LOSS OF MONEY, HEALTH, BUSINESS, CHARACTER, FRIENDS, GOOD CONSCIENCE, FEELING, MIND, LIFE, THE IMMORTAL SOUL.

It is a long and terrible account to run up; but it is an easy one to begin, and I see even boys beginning it at the beer-shops – young men adding to it at the tavern and billiard saloon. Stop! ... Can you afford them in the long run of eternity?[32]

In *The Spiritual Thermometer*, all of life is reduced to a scale from 'Glory' to 'Perdition':

GLORY
Dismission from the body
Desiring to depart and be with Christ ...
Following hard after God
Deadness to the world ...
Looking for Christ. Justifying faith ...
Retirement for prayer and meditation
Concern for the soul. Alarm. Conviction
INDIFFERENCE
Family worship only on Sabbath evenings ...
Family religion wholly declined
Levity in conversation
Fashions, however expensive, adopted ...
Free association with carnal company
Love of novels and romances
Theatre, Races, Balls &c....
House of God forsaken ...
Fornication. Deistical company prized ...
Masquerades; Drunkenness; Adultery
Profaneness; Lewd Songs; Infidelity
Scoffing at religion. Persecuting the pious
Disease and death
PERDITION[33]

Life was conceived as a dynamic progression between moral states, routed either towards heaven or to hell. Tracts dwelt on either/or moral qualities and choices, demanding decision. They called readers 'sinners'. 'You are a great sinner. You were born a sinner. Every day you have been thinking sin, speaking sin, doing sin. Have you not?'[34]

Longer tracts of eight or sixteen pages took time to embrace men's culture with an authentic voice. One dealt with the moral dialectic at Epsom on Derby day: 'the roar and rush of life' with 'bookmakers, tipsters, costers, backers, the purse-trick gentlemen'. 'The showmen on the hill are shouting – "Walk in gents, no children admitted; wonderful freak of nature, walk in sir;" and the preachers on the course are singing "O Calvary, dark Calvary, where Jesus shed His blood for me."' The whole Hogarthian scene was a pan-class moral joust:

> The whole scene is a panoramic medley, the sound a perfect Babel, a mixture of culture and cruelty, of blue blood and blatant black-guardism; a mingling of peer and peasant, of duke and dustman; of prince and plebeian; from castle and from cottage, from the court and the camp; autocracy and democracy hobnobbing in the ignoble sport of gambling; the cream of society and the scum of the earth rubbing shoulders with each other.[35]

Tracts were socially levelling, targeting men of substance as well as of poverty: 'Quickly, ye men of business and might! Your life is more than half gone already. You have passed the crest of the hill, and are looking towards the sun-setting.'[36] Tracts attacked merchants who gave short measures or adulterated produce; true religion would banish 'pebbles from the cotton-bags, sand from sugar, chicory from coffee, alum from bread, and water from the milk-cans', and 'looks on a man who has failed in trade, and who continues to live in luxury, as a thief'.[37] Tracts were written and distributed for specialist sinners: drinkers on the way to the pub, gamblers, smokers, the 'impure', theatregoers, New Year revellers, Sunday traders. In the theatre were to be found 'wicked men, profligates, profane swearers, debauchees, prostitutes'.[38] One tract aimed at London theatregoers said you would find 'the scum of vicious poverty' in the gallery, 'the froth of vicious mediocracy' in the pit, and 'the cream of aristocratic pride, vanity, and scandal' in the boxes.[39] Tracts for every occasion and occupation were available: tracts for railway travellers, cabmen, tram-drivers, publicans, even 'back-sliding professors'. Tracts for and featuring miners and fishermen were common, and notably stories of real-life pit disasters. Six weeks after a disaster at Hartley which killed two hundred men, the *British Messenger* used it as an example for sinners, speaking of how the 'the bodies of the miners were nearly all found clustering close by the root of the old closed shaft': 'In the prison of our spiritual death', it continued, 'most of those who miss eternal life perish in the very act of struggling to force a way that has been closed.'[40] There were tracts which attacked 'our respectable young men, our young men of most gentlemanly manners and appearance, members of most honourable professions' who though 'free from the brand of open profligacy or avowedly infidel principles' were yet addressed as 'thoroughly licentious alike in sentiment and conduct, and alike regards morals and religion'.[41]

In this way, religious rhetoric 'spoke' differently to men than it did to women. Hell was a man's destination, but hardly ever a woman's. Hell 'is called the lake of fire, burning with brimstone. It is a place of terrible torture, dreadful agony, and soul-rocking remorse.' There were to be found 'thieves and murderers, whoremongers and adulterers, swearers and liars; the proud and the vain, . . . the covetous and over-reaching'.[42] In the contest with evil, the salvation economy would always win. A raucous young man at a ball in New England was reported by the *British Messenger* in 1865 as boasting that he would 'raise hell before morning', and then dropped dead in the middle of a dance: 'The still corpse in the ball-room; the blaspheming soul in the bosom of God! Such is the boasted *rational* religion.'[43] To the 'double-death' of dying unsaved was the final apocalypse to come:

> this dying earth
> Ere long shall vanish; all the pomp and splendour,
> Man's many follies, and his empty mirth.[44]

Beneath the bravado, man was vulnerable, and he left the more vulnerable in his wake. Sinful men disowned their godly mothers – a prominent and frequent topic of the evangelical press. 'Young man, have you a mother living still in God's earth?' wrote one evangelical paper in 1862. 'What is she to you? An old woman with wrinkled face and gray locks . . . Are you repaying in her uncheered age, the debt your early years contracted?'[45] The earthly bottom line of man's innate weakness to temptation was the moral and economic pauperisation of his family. 'Did that poor girl who gave her heart and hand to the showy vagabond who stole her affections choose to become a wretched wife? Yet she did choose to marry him; and she did it in spite of reason and conscience, and dearly does she regret the consequences of her choice.'[46] Evangelicals were forced to appeal to physical manliness; when distributing tracts to men, evangelists were advised to adopt a masculine tone: 'Speak of Christ in a bright, manly way,' was the instruction when offering a tract to a taxi driver, 'and he will probably . . . take your book.'[47] The men of the Welsh religious revival of 1904–5 were often portrayed as strong and muscular, shown in kneeling positions with arms outstretched in tensed positions of beseechment.[48]

The rise of 'muscular Christianity' from the middle decades of the nineteenth century was a notable attempt to redefine manhood by marrying physicality to spirituality. Muscular Christianity took on militaristic as well as patriotic overtones in the Volunteers (founded 1860), the Glasgow Foundry Boys' Religious Society (1866), the Boys' Brigade (1883), and later in the Church Lads' Brigade and the Scouting movement.[49] In each of these, sport was an important ingredient. These organisations were in part a response to the crisis of male leadership in existing evangelical organisations. Sunday school teachers declined from being over 80 per cent male in the 1840s to under 30 per cent in the 1870s, and the emergence of male-led uniformed youth movements with a military aura was a change in evangelisation strategy for boys over the age of ten or twelve years.[50]

As Norman Vance has observed, muscular Christianity tends to draw historians' attention more to muscularity than to Christianity.[51] Moreover, its influence was slower to spread from the public schools in the 1850s to a wider acceptance in organised religion than is often thought. The YMCA is a case in point. It was founded in the 1840s and 1850s on a curriculum of Bible study and earnest discussion, but in the 1870s changed towards a revivalist outlook informed by the Moody and Sankey revival of 1873–4. It was not until the early 1880s that it admitted sport as a significant part of its curriculum.[52] In addition, if evangelicals were increasingly speaking to men in a masculine 'voice' by the 1880s, this did not automatically mean that men were being urged to be 'manly' in the sense we understand of muscular Christianity. Tracts were written against games, in part because they were associated with 'Sabbath dissipation', and in part because they were regarded by many as unspiritual, diverting attention from the care of the soul. 'One particular characteristic of the ancient heathen, particularly the Greeks,' one tract of 1853 said, 'was an enthusiastic love of games and races', whilst the chosen tribe of Israel played no games. Modern games were 'most cruel and demoralizing', with boys as young as ten entering races for 'sordid' prizes; to cap it all, tales were told of men who died whilst running.[53] Two decades later, American Dwight Moody was very significant, as he focused evangelical attention on the nature of Christian manhood, especially amongst young men, by targeting them in his evangelisation.[54] Tracts on manhood, such as C.H. Spurgeon's sermon on work among young men, were distributed by his helpers (25,000 in one month in Glasgow alone). When women started attending his services in higher numbers than men, most of his meetings became ticket-only affairs for specific males: clergy, fathers, businessmen and students. Moody's preaching was taken by one evangelical paper as defining a new male Christianity: 'The Christian life he commends is manly and genial, intense, and yet not strained or twisted.'[55] Moody had a dramatic impact on male recruitment to both the mainstream churches and to home and foreign missions. His three visits to Britain between 1873 and the early 1890s became progressively less successful, but he spawned a generation of men who were drawn to be ministers or evangelists – most notably in industrial, fishing and mining communities where they were influential in the Brethren and independent evangelistic organisations. In these and many other evangelical organisations between the 1880s and 1920s, there was little room given to sport. When sport threatened to become a male passion which overrode respect for the Sabbath, the *British Messenger* opined in 1922: 'The passion for sport will tend to overpower the already far too weak sense of obligation to the public worship of God. It may be a trial for boys and young men to restrain their physical energies on Sunday, but such restraint is highly beneficial for them morally, we believe also physically.'[56] And even when sport was utilised by evangelicals, as in the Boys' Brigade, there was no complete ditching of the attempt to androgynise Christian manhood. In the 'BBs', the curriculum may be regarded as perceptibly gendered, with compulsory attendance at the weekday prayer meeting qualifying the boys to participate in the Saturday football and drilling activities.[57] An act of (feminine) piety was required before admission to the (masculine) sport.

Much discussion took place in the 1880s and 1890s on how to Christianise men. Some churchmen felt that men had a specific problem about believing in miracles, but their approach of allowing Christ to be viewed as merely 'a historical figure of the past whose lessons are fitted for our moral guidance' was much criticised by others.[58] The essence of the discourse on male religiosity was to problematise masculinity, and to divert men away from their 'natural' state. Encouraging militaristic and sporting activities was not a caving-in to this, but was an attempt to contain, capture, restrain and discipline masculinity. Muscular Christianity was never unreservedly accepted in evangelical discourse on male piety because it was too closely associated with the sins of gambling, drinking and rough culture. Organisers of sport, especially commercial sport, became tarnished with the same brush as bookmakers and brewers.[59] From the evangelical standpoint, muscular Christianity was no more than an experiment and not a fundamental change to a dominant negative discourse on male religiosity.

THE PROBLEMATIC PIETY OF EVEN HOLY MEN

This negative discourse was so powerful that it was the main theme in biographies of pious men. Exemplars of holy women abounded in religious literature between 1800 and 1950. Every woman, from humble cottage or workhouse to suburban mansion or aristocratic country house, was capable of being used to represent piety. Holy men, on the other hand, were in rather short supply. It was the clergyman, especially of the dissenting denominations, who came to dominate representations of the holy man, and his piety was represented as a constant problem.

Clergy were prominent, popular and in some cases mobbed by admiring crowds. Some received huge amounts of mail from admirers. When R.W. Dale, the Congregationalist minister from Birmingham, left for a six-month trip overseas in 1887, he notified the public that letters would not be answered, and his return was the subject of great coverage in the religious press.[60] Thomas Chalmers recalled to a House of Commons select committee the popularity he had in his first urban charge in Glasgow in the mid-1810s: 'I was very much surprised at the unexpected cordiality of my welcome, the people thronging about me, and requesting me to enter their houses. I remember I could scarcely make my way to the bottom of a close in the Saltmarket, I was so exceedingly thronged by the people.'[61] Touring preachers like Joseph Parker of the 1880s were mobbed nearly everywhere they appeared.[62] Nineteenth-century clergy had the capacity for achieving incredible popularity. Their photographs were widely circulated and in some papers printed in full or even double-page formats, making them quite literally 'pin-ups'.[63] Even when not nationally famous, clergy were in a key position of influence and responsibility in public piety. The minister was frequently portrayed as the agency for the conversion of women. In 1866 the obituary of a Wesleyan Methodist woman acknowledged that 'Her conversion was the fruit of pastoral visitation,' whilst clergymen's published diaries show their own primacy in women's salvation: 'Friday, Feb. 9. I preached at Shapton; the power of God was amongst us. We held a prayer meeting. There was one mourner, but she did not get into liberty . . . On my way to Cawthorn, I called at Royston, and met with a woman mourning under a sense of her sins. I prayed with her, and God heard prayer and set her soul at liberty.'[64]

Clergy were unique and obvious exemplars of piety. However, a crucial and very prominent element in the portrayal of clerical piety was that their learning, status and bearing were critically mediated by two forms of vulnerability: first, vulnerability as economic and social victims, and second, vulnerability in piety.

The classic evangelical male biography started in the eighteenth century with the establishment of the narrative of the clerical hero-victim of dissent: notably the Methodist preacher in England and Wales, and the dissenting presbyterian minister in Scotland. John Wesley was the most prominent hero-victim in England, but the Scottish evidence is instructive. The clergy of the Scottish Secession and Relief churches, formed in 1733 and 1756 respectively, became mythologically established as the successors to the Covenanters of the seventeenth century who had resisted the Catholic and episcopal intrusions of Charles II and James VII.[65] The Seceders established a very thorough 'victim culture' from the 1730s, their puritan millenarianism evident in the culture of the fast days – the day of 'fast and humiliation' which preceded the day of communion for which manifestos were issued decrying 'the many other spiritual strokes we are lying under – while there is no suitable viewing of the Lord's hand in these strokes'.[66] The Seceders were the object of much criticism from the Church of Scotland, having no doctors of divinity amongst their number; in response, one Secession minister openly acknowledged: 'their ministers have been too poor to purchase the title and too illiterate to deserve it.'[67] Victim culture extended to members of the Church of Scotland where clergy had a whole catalogue of complaints with patrons and heritors. They complained of parsimonious heritors leaving their manses and churches in dilapidated condition; as one minister from Argyllshire wrote in 1790, 'with us of the church of Scotland, many of our country kirks are such dark, damp and dirty hovels, as chill and repress every sentiment of devotion'.[68] As a result, the minister became one of the first 'hero-victims' of the Scottish novel from the 1810s. Extremely influential in this was John Galt's novel, *Annals of the Parish*, published in 1821, in which the Revd Micah Balwhidder relates the parishioners' hostility to him for being 'put in by the patron' and how, on his installation, he was guarded by soldiers on the way to the kirk: 'The people were really mad and vicious, and flung dirt upon us as we passed, and reviled us all, and held out the finger of scorn at me; but I endured it with a resigned spirit, compassionating their wilfulness and blindness.'[69]

Whilst clergy of established churches complained of low rates of pay and parsimony on the part of powerful patrons, dissenter clergy (and their wives) made moral capital out of frugality and thrift. The loss of church members through schism is tackled in most biographies very diplomatically; the Revd Fergus Ferguson of the Evangelical Union lost large sections of his congregation twice in two years, and his biographer notes that 'the pastor acted in the kindest way, as they left and implored the divine blessing on their enterprise'.[70] One remarkable and popular Scottish biography of 1877, *The Life of a Scottish Probationer*, was actually about a man who failed, a 'stickit minister' who had graduated in divinity but who never received 'a call' to a congregation; instead he wrote poems and ended his life as an invalid. 'It would be unjust to [Thomas] Davidson', wrote his biographer, 'to represent him as having been a professional failure. The fact that he did not receive a call is neither to be attributed to his lack of power as a preacher, nor altogether to lack of ability, on the part of the congregations to which he preached, to discover and appreciate his gifts.'[71] At the other extreme, some clergy formed family dynasties which were eulogised in public esteem. From one generation to the next, they symbolised the great urbanisation and industrialisation of the nation, spreading out with each generation to new centres of industry and spiritual prosperity.[72] Each clerical auto/biography was a personal melodrama against temptation and congregational fickleness.

Piety never came easy to the clergy of the evangelical century. From the 1830s and 1840s, 'model ministers' were objects of public discussion in the cheap, popular 'improving' magazine, the religious tract-magazine, and the book-length autobiography. Thousands of ministerial biographies appeared between the 1840s and the 1920s, with those of Nonconformist and Scottish presbyterian clergy tending to make great play of lives begun in godly and dignified poverty, often in rural cottages. One biographer said of his subject: 'It was no slight advantage to the future minister that his education was thus begun at a common school and in the companionship of the children of the poor.'[73] They were invariably portrayed as good boys: 'While Robert Hood bore a good character outside his home, he also bore a good character inside it. It was the testimony of his mother than he never once said no.'[74] Henry Drummond was described as a lad: 'He was known as "the man with a secret", because he was so happy and good.'[75] Struggle through university and divinity school led on to issues of evangelical conversion and continual rebirth. These become the dramas – the personal melodramas – upon which the life-stories of the clergy hinged. For some it was a process, beginning: 'His conversion was not a sudden thing, but a gradual growing into the light. Some conversions come like a flash of lightening across a midnight sky, while others come like the sunrise. Robert Hood's conversion came like the sunrise. He had always been good, with his face towards the sun-rising, and at last the blessed beams of the Sun of Righteousness arose upon his soul.'[76] There then followed the evangelical themes of temptation, resistance and sustaining the state of grace: 'When he would be on his way to visit among the closes and alleys on a fine summer evening, he would see hundreds of young people like himself betaking themselves for a walk in the outskirts of the city. On such occasions the devil would say to him, "Why can't you go and have a walk too?" But he always told the devil to get behind him, saying, "No; Christ's work is first." '[77] A leading minister in the Free Presbyterian Church, Donald Macfarlane, wrote in his diary of three years of temptation from atheism after he left divinity college, 'a temptation from the evil one. It left me as weak as a feather before the tempest. It was only gradually I got rid of it.'[78] Biographies and diaries were used in published form to give full exposure to weakness and the self-remonstrance of the minister: 'I have got a most irritable temper. I have got a loose way of talking and of using slang words, most unbecoming my profession.'[79] In 1872–3, the *British Messenger* provided an intense voyeuristic revelation of the Revd James Calder's spiritual struggles about 'the state of my own soul', starting in 1735 when he reported that 'a sullen gloom and unrelenting damp sit heavy on my soul'. Thirty years later he was still in constant self-remonstration: 'Oct. 19th 1762. Alas! I've offended the Lord and provoked Him to deny His usual presence and countenance, by my shameful wasting an hour of precious time before worship in an amusement innocent in itself, but unnecessary and unseasonable, and therefore sinful and offensive at a time when I ought to be employed to better purpose!' He reported in 1763 that 'I have not trembled, and wept, and mourned in secret . . . as I ought to have done.'[80]

In this way the weakness of 'holy men' was most publicly paraded. The spiritual turmoil of clergy, even of the most famous and revered, became an obsession of popular religious magazines. They became an obsession too of Victorian fiction. In Elizabeth Gaskell, Charles Dickens and Anthony Trollope, crises of personal faith were inherent elements in the religiosity of men; as Elizabeth Ermarth has said: 'Doubt or even disbelief were themselves key features of religious experience, an often-necessary stage on the personal pilgrimage to God.'[81] And it was always men, not women, who were afflicted in the Victorian novel: evangelicals like Mr Slope in the Barchester novels, the Methodist minister in George Eliot's *Adam Bede* (1859), and Mr Chadband in Charles Dickens' *Bleak House* (1852). The best of men, the most Christianly 'manly' of men, were being shown to be weak before their Lord. Masculine strength and power was constantly being undermined in evangelical discourse. This continued in the more affectionate and humorous clerical novels of the late nineteenth century, such as the 'Kailyard' school of Scottish romantic stories of J.M. Barrie, S.R. Crockett and Iain Maclaren. Many of the these were fiction-alised versions of the ministerial biography, encompassing the same themes and dramatic structures. Crockett, for instance, wrote a volume of twenty-four short stories in which nearly every one featured presbyterian ministers as 'common men' – men whose poor parents struggled to pay their son's way through parish school and university, and who then faced penury as 'stickit' ministers.[82] In such stories, the minister faced parsimonious, argu-mentative and tale-bearing congregations whose gossip 'brought with them the foul reek of the pit where they were forged, paralysing his work and killing his usefulness'.[83] J.M. Barrie's trilogy of Thrums novels, *Auld Licht Idylls* (1887), *A Window in Thrums* (1889) and *The Little Minister* (1891), were probably the most well-known of all clerical novels of the Victorian period, focusing on the life of a small dissenting congregation and its min-ister, the Revd Gavin Dishart, and their struggles to pay him. The parish-ioners, nearly all weavers, were said in the 1840s to 'have been starving themselves of late until they have saved up enough money to get another minister'.[84] When they lost a minister, 'They retired with compressed lips to their looms, and weaved and weaved till they weaved another minister'.[85] The piety of the minister was located by Barrie in the context of women. It was taken 'for granted that a minister's marriage was womanhood's great triumph and that the particular woman who got him must be very clever'.[86] Dishart fell for the bohemian 'Egyptian woman', Babbie, who emerges as a device for exploring the moral strains and contradictions of the clergyman. Initially criticised by the congregation for the liaison with Babbie, the minister in the end 'preached to them till they liked him again, and so they let him marry her, and they like her awful too'.[87] *The Little Minister* explored personal conduct in the context of 'old-time religion', liberalising values and sexual attraction, and, with a melodramatic conclusion set in a flood, it had widespread resonance on both sides of the Atlantic. The book proved so popular that it was turned into an oft-revived play in both Britain and the United States, and generated three American film versions.

The clergyman was the core figure in discourse on the evangelical 'holy man' of the nineteenth and twentieth centuries, but there were other candi-dates deployed. Primary amongst these were the foreign missionaries (notably David Livingstone) whose heroic exploits started to become well-publicised in both religious and secular press in the 1840s and 1850s, paving the way for more secular imperial heroes. A parallel development was the rendering of ordinary 'manly' life as heroic Christian melodrama. Christian heroes could have many occupations, discursively portrayed in vignettes which combined piety with masculine qualities. A good example of this was the work of Samuel Smiles who combined his books on moral virtues such as *Self-Help* (1859), *Character* (1871), *Thrift* (1875) and *Duty* (1880) with a vast number of moral biographies, nearly all of them about engineers and scientists: *The Life of George Stephenson* (1857), *Lives of the Engineers* (three volumes, 1862, extended to five in 1874), *Boulton and Watt* (1865), *James Nasmyth, Engineer* (1885), and *Josiah Wedgwood* (1894). As Adrian Jarvis points out, Smiles used the genre of the detective story or melodrama to turn the biography into 'the lives of the saints' in which martyrdom to science was a frequent simile, and the engineers performed miracles of science. Smiles' biographies, like evangelical ones, were constructed as novels with liberal use of direct speech, and the stories of invention, discovery and application of science were quite incidental (and often skirted over) in preference to the study of personal character and the 'substantiation of saintliness'. As scientists, they were models not of science but of moral, and specifically Christian, lives, pursuing a moral worth which resonated with those of the readers.[88] Inventions brought moral good: the coming of new road-making techniques, said Smiles, not only changed 'the industrial habits of the people' but also 'the moral habits of the great masses of the working classes'.[89]

Just as the evangelical call was democratic, so too were male exemplars. One story recounted how at a copper mine in Cornwall in the 1860s a faulty fuse left two miners seconds to escape a detonation of explosives. One pushed the other up a ladder saying: 'Up with ye! I'll be in Heaven in a minute.' When both survived, he explained he had done this because 'I knowed my soul was safe', whilst 't'other lad was an awful wicked lad, I wanted to give him another chance'.[90] But for occupational frequency, military men – especially senior officers – outnumbered others as heroes in evangelical literature. With their masculinity assured, the converted soldier displayed the meekness of feminised piety. In 'the conversion and happy death' of Lieut. Col. Holcombe, the hero read a well-known tract, *The Sinner's Friend*, and 'he saw that, vile as he had been, he might be saved. He became a new creature, trusting in the blood of Christ for pardon of accumulated sins during a period of sixty years'.[91] The religiosity of officers in the Great War was much asserted: 'There is no doubt all our greatest generals are religious men', said the *British Weekly* in 1919.[92] Indeed, men achieved a new status in evangelical literature during wartime. In World War II, a large number of tracts and story books were produced for children which depicted their fathers on active service as heroes of

Biblical qualities: 'From his boyhood, David was a brave and daring soldier, just like our Commandoes to-day. He realised he was a sinner and needed to be cleansed. Your earthly father is far away, on Active Service for his King and Country. You, his son or daughter, want to be the very best you can be for your Daddy's sake.'[93] Christian virtues were found in the most unlikely places in wartime. An evangelical book of 1944 entitled *Men of Destiny: Christian Messages from Modern Leaders*, identified Stalin and Chiang Kai-shek as not just 'great men', but inspirational examples for the Christian.[94] Equally, though, war brought challenge to the relationship between masculine sacrifice and piety. In 1917, a story by Annie Swan cast doubt on the war and the loss of men's lives: '"Sometimes one wonders whether it is all worth while," said Gifford, sitting forward, when he was alone with his host in the library [of the manse]. "This tremendous sacrifice, I mean."' [His elderly clerical host replies:] "We have been taught here [from the pulpit] that it *is* worthwhile; that God has accepted and sealed our sacrifice."'[95]

World War I introduced considerable reflection on male piety and man's culpability in sin. At the outset, war seemed to offer clear-cut guides to gender roles: 'We do not want manly women and we do not want womanly men. True religion tends to make each the best of its kind. . . . The primary duty of your young Christian manhood to-day is to offer yourself for active service'.[96] Later in the war, more reflective views emerged from massive church inquiries into God and the soldier. Whilst the Dean of Durham Cathedral felt that 'organised Christianity does not come well out of the world crisis',[97] it was the nature of male piety that was perceived as changed by the war, with a 'trench religion' of instinctual superstition towards a greater being deciding men's fate.[98] 'The soldier has got religion, I am not so sure that he has got Christianity'[99] was a common observation. But there was conscious self-reflection by many clergy on 'misrepresentations of the Christian ideal' during the Victorian period, previously falsely regarded as 'the apex of human goodness'. The 'good man' was reassessed in the light of the Great War: 'A standard was set up, which, it was alleged, was too negative, too bloodless, too safe. Respectability in its narrower aspects was over-worshipped.' As a result, the Christian life became too narrowly associated with feminine qualities, and the churches lost the men during the war. As two churchmen wrote in 1917: 'One began to understand why, apart from scriptural grounds, the Church is described as "she".'[100] Yet, the largest interdenominational study of the impact of war upon the religiosity of male soldiers, published in 1919, brought new hope. There was a 'trench religion', an elemental religious experience, which introduced 'fine qualities'. One officer reported: 'The war has created a new tenderness between man and man, a new sense of fellowship and social sympathy, i.e. within a circle embracing the nation and friendly aliens.'[101] But with this humanity, a new 'real man' was anticipated from the war, changing 'nice boys' who were 'polite and delicate in feeling' into troopers with 'more real backbone than in the days when they were so nice'.[102] Yet, such inquiries in 1919–20 concluded that the innate shortcomings of masculinity, 'the unruly heart of man', still lay at the heart of the problem of piety: 'A man's conduct cannot always be explained simply as the outcome of his circumstances and training.' It was 'the man himself – the man who is quite capable of saying "I will do evil"'. This was 'the root difficulty', the essential ability of man to be ultimately untrainable, unquellable in his choice of evil.[103]

So, the return to peace brought the resumption of the evangelical discourse on the essential femininity of piety and the essential irreligion of masculinity. Through the 1920s, 1930s and 1940s religious literature continued to pump out tracts, novels and magazines in which the feminine romance of piety was contrasted with the susceptibility of men to temptation. The literature sustained its obsession with drink, though it gave new force to gambling and to the 'lounge lizards' who preyed on women's virginity. The evangelical press started to lose readership, and though sustained by wartime emergency in 1939–45, most religious publishing houses folded in the 1950s, with most of the survivors closing in the later 1960s. But the divergent male–female discourses on religiosity did not immediately disappear in the 1920s. They was sustained in the 'secular' press of popular magazines and books – the main site of exteriority for evangelical discourse.

TELLING STORIES ABOUT MEN

In evangelical stories about piety, women appeared throughout as good but not always converted; men, by contrast, almost always appeared as in a perilous sinful state until near the end. Men were the problem, given to manifold temptations: drink (nearly always), gambling (increasingly after 1890), and 'rough' in overall cultural terms. They lived dissipated lives which caused suffering and ruination to mothers, wives and children. Nowhere did evangelical literature have such a powerful influence in the public domain, including in 'secular' fiction, as in its demonisation of men.

Collier Jack published around 1900 is set in a village near Barnsley where a struggling model-mother dies:

'I am leaving you, my children,' she had said, with failing breath – 'leaving you behind, but m-e-e-t me in h-e-a-v-e-n. There'll be no parting there – no s-o-r-r-o-w th-e-r-e. Thank G-o-d, it will s-o-o-n be past ... Richard,' she had said, addressing her husband, 'come near me. Give up the d-r-i-n-k, it is r-u-i-n-i-n-g you; I f-o-r-g-i-v-e you for all the p-a-s-t. M-e-e-t m-e th-e-r-e;' and she pointed upward with her thin, wasted hand. 'Hark, the music is s-o-u-n-d-i-n-g,' she added. 'G-o-o-d n-i-g-h-t! J-e-s-u-s, I a-m c-o-m-i-n-g.'

Her son Jack, like the other miners, was a natural drinker, consuming vast quantities in the pub. But he heard the call at a religious meeting, and, though he tried to live a religious life, he suffered the taunts of his fellow miners. But there was an explosion at the pit with many dead and injured, and a long rescue operation. Under the stress, Jack lost God, returning to his old temptations. However, after a long struggle, he reconverted in the end.[104]

The male-centred evangelical narrative had important characteristics. There were two structures in use between the 1850s and 1930s: the 'son structure' and the 'husband structure':

The 'Son Structure'
A. Son lives with virtuous, struggling mother
B. In late teenage years, son feels temptation of drink/gambling/womanising
C. Son becomes sinner, leaves home
D. Mother becomes ill or son meets virtuous woman-reminder of mother
E. Son converts
F. Chance event, threatening conversion
G. Conversion reaffirmed

The 'Husband Structure'
A. Husband lives with virtuous wife
B. Husband is drunkard/gambler/wife-beater
C. Wife and children suffer in poverty
D. Chance event (often an accident to husband)
E. Wife nurses husband in Christian way
F. Husband converts
G. Family happier, if not richer

As with the structure of the women's narrative studied in the last chapter, the narrative order might change, especially the chance event which could move up or down the sequence. The event was sometimes a mother's death, or an accident to the central character. In a story of 1924, a young Irishman called Jock was raised by his struggling mother, but he disappointed her despite her continuous prayers: 'Jock grew up to be a man; but alas, got in with bad company, and there he learned to drink and gamble. She never went to bed till he came home . . . She felt sure prayer would be answered for her boy.'[105] Yet 'Jock went deeper and deeper into sin', enlisted as a soldier and left home, where he fell in with barrack-room sin of every description and neglected to write to his mother. When a message came that she was very ill, he was shocked and given leave to return home, but arrived at his mother's deathbed moments too late. As a result, he found

Christ. In another story from 1926, a handsome young man of twenty years left his mother to go abroad to seek fame and fortune, but he became ill, bedridden and crippled, finding Christ only in this weakened position of lost masculinity. Manly lust for destiny was brought down: 'man proposes, God disposes'.[106] In evangelical stories, men's conversion was often portrayed in states of illness, paralysis or broken limbs, unable to pursue trade or fortune. Masculine strength removed, usually by the chance event, the man came to a realisation of his own vulnerability, his lack of real enduring strength, especially if nursed by his mother or wife. Stories of real conversions amongst men in heroic occupations were eagerly used by the evangelical press: John Craigie, a sea captain, 'a sinner saved by Grace in mid-life, through the dying testimony of his little daughter', Commander Wolfe-Murray RN, 'a typical Naval Officer who, after seeking God in several wrong ways, found Him simply enough', and in another conversion story, 'a paratrooper's testimony'.[107]

A large proportion of evangelical stories of men centred on the destruction of families by male evils. Adverts for such stories proclaimed: 'a powerful story, showing the terrible havoc made by the gambling fever in happy homes and hearts, and how the grace of God enabled one man to overcome the power of heredity.'[108] Gambling became a particular target for evangelical attack in the 1920s and 1930s when forms of betting, both legal and illegal, were mushrooming in Britain. Indeed, gambling was by the late 1930s even overtaking drink amongst some evangelicals as the primary 'social evil'; the *British Messenger* in 1937 carried a photograph of a street card game with the caption 'At the Heart of Empire'.[109] But from the 1840s to the 1950s, drink remained the single most important social evil in the evangelical lexicon. A tract story from the 1850s featured a soldier in prison in India awaiting execution for murdering a black man. A missionary visited and asked if he had a Bible: '"But, oh!" said he, "I sold it for drink! It was the companion of my youth. I brought it with me from my native land. Oh! if I had listened to my Bible, I should never have been here!"'[110] In the aftermath of World War I, men turning to drink became a common theme. In 'The Absinthe Drinker' of 1920, it was stated that this beverage 'wholly takes possession of a man's mind, and completely stupefies him and his conscience, and overcomes his morality; and, as a result, a man becomes a beast'.[111]

Sport features in many evangelical stories as an 'evil' alongside drink and gambling. A religious story book of 1902 told the apparently true tale of William Easton, a sixteen-year-old boy who in 1882 injured his knee in a football match, and who nine months later died from the wound. With cover pictures of a football match, the tenor of the tract's appeal to boys was obvious, but its moral was the inconsequentiality of sport and William's protracted deathbed conversion.[112] But if evangelical support for sport was equivocal, appeal to manly moral strength was common. Stories for boys exaggerated the masculinity of David, 'the kingly man of war', and 'the soldier-stories of the Bible – full of life and adventure'.[113] Indeed, from the 1880s to the 1930s there was an almost obsessive focus on David in evangelical literature for boys, quite relegating Christ.

However, exploration of the role of femininity in piety was never far from the surface in most evangelical literature about men. Religious stories explored the discourse on the feminised nature of the born-again man. In Sydney Watson's *Disloyal* of 1891, Frank Holson was converted by the Christian love of his wife, and became 'a constant source of wonder to all who knew him': 'His friends in his own wide circle talked of him pityingly behind his back. The *blasé* men, the thoughtless women tapped their foreheads significantly when his name or his piety was quoted, and said "Poor Halson! he's clean gone, don't-cher know!"' Frank was oblivious, having no thought but 'to glorify God among his fellow-men': 'His Christianity was a real, robust life; there was nothing namby-pamby about it; while a more humble-minded, meek follower of Christ could not be found.'[114] Another story of 1896 told of men who refused to help look after their babies – men who 'would yet never relieve their poor wife of a bit of her load when they go out for the day', and would not be seen carrying a child. It featured one father whose sense of good outweighed his concern for manly image, carrying his child and suffering being called 'a dry nurse' by his mates.[115] Sexual impurity was delicately tackled. To become a Christian, a mother told her son in one story of 1890, a boy had to restrain his urges, his body having 'doors on all sides leading to your inner man'. God's command through life 'will come to you, sharp, stern, and imperative, "Shut the door!" and only your instant, prompt obedience will save your soul from being sullied.'[116] Stories returned repeatedly to warning the Christian boy that he would suffer by 'not following the crowd' and would be jeered at for his total abstinence. In short, the true Christian man had to show a restraint which others might take as effeminacy. His main sacrifice would be having to endure the ridicule of his own sex.

EVANGELICAL NARRATIVES ON MEN IN THE SECULAR PRESS

Victorian and Edwardian secular fiction fed off the moral polarities between men and women. Moral description was the very basis of social description.[117] On the dark side, the drunken, gambling, dissolute wife-beater of the 'slums' was one of the most familiar characters of British public consciousness, whilst just as familiar was the comic 'toff' – the gentleman of independent means who spent his life in leisure. Both of these were important objects for discursive disapproval in the religious and secular press. The 'moral man', meanwhile, was a more complex character. Indeed, the discourse on him was confused, ambiguous and ambivalent. Nowhere in evangelical narratives was there greater uncertainty than with the religiosity of the secular hero.

Popular reading for men did not have the same intensity of moral rhetoric as that evident in women's or children's magazines and books. The man's world of business, industry, politics and sport did not have the same narrow focus of the domestic sphere, the home and children, which so dominated female reading. Instead, the world was men's oyster, and the themes of improving reading were wide and varied. Technical journals for artisans like *The English Mechanic* appealed to skill-based learning, the working of machines, accolades to the technological prowess of the skilled working class, whilst even the earliest general magazine for men, *The Penny Magazine* of 1832, promoted 'improvement' as a technological and economic phenomenon rather than a moral one.[118] Specialist magazines reflected elements of the discourse on moral men: the nobility of knowledge, industry and skill, strength and physical courage. They implicitly put in relief parallel values: thrift and sobriety, civic responsibility and moral courage, and it was in general improving literature that the meeting point of values of the male domain was to be found. In biographical sketches, historical series and short stories, a moral conjunction was created at which the virtues associated with the male worlds of science, industrial skill and power (virtues of hard work, independence, self-reliance, and education) were placed within the overarching framework of female piety where they met the moral virtues of home and family (virtues of self-sacrifice, parenting, sobriety and thrift). The conjunction was a discursive minefield, for it was the point where the 'masculine' world met the 'feminine' world; the two had to be 'merged' in the evangelical conversion as the core of the exemplary man.[119] It was here that gendered virtues clashed, where heroes and villains were drafted as moral beings, where masculinity and femininity were married. This required the feminising of maleness – a difficult and perhaps impossible task.

The major site for this clash of gender opposites within male sexuality was in the general improving magazine. For adult males, such literature was rarely designed to be men-only, but it was overwhelmingly family centred. The pioneer of the family improving magazine was *Chamber's Journal*, founded in 1832 as a weekly 'threeha'pence' paper for all the family. As a family journal, it differed quite radically from women's magazines in having a much greater focus on men's issues in a mixture of short stories, science news, social observation, 'moral essays' and biographical sketches of prominent men. The style of holy men found in evangelical reading had enormous influence on the construction of 'secular' heroes in popular improving papers like *Chamber's Journal*. The use of the life biography and the obituary was particularly common, though the fictionalised story was less-often used with men as the central character. Thus, discourses on exemplary men were invariably real-life. Biographical sketches of one or two column lengths were a favourite device for portraying heroic men: men of arms, heroes of imperial expansion, missionaries and scholars. In autobiography, sketches focused heavily on moral virtues as the crux of 'rags to riches' stories. They characteristically concentrated on the period of youth and poverty where virtue was both most dissonant with circumstances and most critical to 'personal progress'. *Chamber's Journal* in 1832 featured Alexander Murray, 'the son of a poor Galloway shepherd, who finally died professor of Oriental languages in the College of Edinburgh'. Born in 1775, his father had only three scree sheep and four cows: 'He had no debts, and no money.' His only possessions were a catechism and a psalm book his father gave him at six years old, lighting a thirst for reading which was thwarted when banned from using the family Bible.

> I at length got a New Testament, and read the historical parts with great curiosity and ardour. But I longed to read the Bible, which seemed to me a much more pleasant book, and I actually went to where I knew an old loose-leaved Bible lay, and carried it away piecemeal. I perfectly remember the strange pleasure I felt in reading the history of Abraham and of David. I like mournful narratives, and greatly admired Jeremiah, Ezekiel, and the Lamentations. I pored on these pieces of the Bible in secret for many months, for I durst not shew them openly.[120]

Living 'in a wild glen' five miles from the nearest village, his father could not afford to send him to school, but instead worked him as a shepherd where he scraped money together to buy ballads-sheets and 'penny histories': 'I carried bundles of these in my pockets, and read them when sent to look for cattle'. At twelve years of age he found work as a private tutor to young children, at which point the biographical sketch effectively ends as the 'hero' starts on the road to university and academic fame.

The useful and rational use of time was at the crux of the discourse on the secular hero. Religion and piety were devices of rationality which furthered learning, skill and self-improvement. Improvement was the emblem of the democratic free society; wealth was an inhibition to personal achievement:

> ... there is no condition in which the chance of doing any good is *less* than in the condition of leisure. The man fully employed *may* be able to gratify his good dispositions by improving himself or his neighbours, or serving the public in some useful way; but the man who has all his time to dispose of as he pleases, has but a poor chance, indeed, of doing so.[121]

A man's time had to be used to personal profit; a man had to increase 'the capacity of doing', to be in an 'habitual course of exertion' to experience 'the majesty of industry'. The wealthy man was an idle man: 'The *gentlemen* must think of it. They must be up and doing.' Laziness was as much a characteristic of the poor man as of the wealthy. In a short story of 1832, Miles Atherton was married with two children and was so given to idleness that he sold his son into 'slavery' with a chimney sweep.[122] Talking with friends was explored as a potential source of immorality. Men talking with men produced 'vices of conversation', where discussion of everything from philosophy to general dialogue could lose moral worth through the lubrication of alcohol which men craved.[123] The abuse of alcohol was one area where the 'secular' improving magazine often outshone the religious journals in fervency. Indeed, the central theme of many improving magazines created in the 1830s and 1840s appeared to be support of the total abstinence movement. They endlessly cited the 'moral statistics' of drinking in Britain, especially in the cities; in 1853, according to *Chamber's*, there were in Scotland 149 people to every dram shop, 981 people to every baker, 1,067 to every butcher and 2,281 to every bookseller.[124] Equally fascinating to its readership seems to have been the statistics of crime and punishment. Where the popular 'unimproving' press dwelt on crime, the improving press dwelt on punishment: the numbers in prison, the types of punishment, and the extent of ratepayer's burden for maintaining police forces.[125]

The popular press was just as much interested as the evangelical journals in exploring masculinity and morality. One article in 1833 on 'The Domestic Man' described effeminate men who wore petticoats long after they had left the nursery, who helped with domestic chores and did the cooking; it was literally an exploration of a caricature, and arrived at no particular judgement.[126] Improving magazines quite openly fostered a feminisation of virtuous sensibilities in men. *Chamber's Journal* addressed itself to the 'whole moral and intellectual nature of its readers', impressing 'sound moral lessons and elevating human character as far as possible above its grosser elements' of animalism and 'low enjoyments of all kinds', whilst cultivating 'a taste for more refined and innocent pleasures, especially for those of polite literature'.[127] In so doing, manly virtues of muscular quality were constantly being mediated. A long article on 'Courage' in 1836 explored the various forms this evident virtue could take, and argued that its supreme form was not a physical but a moral entity: 'It has been by the exhibition of strong moral courage that almost all the social improvements we know have been affected.'[128]

From the 1840s, secular magazines developed different literary genres as gender-specific methods to deal with religiosity. The use of fiction in family magazines was primarily aimed at the female readership, but melodrama was used from the 1860s to upgrade the appeal to men. By 1860, *Chamber's*

Journal was running serialised murder mysteries about women of 'unselfish love' and cruel, vindictive husbands.[129] Poetry, on the other hand, was much less useful for the male audience. As Fairchild observed, Victorian poetry which dealt with religion was 'torrentially abundant', yet its evangelical variety was 'poetically sterile in the nineteenth century'; it was 'too suspicious of any writing which is not motivated by the wish to convert or edify'.[130] Much Victorian poetry was evangelical pulp, shamelessly proselytising and most often written by women for women, relating women's virtues and sensibilities to Sunday dress and behaviour. By contrast, male poets like Charles Kingsley who dealt with religion tended to dwell on its impact upon the rhythms and symbols of everyday life:

> Now the bells are ringing loud
> People rising very early–
> Boys and girls are dressing now,
> And now they go to Sunday School
> To Church–and then come back again.
> Everybody does not work,
> But idle people do not read their Bible
> And God punishes them.
> Now Sunday evening thus comes.
> Everybody goes to bed,
> Boys and girls still remain reading their Bibles
> Till the time they go to Bed.
> Then Monday morning
> Men and women return to work.[131]

Robert Louis Stevenson wrote a long and much revered narrative poem on 'The Loudon Sabbath Morn', evoking similar sentiments to those of Kingsley. Male poets tended to dwell on how, despite its romantic role in community life, the Sabbath was a suppressant of normal male life: of games and play, conviviality and conversation, a day of men at the arm of women in Sunday best. Sunday forced men to the side of their women. Where male poets sought to explore more deeply man's religious purpose, there is frustration, as with Robert Browning:

> Man's work is to labour and leaven–
> As best he may–earth here with heaven;
> 'Tis work for work's sake that he's needing:
> Let him work on and on as if speeding
> Work's end, but not dream of succeeding![132]

Where poets of the eighteenth and early nineteenth century explored Christian sentiment and doctrine in some considerable detail,[133] the evangelical message was less easily transferred from the Victorian melo-dramatic narrative to the poem without losing stylistic credibility. Indeed, in the hands of Victorian evangelicals, the poem became an aesthetically feminised medium, purilely sentimental, romantic and 'unmanly'.

There were no morally improving, religious-based popular journals solely for men. They did not exist. Men would not read them, and there was no suitable diversity of literary genre in which articles in such a journal could 'speak' to men. There were only three ways to circulate religious discourse to men: in negative and challenging form (in tracts for instance), in the elliptical moral format of autobiographical heroism (in the format popularised by Samuel Smiles and some men's occupational magazines), or through exploration of male piety in the context of women's and children's magazines. Only the last of these could be truly exploratory of male religiosity, for it was in men's relations to the family that the key to issues of their piety and impiety lay. In the family-centred improving magazines which flourished from the 1860s to the 1910s (magazines such as *Household Words* and its 1870s' successor *All The Year Round, The Strand Magazine, The Leisure Hour, Cassell's Family Magazine Illustrated, Chatterbox,* and *The Sunday at Home Illustrated*), men's interests were catered for in stories of adventure and bravado and in scientific news. But, by its very form of multiple readership, the family magazine affirmed men's piety within a family setting: in other words, the *form* of the family magazine was as discursively active as its content. By the 1920s and 1930s, family magazines had in general become segregated into women's, boy's and girl's titles in which discourse *on* men remained little changed. However, outwith evangelical literature, popular religious discourse which spoke *to* men rapidly secularised. Men's popular magazines were by the inter-war period largely devoid of serious exploration of piety, being engrossed with sport, militarism and science. For boys, magazines like the *Boy's Own Paper,* founded by the Religious Tract Society in 1879, provided strongly evangelical messages of Christian purity into the 1890s, but from the 1900s it gave a more virile conception of masculinity in tales of derring-do, militarism and imperial patriotism, and by the 1920s it amounted to an endless flow of items on adventure and hobbies.[134] By comparison with the *Girl's Own,* the *Boy's Own Paper* of the 1920s was devoid of evangelical discourse, with tales of war heroes, historical heroes, and items on how to build a wireless.[135] The domain for circulation of discourse on male morality was becoming exclusively located amongst women. By the late 1930s, the contented and self-assured girl portrayed in the *Girl's Own Paper* grew to adulthood in Mrs Miniver's contented home where anxiety about men's conversion was disappearing. Part of this process may have been the tendency in the 1930s for the state to become markedly more relaxed about sites of male immorality; the prohibition cause withered (and many temperance organisations declined), gambling law was eased (and perceived to be a liberalisation) in 1934, and though moral panics continued about popular culture, their impact on both public and politics tended to become localised and temporary.[136] The impact of mass unemployment in the 1930s may have contributed to a reduced demonisation of male immoralities.

Nonetheless, the transition of the 1930s was far from complete. Not only did discourses on religious identity remain gendered within popular culture, but pre-1930 evangelicalism had contributed profoundly to the gendering of cultural forms. Media read, seen or heard by women tended to emphasise the vulnerability of male piety, and had established a tradition of portraying men as the moral villains of the piece. Media consumed by men, on the other hand, became increasingly focused, especially after 1870, on how men might be 'secular' heroes. What was starting to change in the late 1930s was that men were no longer being targeted for the induction of moral or religious anxiety. Women were no longer being required by discourse to *challenge* men into submission to a pious domesticity, but to *provide* a contented domesticity for them.

CHAPTER SIX

PERSONAL TESTIMONY AND RELIGION 1800-1950

—— ·◆· ——

MEMORY, DISCOURSE AND IDENTITY

This chapter explores how personal testimony relating to the period 1800 to 1950 was reflexive to the power of evangelical discourses on piety. Oral testimony, autobiographies, and letters to newspapers or public figures, have been extensively used by historians to provide illustration of personal social experience.[1] But in addition, as Penny Summerfield has said, 'personal narratives draw on the generalized subject available in discourse to construct the particular personal subject. It is thus necessary to encompass within oral history analysis and interpretation, not only the voice that speaks for itself, but also the voices that speak to it, the discursive formulations from which understandings are selected and within which accounts are made.'[2] This chapter deploys this formula, but also expands upon it. The subjectification of discourse is customarily taken solely at the level of reflexivity to discourse.[3] Here, three separate techniques are used in relation to the material examined in the last two chapters. Personal testimony (autobiography, oral evidence and letters to newspapers) is analysed to explore, first, reflexive evidence of discourses on piety, second, evidence of the evangelical narrative structure being used in intertextual exchange by the individual to construct her or his life, and third, for evidence of religious activities, organisations and motifs – the 'salvation economy' – in their lives. In Chapter 8, we return to these techniques to explore the revitalisation of religious discourse, evangelical narrative structure and the 'salvation economy' in the 1950s, and then its breakdown from the 1960s.

In exploring individuals' reflexivity to discourse change, it is obvious that the discourses of times remembered may be very different from the time within which the memory is being recalled and testified. Fundamental to this book is the argument that the evangelical narrative structure and the discourses within it had a powerful continuity between the late eighteenth century and the mid-twentieth century, but that both structure and discourses then radically changed in the 1950s and 1960s. Accepting this proposition for the moment, it is obvious that oral-history testimony given after the 1960s, whilst referring to an earlier period, will have been greatly affected by that change in the moral climate. This was nowhere more apparent than in attitudes to religion in people's lives. The liberalisation of religious values, and loss of the 'religious life' which the vast bulk of oral interviewees experienced in their childhood and young adulthood of the late nineteenth and first half of the twentieth century, became radically 're-remembered'. This becomes evident in oral testimony in the form of laughter, self-derision, grief or even bitterness at recollections of the religious regimes they had followed without question as youngsters. This is not a mere product of aging; this is a product of moral turn.

The effect of this moral turn in oral testimony on religion is evident in another way. The interviewer is younger and, in many cases, someone trained either implicitly or explicitly in social-scientific inquiry. In many oral-history collections, the interviewers are often both personally 'less religious' than their interviewees, and less experienced in their own lives of the moral framework of the evangelical narrative. Most disconcerting, both questionnaire-writers and interviewers in follow-up questions are deploying different, modern and stunted discourses on the religiosity of fifty, seventy or a hundred years ago. There are other discourses, the mythical discourses of received historical wisdom gleaned from social-history books and university classes, which have unrefined and 'unlived' notions of Victorian and Edwardian religiosity. For instance, oral history questions in the 1960s and early 1970s focused heavily on the social (or class) divisions between church and chapel (Church of England and dissent) in England and Wales, and elicited suitable remembrances within this left-wing, Marxist-derived structural approach to society which so dominated British social history and sociology at that time. This then rendered the history of religion as an adjunct to class struggle, adding oral testimony to documentary evidence of religion's power to divide society along class fractures.

As we move into the later 1980s and 1990s, oral interviewees were less drawn to put their memories within this divide. Questioning in oral research in the 1990s changed with the impact of new ideas from post-structuralism. Unfortunately available oral testimony on religion has not yet drawn on the new emerging tradition – in feminist scholarship especially – of the necessity of engaging with the mutual reflexivity of subjectivities between interviewees and interviewers. In this the subjectivity of the interviewer (drawing on its own moral framework of constituent discourses) is inevitably transformed in response to that of the interviewee, and vice versa.[4] The oral history material used in this book was mostly produced between 1968 and 1988 without the benefit of these modern methods. This presents apparent problems. The oral interview of necessity imposes the interviewer as a mediator between the interviewee and the ultimate testimony: the interviewer poses questions, setting the agenda and, most importantly, providing the vocabulary and conceptual frameworks within which informants are invited to respond. This is literally a process of 'putting words into the mouth' of the interviewee, a process which can simplify or alter the vocabulary of the interviewee. This is a particularly acute issue in relation to religion where questions posed by the generation of social-science researchers of the 1960s and after tend to be simplified in their conception of Christianity. Religion is reduced to church, Sunday school, 'being religious', posing issues of belief and life rhythms which interviewees did not naturally look upon from the 'distance' of those words and concepts. Interviewees had lived these issues, not analysed them in social-science terms. They had tended, especially during youth, to look upon these as intimate issues related to sometimes complex Christian doctrines in which they had been extensively schooled. Oral interviewing can be reductionist in relation to religion: it can stunt the detail of religious discourses because the interviewee may alter answers knowing that the interviewer (and the question-setter) will either not understand them or will be uninterested in them. However, this should not be looked upon *merely* as a problem. It is also an opportunity, for it is a product of the testimony, observable in the disjunctions between interviewers' questions and interviewees' answers. The result is that the interview is a confrontation between two modes of understanding religiosity that informs us about *both* and about their relationship – the chronological cultural transformation represented by the 'religious distance' between their respective historical ages.[5] There are, if you like, two interviewees in an interview. The one holding the microphone is telling us as much about discursive domains as the interviewee.[6] One aim is to combine the evidence in this chapter with that in Chapter 8 to exploit this process through re-examining oral testimony of the 1960s, 1970s and 1980s in respect of change to discourse and narrative structure.

Autobiography may be exploited for the same end, but it requires slightly different handling. Autobiography is widely acknowledged as a most revealing historical source for the social historian. It provides a platform where the people themselves can write the agenda of their lives, revealing the concerns which they themselves felt. In this process, the conceptions of 'the self' and the life that has been lived reveal a reflexivity to the discursive world in which the work was written and in which it was read. The reflexivity operates in part through both publishers' and readers' expectations (the operation of commercial factors).[7] But another characteristic is intertextuality with other genres (such as biography and fiction).[8] The way in which the autobiography has introduced religiosity has undergone dramatic change in the last two hundred years, reflecting changes in discourse (and remembrance of it), in how the 'self' has been composed from discourse, and in the structuring of the life narrative and religiosity's place within it. The added advantage of autobiography over oral testimony is that it can reveal discourse change further into the past (towards the start of our research period in 1800). Chapter 8 tackles discourse change itself, but the present chapter looks at the evangelical narrative within personal testimony.

THE EVANGELICAL NARRATIVE STRUCTURE

Ronald Walker[9] was born in Leeds in 1902 before moving to Harrogate. His father was a prosperous director of Hepworth's, a wholesale clothiers, and of at least two other Leeds firms. With four live-in servants and a nanny, he was born into an upper-middle-class household of some substance. The family was Methodist, belonging to the richest of Harrogate's three Wesleyan chapels. For all the material comfort of his upbringing, this man's recollections were dominated by issues of religiosity and morality. Religious conceptions entered unsolicited into wide areas of the interviewee's recollections, but they were located within a highly charged critique. In an articulate testimony, Ronald Walker had clearly dwelt for many decades on the psychological legacy of his youth. Early in the interview, he was asked whether his mother gave any moral guidance to her staff:

> Yes, she insisted – and this is strange in the context of 1970, but she insisted that they went to chapel on Sunday nights, because they couldn't go on Sunday mornings because they had to work. But she was very keen that they should go on Sunday nights and she was – mind you, I was brought up in a Nonconformist teetotal atmosphere, and she was keen on abstinence from alcohol in the servants and was always telling them the dangers of that sort of thing. And on one famous occasion we had a very good cook who, for 12 months at a time would be a very good cook, then for 12 months she'd break out on gin and we'd find her flat on the kitchen floor. Mother used to search her room and find hidden bottles of gin in her wardrobe, and she with great ceremony poured this down the sink, and we put up with this, and so forth. Poor Sarah, they called her, she finished up in an inebriate's home I'm afraid to say.[10]

This passage set the thematic tone and the narrative structure for the rest of Ronald's lengthy interview. In it he posits a number of oppositions: employer–employee (or 'upstairs–downstairs'), loyalty–disobedience, sober–drunk and teetotalism–drinking. These are value-types, engrossed within an overarching moral opposition which is immediate and universal, and drawn from evangelical discourse. The moral opposition is used to define the atmosphere of the household, constituting a discursive framework of puritan chapel-going nonconformity and its values. Within it is told the melodramatic discovery of the drunken cook with his mother's 'great ceremony' of pouring the gin down the sink. However, the house's moral rules and the cook's fall from grace are recounted with a cynic's post-teetotal, post-puritan 'edge'. It is a story drawn straight from the narratives of early twentieth-century puritan teetotalism, but in its telling in 1970 it is 'cynicised' for consumption by a younger listener, someone assumed alien to the world of the description. The story works because it is recounted within its historical, early twentieth-century puritan discourse, permitting the evangelical 'narrative machine' to move relentlessly between its polarities. If the cynicism were to be removed, it reads exactly like a teetotal tract.

This is an oral-history interviewee moving between two discursive worlds: that of the evangelical discourses of his youth in the 1900s and 1910s and the non-evangelical discourses of 1970. At the age of 68 years, Ronald Walker is sharing with a younger interviewer the 'strange' world of his past, a world which for its time was hegemonic upon his life, and to which as a young man he owed an unquestioning allegiance. He is sharing with the interviewer a window on the past, and assuming (perhaps rightly) that the interviewer would be fascinated and educated by this revelation. It is a confessional memory rooted in that moment in 1970 when the discursive world of his youth was not just anachronistic to his listener but was, on the face of it, anachronistic to him also.

Yet, his testimony reveals the evangelical narrative as far from anachronistic to the way in which he constructs his past. His entire and very lengthy interview develops from this early start into an exploration of the discursive gap between present (1970) and past (1900s, 1910s and early 1920s). It is intense in its exploration of the evangelical moral structure of his childhood and youth.

> Q: Did your parents bring you up to consider certain things important in life?
>
> A: Yes, in a narrow Nonconformist tradition. Lying was the unforgivable sin, so I'm afraid I've been unforgiven a few times. Turning the other cheek was regarded as a good thing. They would have been pleased if I'd shown any interest in the Methodist ministry which, of course, I didn't. . . . And respect for elders. I'm talking about the usual Victorian traditions, which was common.[11]

The young man was being raised by parents with a high expectation for his piety. The family met round the family piano on Sunday evenings for hymns and carols, read Dickens, Thackeray and Scott, and magazines of a light but mostly 'improving' character, with mother taking the 'the family magazines, you know, the predecessors of the present glossies': *Home Chat, Pearson's Weekly, Titbits, Chums, The Scout* and the *Boy's Own Paper*.

'Modern novels had to be approved of in the reviews of the decent news-papers before they were allowed in, but if they were given a good review, [they were] allowed in the house.'[12]

The chapel defined the family's circle, and indeed defined the extended family: 'And it was a very close Chapel community. A lot of people who were not related we called Uncle Sam and Uncle Dick, who weren't our uncles, and so forth, but we were on that sort of relationship with them.'[13] Sundays were a day of supposed fervent loyalty to the family's moral code. Ronald Walker went with the family to chapel in the morning and to Sunday school in the afternoon. He wore a boy's 'Sunday best' outfit:

> I was dressed, Heaven help me, in sailor suits, dark blue in winter, white on summer days in summer, when you haven't to sit down anywhere for fear you'd dirty your backside, until I got – I don't know, 8 or 9, and then I was out into, of all things, an Eton suit for Sundays. And these were very much our Sunday clothes.[14]

But Sunday sanctity in his family was, perhaps surprisingly, more in the appearance than in the observance. The children were allowed to play games in the house, so long as they were quiet games like cards: 'This whole idea of "having a good time but don't let the neighbours next door know you're having a good time" attitude. I'm being cynical here.'[15] In public, his parents considered it wrong to ride on a tram on a Sunday, and wrong to work 'except for servants, of course. It was part of the condition to which they had been born for them to work, but other work had to be very neces-sary and then it was excusable, but unnecessary work upstairs was regarded as not the thing.'

> I don't think their mental attitude included the thought of pleasure on a Sunday, it was more duty. I've recited [at] chapel morning and night for them and they took their turn in bringing the parson home for lunch, which was another great trial for we kids. But when we were in Bridlington on the Parade, they would walk out on a Sunday afternoon and listen to the band, but anything exciting, or going off on trips, or anything of this sort was not a very good thing.[16]

Ronald's memories sustain their embittered quality as the interview proceeds. The moral oppositions become hypocrisies which he doesn't merely laugh off, but at which he cavils:

> I was taken by the scruff of my neck very early in life and told to 'sign here', where I pledged total abstinence for the rest of my life, and I satisfied my conscience when I grew up that that was got under duress and I'm afraid I'm not a teetotaller and I'm not ashamed of the fact that I was made to sign something that I did not quite under-stand at the time.[17]

Religion textured nearly all his recollections: the chapel anniversaries with ladies dishing out plates of boiled ham and tea from urns; and the temperance club tea parties for youngsters with more boiled ham and tea: 'boiled ham seemed to come very much into the picture, doesn't it. [*Laughter*] Tea parties of this sort and little lectures on the evils of drink.' But he adds that these were not 'a lot of horrible people, they were very nice people who did these sort of things, but terribly narrow, but believed quite firmly in what they were trying to do for us'.[18]

Underlying the embittered narrative is the issue of his own piety. Ronald Walker's father had wanted him to become a Methodist preacher, and when in his later teens he showed no interest in that, his father deflected his expectation towards a substitute piety – medicine. Ronald had no choice in this, and he was entered at Leeds University to train as a doctor, but failed his first-year exams in part, at least, because of taking up interests in competitive swimming and athletics. A mounting rift developed between him and his father as he appeared to slide from both his faith in religion and his father's vocational expectations for him. 'His children, my generation, I'm afraid we were falling away from this sort of thing. We went to chapel because we had to. I remember we didn't *have* to, we went there to please our parents, but I don't think any of my sisters or myself had, at that time, any – we were losing our childish convictions and hadn't got any others.'[19] Yet revealingly, as the interview arrived at the end of the narrative of Ronald's *own* life, he returns to the end of his *father's* life for the conclusion:

> I think they were very sincere in their beliefs. I don't care to discuss whether their beliefs were right or wrong, but they were very sincere about it. All their lives they prayed together. Every night my father read a portion of the Bible to my mother, late at night, and on his deathbed [in the late 1920s] he sent for us all – typical of the time ... he knew he was dying and most embarrassingly he confessed himself a great sinner before he died. He had a feeling this was the sort of thing to get off his chest.[20]

His father sought to conclude with the deathbed scene of evangelical discourse. But his children were perplexed. They had undergone a 'spiritual turn' from their father's world. Bitterness and confusion over personal values ooze from Ronald's testimony. At one and the same time he was rejecting and almost *blaming* the discursive world of his youth, whilst yet still moving into that world, affirming how much he owed to it, and returning again and again to discuss his father when the questions were actually about himself.

That interview reveals the disjunction between the different discursive worlds of interviewee and interviewer, and between those of an interviewee's own past and present. Such disjunction tends to be at its most pronounced during recollection of religious trauma. Another interviewee, Norris Thompson from Gravesend, was born in 1905 into a Nonconformist shopkeeping family in which religion was vitally important, his mother spending enormous time evangelising amongst poorer people.

> And of course I was very frightened too. You see I believed in the second coming of Christ. And they [his parents] felt it was quite imminent you see. Well, and it created a real fear in my early – because I knew I wasn't good enough to go up, you see. And I always thought my mother and father, they would go, they were so good you see – and it was a real fear. Yes, yes. I don't think I ever told this to my parents, I have never told it to anybody, but it was always within me. If they were late, you know, coming back from anywhere: 'Where have they gone?'[21]

Religious fear was not limited to Nonconformists. Maude Baines, a woman in Highgate in London born in 1887 into a Church of England family, was read stories at bedtime by her father as she was a poor sleeper: 'I was terribly afraid of going to hell, you see, and I was afraid of going to sleep in case I burnt up. I suppose, you know, I was brought up in the old way of the hell-fire and all that, and being a very imaginative child I was terrified of going to sleep. I tried not to go to sleep and used to get hysterical and father used to come and sit and – and read to me a little and pat my hand and he was very tired.'[22]

The most obvious way in which oral testimony reflects the evangelical narrative is from the starting point of a 'religious' childhood which has been 'lost'. However, testimony could start from the other, 'irreligious', end and travel the conversionist route to 'salvation'. Born in 1889, Elizabeth Ormston from Leigh in Lancashire lost her first stepfather, a butcher, at the age of ten when 'he killed hisself with drink' going on 'the flash' or binge drinking with other men. But the family then moved to Bolton where her mother married a teetotaller, a man who played in the Aspull Temperance Band. She was then brought up 'very religious', her mother ensuring she went to Sunday school and also attended church, twice every Sunday. She was forbidden from so much as stitching a button on that day, and was sent on weekday evenings to the Band of Hope and Christian Endeavour. To add to the polarities, her new stepfather was poor and teetotal, but his sister married the very wealthy clerk of works at a brewery: 'they lived in a big house on Junction Road, stood in its own grounds, so hadn't any time for us'.[23] Elizabeth structured her narrative of childhood years between the bipolarities of the evangelical discourses on male immoralities, their destruction of family life, and their redemptive opposites: the drunken stepfather succeeded by the teetotal stepfather, the rich and aloof brewery manager versus his poor, respectable and abstaining brother-in-law.

The same structure was evident in the searing testimony of Arthur Turner from Lancashire, interviewed in around 1970 while living alone in deep poverty in Manchester. He was born in 1894 into a very poor family in Hankey Park, his father a blacksmith striker and his mother a weaver before she married. They were so poor that their food was of extremely low quality (their special Sunday lunch being 'lips and lugs', the lips and ears left over from the butchers). He went to school in bare feet (with clogs reserved for Sundays), and attended ragged schools to get free 'soup and stuff at night time'. Though 'nearly everyone in street went to church Sundays', neither his parents nor he ever went, not even to Sunday school. Yet, he wore clogs and 'a little sailor suit' specially on Sundays. He had a brutal upbringing, being beaten heavily by his father and harassed by the police for innocent games. Arthur became a young man torn by resentment at unfair treatment, developing in his teens as a street fighter, and at the age of sixteen he did seven days in Strangeways Prison for loitering with intent. He became repeatedly arrested for the same offence – on every occasion, as far as he was concerned, trumped-up charges by policemen who didn't like him. He joined the Royal Navy where he was birched, and ended up in his twenties as a chimney sweep. But this brutal, alienated and characteristically 'rough' youth changed in 1923 when he married. Arthur had three children who went to Sunday school, and he and his wife took them regularly to an Anglican Church. They said grace at meals and he taught his children family prayers. He gave up smoking and drinking, but though he and his family remained poor, he recalled his marriage was much happier than that of his parents. But things gradually changed again. By the late 1960s his wife and most of his children had predeceased him and he entered a lonely and impoverished old age. His narrative had become a circular route through life: from brutal childhood and early manhood in the navy, through happy but poor marriage with a family, to lonely and poverty-stricken old age. It was also a moral circular tour: from unchurched, unhappy childhood and early manhood, through a 'moral', teetotal, churchgoing and Christianised family life, to an old-age solitude devoid of relatives, friends and comfort. In his poverty and declining years, religiosity and morality had no context, no place and no purpose; they were located in memories of marriage. Finding the interviewee living alone in the front room of a dirty and very cold flat, surviving on dry bread and tea (a diet as bad as that of his tender years in the 1890s), the interviewer was deeply shocked. She wrote to the oral-history co-ordinator: 'The complete and utter emptiness of the lives of these people is quite horrifying to contemplate.'[24]

The counterpointing of 'good' and 'evil' in the narratives of the poor also infected a modulation between religion and male-induced poverty. A common characteristic of many interviewees, though especially those from poor backgrounds, is to override the interviewer's scheduled 'slot' for

religious questions and answers to use issues of religious and moral identities as constant points of referral throughout the life testimony of
childhood and youth. This happened with Frederick Green, born in 1886
to a father who 'only ever went to the pub'. Frederick's Salvationist grandfather inspired him to an interest in the Salvation Army and to make a
close friendship with an Army missionary. In childhood he accompanied
his mother to the mission every Sunday night, and got Christmas lunches
for the family by touring charity outlets to obtain as many as four free
breakfasts in paper bags. He went to Sunday school and temperance-
hall lectures, becoming a life-long teetotaller, and teaching himself prayers:
'These little things come over you', he said.[25] When poverty and its causes
were discussed, interviewees tended to raise religion and poverty in either
the same or adjacent passages of testimony. This is evident in the account
of George Hilliard from Lancaster. Born in 1910, his father ran off during
World War I, leaving the very poor family to survive on soup kitchens
and poor-law handouts of coal. His only childhood footwear were clogs
provided by a police charity. Challenged by a priest why he wasn't at mass,
George explained that going up the street in clogs on a Sunday caused him
to fall over and get filthy, forcing him to stop short of the church door:
'You were ashamed of clattering in church with clogs, that was what it
was. They wouldn't take that as an excuse. They didn't understand the
embarrassment of that. God isn't listening to your clogs clattering.' But he
did go to a Wesleyan Mission on Sundays where scholars got a story
book, 'a thick one with a label inside telling you how many attendances
you'd had out of so many and your name on', and got to go to Christmas
parties and outings to the country.[26] In such ways, interviewees from the
poorest working-class backgrounds characteristically placed poverty and
religiosity side-by-side in their testimony. In the Preston home of Henrietta
Isleworth (born 1900), her stepmother hung texts and pictures around
the walls: texts in gold letters of 'God is the Head of this house, the
unseen listener at every meal' and 'Thy Word is a lantern unto my feet',
and fourteen pictures with religious themes hung over the doors: 'They say
they are unlucky now. How poor she was.... She sat up all night and
made a shirt for fourpence to buy a loaf.'[27] Religion acts as the motif of
moral worth, set in relief by the unfairness and suffering of being the victims
of poverty.

Autobiography allows us to follow the same evangelical-narrative routes
as oral testimony and to detect the same moral bipolarities. But being a
longer-established 'source', it also illuminates transition in constructions of
religiosity. There is hardly a single autobiography of anyone, from whatever social background, born between 1800 and 1930 that does not discuss
religion and the moral construction of the individual – whether it's of themselves, their parents or others in their communities. Some autobiographers,
notably male socialist autodidacts, record their repulsion from religion

and their journeys into atheism. Many from poor backgrounds, notably women, recall with anger the religious-moral regimes of their communities which condemned their parents unjustly for various moral lapses (from drinking or socialism to giving birth out of wedlock or 'unnatural' sexual appetite, even within marriage). But those that did so are revealing the inescapable power of religious discourses within periods of their lives. Men made life-journeys dominated by the pursuit of 'useful knowledge' and awakening to the personal freedom, the personal democratisation of the intellect, which learning brought. David Vincent has noted the common sequential progression from childhood helplessness (because, for instance, of drunken fathers) to moral improvement through education and then marriage to a 'good woman'.[28] Sunday was the great day for 'improvement'; it was the one day of freedom from work, and Sunday school and chapel provided an important venue and motivation for the life odyssey to start. Chance events, disaster and salvation – all were common ingredients in the autobiography lifted from the evangelical narrative structure. So too was the system of bipolarities: of drink and sobriety, rough and respectable.

Even in the early nineteenth century, religious cynics abounded. One such was Alexander Somerville, the son of a border shepherd, yet he gave vivid accounts of attending church assemblies as 'intellectual treats'.[29] But with autobiographies published from the 1850s onwards, lives were increasingly constructed within the evangelical narrative structure that had come into play in their childhood. Christian Watt, a woman born in the 1840s into a poor fishing family on the Moray Firth coast, wrote her memoir for a doctor in the mental asylum she entered late in life. She lost her father and many brothers to the sea, worked as a fisherwoman selling fish from a creel she carried on her back through the countryside, and worked for spells as a domestic servant in London and the United States. She recalled how she lost her virginity in the 1850s to her betrothed in her parents' bed whilst they were away; she was spied on by a female neighbour from behind a curtain, and when a child was born out of wedlock, and she faced church discipline for fornication, she underwent conversion. Her account contains all the sought-after ingredients of the evangelical narrative: suitable husband, financial security, love. It also contains chance events by the score, but throughout there is the longing journey which is answered by salvation, the return of doubt, and a second conversion experience. Always a rebel against the burden of 'official' and community Christian morality, she nonetheless found supreme joy in her rebirth which then reinforced her rejection of that enforced Christianity.[30]

For some autobiographers, the starting point was the irreligion and immorality of parents, usually fathers. Henry Hetherington's father gave up being a master tailor around 1800 to rent a public house where 'his love of company' and 'his unconquerable propensity for drink, effectually weaned him from his home', leading to dissipation, death and the debt of all the family.[31] The Victorian 'life' was invariably a journey away from, or in fear of, such moral and economic destruction. The male artisan – respectable, pious and home-loving – was a common self-portrait, but invariably set as the outcome of a life's journey through the temptations of drink and gambling. After an apprenticeship following railway engineering jobs (and manly temptations) around the train depots of Britain, Peter Taylor married and settled in Paisley where, because of young children, many families could not attend church services: 'so we had one of our own in each other's houses, week about. I have carried my first-born in his cradle upstairs, and Maggie coming up behind with the Bible. Ach, it was not only grand, it was glorious.'[32] The act of writing one's own life was an affirmation of moral worth. So, too, were diaries. John Sturrock, a millwright in his mid-twenties, recounted in the 1860s his fastidious teetotalism, his search for a Christian congregation to suit his tastes, and his need to record his life in a diary so that 'I may be able to form an estimate of how I have spent my leisure time, whether I have been trifling it away or turning it to any particular advantage'.[33] References to religious literature (especially *Pilgrim's Progress*), and biblical quotations and allusions, abound in the nineteenth-century working-class autobiography. Many working-class autobiographers were active in church, Sunday school or home-missionary activities, and most feature periods of searching for salvation, periods of waiting for the Lord. They deploy the moral polarities of drink and sobriety, improvidence and thrift, rough and respectable, irreligious and pious as the discursive structure of their accounts.[34] Women's published autobiographies, though rarer than men's, were often so intensely bound-up with religiosity that they were indistinguishable in rhetoric and narrative structure from evangelical fiction.[35] A minority of autobiographers experienced religious crises, but even here few lost Christian faith completely, rebelling more against the churches than against belief and the narrative of the moral life.[36]

The discursive power of religious narrative was noted by early religious psychologists in the 1890s in studying the evangelical conversion. Using interviews and questionnaires, psychologists discovered that what they called the 'conversion narratives' of 'very commonplace persons' kept true to 'a pre-appointed type by instruction, appeal, and example'. They noted how in the eighteenth century Jonathan Edwards, to whom the modern evangelical conversion owes much for its narrative, had spoken of conversionist testimony as in 'an exact conformity to the scheme already established in their minds'.[37] The same conversion narratives were apparent in personal accounts of coming to Christ at the Billy Graham London crusade of 1954 (which attracted almost two million attenders), and in early 1980s oral-history testimony of the 1949 religious revival on the Isle of Lewis.[38] The evangelical narrative structure was familiar discursive terrain to be readily and expectantly drawn upon in personal testimony. But the way in which the testimony reflected that discursive power was significantly gendered.

WOMEN'S NARRATIVES

In the autumn of 1904, the *Daily Telegraph* published a massive readers' correspondence instigated by one letter which asked of Christian Britain: 'do we believe?' A collection of 242 letters from the correspondence received was published in book form the following year, in which 239 writers were divided into those professing Christian 'faith' (130), those professing 'unfaith' (57) and those professing 'doubt' (52).[39] The correspondence was dominated by men of the 'establishment', the upper echelons of Edwardian society, mostly from London and the Home Counties, with strong representations from Anglican clergy, lawyers, and doctors, with the odd mayor, rear admiral and banker thrown in. Irrespective of their attitude to religion, they represented the issue of 'believing' as an overwhelmingly intellectual issue, debating the nature of Christian religion in terms of doctrine, science, comparative religions and logic. This was an exercise in intellectual machismo – powerful men applying 'reason' to religion, whether for or against, and signified by many of the 127 anonymous letter-writers adopting self-consciously Latinised monikers: Oxoniensis, Homo, Cantabrigiensis, Etonensis Credens, Credenti Nihil Difficile.

Only seven of the 239 correspondents were identifiably women. Their manner of writing was very different. With them the issue of morality dominated, the prime concern being the impact of unbelief upon women's moral stature. 'Gambler's Wife' contributed a letter-length autobiography of the 'cruelty, wrong, and oppression of men' wrought on her and her children by her husband, a rich landed heir, who had spent his fortune and impoverished and abandoned his family. She had struggled to bring her children up in respectability before God and society, but had failed in the face of 'the leaders of society, who have not the manliness to defend the right': 'My life has been a living death, and I long for the end.'[40] At the other extreme from this was another letter, signed 'A Very Happy Woman', who confessed herself 'incompetent' to discuss belief 'either theologically or scientifically', but offered her personal conviction of an 'undefined religion' based on 'life, love and peace'.[41] Many male correspondents asserted that 'women worshippers who attend services believe . . . but the immense majority of men do not'.[42] In response, a woman from London, signing herself in mock intellectual submission as 'Amoebe', spoke of 'the large number of thoughtful women who do not believe' because of the expectation that women must be religious in order to be moral. She had abandoned Christian belief after reading widely in science and theology. This, she wrote, shattered her:

> At first my whole motive in life seemed gone, and I felt that the morals which hung upon that motive must go too. For a long time I was absolutely miserable. I have recovered. I never pray now. I only feel and think and act. But I am sure all who know me would say that my character is superior now to what it was then, because it is richer, more sympathetic. I may also say that I do not find resisting temptation any more difficult, relying on my own strength, than I used to do when I prayed for help.[43]

Eschewing 'male' reason, these women had been forced to engage with religious doubt within the evangelical discourse on female piety. Even then, they could not shed it; the implications were too great. A man might gain respect for professing 'unfaith' with intellectual vigour, but for a woman to maintain her 'character' outside the profession, or the semblance, of Christian belief was a difficult and often heroic enterprise. If a woman shed her religion, she could shed her reason for being.

Few women before the mid-twentieth century could even attempt to throw off these shackles of their moral identity. Those who did were, as in these cases reported in the columns of the upper-class *Daily Telegraph*, overwhelmingly aristocratic, upper-middle-class, or bohemian and artistic. But for the 'ordinary' woman to contemplate revolt against evangelical discourse was, as with 'Amoebe', to endanger *being* a woman: 'My whole motive in life seemed gone, and I felt that the morals which hung upon that motive must go too.' Clinging to or acquiring the status of being 'a Christian' was a *sine qua non* for most women between 1800 and 1950. In the nineteenth century, this could mean a conversion experience; Mrs Sydney Watson left a Bible class meeting determined to get a share of God's love and resolved 'more earnestly than ever to be good'.[44] After 1900, it tended to be a social rather than salvationist goal; Margaret Penn and Alice Foley from north-west England were almost driven to despair in the early twentieth century by their desire for acceptance in church and Sunday school.[45] But throughout the period, few women could ignore the discursive power of religion to their womanhood. Winifred Foley's father was a miner with little interest in religion who felt that 'organised religion was the opium dealt out to the masses by the cynical few, to obtain for themselves their own heaven on this earth'. Husbands only went occasionally to church in her village, being able to disengage themselves intellectually, politically and discursively from religion. But Winifred's mother, like most women in the village, went to church regularly, though the poorer wives only went once a week because they couldn't afford good clothes.[46]

Being a practising Christian was for a woman a richly feminised experience. Young women and girls aspired to and emerged into womanhood within a series of signs and symbols located in church and faith. Oral and autobiographical testimony comes alive when women recall late Victorian and early twentieth-century religious events. The theatricality of the revivalist preacher, and of the call to the saved to come forward, appears frequently. Molly Weir speaks of the attraction of Jock Troup's tent preaching in Springburn in Glasgow between the wars. He was such 'great value' that he could 'make the flames of hell so real, we felt them licking round our feet, and the prospect of heaven so alluring we often stood up to be saved several times during the week'; once home, she re-enacted the service to her Grannie.[47] Margaret Penn in Lancashire and Flora Thompson in Oxfordshire, like many children of the late nineteenth and early twentieth centuries, attended services or Sunday schools of different denominations, but favoured Methodist worship over Anglican for its evangelical excitement.[48] Aesthetic sensibility features powerfully in elderly women's testimony of remembrance of Sunday school and church services when they were young girls. Henrietta Isleworth from Preston recalled: 'I always remember we got white silk dresses on for Good Friday, they must have been lovely, and they took us for a long walk'.[49] Isabelle Jones (born 1900) from the same town went to a Methodist Church four times every Sunday as a child; 'We never thought – we thought it was lovely, we never thought anything about it. We would be dressed in our best, you know.'[50] At the teetotal meetings of the Band of Hope in the 1910s, Jean Kennedy recalled:

> We would meet in the Band of Hope. There was an old Church stood in the middle of the Brae and it was a lovely, *beautiful* Church and the velvet where the – preacher stood was just – oh, it wasnae much broader than that cabinet and it was red velvet, I can mind. And we had cantatas and things like that.... Peggy and I used to sing – oh what was it? 'Count your blessings', and we'd stand as proud as be. And we had white frocks and because I thought I was the king – the queen of everything. Mine was lacy and Peggy's was plain. Oh, we used to rival in good fun.[51]

Religious worship was a vital venue for young working-class girls to express their femininity. Their testimony sparkles when discussing the 'Sunday best' dresses. Kate Langholm born in 1914 recalled:

> Well, Sunday was my day because Sunday I was up and I was born, I mean brought up a Protestant, but on a Sunday morning I got dressed – you had a Sunday outfit you see, you only wore it on a Sunday, no other day except a Sunday. Well I went to my two pals, they went to the Catholic Church, so I went with them to mass on a Sunday morning so's I'd have my Sunday clothes on. When I came home I'd go to the [Protestant] church with my mother and then

when I came home from that I kept on my clothes because I was going to the Sunday school, and then we went to Bible class at night. And the reason I went to all that was because I got wearing my Sunday clothes. As soon as I was finished from the Bible class you'd to take them off, hang them up and put on your ordinary clothes. You weren't allowed to wear your Sunday best for playing with. So the one [day] I looked forward to is a Sunday just for that – to keep my Sunday clothes on.[52]

Hetty Beck born in 1879 in London recalled the special Sunday dresses she wore as either white or very pale, used for church and Sunday school anniversaries and for Sunday evening walks with friends, in stark contrast to the black she wore after funerals during the long mourning time.[53] It was the same for young Catholic girls. 'Sunday-best' dresses were bought annually, usually in spring, as Maria Nolan (born in 1910) recalled:

First Sunday in May, that's when you got your summer clothes bought. . . . And all you did was, she [mother] did was, to go down to the village shop; they were Baptist folk, and very nice people . . . Mrs Bingham would get the order and she would go to the Glasgow warehouse, and just exactly, she just took a tape and measured us, and she brought back the beautifulest clothes. It was the talk of the village. 'I wonder what the Nolan girls will have this May?' Sometimes be shepherd's tartan with velvet; another time it would be green velvet.[54]

The dresses are remembered with great clarity: the parade to church in 'our button boots and our parasols . . . black button boots we had on, and eh a black dress. It was awfy fancy made with frills, puff sleeves and everything.'[55] One woman recalled being taken for a new Sunday-best outfit, but after making a scene in the draper's shop about dress colour (she wanted green), her mother threatened her with the very real punishment of *not* going to church.[56]

Sunday-best dress was a signifier of both feminine and religious apprenticeship. Churches were privileging women's and girls' sense of their own identity. But they were also privileging women as vulnerable. The Band of Hope's magic lantern stories of female victims of male drink were widely recalled in first-hand testimony:

You would see the mother would probably be in bed, and she'd either just had an addition to her family or she was ill with tuberculosis. And you usually saw the father who had been drunk, and it was always perhaps the eldest sister was looking after, you know, a big family. And this was brought home to you about, you know, drink, you know, how it was the downfall of your eh – So, with the result that when you would go to these things, you know, you'd sometimes come away with your face all tear-stained. . . .[57]

In Glasgow in the 1920s, Molly Weir related the lantern slide temperance message of the evils of strong drink to the reality around her, especially on Saturdays; children were 'noting with a shudder every detail of the poor wives and children being thrown into the streets because the husband had drunk away the rent money'.[58] In the evangelical and temperance movements, women were both the moral guardians and the moral victims of fathers, brothers, husbands and sons. These discourses were not just circulated through passive mediums like books and magic lanterns. Placed at the head of the 'White Ribboners' parades of the British Women's Temperance Association were young girls, dressed in white, deliberately selected as the daughters of drunken fathers who, it was hoped, would see them and take shame.[59] Virtue and piety were on parade, and they were female.

Until the mid-twentieth century, religion was the primary, and usually the only, focus of formal recreation for older girls and young single women, including domestic servants.[60] Large numbers of female oral interviewees and autobiographers, most not professing to being especially devout or 'reborn', became – sometimes to their own surprise – Sunday school teachers.[61] In Barrow in the 1940s and early 1950s, the parents of Nelly Messenger were non-churchgoers, but she became very active as a youth leader in the Church of England, the Brownies, the Girl Guides and the Scouts. She went to church parade every Sunday morning, and in the afternoon and evening 'knocked about together' with two or three of her female friends, touring the different churches of the town:

Q: Why did you do that?
A: Just to see what they were like. We would go to the Salvation Army one week, we would go to the Gospel Hall another week and the Methodist church another week, and one week we went to the Catholic church and it was absolutely full. And they showed us to the front row, and of course we had no rosaries or anything.[62]

Huge numbers of girls and young women *savoured* church services between the 1850s and 1950s. A woman from Stirling regaled her interviewer with a battery of churches and organisations she attended in the 1920s and 1930s: the Railway Mission ('a lovely wee mission hall'), the South Church Sunday school ('I chummed with the same wee girl going up to school') as well as other Sunday schools, the Salvation Army ('I was a Sunbeam'), and the Baptist church meetings (where 'another pal of mine, her father was a caretaker'). 'Oh yes, it was all religion', she concluded; 'I don't know why we didnae sprout wings! [*laughing*]'.[63]

Between 1850 and 1950, young women and girls prepared for church on a Sunday in the same way that they later prepared for going out on Saturday nights to the cinema and the dancing. At the chapel in Jim

Bullock's mining village in Yorkshire in the early twentieth century, 'girls wore frocks and pinafores, and their hair hung down in long curls, the result of wrapping it in curling rags on Saturday night'.[64] A major reason for this was romance. Church and religious organisations were the 'singles bars' and dating agencies of their time. Molly Weir recalled:

> All our romantic attachments were formed with those boys whom we met through the church. All our religious observance, which played so large a part in our lives, became more thrilling and exciting when we could peep across at the lads under cover of our hymn-singing, and later we joined up with them for a few delicious moments on our demure walks over Crowhill Road after evening service.[65]

Church, chapel, Sunday school and mission hall were important locations for romance. Henry Elder's mother met her husband, a piano finisher, in Field Lane Mission in Rosebery Avenue in central London in the early 1890s where he preached and where his sister played the organ.[66] David Mitchell, born in 1899 to non-churchgoing parents, spent all his life in Salvation Army organisations where he met his wife.[67] Percival Chambers (born 1894) changed from going to the Church of England to the Baptist Church because 'there was a young lady I knew went ... and that enticed me and kept me there for a long time'. He then switched to a presbyterian church because there was another lady he liked, and took a short period back at the Church of England because of another young woman.[68] Patricia Quigley (born 1906) met her husband at the Sunday school of her Church of Scotland in Stirling: there was, she recalled, 'a superintendent in the primary who prided herself in getting young couples together, you know ... And I was the pianist, in the primary Sunday school, and she was a great one for making matches. And that was where I met my husband when we were seventeen.'[69] Sunday was not only a day for dating but a day for consummating romance. In England, Sunday became the most popular day of the week for church weddings. Most English weddings took place in the Anglican Church (accounting for between 80 and 94 per cent of all marriages in sample parishes in Birmingham, Manchester and Blackburn), and Sunday was its leading day by the late Victorian period. In Bristol Sunday was the leading day for nuptials throughout 1790–1911 (with from 29 to 37 per cent of all marriages taking place on that day). But in other cities it jumped in popularity: in Birmingham Sunday weddings rose continuously from 18 per cent of all marriages in 1791 to 51 per cent in 1911; in Manchester the figures rose from 21 per cent in 1790 to 35 per cent in 1871, only to be stalled by an apparent change of local clerical policy which pushed them on to Wednesdays, whilst something similar appears to have happened in Blackburn in the 1880s, when couples seem to have been directed to substitute Thursdays or Saturdays for Sundays.[70]

However, once married, the woman of the working classes usually changed her relationship with Sunday churchgoing. Sunday was a highly gendered day for parents. Characteristically, in households without domestic servants, mothers remained at home in the morning to look after young children and prepare Sunday lunch, whilst older children and the father went to church, chapel or Sunday school. A man from Essex recalled in the first two decades of the twentieth century how in the morning the children 'went to the Sunday school, and then from Sunday school into chapel. Father went Sunday morning in the morning, Mother stopped at home to cook the meal.' The children went back to Sunday school again in the afternoon, and after tea at home went back to chapel, this time with Mother.[71] Tom Willis' mother said to him in around 1930:

'You don't have to go to church, do you? I mean you can live a decent life without all the rigmarole, can't you? Strikes me that half the people who go to church are humbugs anyway, Sunday Christians.' She smiled. 'No, I don't think He'll hold it against me. When I get to the pearly gates He won't hold it against me, I'm sure of that. And if He does, I'll tell Him straight. I was too busy on Sundays getting dinner and tea for you bloody lot to have time to sit on my arse in church.'[72]

Domestic ideology expected women to cook meals, and the most important meal of the week in virtually all households in nineteenth- and early twentieth-century Britain was that at Sunday lunchtime. Even for poor and working-class families it was the day for meat, the best that could be afforded. In Barrow in Lancashire one interviewee recalled: 'We always had a big joint which used to do Monday as well of course, but we always had cold meat for supper on Sunday night, always. We had all the trimmings of course with Yorkshire pudding. Yorkshire pudding first and then you'd have your joint after and always a pudding after that if you wanted it, milk pudding after that.'[73] Such meals took time to prepare, and for Protestants without domestic servants this meant in almost all cases the woman of the household missed Sunday morning worship, which in most churches was timed at a single service starting at 11 am and finishing at anytime between 12.30 pm and 1.30 pm. This meant that women's attendance at morning worship was dramatically reduced – an issue we explore in statistical detail in the next chapter. Even in Scotland, Sunday lunch was, by the start of the twentieth century, an important ritual in most families. In the inter-war period one woman recalled that 'my mother wouldn't have thought Sunday was Sunday without a joint of meat', whilst the mother of another couldn't afford proper 'butcher' meat but still laid out 'a wee bit meat and maybe our soup and tatties'.[74] If the family was strictly sabbatarian, then the food would be cooked on Saturday night and reheated.[75] Arrangements in the Catholic Church were different. There were multiple morning masses between 9 am and 12 noon to choose from, allowing a much greater female attendance which characteristically occurred at the early services so that they could get home in time to prepare Sunday lunch.

Meals had what Camporesi calls 'dietary protocols',[76] and Sunday lunch had developed by the late nineteenth century as an essential symbolic resource in the British family. The aspiration was to a joint of beef, roasted with 'all the trimmings'. In the north of England by 1900, and even in much of the south and in Scotland and Wales, the key trimming was Yorkshire pudding, served very often as the savoury preliminary course to the meat and eaten separately. With soup and a dessert (bread-and-butter or milk pudding being common), this was the aspirational working-class Sunday lunch. For the middle classes, the roast joint and soup also featured, but the dessert was often cake- or sponge-based. Oral and autobiographical testimony is universal on the special significance of Sunday lunch, and even in the poorest of houses some special meat, be it only 'lips and lugs', was obtained. Lunch was a weekly affirmation of family life, its relative 'luxury' over the diet of the rest of the week subscribing each family member to complex religious, family and community values.

Sunday lunch and Protestant Sunday worship clashed. The ironic situation arose in nineteenth-century Britain that evangelical discourses put extra pressure upon women to be 'religious' yet deprived them of a convenient morning time for worship. Many Protestant clergy sought remedies for this. Special afternoon services for women were extremely common in Scotland, and many Nonconformist and Anglican clergy and missions did likewise in England. In one Scottish parish the women's afternoon service was held at the front of the church whilst their children were taken in Sunday school at the rear.[77] Many female interviewees had contact with church out-reach agencies aimed specifically at women, including missions. Doris Tarlking of Finsbury recalled that in 1910 she was befriended by a wealthy woman who did 'a lot of good works', and who invited her to a Sunday afternoon women's mission meeting she conducted. Doris slipped in a rear pew where the attitude of other attenders made her cynical: 'there were three old ladies in front and I heard one say to the other: "Just butter her up, dear, and she'll give you anything you want." '[78] Special afternoon worship only accentuated the sense of 'otherness' amongst poor female attenders.

If women's narratives illustrate the problems of working-class women attending church, they show that the moral construction of womanhood was subject to irresistible community and family pressures. Edith Hall recalled that in inter-war London 'the greatest stigma against a woman was to be considered lazy',[79] and those single young women who failed to work were considered unrespectable. Finding a husband – and being seen to want a husband – was the most serious area of application. Those who did not get married in Grace Foakes' community 'were looked upon with pity', but those who tried too hard courted the label of 'gutter-snipe', 'promis-cuous', or 'asking for trouble', and would be restrained by mothers who advised to 'keep Pure'.[80] In turn, these moral issues were inseparably linked, most often by mothers, to religious morality. This might be the simple avoidance of blasphemy and Sabbath desecration, or could be the avoidance of pregnancy out of wedlock. Winifred Foley recalled a ditty current among her peers which she said to herself when tempted by her first sexual encounter:

> There was a young lady so wild
> She kept herself pure undefiled
> By thinking of Jesus
> Venereal disease
> And the dangers of having a child.[81]

Discourses could be turned into rules by churches. A woman who had a child out of wedlock was frequently unwelcome: the Girls Friendly Society, one interviewee recalled, 'had a very, very strict rule because they wouldn't accept as a member any girl who had fallen ... They were there to keep out anyone who had made a mistake. They should have been trying to lift them up again, I thought.'[82] Where before 1800 the church would have sought the woman in church to 'purge the scandal', a hundred years later she was summarily excluded.[83] But popular religious discourse on female behaviour was in many ways more severe, more uncompromising, and less forgiving than official ecclesiastical censure. Official religious discourses on female morality were powerfully enforced – by the role of gossip, parental supervision and peer-group pressure.[84] A woman's destiny in life was heavily hedged in a maze requiring finely balanced judgements. Individuality could be suppressed to a degree to which men were not expected to submit.[85] Indeed, autobiographies tend to recall evangelical discourses as a community product, not one from pulpit, tract or magazine.

Oral history has recently demonstrated the existence of a much more complex world of women's religious ritual which reveals what Sarah Williams has called 'the elusive and eclectic dimension of religious belief'.[86] Both women and men alive in the late twentieth century recall the obser-vance of a myriad of practices to ward off bad luck, but it was women who had the most varied liturgy, adhered to it most fervently and passed it on from mother to daughter. This world was composed of liturgies recalled by Christian female interviewees within a narrative structure of drama and even melodrama which linked women's bodies, health and piety. Birth rituals were the most potent and widespread, centred on the act of 'churching' a woman after giving birth, a ceremony without which women were barred (seemingly entirely by other women) from entering many homes. One informant recalled in dramatic terms how for hours, one day in November, she led her sister with her baby round London in thick fog trying to find a church that was open for the sister's churching.[87] Churching had been a formal Church of England service until 1645, and although restored in 1660, it seems to have withered in elite circles and amongst Nonconformists. But oral-history evidence from Lancashire, Dudley and from London demonstrates both how widespread the practice was until the first half of the twentieth century, and how its survival rested with plebeian women themselves who enforced a discourse that, without it, bad luck would befall both the 'unclean' woman and the household that admitted her.[88] Melodrama also features in the long story told by Mary Manson in Shetland of how her mother travelled on foot with a sick female cousin across two barren islands and made a perilous sea-crossing to find a wisewoman for a remedy. The woman locked them in a dark box-bed whilst she prepared a potion and sent them away to administer it with considerable ritual.[89] A variety of studies have demonstrated, using oral and documentary evidence, that complex religious observances based on amulets and rituals, many kept secret and furtively observed, existed in Britain until the middle of the twentieth century. This constituted a highly gendered religious world, mostly rooted in Christian belief. Williams concludes that 'apparently incompatible narratives of religious belief' coexisted for women, drawing upon both church and folk customs of some considerable longevity.[90]

Women had to negotiate complex and competing Christian protocols. To borrow an observation from Stanley and Wise, the gender 'role' ascribed by religious identity to women was not fixed and immutable, not 'gender socialised *in* someone' but was 'situationally variable', meaning that the 'self' was and is 'relationally and interactionally composed, its construction being historically, culturally and contextually specific'.[91] The moral and religious 'self' was a negotiation between sometimes contradictory protocols of discourse, as they interacted with economic and family circumstances. To be both pious and feminine was very difficult.

MEN'S NARRATIVES

The structure of male narratives reveals important facets of masculinity as a social construction. Significant numbers of male interviewees recall pressure from parents to become a parson, minister or priest. The testimony of Thomas Brennan, born in 1896, revolves around two central episodes in his life – the choice in his youth of becoming a Catholic priest, and his years of war service in the armed forces. Raised in Liverpool of fairly devout Catholic parents, he was trained as an altar boy, and looked on the clergy 'as real fatherly figures – very kindly, oh yes, yes', and his parents hoped he would go into the priesthood – a profession 'that was drilled in you' as 'something out of the ordinary' and due 'a very great respect'. However, self-doubt that 'I wouldn't make the grade' led to him turning down the offer to join a priest going to South Africa, a decision he clearly regretted. He recalled instead his religious life outside the priesthood in the Catholic Young Men's Society, Sunday evening concerts, and his continuing work for the church: 'And you think to yourself, well, I must make the grade. I must save my soul if I can.' His testimony then changes gear as he moves into many pages of uninterrupted recollections of war service, standing as an alternative and consummated identity that he delivers with vigour and free from doubt or regret – an area of identity where he did 'make the grade'.[92]

In evangelical households, boys were strongly encouraged to look upon clergymen as heroes to emulate. Caradog Wells, born in 1903 in the Rhondda, was told by his mother to model himself on his uncle from farming stock, who 'turned out eventually to be a local preacher' with the Wesleyans. 'And she used to – always – when it came to be a question of referring to anybody who we should follow and grow up and act like, it was always my uncle Emmanuel.'[93] From 1800 to the early twentieth century, young boys in Wales and in the Scottish Highlands were known to play at being preachers, by exhorting to dogs and livestock in the manner of their favourite pastors.[94] Clergy were sometimes affectionately satirised. Dolly Scannell's family played a Christmas game called 'Confessions' in which her brother 'dressed up as a vicar, and as each person entered the room he had to kneel in front of the priest and confess his sins, and when the priest bent to give him absolution so of course he would be soaked with water'.[95]

One of the main attractions of the Church of England for young boys was singing in a choir. Anglican choirboys were paid, and even those with non-churchgoing parents were to be found in a choir. Lazarus Cox from Oxford went to church three times on Sundays because he sang in the choir, 'and then that was a farthing a time, and if you mis-behaved your-self you was in the chancel. The old vicar used to say, when we got down: "sixpence off your money Cox, for talking".'[96] Thomas Upton, born 1904, sang a great deal in church choirs: 'I used to enjoy that thoroughly, but I don't think that made me particularly religious, but it took me to church.'[97] Music was an important religious connection for working- and middle-class men. In the Church of England, a surprising number of male oral interviewees were bell-ringers, while an even larger group were in the church choir as men and boys. Many in the working classes were in brass bands, where religious and temperance music was located in an all-male venue. But even more important was the vital familiarity which working-class neighbourhoods had with religious music. Before 1920, temperance bands, works bands, club and lodge bands, and Salvation Army bands were familiar and common, not just on Sunday afternoons playing at bandstands in public parks, but on Saturdays and weekday evenings playing at street corners. Mr J. Partridge recalled how in Hackney during his childhood in the 1900s 'Salvation Army bands on a Sunday morning, used to come and play, and you'd all turn out and listen to that or open your windows'.[98] Their repertoire was dominated by religious hymns and psalms, and their familiarity made them well known in daily life. Interviewees recall the singing of hymns on works outings and even in workplaces, especially among women millworkers, pitbrow lasses, fishermen, fish gutters and miners.[99] Music was one of the important male connections to religiosity. The rise of the brass band from the 1870s in the working-class communities of the Midlands, northern England, South Wales and central Scotland created a characteristic male world, combining the masculinity of militaristic uniforms, the machismo of the brass instrument, and the religious content of the sacred music. To this was added the male voice choir in Wales which, uniquely in Britain, developed a strong and enduring association with Nonconformist religion. And organ music was not confined to churches. When the movies came to Barrow-in-Furness in the 1900s they were screened at an open-air fairground in the Market Square with 'a beautiful organ on the front, a huge organ right across the front of the marquee' playing 'gorgeous' hymns and classical music which attracted people in their hundreds.[100] Even modern cultural forms, with 'secular' content, could be surrounded with religious symbols.

Music was also an important religious theme in the home. Many interviewees, mostly of upper-working-class or middle-class parents, recall Sunday evenings between the 1870s and 1910s around a piano or harmonium singing psalms and hymns. Religious music in the home was not just an addition but sometimes a substitute for formal church connection – as a Scripture Reader discovered whilst door-to-door evangelising in Islington in about 1898:

> 55 Popham Road: Mrs Hooker. Had conversation upon spiritual matters. Is rather sceptical: sometimes thinks there is a heaven, and sometimes she thinks there is not, but she certainly did not believe there is a hell. She does not attend a place of worship; they generally had some music at home, which she thinks is as good as going to church.[101]

Reginald Collins from Liverpool recalled the family singing in the 1900s and 1910s: 'We used to sing together but not organised. Me dad used to sing. He used to – he used to sing some wonderful songs. Moody and Sankey's hymns, you know. And "Blind Boy", I remember him – remember him cry – we cried over that, yes.'[102]

Boys, however, had severe problems with churches. Whilst girls loved wearing Sunday-best dresses, and revelled in the recollection in oral testimony, boys generally hated their Sunday-best clothes. These were dominated by two types: the sailor's suit, and the Eton suit. The latter was extremely common amongst all social classes. In the upper-middle-classes, Ronald Walker blanched at the memory of being dressed as a boy in Harrogate with a dark-blue sailor suit for winter and a white one for summer, with an Eton suit as an alternative. The working classes and the poor still equipped their boys aged seven to twelve years in such things. Thomas Brennan and his brothers from Liverpool, brought up Catholics, were supplied by their father with new knee trousers and stockings every year for their appearances in the church choir. Reginald Collins, the son of a Liverpool dock labourer who had long periods of unemployment, wore an Eton suit on Sundays, whilst Arthur Turner, despite a very brutal and poor upbringing in Manchester's Hankey Park, had a sailor's suit.[103] Religious clothes changed for funerals. In Wales, William Pugh recalled that it was the custom for the people organising a funeral to give on the morning of the burial a black tie and a pair of black gloves to everyone invited.[104] Not one male oral interviewee recollected this sartorial regime with affection. If the religious signification of girls' Sunday-best dresses supported their own signification of femininity, it did not do this for boys.

For boys, Sundays were days of encasement in suits of stupefying grandeur and pretension, suits which imprisoned the spirit of the carefree physicality of puberty and adolescence. Boys were frequently deprived of a churchgoing role-model father; oral interviewees from many Church of England families report that their fathers were not churchgoers. Lazarus Cox was born in 1879 in Oxford, his father an illiterate and non-churchgoing builder's labourer, and it was his mother who 'always saw that we gone to church all right' where he became a choirboy.[105] Boys were being trained to be 'religious' by mothers, and it was mothers who 'dressed' boys in Sunday best. Boys' Sunday-best clothes were seemingly uniformly detested, in large part because they represented a cultural imprisonment symbolic of the virtually universal ban on Sunday games. Ball games and especially football, the emerging adoration of males of all ages and social classes between the 1880s and 1920s, were banned from public spaces by bye-laws and community expectation. Men were trained to perceive their masculine tendencies, even those promoted by muscular Christianity, as curbed on the Sabbath. Sunday was feminised, and men's games were rendered immoral and criminal.[106]

This was only part of a much wider phenomenon – the way in which evangelicalism was designed to induce guilt in men for their manly pleasures. Religious discourse on drunken men and impoverished families, on male tendencies to dissipation, sexual impropriety, gambling and 'rough' behaviour, threw blame for immorality on men. This intensified from the 1850s to the 1920s as men were increasingly demonised by the publicity campaigns of religious pressure groups, leading to new laws restricting their pastimes, especially on Sundays.[107] Men's pastimes, especially drinking, gambling and smoking, were increasingly the object of evangelical campaigning and parliamentary enactment.[108] Men were made into the culprits, and their relationship to religion by the late Victorian period was surrounded with anxiety and tension.

RELIGIOUS SYMBOL AND MOTIF

Estimates of churchgoing in late Victorian and Edwardian Britain compiled from oral-history archives have universally exceeded the figures obtained from censuses of church attendance. Hugh McLeod's analysis of oral testimony showed that 40–50 per cent of interviewees were brought up in a family where at least one adult was a frequent churchgoer, but there was wide regional variation – from over 50 per cent of the interviewees in Scotland and Wales claiming their fathers were regular attenders, to lows of 20 per cent in London, the Potteries and the north Midlands.[109] Problems with these samples may exaggerate the regional variations,[110] but they undoubtedly reflect basic regional differences evident from other sources. In a moderately high churchgoing area like Stirling, for instance, a socially balanced sample of elderly women interviewed in 1987–8 produced 27 per cent who said that both parents had attended church every Sunday in the late nineteenth and early twentieth century, a further 40 per cent reporting regular attendance, 11 per cent saying that their fathers only (and 9 per cent mothers only) attended regularly or every Sunday, and a mere 13 per cent stating that neither parent attended church.[111]

If oral testimony upgrades estimates of churchgoing among working-class adults (the interviewees' parents), it does this even more strikingly for their children (the interviewees themselves) of the period 1900–40. Interviews show that Sunday school attendance was widespread. Amongst the Stirling archive of 76 female Protestant interviewees, 73 per cent claimed to have attended Sunday school, 45 per cent attended weekday meetings of teetotal organisations (the Band of Hope, the White Ribboners or Good Templars), 13 per cent were in church-affiliated uniformed youth organisations, and 14 per cent were in church choirs.[112] Most of those who didn't attend Sunday school or uniformed organisations lived in rural areas where either these organisations did not exist or travel to church was extremely difficult. The sheer weight of testimony towards children's patronage of church organisations is compelling. If the level of child association was extraordinarily high, the *intensity* of their connection was remarkable. The researcher in an oral-history archive comes away overloaded with accounts of entire Sundays, and two to three weekday evenings, devoted to religious meetings. Mr Darling, born 1889 in Warkworth in Northumberland, recalled his presbyterian upbringing with his father, a bailiff:

And when we were old enough we had to go to church with him [father] on a Sunday morning. We used to walk four miles. We were all brought up, right from children, to go to Sunday school, and you never forget it, no.... We weren't allowed to gallivant about on a Sunday, you know. Oh no. You had to get a book and sit. Oh there was nothing done on a Sunday.[113]

In Roman Catholic communities, chapelgoing by the late nineteenth century was very strong. Arthur Turner from Hankey Park in Manchester recalled: 'Well, nearly everybody in street went to church Sundays you know. Oh aye, nearly all Catholics near there.'[114] William Pugh recalled life in a North Wales farming valley where virtually every living soul was shackled to the chapel. On Sundays, with a three mile walk to chapel, his sixty-nine-year-old grandfather went in the morning, both his parents went morning and evening, and William went three times (attending the Sunday school in the afternoon). His father led the chapel singing, there was family worship morning and night during the week conducted by his grandfather, and grace was said before all meals. For household reading the family took the evangelical newspaper *The Banner* and, though mother was too busy 'from rise to bedtime' to read, 'my father and grandfather used to sit by the fire and read. And they'd read biographies. The stories of people.'[115]

Between the 1880s and 1940s, many homes had important religious arte-facts. The family Bible was common, and multiple Bibles for different members of the family were usual in better-off families. Households had some special books brought out on Sundays 'as a treat': 'the very big Bible with the pictures in. Oh David, the very big giant with blood gushing out of his forehead where the stone had hit him, you know, and it was marvel-lous. I loved that.'[116] Magazines of a religious, 'improving' and domestic nature were widespread: *The Christian Herald*, *Home Journal*, *Home Words*, *Home Notes*, *Good Words*, *The Penny Illustrated*, the *Boy's Own* and *Girl's Own Papers*. Dora Bucknell born in 1882 in Hull recalled *Horner's Penny Stories*: 'They were very sentimental. Very sentimental sort of love stories, and a bit of religion in them as well, these books had. I used to skip the religion and the romantic bits and get on with the story [*laughter*].'[117] Asked if there were any books in her household, a woman from a very poor family in Preston recalled: 'We had our books. We got a Sunday school prize, you see, and we had to read them and the first book I ever remember reading was Jessica's First Prayer, or something like that. I had that book for years.'[118] For books, Dickens, Scott and Thackeray, usually recited as a threesome, clearly outnumbered the rest in the British household of 1900. Decoration was also important. Whilst Catholic and some Anglican homes displayed crucifixes, many Nonconformist homes had religious pictures. Mr Wash, born 1899 in Halstead in Essex, lived in a Congregationalist home where wall pictures tended to be religious subjects 'such as John Wesley's house on fire, you know, and that sort of thing. He'd got his children round him, and making some pronouncement about "let the house burn, I am rich enough", you know, that sort of thing.'[119]

In London, where rates of churchgoing were lower than in most of the rest of Britain, the churchgoing family had a certain status: Hetty Beck recalled of the 1880s and 1890s that 'in those days, if you went to church, well then you were regarded as someone of – er – a certain amount of importance'. People 'who really looked to the serious side of life went to church or chapel or Salvation Army or Church Army', people you 'would – er – deal with and have a good deal of conversation with really'.[120] Churches represented a 'well-off other' to many families. Working-class religion, as Hugh McLeod has said of London, was 'severely practical', with an epigrammatic and pragmatic view of both God and the churches. Those who held a strong faith were seen by others as self-reliant individualists and thus outsiders to the majority of working people; the practical was prioritised over the other-worldly.[121]

Yet, what made Britain a Christian nation before 1950 was not the minority with a strong faith, but the majority with some faith. The families in which one or both parents did not go to church are important in any study of religious decline. The numbers of families with no regular parental churchgoing emerges from McLeod's review of oral testimony as quite high (50–60 per cent), whilst an analysis of the Stirling archive produces a much lower figure (13 per cent). The oral testimony which chronicles these families is fascinating, for they reveal more church influence than the bald figures suggest. James Mahoney (born 1899) was brought up in Poplar and East Ham, both areas of low church attendance, his father a lapsed Catholic stevedore and socialist and his mother nominally Church of England. His 'mum and dad were not churchgoers, so, but we were made to go to Sunday school always." He described his parents as 'Hundred per cent Christians but not churchgoers', teetotallers who never gambled and who made their children say prayers at night and memorise the Lord's Prayer.[122] Probably the majority of interviewees born between the 1870s and the 1920s with non-churchgoing parents participated in church activities themselves. In some cases they imply that they were 'sent' by parents, but many found religion for themselves.[123] Leah Ward's parents weren't churchgoers in their Nottinghamshire mining village in the 1880s, but she went to Sunday school, Band of Hope and Methodist Church services, and when she was thirteen her father joined the Christadelphians.[124] David Mitchell was brought up by parents who only went to church to christen their children, but yet they celebrated Sunday as strictly as most churchgoers: they had a big Sunday lunch, his dad wore a Sunday-best suit to lead a family walk, and no games were allowed. In turn, David became highly involved in church activities: a Church of England Sunday school and Thursday evening Bible class, a member of the Salvation Army Band of Love temperance organisation and its Young People's Band, attending three Army meetings a week, concluding his account: 'Spent practically all my life at the Salvation Army.'[125] The parents of Percival Chambers (born 1894) were not churchgoers, but in West Norwood, London, he went to a massive range of religious organisations, including Sunday school, Band of Hope and the Church of England where he was a choirboy, before becoming a Congregationalist during his mid-teenage years and a Baptist in his late teens. He was, he said, attracted by young ladies and by fine preaching.[126] The parents of Mr F. Sunderland in Keighley in Yorkshire were not churchgoers in the 1900s, but they kept a strict Sabbath with no games, play or work, and clean and special clothes to be worn.[127] In the same town, Norman Potter's parents never attended church, but he became engrossed in the 1900s with church activities and those of the Pleasant Sunday Afternoon movement, and kept going to church during his adult life.[128]

So common was this pattern of activity amongst English interviewees born in the 1890s and 1900s that it deserves attention. Children of non-churchgoing parents were becoming involved with real intensity, overwhelmingly at their own volition, in church and Sunday school activities. But what of the parents? Some of the interviewees reveal that their parents had been churchgoers when they had been in their childhood and teenage years, had got married in church (or in Scotland, with different legal arrangements, by the minister in any location – such as the bride's home, the manse or an hotel or ballroom), but had stopped attending church after the birth of the first child. While returning to be 'churched' and to christen babies, their attendance at church stopped. Sarah Cookson born in 1887 in Keighley is typical in her account of her parents: 'In their young days – they were Church of England, really both of them – but in their young days before they was married they both attended the Salvation Army ... [T]hat was before they were married, and I think they'd get married when they were going there.'[129] They then stopped attending church when their family started, and Sarah became heavily involved in church activities. This was an extremely common pattern of a child having major connections to church organisations when neither parent attended church at all. Out of a small sample of 39 transcripts that referred to non-churchgoing parents in the Qualidata Archive, this pattern applied to 14 interviewees – just over a third, all of them from England and none from Scotland or Wales.[130] There was a family cycle to church connection in England in the late nineteenth and early twentieth century. In working-class families, church connection was something entered into in childhood and teenage years, enjoyed during courtship (with many romances beginning at church, chapel or Sunday school), and then was put into suspension in the early years of marriage when there were young children. In those cases, either one or both parents stopped attending church, and more often than not it was the mother who stopped going, being compelled to use Sunday mornings to prepare Sunday lunch. Other forms of religious observance were sustained: both children and adults observed the no-games, no-work rules, Sunday best was worn by children and fathers, family walks were taken in the afternoon or (in summer) in the evening, and there was special food for Sunday meals. Prayers and grace were often said in the home. Some then returned to Sunday worship when the children had left home, notably women who joined Mother's Groups or similar organisations.[131] Critically, what kept young married working-class women from church was the need to prepare Sunday lunch and look after babies.

Christian signification is strong in personal testimony relating to the period before 1950. In oral sources the evangelical narrative structure and discourses on gendered piety were widely used in conceiving individuals' lives. Dissonance between interviewees and interviewers, and between interviewees' present and past, intimated substantive change to discourse on Christianity. Popular autobiography, a genre which by the 1970s and 1980s was dominated by women writing for a predominantly female readership, focused on lost 'community' (both urban and rural) and lost values in which religiosity was a prominent motif. The world that was lost was a female one. This is nowhere more apparent, in both types of source, than with Sundays – a woman's day which retained much of its Protestant strictness in many parts of Britain until the 1940s.[132] Celia Davies recalled:

> We accepted Sunday and all that went with it, just as we accepted the seasons of the year. . . . I believe we even had Sunday hair ribbons. Nearly all our toys were put away, except books of bible stories – anything in the nature of a game was forbidden. When we went out for a walk we were not allowed to run or skip, or trail our feet in the autumn leaves. We walked sedately on either side of the pram, with that 'Sunday' feeling inside us.[133]

The Sunday 'feeling' was the great female sensibility. In Norfolk the Sunday routine of church, chapel and Sunday school was undimmed in the 1930s from the Victorian period, with the strictest houses eating only cold meals (thus allowing women to all services), and the Sunday school festival being the major calendar event of the summer.[134] If conversionism and anxiety had diminished, the discursive symbolism of evangelical religion had not. Far from being privatised or dimmed, Christianity lay at the heart of the contented and woman-centred family life into which British society had by the eve of World War II funnelled Victorian moral values.

CHAPTER SEVEN

'UNIMPEACHABLE WITNESSES': THE STATISTICS OF 'CHRISTIAN PROGRESS' 1800–1950

—— •◆• ——

URBANISATION AND RELIGIOSITY

Church historians are privileged by the volume of statistics they have at their disposal. There is no other area of popular culture for which such data are so profuse. One consequence is that scholars have tended to privilege statistics of religion in their research, following the maxim of one English investigator of 1904 who wrote that figures were 'unimpeachable witnesses to vigour, progress and interest' in the Christian condition of the nation.[1] The Victorian and Edwardian churches, social investigators and newspapers attached great evangelical discursive power to their creation, and academics reciprocated that faith by attaching to them social-science power in the late twentieth century. This chapter explores and questions the use of statistics by churchmen and academics in apparently 'proving' the unholy nature of the Victorian city and the working-class 'heathens' within them. Instead, it offers an alternative 'reading' of the data which raises *gender* to primacy in understanding the social history of British religion, and concludes with a revised statistical chronology to secularisation. This quantitative exercise might seem out of place in a book which locates statistics as part of the Enlightenment project which the author seeks to eschew. But statistical method still has its place in modern cultural theory, especially when investigating the impact of discourse change upon the protocols of people's behaviour.

Nineteenth-century churchmen were convinced that the growth of cities was undermining religion. Thomas Chalmers was the first to come up with data which apparently 'proved' this issue. He published results of surveys in the late 1810s of church sittings taken in selected areas of Glasgow. As Table 7.1 shows, these results were varied, but were interpreted by Chalmers as showing higher non-attendance at church in the industrial working-class suburbs of cities. In one suburb, where dissenters made up 77.9 per cent of all pew-holders, he wrote that were it not for them 'there would have been a district of the city ... in a state nearly of entire Heathenism'.[2] Chalmers took Glasgow as representative of British cities,

Table 7.1 Proportion of church sittings occupied in Glasgow, 1816–20

Area	Population	Seats taken (%)
Central city:		
Tron Parish	10,304	28.4
Goose-Dubbs	945	11.2
Part of Saltmarket	387	15.8
Clay-Braes	319	20.1
Part of Bridgegate	209	3.3
Inner suburbs:		
Unnamed	875	21.7
Suburbs:		
Parts of Barony Parish	2,689	21.7

Source: Figures calculated from data in T. Chalmers, *The Christian and Civic Economy of Large Towns*, Glasgow, 1821, pp. 110–13.

and argued that it was 'the magnitude of those suburb wastes, which have formed so rapidly around the metropolis, and every commercial city of our land' which created a 'lawless spirit', 'the great and the growing distemper' and 'families which, from infancy to manhood, have been unvisited by any message from Christianity'.[3] These were the first widely publicised figures to be used as evidence of high non-churchgoing in large towns, and especially in districts dominated by the poor and working classes. Chalmers said that given the closer distance of people to churches in cities than in the countryside, there should be a higher rate of attendance:

> Let it be premised, that, in a country parish, the number who should be in attendance upon church, is computed at one-half of the whole population. In towns where the obstacle of distance is not to be overcome, a larger proportion than this is generally fixed upon. We think it, however, overrated at two-thirds, and shall therefore assign the intermediate fraction of five-eighths, as the ratio which the churchgoing inhabitants of a town should bear to the total number of them.[4]

Setting his expectation at over 60 per cent attendance in urban parishes but only 50 per cent in rural ones, Chalmers could easily point to churchgoing rates of around 22 to 28 per cent as confirmation of the rising irreligion of cities. From a modern statistical standpoint, of course, the data are highly problematic, are analysed according to quite arbitrary rules, and do not provide satisfactory 'proof' of the hypothesis. The 'reading' is highly partial.

Conclusive statistical proof of the applicability of this argument across mainland Britain appeared to come from the government's census of churchgoing in 1851. The census compiler, Horace Mann, told parliament: 'more especially in cities and large towns it is observable how absolutely insignificant a portion of the congregations is composed of artizans'.[5] Social-science scholars of the 1960s used the census data to support the same interpretation. Pickering grouped towns according to their level of church-going in 1851, and deduced that 'within given bounds, church-going is *broadly* inversely correlated with the size of an urban population'.[6] Perkin carried out a similar exercise and came to the same conclusion.[7] McLeod produced various statistical exercises which showed that English towns had lower rates of churchgoing than rural ones, and that industrial zones had lower rates of churchgoing than agricultural zones.[8]

More recent revisionist work has, however, challenged this enduring interpretation. For while the 1851 census' published data showed that churchgoing was higher in rural than urban places in England as a whole (but not in Scotland), detailed research (including on unpublished data which can allow more precise distinguishing of rural from urban) tends to show results of low significance. This is certainly the case in the English north Midlands (Derbyshire, Lincolnshire, Leicestershire, Rutland and Nottinghamshire) where the correlation of churchgoing with level of urbanisation produced a low negative correlation ($r = -0.157$) and an even lower positive correlation with level of ruralisation ($r = 0.147$).[9] These indicate that urban and rural conditions were not determining factors in churchgoing levels in the north Midlands; if the correlations are turned into regressions, each produces statistically insignificant figures (in each case, $R^2 = 0.02$). In Scotland, towns had higher churchgoing rates than rural areas and virtually all large cities had higher attendance rates than their surrounding rural counties.[10] Revisionist research results are not limited to regional case studies. The present author undertook regression analysis on all the urban data (for 116 towns) in the published 1851 census, and found that in England and Wales there was no statistically significant relationship between town size, or rate of growth of towns over ten or fifty years, upon churchgoing rate ($R^2 = 0.04$, t statistics $= -1.61, -1.35, -0.65$). However, in Scotland rate of growth of a town over fifty years explained a quarter of variations ($R^2 = 0.26$, t statistic $= -4.21$).[11] These results were challenged by Bruce, who used a 56 per cent sample of towns from the census, but despite employing methods to improve his results (log 10 arrays and omitting the outlier London), he showed that even at its best only 14 per cent of the variations in churchgoing rate amongst his sample towns could be accounted for by town size.[12] Admittedly, church attendance rates for English cities in the nineteenth century generally compared unfavourably to those of country areas, but there were largely unrecognised, in-built reasons exaggerating this. First, urban church services – especially between the 1850s and the 1930s – were much more spread out amongst a variety of types of places of worship which enumerators, frankly, had difficulty in locating. Urban religious occasions could be exceedingly diverse, including not just a myriad of mission and Bible groups on weekdays as well as Sundays, but events such as the Pleasant Sunday Afternoons for men and Pleasant Monday Evenings for women in the Edwardian period.[13] Occasions of religious worship in towns were held at more irregular hours in more diverse types of place than in country areas, and were often ignored by enumerators. Sunday schools, which were more important in urban dissenting areas than in rural Anglican areas, were characteristically not counted in religious censuses after 1851, again exaggerating the difference in religiosity between town and country.

The most impressive evidence of such problems comes from the *Daily News* census of churchgoing in London in 1902–3, probably the most accurate and full census ever undertaken in Britain. As an experiment, Chelsea was the only borough in the census where every detectable church service at all times of day on a Sunday (and Saturday for Jews), though not on other days of the week, was subjected to enumeration. The results showed that 17,061 attendances were recorded at 'ordinary service' times in mid-morning and evening, but a further 7,263 attendances occurred outwith those services. Of these, 5,348 were attendances at Sunday schools. Although some of these children are likely to have also attended worship (and been already counted), it still means 42.6 per cent extra attendances. Applying these ratios to the total for the County of London, as shown in Table 7.2, would raise the census compiler's overall final attendance rate for the capital from 18.6 per cent to 25.8 per cent of population. This indicates a serious underscoring of religiosity in the capital, Britain's largest

Table 7.2 How contemporaries underestimated churchgoing: adjusting the results of the London Religious Census of 1902–3

Total population of London County	4,536,451	
Crude church attendances and rate	1,003,361	22.1%
Adjusted crude attendances and rate	1,430,793	31.5%
(+42.6% of attendances to allow for un-enumerated services)		
Adjustment to exclude residents of institutions[1]		32.0%
Adjustment for 39% of attendances being by 'twicers'[2]		25.8%
Census compiler's adjusted attenders' rate[3]		18.6%

Source: Figures calculated from data in R. Mudie-Smith, *The Religious Life of London*, London, Hodder & Stoughton, 1904.

Notes
1 66,237 people lived in residential institutions where attendances at services were not enumerated. Discounting these leaves a net population of 4,470,214.
2 The adjustment involves deducting 39% from the total morning attendances. The calculation by the census investigators to make this adjustment for their total figure for London County is either wrong or involved some further unrecorded adjustment.
3 This excludes the 42.6% increase.

and most notorious low churchgoing area of the nineteenth and twentieth centuries.

The implications of this exercise are statistically very important. If the problem of under-recording of church attendance was so severe in the best census, it was much greater in less accurate censuses. It was particularly acute in urban areas where the times and forms of religious worship were much more varied than in rural areas, and proportionately more difficult for census-organisers to ensure the presence of enumerators. The more social-science method is examined closely, the less convincing is the case that cities were uniformly more secularised than small towns, and that towns were more secularised than rural villages.[14] Equally, the evidence from Chelsea in 1902–3, in the best churchgoing census ever taken in Britain, demonstrates that both contemporary churchmen and later historians have placed unwarranted faith that social-scientific method was able to deliver percentages of churchgoing, those 'unimpeachable witnesses', which could present a true impression of religiosity in the supposedly 'unholy city'.

CLASS AND RELIGIOSITY

Since 1800, social class has been the obsessive focus of statistical inquiry into religion in Britain. The absence of any significant data on the social class of churchgoers in the 1851 religious census did not stop its compiler Horace Mann from branding the working classes 'unconscious Secularists': 'These are never or but seldom seen in our religious congregations.'[15] Such statements constituted the 'official' discourse on the irreligious city, establishing that the working class were irreligious, and that the middle classes were the churchgoing bastions of civil morality. Modern scholars who use statistics have almost uniformly tended to agree. Hugh McLeod, in analysing the different levels of churchgoing across London in 1902–3, concluded that 'the most important differentiating factor was class',[16] reflecting what has been the burden of most writing on the social history of religion from the late 1950s to the mid-1990s.

Sometimes the religiosity of middle-class parts of towns and cities was the result of deliberate religious engineering. Hampstead was developed between 1850 and 1914 by the landowners, Eton College and the Dean and Chapter of Westminster, to exclude Nonconformists in an attempt to create 'an exclusively Anglican colonisation'.[17] In Glasgow, it was widely reputed that when Cambridge Street United Presbyterian Church moved in the 1860s to a more palatial church in the west end it was a deliberate attempt to exclude the less wealthy members of the congregation.[18] Instances like this probably abounded in Victorian Britain, but the social scientist should not take this as evidence that the working classes were irreligious. However, between the 1950s and 1970s most did precisely that. John Kent concluded that 'in the first half of the nineteenth century the churches were failing to form the habit of church-attendance in the majority of the urban working class', and in the century as a whole 'the Protestant churches had almost lost any claim to express the religious aspirations of the working class'.[19] Edward Norman wrote that 'Church leaders of the mid-century continued to build more churches in the populous districts, and the masses continued to decline to attend them'.[20] 'Outside the church organizations', David Mole said of Birmingham, 'lay the vast masses who rarely went to church.'[21]

Hugh McLeod has argued most strongly for there being a link between class and formal church connection. His work on London between the 1870s and 1914 is central to this case in which he argued that 'the poorest districts thus tended to have the lowest rates of attendance, those with large upper-middle-class and upper-class populations the highest'. He continued: 'Except among Irish Roman Catholics, only a small proportion of working-class adults attended the main Sunday church services.'[22] He used a wide variety of social statistical data to lend support. McLeod applied averaged ranking social data on London boroughs (as distinct from the absolute values) to produce correlations which appeared to show that in 1902–3 social class had a highly significant relationship with churchgoing levels at all churches (reaching Spearman Rank Correlation coefficients of 0.70 for Greater London, 0.90 in Metropolitan boroughs, 0.85 for Anglican services, and 0.56 at Nonconformist chapels in Greater London).[23] This was supplemented by comparing maps of church attendance rates for London boroughs with a map of proportion of large houses (of six or more rooms) in 1911. He concluded from a visual analysis of these maps that there was a close positive relationship, and this indicated a positive 'relationship between class and religious practice', one especially strong in the case of Anglicanism whilst Nonconformists appeared to be strongest in the parts of London which were predominantly composed of those in the middle orders of society.[24] McLeod's evidence seemed impressive, but was weakened in two ways. The first was his use of ranking correlations rather than the absolute values of social and religious indicators; ranking data fails to convey the degree of difference between cases. The second weakness was that the social indicators which McLeod amalgamated in a social index have remarkably poor relationships with each other based on absolute values (rather than rankings of combined indexes of social indicators),[25] and reduced the social composition of a large borough to a mean (or average) which poorly reflected the social diversity of each borough by being sensitive only to levels of wealth and not to levels of poverty or deprivation.[26] Nonetheless, both this research and McLeod's later work presents the most sophisticated and sustained case for social class being the principal variable explaining differences of churchgoing and church affiliation in nineteenth- and early twentieth-century Britain.

In the 1980s and 1990s, social historians of religion, including McLeod, pursued a much more nuanced approach to class and churchgoing. A plethora of studies, many based on London, argued for a much greater degree of active working-class connection with the churches, especially in the late Victorian and Edwardian periods, than had previously been thought.[27] Some argued that what was happening between the 1870s and 1930s was a decrease in weekly worship, perhaps especially by working-class churchgoers. Clergy at the time reported increasing non-weekly attendance by worshippers, say every month, meaning that the proportion of the population recorded attending church on a single Sunday may not have revealed the true extent nor the true social balance of the churchgoing population.[28] However, most historians would still say that the working classes were under-represented in the majority of church congregations compared to their numbers in local communities. Class remains the principal factor attributed by researchers to account for variations in church connection, with the working classes attributed both with having lower levels of churchgoing that the middle classes and with causing a lowering of church connection in the nineteenth and twentieth centuries.

The *Daily News* census of churchgoing in London 1902–3 provides the most reliable and complete data to explore the statistical reliability of social-class indicators as determinants of churchgoing. Despite its shortcomings, especially its undercounting of less formal church worship (attended probably by the working classes), it provides a unique opportunity to apply class and other variables to test causative relationships. In the first instance, a series of correlations (which test the existence of relationships) and regressions (which gauge the extent to which one variable determines another) were applied to the data in the London census. If class was such a significant determinant of who went to church on a given Sunday, we should expect there to be high correlation and regression coefficients.

Table 7.3 gives the results. These show that every variable had a relationship with church attendance rate, but the degree to which each factor actually *determined* the church attendance rates was in all cases between poor and insignificant. In Metropolitan London as a whole (excluding the City, where the figures were heavily distorted by low residential population and high in-migration of church attenders on Sundays), levels of servant-keeping and opulent housing determined 26 and 32 per cent of churchgoing rates in positive relationships, and house overcrowding determined churchgoing by 16 per cent in an inverse relationship. In the Set C equations, death rate emerges as determining only 12 per cent of churchgoing levels in an inverse relationship, but infant mortality rate determined a very important 48 per cent; however, these must be treated with caution as they come from a small sample. Servant-keeping is shown in equations 8 to 11 in Set D to be a much more subtle indicator of churchgoing habits. They show that servant-keeping had a positive relationship with determining churchgoing in the lowest three quartiles of the 28 boroughs (that is, in the most working- and middle-class boroughs), but

Table 7.3 Churchgoing and social indicators: correlations and regression analysis of factors influencing church attendance rate

	Correlation coefficent (Pearson) r	Regression		
		Coefficient of determination adj. R^2	t statistic	sig. 2-tailed
Set A: 28 boroughs of Metropolitan London				
1. Domestic indoor servants as % of households	0.5373	0.26	3.25	.003
2. % population living in houses of > 7 rooms	0.5856	0.32	3.69	.001
3. % population living more than 2 per room	−0.4359	0.16	−2.44	.022
Set B: 25 boroughs of Greater London with significant male industrial workforces:				
4. % occupied males working in industries characterised by large-scale production	0.3966	0.12	2.12	.045
5. Domestic indoor servants as % of households	0.3592	0.09	1.89	.072
Set C: sample of 12 boroughs of Metropolitan London drawn equally from north, south, east and west of the city:				
6. Death rate	−0.4472	0.12	−1.59	.143
7. Infant mortality rate	−0.7211	0.48	−3.32	.008
Set D: quartiles of 28 Metropolitan boroughs ranked by domestic servants as % of households				
8. First quartile (lowest proportion of servants)	0.5869	0.21	1.62	.166
9. Second quartile	0.3009	−0.09	0.71	.512
10. Third quartile	0.6054	0.24	1.70	.150
11. Fourth quartile (highest proportion of servants)	−0.4179	0.01	−1.03	.351

Sources: Figures calculated from data in R. Mudie-Smith, *The Religious Life of London*, London, Hodder & Stoughton, 1904, and H. McLeod, *Class and Religion in the Late Victorian City*, London, Croom Helm, 1974.

that in the fourth quartile (the most wealthy of London) servant-keeping had a *negative* relationship with churchgoing rate. In other words, in the parts of London with the upper classes and multiple-servant households (Hampstead, Kensington, Westminster, Chelsea, Marylebone, Paddington and Lewisham), the wealthier the borough the lower was the rate of churchgoing. This suggests that as house size increased from upper-middle to upper class, churchgoing went down; residents of upper-class districts were less churchgoing than those of middle-class districts. In short, class did not act as a uniformly stable indicator of variations in churchgoing in all major sections of the social spectrum.

The equations show further problems with social class as either a stable or significant determinant of churchgoing. In Set B, equation 4 shows the extraordinary result that amongst the 25 boroughs in Greater London with more than 7.7 per cent of the male workforce employed in industries characterised by large-scale production, the proportion of men working in those industries determined 12 per cent of the variations in churchgoing in a *positive* relationship; in other words, as male industrial employment rose, churchgoing rose too. This applied only to those 25 (out of 51) boroughs, but is highly suggestive of the influence of an industrial as distinct from non-industrial male workforce. This should not be taken to imply that industrially employed *men* were necessarily more churchgoing than their non-industrial counterparts, but may indicate something about the churchgoing habits of the women, children *and* men in such households. It would suggest a cultural differentiation between industrial and non-industrial families. Turning to infant mortality and death rates, they appear from these regressions on London in 1902–3 as significant predictors of churchgoing rates. This seems to be supported by the work of Chadwick on Bradford in 1881 where she used the same types of data to argue that churchgoing was higher in middle-class as compared to working-class areas, concluding that the Bradford churches were failing to attract the lowest social groups.[29] However, regression analysis on her data does not support her interpretation. Using her fifteen wards of Bradford and district, both independent variables produced results which showed no statistically significant relationship with church attendance rate. (Death rate: adjusted $R^2 = -0.059$, t statistic = 0.46, sig. = .651; and infant mortality rate: adjusted $R^2 = -0.075$, t statistic = -0.16, sig. = .873.)[30]

The lesson from this is that social indicators may be important, but they comprehensively fail to provide a universally reliable predictor of churchgoing rates. Even at their best, social indicators fail to account for a majority of the variations in churchgoing between different parts of a town or city. In any event, the major shortcoming of this approach is that social indicators are merely *surrogates* for social class – that is *indirect* indicators – and no substitute for the direct evidence of social composition analysis.

It was only in the 1960s that real sociological techniques of social-composition analysis started to be applied. This has produced a raft of different studies, often with varying social-classification systems which makes comparisons a little difficult. Fortunately, the results are sufficiently clear-cut to override technical problems. Gilbert analysed the occupational structure of 10,997 English Nonconformists between 1800 and 1837, and found that 59 per cent were artisans and 17 per cent other manual workers – a total of almost 77 per cent working class.[31] Hillis showed that 61 per cent of 3,666 presbyterian church members in Glasgow between 1845 and 1865 were working class, with nearly 50 per cent being accounted by artisans and other skilled workers.[32] Field and Snell have shown in separate studies the dominance of the working classes in Methodism – nationally 80 per cent of Wesleyans and 76 per cent of Primitives, and in the north Midlands between 1800 and 1894 figures of 72 per cent for Wesleyans and 91 per cent for Primitives.[33] In Bradford in the late Victorian period, the working classes made up the majority of church members in nearly every congregation, with skilled manual workers the largest single social group making up from 30 to 45 per cent of the total.[34] In seven Stirling congregations between 1849 and 1908, an average of 52 per cent of male communicants and 47 per cent females were skilled working class.[35] In virtually all of these studies, the skilled working classes dominated, but in certain churches (such as the Primitive Methodists) and in certain places the unskilled could make up the majority of churchgoers. Hopkins calculated that in two Black Country villages in 1851, 42 per cent of the working classes attended church (or 50.5 per cent if an allowance were made for it being Mothering Sunday). Moreover, he argued convincingly that those in dissent were not mainly skilled or even semi-skilled workers but were nailers, 'the lowest strata of the working classes, many of them notorious for their rough and uncivilised mode of life'.[36] Certainly, Jeffrey's work on Stirling suggests that we should not underestimate the significance of the unskilled working class in congregational life: they made up on average 20 per cent of male communicants and 24 per cent of females, and participated in congregational activities and duties.[37] Dennis' study of one Congregational Church in Huddersfield showed that 68.6 per cent of members were drawn from the working classes (families of tradesmen, craftsmen, textile workers, servants, laundresses, dressmakers and one pauper).[38] The evidence from the twentieth century tends to indicate the same. Seebohm Rowntree considered that the proletarian–bourgeois balance in York churches was roughly representative of the population of the town as a whole: a 66:34 split between working and middle classes in 1901, and a 83:17 split between 'non-servant-keepers' and 'servant-keepers' in the 1930s.[39] Field showed that the proportion of Methodists who were working class fell slightly during the twentieth century, but in some congregations it was the middle classes who declined.[40] In most studies of the 1960s, congregations were still occupationally structured in roughly equal ways to the nineteenth century: in Falkirk, between 50 and 66 per cent were skilled working class, a further 5–20 per cent were unskilled, and the remainder were middle and upper classes.[41] This evidence is of its nature piecemeal, but it is very significant. Every major study based on social-composition analysis of churchgoers or members shows for every part of Britain from the late eighteenth to the late twentieth centuries, for every denomination, that the working classes were in the majority.

Church statisticians of the nineteenth and twentieth centuries have argued about the impact of all sorts of other, non-class factors on church-going levels: the weather, the time of the year, availability of pews, and distance from church. The impact of the first and second of these was certainly exaggerated. An analysis of the most extensive data, contained in the London census of 1902–3, produced correlations between levels of churchgoing on the one hand, and variations in the weather and in the month of the year on the other, with extremely poor figures (of –0.1752 for weather and –0.2905 for month) – poor enough to conclude that neither determined variations in churchgoing levels within the capital.[42] The numbers and pricing of rented pews was thought by many Victorian commentators to be a factor keeping attendances in some cities low, and for keeping out the working classes and the poor. Bradford was identified in 1858 as the most deficient for Anglican church accommodation in England, and this was still thought by many in the late Victorian period to be the cause of working-class alienation.[43] Certainly by 1881, the availability of pews was *not* a factor which determined levels of church attendance in different parts of that city; the difference between the proportion of Bradford people and proportion of Bradford's pews located in each of the fifteen wards produced poor results (adjusted $R^2 = -0.05$, t statistic $= 0.59$, sig. $= .565$) when regressed against church attendance figures for each ward.[44] Yet, availability of church accommodation was probably an important issue before 1850, when church provision in new industrial centres was often slow to develop, and was low in some rural areas (such as the Highlands and Hebrides). The issue in such cases was also the distance from church. Dennis' study of Huddersfield has produced data that show that as towns grew in the second half of the nineteenth century, *existing* congregations increased the proportion of their flock who lived under 1 kilometre from the church – on average from 73 per cent in 1851 to 82 per cent in 1880 – whilst *new* congregations resulting from suburban growth after 1851 started with initially high figures of around 80–98 per cent living close to their church, but then declined slightly to stabilise at an average of 74 per cent by 1880. Though Dennis uses this as evidence that churches 'facilitated the disintegration of territorially defined communities', the uniformly high proportion of church members living less than a kilometre from their church (ranging from 52 per cent to 100 per cent in his data, with the figure being over 70 per cent in 20 out of 30 data points for thirteen Huddersfield congregations),[45] it is striking how strong is the obverse argument – namely, that congregations provided intensely local foci for the vast majority of churchgoers as the scale of urban communities grew in the late nineteenth century.

Overall, the factors so far considered are poor predictors of churchgoing levels in the population. Social class appears as notionally significant in correlation for some places (notably London) but poor in others, whilst everywhere it is a hopeless determinant in regression analysis. The working classes made up the majority of churchgoers in virtually every denomination in every period from 1800 to the 1960s, with the skilled working class of artisans and tradesmen being particularly numerous in congregations. The unskilled were far less numerous, and indeed were the least churchgoing of all social classes in most places (though, as the Black Country may indicate, not all). However, evidence from churchgoing censuses that lower proportions of the working classes (skilled and unskilled) attended worship compared to the middle classes may be the result of different attendance patterns – such as less frequent Sunday attendance, and more attendance at under-recorded weekday and non-regular religious gatherings – and not of being any more 'unchurched' than the bourgeoisie. Equally, the data from 1800 to the 1960s fail to identify a period in which there was a working-class haemorrhage from congregations, tending to undermine the notion that working-class evacuation of the churches led secularisation at any point. With the whole picture complicated by regional variation, and by the possibility of increased male industrial employment having a positive influence upon working-class churchgoing, we are left with the conclusion that social class on its own fails to explain church decline in Britain between 1800 and the 1960s.

GENDER AND RELIGIOSITY

Women have tended to dominate church memberships and churchgoers during the last three centuries. In the membership of Baptist and Congregationalist churches between 1650 and 1980, women outnumbered men by a factor of two to one, though by somewhat less within Nonconformity as a whole. In Bradford in 1881, 71 per cent of members in twelve Nonconformist congregations were female. In West London in 1902–3, 68 per cent of Church of England morning worshippers were women and 69 per cent of evening worshippers. In the whole of the capital in those years, with the inclusion of children, adult men made up only 23.9 per cent of Anglican worshippers, whilst women made up 60.8 per cent of all adult churchgoers to all denominations.[46] However, in Stirling between 1849 and 1908 women made up only 59 per cent of communicants, the result of seemingly high working-class male church membership.[47] Nonetheless, religious worship was more often than not a highly feminised environment. However, the way in which churches were gendered had a complex interaction *with* social class.

To explore these issues, a new social index of London in 1902–3 was created by merging three variables: female servants as a percentage of house-holds, the percentage of houses not overcrowded (with less than two persons per room), and the percentage of persons living in houses of eight rooms or more.[48] This index improves on that of Hugh McLeod by, first, using absolute figures and not rankings, and second by including a sensi-tivity to deprivation in the form of house overcrowding (resulting in a significant change to the rank ordering of the boroughs from McLeod's index). This new social index produced a correlation of +0.5907 when related to the church attendance rate for the twenty-eight London boroughs. This suggests a firm (though not strong) positive relationship between these two variables, indicating that churchgoing tended to rise as the social composition of a borough rose. But using it in gender analysis of the census data produced highly interesting results. Correlations with the proportions of men and of women in the population who attended church gave results of +0.6235 and +0.4217 respectively, indicating that the social index was much more important in determining adult *male* church-going levels than that of females. In short, female church attendance, in direct contrast to male, was markedly less affected by variations in social class composition of a borough.

Even more detailed analysis of gender attendance at Sunday worship by time of day was instructive. The results are given in Table 7.4. These indi-cate that the social status of a borough was a highly determining factor upon levels of morning churchgoing, but was markedly less influential upon male attendance in the evening and of almost negligible influence upon female attendance in the evening. Bearing in mind that the data on Catholic churchgoing will tend to moderate the results of all other churches (because of its predominance in the morning), these correlations suggest that church-going in virtually all remaining denominations was a socially determined experience in the morning, resulting in characteristically bourgeois congre-gations, but a socially democratic experience in the evening. The results of equations 5 and 6 increase the intrigue. They indicate that if the propor-tions of men and women attenders who went to church in the evening are correlated against the social index, then it reveals negative relationships which, in the case of women, was strong. This shows that there was a strong propensity for women in boroughs of lower social status to attend church in the evening rather than in the morning. The lower the social status of a borough, the greater was the tendency for female churchgoers to attend in the evening. Conversely, the higher status boroughs saw a greater proportion of their female attenders going in the morning.

Table 7.4 Church attendance, gender and social class in Metropolitan London, 1902–3: correlations and regressions

Dependent variables correlated and regressed against the social index for 28 boroughs

		r	Adjusted R^2	t statistic	sig.
1.	% male population attending in morning	+0.6509	0.401	4.369	.000
2.	% male population attending in evening	+0.4833	0.202	2.803	.009
3.	% female population attending in morning	+0.6627	0.419	4.522	.000
4.	% female population attending in evening	+0.1731	−0.006	0.911	.371
5.	% male attenders going in evening	−0.4963	0.217	−2.911	.007
6.	% female attenders going in evening	−0.7784	0.591	−6.329	.000

Where women were more numerous than men in the population, churchgoing increased. The proportion of women varied significantly between the London boroughs, reaching a high of 64 per cent in Kensington. Correlations of churchgoing levels in west London boroughs set against the proportions of men and women in the adult population of each of those boroughs produce a positive correlation for women and a corresponding and equal negative correlation for men.[49] In short, the more women there were in a population, the higher was the churchgoing. Moreover, regression analysis of those west London boroughs shows that variations in the proportion of women in the population determined 78 per cent of variations in the proportion of women amongst adult church attendances.[50] The implication of this is that a high sex imbalance towards women in a community tended very strongly to increase churchgoing *by* women, which in turn tended to increase overall churchgoing. Equally, the converse was also true; relatively high levels of men in a community (even a variation of a few per cent) tended to reduce overall churchgoing levels. High churchgoing was thus strongly associated with highly feminised communities.

The position of children further illuminates the importance of gender to churchgoing. Of 1,003,361 recorded churchgoers in London in 1902–3, 32.3 per cent were children, of which just over half – 57.2 per cent – went in the morning. Their attendance patterns also varied between boroughs. Amongst factors influencing these variations, the social index showed a correlation of –0.6284, levels of male churchgoers attending in the evening

+0.6163, and levels of women churchgoers attending in the evening +0.7183. These results indicate that churchgoing by children was significantly weighted towards the mornings in high-status boroughs and towards the evening in low-status boroughs, and that the proportion of women attending in the evening was the most influential factor (producing an R^2 of 0.52). Taken together, these results demonstrate that children's attendance at church in high-status boroughs was more likely to be in the morning – when, as we saw earlier – women in those boroughs tended to attend, whilst in low-status boroughs they tended to go in the evening when women did.

Overall, the London data for 1902–3 show that women were critical to the churchgoing habits of the population as a whole. Where women went to church more, men and children tended to go more. Where women were more numerous in the population, overall churchgoing was higher. Where a borough was more strongly working class in character, women tended to go in the evening and to attract children with them. In those boroughs that contained a strong representation of high-status households, women's morning attendance was higher than elsewhere and, again, they attracted children with them. In short, women were the pivotal factor in determining the churchgoing habits of the people as a whole.

This throws considerable importance upon the way in which women organised their Sundays. One factor that many contemporary commentators and later social historians highlighted was the role of domestic servants. The numbers of domestic servants as a proportion of households in London in 1902–3 varied between a high of 80 per cent of the number of families in Kensington and only 5.7 per cent in Shoreditch. As we saw earlier, the level of domestic servants per household produced a significant correlation with churchgoing levels of +0.5373 (and an adjusted R^2 of 0.26), but this was not the strongest single variable. However, further investigation shows that the influence of female servants was critical to distinguishing church attendance patterns for morning and evening services. Table 7.5 shows that in Metropolitan London in 1902–3, the proportion of servants per household determined 44 per cent of the variations between the boroughs in the total church attendance at morning worship, but a statistically insignificant amount (3 per cent) in the evening. In the morning, it is clear that variations in domestic servants between boroughs was vital in varying the levels of male, female and child attendance. This impact was almost equally noticeable upon women and men in the morning, but in the evening it had a slight impact upon men but absolutely none upon women.

The implications of this are far-reaching. It indicates that the single largest occupational group amongst women – domestic servants – was critical to determining variations in morning churchgoing between communities. It shows that churchgoing was closely related to the nature of the

Table 7.5 Impact of female servants on churchgoing, London, 1902–3: correlations and regressions

Dependent variables regressed against % female servants per household for 28 Metropolitan boroughs

		r	Adjusted R^2	t statistic	sig.
All 28 boroughs					
% women attending	Morning	0.6067	0.345	3.900	.001
church	Evening	0.0546	−0.035	0.286	.777
% men attending	Morning	0.6163	0.355	3.982	.000
church	Evening	0.3501	0.088	1.896	.069
% total population	Morning	0.6759	0.437	4.683	.000
attending	Evening	0.2648	0.034	1.400	.173

household economy, with the presence of servants releasing large numbers of middle-class women to attend church who, in their turn, allowed and cajoled their female servants to attend church later in the day. As Arthur Sherwell noted in 1904, domestic servants were heavily concentrated in west London where their employers were mostly Church of England and where they were accustomed to be sent to church, often as a condition of employment. According to Sherwell, the servants characteristically went to church in the evening, and the boroughs with the most intense levels of female servants – Kensington, St. Marylebone and Paddington – created the unusual anomaly of higher female churchgoing in the morning rather than the evening, and also accentuated the high level of Church of England attendance in those boroughs.[51]

If the female domestic servant enabled the distinctive morning-centred pattern of middle-class churchgoing, the role of the wife-mother in the working-class and servantless household was just as important. The critical factor in both cases was Sunday lunch. In the middle- and upper-class household, the servants were expected to stay at home in the morning to prepare lunch for the family and to look after babies. In the working-class family, it was the wife-mother who performed this function. As we have seen in the last chapter, autobiographies and oral testimony demonstrate both the symbolic importance of Sunday lunch and the role that the wife-mother played in staying at home to prepare it for the rest of the family. Sunday lunch thus becomes the key to understanding the low attendance of women at Protestant church services, especially in England, between 1800 and 1950. If a woman did not go to church in the morning, the mildly apathetic man would also not go. In London in 1902–3, the most working-class Protestant denominations saw women attending worship overwhelmingly in the evening. Evening worship accounted for 87 per cent of women attenders at the mission stations of all the major denominations, 80 per cent at the Bible Christians, 76 per cent at the Salvation Army, 74 per cent at the Primitive Methodists, followed by figures of 66, 62 and 60 per cent respectively for the fairly working-class Baptists, Congregationalists and Brethren. Only in the solidly working-class Catholic Church did 77 per cent of women attend at one or other of the morning masses. By contrast, in the Anglican Church, the denomination which contained the highest proportion of middle and upper classes from the wealthy boroughs of the west end, only 53 per cent of women attended in the evening.[52]

The results of this investigation are highly significant. What has been revealed about London in 1902–3 is highly likely to mirror the characteristics of churchgoing elsewhere in Britain in the nineteenth and first half of the twentieth centuries. It reveals the key role of women in determining family churchgoing, mediated by the social status and servant-keeping capacity of the household. It indicates an important irony. While women attended church more than men, they were called upon to sacrifice the primacy of that act to the needs of Sunday lunch and baby-minding. Virtually all Protestant churches held their Sunday morning service at 11 am, the exact time at which the preparation of a hot Sunday lunch required to start. If faced with the choice, Sunday lunch was a more important ritual in households of all social status than going to church. Only in the Catholic Church were women able to go to worship early and then return home to cook; by the early twentieth century the number of services in the larger parishes had grown to the point where there could be nearly hourly masses between 7 am and 11 am.[53] The holding of Protestant morning church service at the time when Sunday lunch required a woman's preparation emerges as a most significant cause of the variations in churchgoing habits between Britain's social classes.

LONG-RUN CHANGE IN BRITISH RELIGIOSITY

So far in this chapter, we have looked at possible causes of secularisation in the form of factors determining levels of non-churchgoing. This final section looks at the statistical story of secularisation in Britain down to 1950 and beyond.

It is extremely difficult to use data on churchgoing to construct accurate time series. However, a number of points can be made. It seems clear to most specialists in the field that the levels of churchgoing revealed in the 1851 religious census were historically very high. In England, attendances at church on 30 March that year represented 59 per cent of total population; if adjusted for individuals making multiple visits to church, and if children are excluded, something like 40 per cent of adults attended church on that one Sunday. In Scotland, the figures were marginally higher despite a markedly higher number of non-returns from enumerators.[54] Given that some people were ill or detained by family matters, the numbers of regular attenders would have been higher. By the known standards of churchgoing in mainland Britain for all periods of history, the results of this census showed a high level of Sunday worship. Levels in the previous fifty years may well have been lower; reasons included the paucity of churches in upland and island areas of the Scottish Highlands, the rapidity of urban and population growth, and the sluggishness with which new churches were erected in rising industrial centres. After 1851, rates may well have continued to rise for a decade or two as church building blossomed, financed by the mid-Victorian boom.[55] But there is some evidence of decline. Evidence from a variety of local censuses – in Dundee, Bath, Bristol, Coventry, Leicester, Nottingham, Bradford, Liverpool and several others – suggested a decline in the region of 20–30 per cent between 1851 and 1881.[56] However, evidence from other places showed little change over thirty years, and in the case of Bradford it has been suggested that the proportion of individuals attending church rose.[57] Evidence for decline in churchgoing after the 1880s is stronger, though decline in double attendances on a Sunday accounts for some proportion of it. Nonetheless, all the evidence suggests a fall in churchgoing from before 1900 which was sustained at a steady, though not spectacular rate, until the 1940s.[58] However, given the strong indications that much of the decline until the mid-twentieth century may have been caused by individuals attending church less frequently, the astute observer should refrain from equating a decline in churchgoing with a rise in the number of non-churchgoers.

Church membership is a different measure of the people's attachment to the churches, and it provides a wider availability of time series data. It is not really until the 1850s that sufficient data on church affiliation becomes available from British churches, and even then major denominations (notably the Church of England) only collected usable national data from later and the quality was poor. Even when data was collected earlier by some denominations, the concept of church affiliation (or 'membership' or 'adherence' as different churches called it) was still in its infancy as the notion of churches as discrete 'clubs' was still developing. In this way, we are highly limited in what can be deduced from such data. In the case of most churches, adherence or membership is measuring some form of 'passive' association with a church rather than an active one like churchgoing. Nonetheless, church adherence is an important form of religiosity, a measure in itself which churches regarded as important and which, as plentiful oral evidence suggests, many ordinary worshippers regarded as indispensable. It became all the more important during the twentieth century.

A study of church membership reveals that its pattern of decline was very different to that of churchgoing. Despite the problems with the data, it is possible to say with reasonable certainty that church membership per capita grew from the 1840s (the earliest point when it can be sensibly assessed) to reach a peak in England and Wales in 1904 and in Scotland in 1905. The growth was rapid until 1863, then lessened until fluctuations between growth and decline set in during the 1880s and 1890s, until the peak membership rate in 1904–5. This growth took place during the most profound growth of towns and cities in Britain, posing further contradiction to the tenet of secularisation theory that urbanisation caused religious decline.[59] The patterns of individual churches' growth varied considerably; for example, the Wesleyan Methodists peaked as a proportion of population in 1840, the General Baptist New Connexion in 1851–63, the Congregationalists in 1863, the Particular Baptists in 1880, the Church of England in 1904, the Scottish Episcopal Church in 1914, the Church of Scotland in 1925, and the Roman Catholic Church considerably later – in Scotland in 1981.[60] But aggregating the data shows that the British people as a whole attained their highest levels of church adherence in the Edwardian years. This is confirmed by analysis of the long-term aggregate data on church membership, augmented by estimates, produced by Currie, Gilbert and Horsley, which shows that in Britain as a whole church membership per capita grew continuously from 1800, when it stood at an estimated 11.7 per cent of total population, until 1910, when it peaked at 19.3 per cent. This pattern was also confirmed for Protestants alone, whose church membership as a proportion of the non-Catholic population rose from 10.6 per cent in 1801 to a peak of 14.7 per cent in 1910.[61]

Between 1900 and 1955, most British churches showed declines in church membership, but it was relatively modest decline, and much slower than the decline that is likely to have occurred in churchgoing. In the Church of England, as shown in Figure 7.1, the high points in Easter Day communicants as a proportion of population occurred in 1903 and 1913 from when there was only modest decline of 11.7 per cent to 1939. World War II then caused a fall followed by a modest recovery to a post-war high in 1956, by which date the net loss since 1903 had been 21.4 per cent. That amounts to an average annual loss of 0.26 per cent of communicants over 81 years. This was as nothing compared to the loss of 1.3 per cent per annum (a total of 36.4 per cent) which ensued between 1956 and 1984, reaching a level in 1995 some 60 per cent lower than at the start of the century. The same story can be obtained from data on the Church of Scotland (which includes its pre-1929 constituent, the United Free Church) as shown in Figure 7.2. This shows that its high point of adherence came in 1905, and then fell only slightly to revitalise to a marginally higher figure in 1956; then it lost 33.4 per cent by 1984 (a loss of 1.2 per cent per annum), reaching a level in 1998 some 48 per cent lower than in 1900. The similarity is

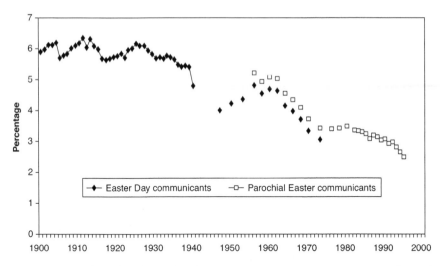

Figure 7.1 Church of England communicants as percentage of total population, 1900–95

Sources: Figures calculated from R. Currie, A. Gilbert and L. Horsley, *Churches and Church-goers: Patterns of Church Growth in the British Isles since 1700*, Oxford, Clarendon Press, 1977, pp. 128–9; *Church of England Yearbook*, 1979–2000; B.R. Mitchell and P. Deane, *Abstract of British Historical Statistics*, Cambridge, Cambridge University Press, 1962, pp. 12–13; Office of Population Censuses and Surveys; *Office of National Statistics, Annual Abstract of Statistics 2000*.

striking: in England, Scotland and Wales, the historic established churches experienced an almost identical set of trends of roughly level membership status from 1900 until the mid-1950s, and then declined at roughly identical rates to the end of the century.

The scale of decline in overall church membership between 1904–5 and 1950 was relatively minor. From a high of 19.3 per cent in 1910 for church membership in the British population as a whole, the figure fell to 19.1 in 1920, recovered to 19.2 in 1930, and then fell to 18.1 in 1930 – a fall sustained to 17.6 by 1950. This gives a figure for the net fall in church adherence per capita of only 7.9 per cent in Britain over the period 1910–50, with a slightly higher proportion of this fall seeming to come from high-membership zones like Scotland where the loss was 11.1 per cent.[62] What was happening to church affiliation between the 1910s and 1950s was far from clear-cut. Year-on-year data indicates short periods of decline and growth succeeding each other within each decade, with the detailed data from Scotland indicating that adherence grew in years of economic downturn and declined in years of economic recovery. The two world wars had caused disruption to many churches as men and women left their own congregations through wartime service, but there were signs of clear

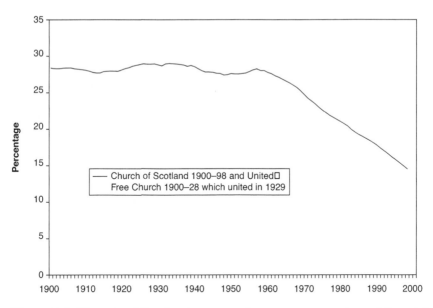

Figure 7.2 Church of Scotland communicants as proportion of Scottish population, 1900–98

Sources: Figures calculated from R. Currie, A. Gilbert and L. Horsley, *Churches and Churchgoers: Patterns of Church Growth in the British Isles since 1700*, Oxford, Clarendon Press, 1977, pp. 133–5; *Church of Scotland Yearbook*, 1971–99; B.R. Mitchell and P. Deane, *Abstract of British Historical Statistics*, Cambridge, Cambridge University Press, 1962, pp. 12–13; *Registrar General for Scotland, Annual Reports*, 1971–98.

recovery, especially after 1945.[63] In short, despite problems in some denominations (notably the Methodists), the first half of the twentieth century witnessed no great haemorrhage of church membership in Britain.

This creates a picture of a twentieth-century society in which church-going was seemingly in decline whilst church affiliation was much more resilient: a society of religious belonging without high worshipping. How-ever, the crude data are partly misleading. The oral evidence considered in the previous chapter showed that church attendance figures were going down, not because individuals were shedding their church connection, but because they were going less frequently. Various factors were at work here. Twicing, or going to church twice on a Sunday, was clearly very high in the Edwardian period, with as many as 39 per cent of London morn-ing church attenders also going in the evening. This habit was already in decline and continued to decline. In addition, there is clear evidence of a growth of attendance at minor denominations in the inter-war period, with evangelical missions, the Brethren and unaligned congrega-tions benefiting considerably. This is clear from Scotland where minor non-mainstream churches increased their proportion of marriages from 7.3 per cent in 1895 to 9.1 per cent in 1935, only to fall in subsequent years, whilst a similar though less significant trend occurred in England.[64] For others, there was a trend of less frequent churchgoing, a trend largely apparent amongst adults. They were attending church less, but *associating* with it still quite strongly.

This need to associate with a church without necessarily worshipping in it is very important to the understanding of what was happening to religion in the first half of the twentieth century. To take figures from the best recorded part of Britain – Scotland – it seems that by the middle of the century something like a minimum of 44 per cent of the Scottish people had a church affiliation (including Sunday school enrolments), but only about 12 per cent of the people attended church on a given Sunday.[65] This means that about just over one in four of church affiliates attended on a given Sunday, with figures of very similar proportions probably pertaining in the rest of Britain. Large numbers of people were sustaining a relatively inactive church connection. They were keeping a bond between themselves and a church, an act of symbolic attachment. This was most apparent in the people's connections with religious rites of passage. The British people retained a very strong attachment to religious baptisms, marriages and funerals. Figure 7.3 shows that marriage sustained a very important hold on the affections of couples, giving way only marginally to civil marriage between 1900 and the late 1950s. Even more striking from Figure 7.4 was the *growing* popularity of baptism in the Church of England during the first four decades of the century. Similarly, there was an exceptionally high level of Sunday school enrolment (Fig. 7.5), a level about double that of the mid-Victorian period. Though it declined notably in the 1930s, it recovered strongly during 1945–55, and was by then the British people's most common form of participation in organised religion. To these 'official' rites of passage were the unofficial systems of popular religious belief which survived very strongly amongst women.[66] Popular attachment to such religious rites, 'official' and 'unofficial', not only sustained a continuity between industrial and pre-industrial eras, and between urban and rural Britain, but their survival and, in the case of Anglican baptism, *growth* in popularity constituted a critical element in the changing pattern of people's religious identity.

It should be clear, even in this brief chapter, that existing secularisation theory fails to explain the observable statistical data upon which it has been erected for two centuries. In the nineteenth and twentieth centuries, social class was a poor predictor of variations in churchgoing, the working classes dominated the congregations of virtually all denominations, and churchgoing and church membership per capita grew during Britain's most rapid urbanisation between 1800 and 1880. The consequence is that it is an error for the historian or sociologist to conclude from religious statistics that the

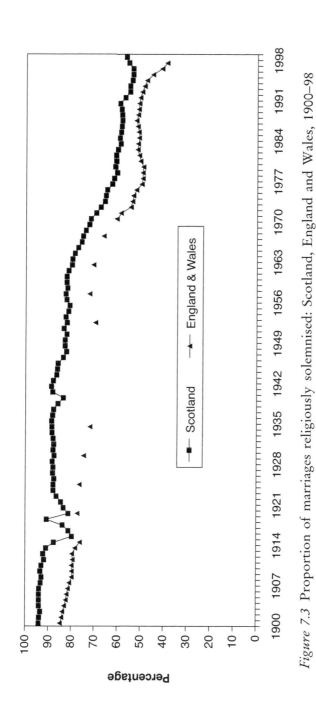

Figure 7.3 Proportion of marriages religiously solemnised: Scotland, England and Wales, 1900–98

Sources: Figures calculated from R. Currie, A. Gilbert and L. Horsley, *Churches and Churchgoers: Patterns of Church Growth in the British Isles since 1700*, Oxford, Clarendon Press, 1977, pp. 223–9; Office of Population Censuses and Surveys, *Marriage and Divorce Statistics, England and Wales*, 1974, 1989; Office of National Statistics, *Annual Abstract of Statistics 2000*, p. 40; *Population Trends 1995*, Spring 1999, p. 57; Registrar General for Scotland, *Annual Reports*, 1971–98.

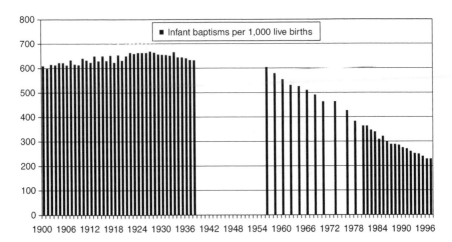

Figure 7.4 Church of England baptism rate, 1900–97

Source: Figures from *Church of England Yearbook*, 1984–2000.

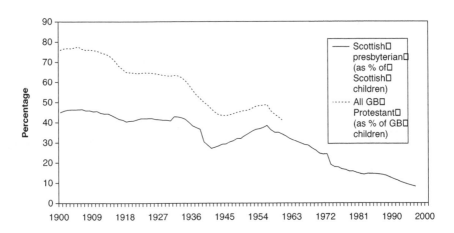

Figure 7.5 British Sunday school enrolment, 1900–96: percentage of 5–14-year-olds

Sources: Figures calculated from R. Currie, A. Gilbert and L. Horsley, *Churches and Churchgoers: Patterns of Church Growth in the British Isles since 1700*, Oxford, Clarendon Press, 1977, pp. 167–92; *Church of Scotland Yearbook*, 1971–98; B.R. Mitchell and P. Deane, *Abstract of British Historical Statistics*, Cambridge, Cambridge University Press, 1962, pp. 12–13; *Registrar General for Scotland, Annual Reports*, 1971–98.

British working classes of the period 1800–1950 were significantly more alienated from the churches or Christianity than the middle or upper classes.[67] Instead, the interaction of gender with social class emerges as the central determining factor. The privileging of female piety in evangelical discourse underlay women's centrality to churchgoing patterns, and the resilience of that discourse ensured the continued strength of popular religiosity in Britain until the 1950s. Certainly, there was change during the period to the balance of ways in which that religiosity was expressed. Churchgoing declined after the 1880s, but this was counterbalanced down to the mid-twentieth century by the popularity of female-centred rites of passage (marriage, baptism and churching), by children's continued and almost obligatory Sunday school enrolment, and by the affirmation of a Christian identity conferred by church membership. Christian Britain survived into the 1950s with a medley of well-observed rites, some of which were stronger than they had been in 1800 or 1850. A vibrant Christian identity remained central to British popular culture, retaining a capability to explode in fulsome self-expression.

CHAPTER EIGHT

THE 1960S AND
SECULARISATION

——— .◆. ———

RETURN TO PIETY: 1945–58

The late 1940s and 1950s witnessed the greatest church growth that Britain had experienced since the mid-nineteenth century. Historians and sociologists have never come to terms with the growth of institutional religion in Britain between 1945 and 1958. Some scholars miss its scale or even its existence because the statistical data have not been scrutinised closely. Most, however, have ignored it because it does not fit their theoretical presumption that secularisation was under way long before, and that Britain was by then a 'secular society'.[1] However, what happened in these years is demonstrative both of the power of discursive Christianity, and of the nature, timing and duration of British secularisation that followed.

The period between the end of World War II and the late 1950s is commonly referred to by many historians as 'the age of austerity'. Despite the rise of the welfare state and comprehensive town planning, and despite full employment and significant growth in standards of living for most social groups, rationing on foodstuffs, furniture and most basic commodities continued until the mid-1950s. It was an age of economic retrenchment in Britain's old basic industries, marked by widespread nationalisation and concern with the fiscal health of a nation that had borrowed heavily during and at the end of the war. The mood of the country seemed dour, unexciting and intensely conservative. Even the rhetoric of the bold, new welfare state was resonant with Victorian religious philanthropy in its talk of educating the working-class girl and preventing juvenile delinquency.[2]

This was nowhere more marked than in the discursive construction of femininity. The end of the war had been marked by the state's promotion of 'pro-natalism', of women's place being in the home where the nation needed an invigorated birth rate to overcome labour shortage. During the war, women had been drafted into a wide variety of industries and agriculture to fill the gaps left by men on active service. But as Penny Summerfield has shown, the way this was implemented did not undermine domestic ideology, and it 'did little to alter but rather reinforced the unequal position of women in society'.[3] Though female participation in the labour market increased, domesticity was revived. In manual occupations, the idea evolved that women could combine paid and domestic work, while for middle-class women there was a significant return to the domestic ideal. For both groups, labour-saving devices could improve domestic efficiency.[4] However, working women became the target of a barrage of official and popular discourses which returned them to the home and hearth and imposed on them guilt and anxiety about neglecting their children and doing them psychological damage.[5] As Liz Heron wrote of the fifties:

> It is seen as the time when women, yielding their jobs to the returning male population as soon as the war was over lost the paid employment that had given them independence; as the time when the family was recemented, when women were redomesticated, their role redefined as that of home-maker; when progress itself had a domestic incarnation, with the kitchen as the centre of the new developments in consumer technology. It is seen as the time when all the outward signs of sexual difference were re-emphasised through style and fashion, and women's femininity pronounced in the clothes of the New Look.[6]

Summerfield has recently analysed women's oral-history narratives on their wartime lives in terms of two dominant discourses: the modernising woman and the traditional woman. The first put the accent of the war's effects on change and opportunity, a welcome liberalising of women's roles. The second pictured the war as something to be endured for a return to normal or traditional female roles. But Summerfield concludes that despite 'real' differences between them, 'the discourse of modernisation was in fact riddled with traditionalism'. Few of those who pushed, or identified with, the discourse of modernisation 'departed from the dominant, traditional view that women's main purpose at the end of the war was to "return home" and recreate a domestic haven'. 'The contradiction', Summerfield continues, 'between this representation and the idea that the war had liberated women was resolved by the suggestion that, later in the post-war years, women would turn their backs on the domestic "cage" and demand the freedoms made available by the war.'[7]

The deferment of women's liberation in the late 1940s and 1950s was apparent in the fervency with which media circulated the traditional discourse on domestic ideology. The film *Brief Encounter* (1945), presciently symbolising the transition to peacetime moral sensibilities, explored a woman's claustrophobic fear of public discovery of her extra-marital love affair. She worried people 'could read my secret thoughts', blushed as a vicar stared at her on a train, and 'felt like a criminal' when found by a policeman in a public park at dead of night. Her final dissolution of the affair affirmed – albeit reluctantly – its sordidness and her unbearable guilt in the face of her role as mother and wife.[8] The return to home and family was signalled also in women's magazines. During the war they had been immensely popular for exploring women's changed wartime roles (in employment for instance), social issues of expanding welfarism, and the new female challenges which shortage and war brought to the home with absent men. But at war's end, magazines which attempted to retain editorial on social-conscience issues like equal pay suffered catastrophic impact on circulation, and a conservatism based on motherhood, cookery and gardening returned to dominate women's popular reading. As Evelyn Home wrote in *Woman* in 1951, 'most women, once they have a family, are more contented and doing better work in the home than they could find outside it'.[9] Women as consumers became a primary 'message' of the press in the 1950s, with advertisers funding much of the income-growth of women's magazines, and demanding editorial content to match advertising copy's judgement of women: 'Yes ... but will she roast bread cubes to drop in your soup?'[10] By the mid-1950s, most women's magazines had arrived at a uniformity of concentration on women's domestic role and the twin goals of finding a husband and raising a family, all done, as Cynthia White noted, 'to the virtual – not to say virtuous – exclusion of all other interests and activities, including paid work outside the home'.[11] It was the virtue, or moral judgement, involved in these goals which was a characteristic reassertion of the 1950s. As late as 1961, a columnist in *Woman's Own* advised:

> You can't have deep and safe happiness in marriage and the exciting independence of a career as well ... It isn't fair on your husband. I believe [any man] would tell you that he would rather his wife stayed at home and looked after his children, and was waiting for him with a decent meal and a sympathetic ear when he got home from work.[12]

The 'hearth and home' formula was reapplied with a vengeance to girls' fiction in the post-war decades. New romance comics like *Marilyn* (founded 1955), *Valentine* (1957) and *Boyfriend* (1959) provided what Cynthia White has described as 'a simplified dream world peopled with heroes and heroines who rushed breathlessly through a series of ill-fated encounters towards the predictably happy ending where "girl-gets-boy"'. These papers were, she remarks, both naïve and 'unimpeachably moral by pre-war standards'.[13]

Traditional values of family, home and piety were suddenly back on the agenda between the end of war and 1960. The churches benefited immediately. During the late 1940s and first half of the 1950s, organised Christianity experienced the greatest per annum growth in church membership, Sunday school enrolment, Anglican confirmations and presbyterian recruitment of its baptised constituency since the eighteenth century. Figures 7.1, 7.5 and 8.1 show the scale of this growth, leading to peaks in membership in the 1955–59 period for virtually all British Protestant churches. Marking the mood, religious revivals spread across Britain, aided by new technology and new forms. The Billy Graham crusades of 1954–56 were especially noteworthy, producing mass audiences in football stadia, military barracks and nightly congregations of tens of thousands in large indoor arenas, with remoter congregations participating in cinemas and churches by the development of closed-circuit radio and television. Radio evangelism was also permitted in the early and mid-1950s on BBC radio. Accompanying all of this was a revival of tract distribution and district visiting on a scale not witnessed since the late Victorian and Edwardian periods.[14]

The demographics of those most affected by this resurgence of organised religion are most instructive. The gross numbers attending crusade events were enormous: 1.9 million people in the 1954 London crusade, and a further 1.2 million in the 1955 Scottish crusade. Yet, the numbers making 'decisions for Christ' or coming forward for spiritual counselling were minute: only 36,431 (2.1 per cent) in London and 26,457 (2.2 per cent) in Scotland. The evidence is overwhelming that it was the young – those who were between 5 and 20 years of age at some point during the period 1945 to 1956 – who participated most fully. And amongst this age group, it was girls and young women who made up those most deeply affected. Of those who 'came forward' in London in 1954, 65 per cent were women and over 50 per cent were under nineteen years of age; in Scotland the following year 71 per cent were women, 73 per cent were under the age of thirty years, and 11 per cent were under twelve years.[15] The events were culturally extremely important. Children were accompanied by adults, especially women, many of whom were dressed in their best fur coats and tippets.[16] Accompanying adults may even have discouraged children from going forward; one boy in his early teens at a packed Billy Graham meeting at Tynecastle football stadium in Edinburgh was prevented from going forward when his aunt put a restraining arm in his way, saying: 'Don't be so silly.'[17] For many attenders these were spectacles in the midst of austerity; for a small number, especially the young, they induced considerable anxiety. This was a return to an older evangelical discursive state.

It would be foolish to overstate the direct impact of church growth and revivalism upon Britons in the fifties. Few were converted and church membership started its decline in the two years after Billy Graham's visits. But the sheer numbers attending were vast, and in this the events both reflected and reinforced discursive and institutional Christianity. Attendances at the Greater London crusade in 1954 represented 21.2 per cent of the resident population, whilst attendances in Glasgow represented 73.7 per cent of the city's population.[18] Even allowing for significant travelling from outside areas (especially to Glasgow) and multiple attendances, the figures show that the events had a powerful resonance to 1950s Britain.

The widespread penetration of the events into the print and broadcasting media, and the demographic density of participation, could not have happened if the discursive power of the evangelical narrative had been seriously diminished. This was especially true of young women and girls who made up nearly three-quarters of those who came forward. Their discursive environment made them highly responsive to the Graham crusades. Girls growing up in the fifties recall: 'Christmas is cribs and paintings of baby Jesus all over the school corridors and the inevitable daily prayers with "Onward Christian soldiers".'[19] Not believing in God was unpopular: a girl who proclaimed her unbelief in the school playground recalled being taunted and called 'a heathen' by her classmates.[20] More broadly, discourses on sexual morality were the commonest currency of community policing and wounded the young. John Lennon's mother 'lived in sin', making him the object of persistent jibes and moralistic name-calling (contributing, some have said, to his defensive and caustic personality), whilst Carolyn Steedman's mother hid her unmarried state and prevented her daughter from proceeding from Sunday school to confirmation class because of the absence of a baptismal certificate.[21]

The 'official' culture of the decade has been described by one writer as a 'psychic dam'[22] imposed by a stolid establishment through the Lord Chamberlain's censorship of the theatre, the courts' censorship of literature, and the Reithian ethos of intellectual elitism in radio and the new medium of television. It was the generation of 'conservative and respectable ordinariness': 'The ordinariness of manners, or please-and-thank-you'd politeness, of being a nice girl, who went to the Brownies and Guides, and for whom the competitions in the annual Produce Association show provided one of the most exciting occasions of the year.'[23] Suburban ordinariness reached its apogee, enjoyed by older generations as the prize for enduring two wars and a prolonged economic depression. The values remained the same – order, duty, thrift and respectability – endured by the young in Sunday school respectability, the Cubs' 'Bob-a-job-week' and the Brownies' 'Purpose Day'.[24] The 1950s sought to recreate in the young not just these values but the evangelical state of anxiety about worthiness: 'I see now,' wrote Carolyn Steedman three decades later, 'the relentless laying down of guilt.'[25]

At the same time there was an alternative discursive world in the making in the 1950s. It was being manufactured by a bohemian and 'delinquent' minority, based around Elvis Presley and rock-and-roll from 1956, and skiffle music in 1958–60, and centred on underground cafes, town hall dances and art colleges.[26] The musical idiom, rather than the lyrics, became signature tunes or symbols of rebelliousness in dress (notably black leather), sexual activity and illegal drugs. To be such a 'rebel' implied important things about religion. Paul McCartney recalled: 'It was during that time, A-levels time, I remember thinking, in many ways I wish I was a lorry driver, a Catholic lorry driver. Very very simple life, a firm faith and a place to go in my lorry, in my nice lorry. I realised I was more complex than that and I slightly envied that life. I envied the innocence.'[27] But the majority of young people were outside 'beatnik' culture in the 1950s. For most children, it was a decade of submission to family values and duty, of boys being good and girls being nice. Personal testimony shows many unchanged features of childhood between the 1900s and 1950s; one oral historian, Elizabeth Roberts, comments: 'They were to do as their parents told them; they were to be honest and respectable; they were not to bring shame on their families by getting into any kind of trouble.'[28] The fifties' Sunday was only marginally more liberal than its Edwardian predecessor: going (or being sent) to Sunday school whether or not your parents went to church, Sunday-best clothes, restricted Sunday games, and with the parkies tying up the swings in the public park. The church, Sunday school and family were memorials to their parents' history which the young endured in that decade. Both change and continuity seemed retrospective. There was the world of the past, still present in Victorian values, in adults' memories of depression, in a war memorialised in bomb-sites, war movies and a father's silence on his war. The past also seemed present in what was new: the welfare state, prefabs and council-housing estates mending the past in its own image. The family home was at the peak of its sanctifica-tion; more homes were demolished and more new ones built than ever before, predominantly one- or two-storey 'cottage' style with front and back gardens.[29] Where change intruded, it remained institutionally and discursively boundaried. Even dances and popular music could be church-mediated. By the fifties, introduction to dances and popular music was often in the church hall: Jenny Kennedy, born 1945, went to coffee bars during the week, the church dance on Saturday night, and only went to Sunday school because her mother stepped in when there was no one to teach the infants.[30] The 1950s were about perfecting Victorian values and finally distributing their fruits. The decade was, as Carolyn Steedman has put it, 'a point between two worlds' where the child was 'a repository for other people's history'.[31]

THE SIXTIES' DISCOURSE REVOLUTION

Secularisation could not happen until discursive Christianity lost its power. From 1800 until 1950, the British Christian churches had no state sanction to force people to be adherents or believers as had been the case before 1800. It had been the 'salvation economy' which had wielded a power over the individual to make the choice to absorb and adapt gendered religious identities to himself and herself. It was only when that discursive power waned that secularisation could take place. The result was not the long, inevitable religious decline of the conventional secularisation story, but a remarkably sudden and culturally violent event.

In the 1960s, the institutional structures of cultural traditionalism started to crumble in Britain: the ending of the worst excesses of moral censorship (notably after the 1960 trial of *Lady Chatterley's Lover* and the ending in 1968 of the Lord Chamberlain's control over British theatre); the legalisation of abortion (1967) and homosexuality (1967), and the granting of easier divorce (1969); the emergence of the women's liberation movement, especially from 1968; the flourishing of youth culture centred on popular music (especially after the emergence of the Beatles in late 1962) and incorporating a range of cultural pursuits and identities (ranging from the widespread use of drugs to the fashion revolution);[32] and the appearance of student rebellion (notably between 1968 and the early 1970s).[33]

However, some modern cultural theorists go much further to argue that the 1960s was a key decade in ending 'the Enlightenment project' and modernity. In its place, the era of postmodernity started to mature.[34] Structural 'realities' of social class eroded, and there was a repudiation of self-evident 'truths' (concerning the role of women, the veracity of Christianity, and the structure of social and moral authority), a new scepticism about the science-derived nature of 'progress', and the disappearance of an agreed 'reality'. Science, social science and Christianity were equally victims in the making in the 1960s. They started to be undermined by the 'linguistic turn' – the deconstruction of the role of language, signification and discourse which had constructed the Enlightenment narrative of history, rationality and progress. As Lyotard wrote: 'The narrative function is losing its functors, its great hero, its great dangers, its great voyages, its great goal.'[35] Just as environmentalism and the anti-nuclear movement started to challenge science in the sixties, so poststructuralism and feminism would come within a decade or so to challenge social science.

But the immediate victim was Christianity, challenged most influentially by second-wave feminism and the recrafting of femininity. In 1959, *Boyfriend* magazine for teenage girls began publication and was an instant hit, starting with a circulation of 418,000. Its format was new, but its message was old. It used a well-known pop song and its singer to inspire a story which delivered a traditional moral discourse on the nature of female virtue. The magazine was short-lived, winding-up in 1965 when its sales had plummeted to 199,000. It was cleared off the shelves by *Jackie*, which started in 1964 when Beatlemania was at its height. Its initial circulation was 350,000 and reached 605,947 by 1976. *Jackie* also took pop songs as the inspiration for its comic-strip stories – 'Meet me at the corner', 'Come fly with me' and 'Where have all the flowers gone?' – but discarded traditional moral language. Stories now focused on the words 'you', 'love' and 'happiness'. Rooted in swinging London, *Jackie* persisted in asserting the separation of sex roles, but acknowledged that women worried over men and accepted that love was not necessarily for ever.[36] What was novel in *Jackie* between 1964 and 1978 was the disappearance of discourses on domesticity, separate spheres, and women's limited career ambitions. The virtuous sexual girl was now a matter for negotiation rather than rigid abstention. Moreover, the home hardly featured at all in the strips. Discourses on feminine identity was now conveyed by everything other than family, domestic routine, virtue, religion or 'respectability'.

The same process, though more carefully modulated, was going on within conventional women's magazines. This market entered a crisis in the 1960s with rapidly falling sales. A few 'traditionalist' magazines like *Woman's Weekly*, with its diet of romantic fiction and homely virtues, succeeded in catering for the older married woman. But many failed, including *Housewife* which declined and ended in merger with another. The future lay with magazines like *Everywoman*, which relaunched in 1966 on the assumption that its women readers were workers as well as house-wives, had shared fashion and beauty concerns regardless of age, and were keener on real-life fiction rather than romance. As Cynthia White suggested, there was a fundamental shift by women readers away from publica-tions which treated them as 'domestic functionaries'.[37] Whilst supporting traditional items such as cookery, clothes and the furniture, there was a decline of features on mending and 'making do', thereby undermining the traditional home-keeping virtues of thrift and being able to darn and sew. In part, magazines became driven by consumer-buying.[38] But they also became less concerned with womanly 'virtues' and developed an engagement with their readers' wider concerns. Some, like *Woman* and *Woman's Own*, made subtle compromises between 'tradition' and 'change', perhaps most noticeable through a new breed of agony aunt. Unlike their predecessors of even ten years before, who had advised women on how to please men in the domestic sphere, 'aunts' like Marje Proops and Clare Rayner were now treating women as equal partners in relationships, and exploring sexual issues in explicit ways by, for example, publishing letters from troubled women (and men) about the myths of sexuality (including the length of penises and the width of vaginas). For the younger woman, there were more adventurous publications. The pioneer *She* (founded 1955) came into its own in the late sixties, treating its readership as intellectual beings with a mix of serious and open-minded discussion of both social issues and 'women's writes'. Its stablemate *Cosmopolitan* (founded 1972) took an even bolder stance, combining a glamorous presentation with a feminist treatment of women's liberated sexuality, careers and entertain-ments.[39] Other magazines and books in the same vein for young women followed: *Honey*, *19*, *Over-21*, and Shirley Conran's *Everywoman*.

The discursive change was swift and dramatic. The fifties' construction of the 'respectable' woman of homely virtues, the last widespread vestige of nineteenth-century female piety, was for the bulk of young people abruptly dissolved. The change in print media was surpassed in speed and pace by the arrival of new signifiers in other media. The rise of the pop group, signalled by the release of the Beatles' 'Love Me Do' in October 1962, introduced the pop concert and female adulation on an unprecedented scale. Over the next three years, the pop record, the pop magazine, radical fashion (including the miniskirt), pop art and recreational drug-use combined to create an integrated cultural system which swept the young people of Britain. Television was ambiguous, straddling the traditional discursive world of the establishment and the conveyance of the new. Its pop programmes ('Ready Steady Go' and 'Top of the Pops') fed 'swinging London' to the nation, whilst its burgeoning youth comedy ('That Was the Week That Was' and 'Monty Python') ridiculed 'establishment' values, pomposity, politicians and Britain's armed forces.[40] International telecommunications, pioneered by the Telstar satellite in 1963, was by 1967 providing same-day coverage of the hippie 'summer of love' in California. Between March and August of the following year, it provided coverage of the major political touchstones of the decade: the Prague Spring, the Cultural Revolution in China, the May revolution in Paris and other cities, and, from America, the Civil Rights movement, the anti-Vietnam war movement and the Democratic Convention riots in Chicago. British television remained the representation of the establishment, yet even in its implied criticism (of sexual promiscuity, drug culture and radical politics) it was signalling profound discursive change.

Central to the signification power of all the media was the pop record. Aided by over a dozen pirate radio stations which were active around Britain's shores between 1964 and 1967, the vinyl record in single and long-playing formats displaced the printed word as the key method by which young people formed their own discursive world. In part, as McLuhan famously said, 'the medium was the message' – its own form being a signifier of a discourse of a new irrationality.[41] In this regard, pop music signified more trenchantly than any magazine a challenge to hegemonies of the establishment. The discourse change was also *within* pop music. The Beatles rose to fame in Hamburg and Liverpool playing mostly other people's songs, including American rock and ballads, dominated by lyrics about dance (rock and roll and the twist) or about romance. As argued earlier in this book, romance was the central area of interaction between religious and secular narrative structures from the 1840s onwards. The Beatles reflected the pop world generally in the early 1960s by sustaining this tradition in popular song (which had stretched from the Victorian music hall to the crooners of the 1950s). The lyrics of all of the 49 songs copyrighted by the Beatles during 1963–4 were about boy-girl romance. Beatles lyrics then changed radically, with romance dropping to 83 per cent of their 1965 lyrical output, 40 per cent of 1966 output, and a mere 5 per cent of 1967 output. Despite a slight rise (to 14, 11 and 20 per cent) in the final three years of their existence, romance had been displaced by complex and varied lyrical themes influenced by amongst other things the anti-war movement, drugs, nihilism, existentialism, nostalgia and eastern mysticism.[42] Conventional morality was not just confronted but in some cases subtly explored in these later songs, nowhere more so than in the oppositional discursive 'voices' in 'She's Leaving Home', about a girl leaving her parents and the symbolic shedding of family, convention and unhappiness:

> She *(We gave her most of our lives)*
> is leaving *(Sacrificed most of our lives)*
> home *(We gave her ev'rthing money could buy)*.
> She's leaving home after living alone for so many years.[43]

Female rebellion – of body, sexuality and above all the decay of religious marriage – was a transition out of the traditional discursive world.

The Beatles were merely one band *circulating* discourse change, not *creating* it. Pop music – buying it, listening to it, dancing to it and making it – released the generation of fifties' and sixties' children from conventional forms of popular culture and conventional discourses. Ray Davies of The Kinks recalled: 'I went to a church school but the closest I felt to religion was not when I was singing in the school choir or when I was at Sunday school, which I always went to, but it was more when I rehearsed with Dave in the front room.'[44] Pop music's impact upon girls, enforced by magazines like *Jackie*, was critical. Women had previously been the heart of family piety, the moral restraint upon men and children. By the mid-1960s, domestic ideology was assailed on many fronts, putting the cultural revolution in collision with not just the Christian churches but with Christianity as a whole. The loss of domestic ideology to youth culture from *c.* 1958 meant that piety 'lost' its discursive home within femininity. Its last redoubt, 'the angel in the house' to use an historian's cliché, was now negotiable and challenged discursive terrain. The distinctive growth in the 1950s of women's dual role in home and work was a major contributory factor, creating a new stress about which model defined a woman's 'duty', upsetting the salience of evangelical protocols, and rendering women part of the same religious 'problem' as men.[45] The reconstruction of female identity within work, sexual relations and new recreational opportunities from the late 1960s, put not just feminism but female identity in collision with the Christian construction of femininity.[46]

The discursive death of pious femininity destroyed the evangelical narrative. This was acutely spotted by the leaders of one denomination – the Moral Welfare Committee of the general assembly of the Church of Scotland. Between 1967 and 1972, the Committee effectively abandoned its traditional promotion of temperance, and offered the Church responses to the liberalisation of British society: to legalisation of abortion in 1967 (which it did not wholly oppose), to decriminalisation of homosexuality in 1968 (a 'distasteful' group of people who were 'sick, and who are in need of a physician, even although as yet no complete cure has been found'), and the liberalisation of divorce (which it approved subject to the promotion of 'Engaged Couples' courses). By 1970 it was quite optimistic, admiring young people's principled opposition to the Biafran and Vietnam wars, and finding virtue even in sexual permissiveness: 'If the sanctions of commandment and convention are gone, people are set free to respond to goodness for its own sake, under no compulsion, constrained and sustained by the love of Christ and not by the fear of a lost respectability.' The Committee considered whether marriage might be on the way out, and felt this was not without historical precedent. 'The spirit of the age with its new found freedoms, and its healthy intolerance of humbug and hypocrisy, challenges Christians to re-think the implications of Christian morality – not a bad thing to have to do.' But then, in a single sentence of its report in 1970, the Committee grasped the central issue: 'It is the promiscuous girl who is the real problem here.' In this utterly sexist statement, the Committee actually understood the central issue – that the 'moral turn' in female sexuality destroyed the entire house of cards. Boys had always been boys, but female permissiveness meant that a generation of young women were turning their back on the discourse of pious femininity. With this realisation, the Committee could not cope, and by 1972 it voiced total exasperation with 'the turbulent continent of morality' and the unfolding 'promiscuous age'.[47]

Many Christian congregations in Britain tried to compromise with the new age of youth in the late 1960s, developing new forms of religious worship using guitars and penny whistles, modern dress and a 'happy-clappy' atmosphere in an attempt to mimic the forms of youth culture. Churches continued to try to absorb rock bands and the new-fangled discotheques within their premises. In Edinburgh, large numbers of fourteen- to seventeen-year-olds (including the author) were members of a considerable 'church-hall' circuit of rock dances and discos, but this had largely collapsed by 1970 as it was shut down by congregations unable to countenance the increasing loudness of the music, the arrival of soft drugs, the visits of the police and, above all, the brazen nature of teenagers' casual sexual liaisons. A hundred and ninety years after Sunday schools first opened, the salvation industry was shutting its doors to an entire generation of youngsters who no longer subscribed to religious discourses of moral identity. Secularisation was now well under way.

SECULAR LIFE NARRATIVES

Secularisation was founded on discourse change. It is discernible from personal testimony in differences between times remembered and the times of remembering, and also between the subjectivities of older interviewee and younger interviewer. We saw in Chapter 6 that those born in the late nineteenth or very early twentieth century generated testimony, especially in the late 1960s and 1970s, composed in an evangelical narrative structure with discourses on piety and morality contained within it. But inter-generational oral-history narratives, in which members of two and sometimes three generations of the same family are interviewed, allow us to see the evidence of discourse change. Moving between the generations – those born successively in the 1900s/1910s/1920s, the 1930s/1940s/1950s, and the 1960s – there is a disappearance of evangelical narrative structure, 'traditional' discourses on religiosity and morality, and a growth of 'stunting' in the conception of religion.

Three generations of the Lowrie family were interviewed in the 1980s. With the oldest, Kevin Lowrie born in 1904, issues of religiosity and morality tend to appear in his testimony in the description of strict parents and family discipline. Kevin's father was 'very, very strict indeed – but a good man' who steered his son into church choirs and solo bass singing in churches around their home city of Bristol. He made the family 'go to church morning, afternoon and evening'. Kevin likened him to the clergy: 'He was very much – [of] course, the churchmen were like that too, you know. I mean they were terrors, especially bishops and that. He was a miserable old so-and-so.'[48] This type of answer is extremely common amongst male interviewees born in the early twentieth century, characterised by a presence of evangelical polarities and the residue of the evangelical narrative structure, but overlain with commentary (ranging from the resentful to the mocking) on illiberal parental attitudes to religion, morality and child discipline.

The testimony of the next generation showed a reduced trace of the evangelical narrative, but instead described a greater equilibrium in family life between morality and humanity in the 1940s and 1950s. Kevin's son, Laurence Lowrie (born 1939), found his father much less strict, indeed entirely liberal, about religious upbringing:

Q: How much would you say religion meant to you as a child?
A: Some. Not a great deal, but also not completely ignored.
Q: Was it ever talked about at home?
A: Not very often.
Q: Would they have minded if you hadn't wanted to go to Sunday school?
A: I think they were fairly lukewarm about it . . .

Q: Did religion mean more or less to you after childhood?
A: About the same.
Q: What does that mean?
A: Well, not important nor unimportant. A fairly medium course if you like. Occasional attender at church as a child.[49]

Among interviewees born after the late 1930s, answers on religious matters are strongly characterised by these short answers. This can be interpreted in a number of ways. On the one hand they exude an air of indifference about religion; the testimony suggests it is a topic the interviewees of that generation devoted little time to in their daily lives or even in their more thoughtful moments. On the other hand, it might be interpreted as a way of rejecting the interviewer's intrusiveness: the short answers might be saying 'this a private matter, it's none of your business'. A third possible factor is the interviewer's (or questionnaire-setter's) 'stunted' conception of religion which fails to provide a question to which the interviewee feels able to respond. There is, however, a fourth issue: the absence of either a narrative structure or a set of terms with which the interviewees are *able* to answer. They are of a generation that has not sustained a training in how to express their religiosity. They may even have a sense of religiosity or spirituality, but they are not familiar – like their parents and their grand-parents – in having to express this. Critically, a very common element is the general absence of the motifs of moral bipolarities (drinking and teeto-talism, strict Sundays and banning of games, gambling and not gambling, strict discipline and naughtiness), as well as an absence of the narrative progression which contained these contrasts. There is indeed a reticence about describing their lives with the same openness as their parents. Constructing a life narrative is less important to them, but equally they do not *conceive* of it as being capable of being rendered in such a format. In other words, the 'stunting' of the concept of religion is *mutual* between interviewee and interviewer.

This last issue surfaces in a new way in the final generation when the discursive change is virtually complete. Maureen Lowrie born in 1967, was the granddaughter and daughter respectively of Kevin and Laurence, and at the time of being interviewed in the late 1980s she was a student. She had attended Sunday school but stopped at the age of ten: 'that was my decision'. Religion meant little to her until she decided to get confirmed, but 'Now that's died off; I seem to have lost that faith, you know.' She became bitter with the Anglican vicar when her best friend's father was sacked as headmaster of the local Church of England school: 'standing on a Sunday morning shaking his hand seemed the height of hypocrisy to me. So, Sundays is kept for my work and also for my parents.'[50] What emerges is the interviewee's stunted conception of religiosity as 'going to church' and not as a wider personal religious identity.

Such transitions in intergenerational oral testimony are commonplace. One Edwardian woman from Enfield was reported by her children as being fairly religious, continuing to attend weekly church events into old age in the 1920s. Her daughter reported in a shorter fashion on her religiosity, but recalled in some detail going to Sunday school weekly in the 1920s and early 1930s. By contrast, her granddaughter reported that religion meant 'nothing at all' in her youth in the 1950s, though she did attend church for a year and continued to attend church dances, the Guides and to wear Sunday best. The fourth generation, the great-granddaughter brought up in the 1970s and 1980s, never went to Sunday school, church, Guides or any church-based activity. No religious or quasi-religious discourse, motif or activity whatever can be discerned in her testimony. Repeated questioning on religion, drawn from the same questionnaire as put to her mother and grandmother, drew blank or disinterested responses; her only comment was: 'I was never religious.'[51] The stunting had become reversed; it was the interviewee, not the interviewer, who had no discussable concept of her religiosity. The 1960s generation had become inarticulate about religion – even more so than the older interviewer.

From early in the twentieth century, there is plenty of evidence from autobiography and oral testimony of men disavowing churchgoing, and even rejecting Christianity.[52] But for women, this type of personal journey away from religion was extremely difficult and comparatively rare before the 1950s. It was difficult because a woman could not just 'drop' religion as a man could; her respectability as a woman, wife and mother, whether she liked it or not, was founded on religion whether she went to church or not. For a woman, religion filled the same place occupied by ignorance about sex. Hetty Beck, born in 1879 into an upper-working-class Church of England family, recalled:

> [T]here was certain things that were not revealed to us in our days – fact – well, youngsters talk about them when they're five years old these days [1960s], but – oh no – things were kept very private, in many ways. But you learnt more when you got older and you got out into the world and mixed with other people, whatever you did really at home – which, perhaps it was best; perhaps it wasn't – I feel – I'm not too sure about it. Now if you look a – er – well of course, life at that time, when we were growing up, life was – you lived a sheltered life. You went to church and Sunday – you went to Sunday school and you'd go to church in the evening . . .[53]

This disturbed broken answer is typical of elderly female interviewees in the late twentieth century who were seeking ways to verbalise the changes in their personal world since childhood. But with these women, it was still an *articulate* engagement with conceptions of religiosity – with the evangelical narrative structure and its discourses – which defined their femininity, rather than a spoken knowledge of their bodies and the 'facts of life'. The site of their femininity had been religion and church which provided a sexually 'sheltered life'. By speaking its very name, such testimony marks its end.

The elderly of the 1970s and 1980s displayed the intergenerational change in another way. Even if they were in transit away from the evangelical life narrative, they were still subscribers to its discourses. When the generation born in the first half of the century discusses why religion has been important in their lives, they characteristically give broken replies in which they resort to relating their own religious activity to that of their parents: 'I had always been used with – well, my father was an organist for a start', and 'Religion was well, my Dad was – They were very religious. I mean, it was a sort of routine we had been brought up to.'[54] When discussing their *loss* of religiosity, on the other hand, they tend to refer to their own children and cultural change. Paula Queen born in 1912 in Edinburgh said in the 1980s:

> I don't know when it [religion] ceased to be quite as important. I'll tell you what I think is wrong nowadays. You see so much about science on these [television] programmes that that – I remember when my son was taking medicine, not one of these students believed in anything. He did join Greyfriars Church initially but when he got further on and so steeped in science they would make you believe that you're just a chemical equation and that when you died it was just the chemical equation ceased working and that was it, you know. It used to depress me when I used to hear it because they could knock down every argument you had. And I'd say 'but the Bible', and my son would say the Bible was written by a man – a man writes a book, he doesn't always stick to fact. And so what could you say to that because I suppose it was written by a man and then I started to listen to programmes on there, scientific programmes, and I really – am torn in two. I can't decide now whether – I don't believe there's a hell, I think you make your own hell on earth . . . I can't believe that there's a heaven where there's angels fluttering about and all that. I can't believe that nowadays, but I'd like to think there's another life . . .[55]

Here is an elderly woman reflectively rationalising her position within discourse change. This is an attempt to justify Christian religiosity both before and after discourse change – an attempt made on the assumption of that change. This is a form of justification which would not, for the most part, have occurred in their younger years. There is a sense of not just confusion over 'what to believe', but grief – discursive bereavement – at the loss.

Instructively, the phenomena observable in late twentieth-century testimony of younger people – reticence about talking about religion, the stunted nature of religious and moral motifs, and the unavailability of a narrative structure – is not replicated in autobiography written in the same period. The post–1945 working-class autobiography, describing lives from the 1880s onwards, shows no reluctance whatsoever in discussing religion. This dissonance between the two primary forms of experiential source is revealing and important.

We noted in Chapter 6 the dominance of religious narrative structure and evangelical discourses in nineteenth- and early twentieth-century autobiography. The autobiography focused on the subject (the writer) as on a life-journey, using notions of progression, improvement and personal salvation, whether within religion or opposing it, as the construction and purpose of the literary work. Working-class autobiographies of the second half of the twentieth century form a revealing contrast in structure and treatment. Dealing with lives begun in the main between the 1860s and the 1920s, they record living through the period of discursive Christianity's greatest power. They discuss religion in great detail and in some considerable length; virtually all went to Sunday school or church, many went to temperance activities such as the Band of Hope, and they remember their lives as children and young adults as infused by religious leisure and recreation. Yet, very few of them deploy an evangelical narrative structure. Few recall conversion experiences or even mention the subject. Religion is recollected as an activity (going to church and Sunday school), as a moral regime (the suppression of Sunday games and wearing of 'Sunday-best' clothes), and as a definer (rightly or wrongly) of respectability within the community. The way this is structured is within a specialist agenda item in the autobiography. Indeed, very large numbers of post-1950 autobiographies pigeon-holed religion in a separate chapter on 'Sundays'. Religion is taken in these as the motif of the past, a feature – perhaps in many the central feature – which distinguishes a world we have lost, in which symbols of religious activity are cited as ciphers for a world of quaint activities. The discursive world of evangelical Christianity of late Victorian and Edwardian Britain had become, for the autobiography of the 1940s to the 1970s, a curiosity. Religion had become something to be remembered and something commoditised as nostalgia, for purchase in paperback. The religious past of Britain had become a best-seller.

The biggest selling autobiographies were those predominantly set in rural and village locations, featuring tightly bound communities with intense relationships between the inhabitants. Books by Winifred Foley (set in the New Forest), Lillian Beckwith (set in the Scottish Highlands) and above all Flora Thompson (rural Oxfordshire) use the high religiosity of their communities as the central symbol of the 'lost worlds' they are selling as literary commodities.[56] Urban and industrial autobiographies also became popular: books by Robert Roberts (Salford), Margaret Penn (Manchester), Molly Weir (Glasgow), Dolly Scannell (London), Jim Bullock (coal-mining

Yorkshire) and many others. Both rural and urban settings provide corrective pictures to popular mythology of idyllic country village and unpleasant city slum: the first was far from an harmonious society, and the second was characterised by neighbourliness in the midst of hardship. The effect is the same: they draw pictures of a lost world to be fondly remembered by the elderly reader or hankered after by the young. A few display considerable antagonism towards evangelical morality and its effect upon the lives of their parents, especially upon mothers, and in so doing convey the stifling community pressure to conform to religious moral codes as late as the 1940s.[57] They are moral tales of community, but they were rarely moral tales about the 'self'. Generally speaking, the autobiographers reveal themselves as lifelong churchgoers and Christians, but their volumes are rarely composed as 'religious lives' in the form of their Victorian and Edwardian predecessors. While they poke gentle and affectionate fun at the moral world of their youth, they still in general subscribe to it. It is a world they regret for its passing, something they and their publishers realise will attract book buyers who can invest in that nostalgia. In this way the autobiography reveals discourse change perhaps more potently than oral testimony: the journey from the construction of moral lives to the nostalgic *reconstruction* of moral communities. The autobiography of the nineteenth century was a construction of the moral journey of the individual to salvation – be it Christian, atheistic or socialist. The autobiography of the twentieth century was a moral museum of community in which the writer was participant observer rather than moral hero. Autobiography was no longer about progression but about loss. Religion – as narrative structure, the cement of community, and as motif – was central to that loss.

This leaves this work with an empirical problem. If people became inarticulate about their post-1950s religiosity, finding it easier, as Charles Taylor proposes of 'modern' humankind in general, to not believe than to believe,[58] how does the historian show this? Silences are now well-known territory to the historian of both the early-modern and modern periods, where failure to mention or discuss major events or issues is in itself a potent research finding.[59] The thing about the sixties is that religion was much discussed, notably the *Honest to God* debate from 1962 and the supposed 'death' of God, to which the elderly responded in considerable numbers.[60] Public debate on television and newspapers was widespread on not just the decline of religion but also on moral change. The problem is that autobiographies and oral testimony of the sixties' generation are relatively few and elite, seem wholly antagonistic to conventional religion, and interested only in experimental religiosity such as eastern mysticism.[61] This is not a product of either insufficient evidence or because the likely interviewees are too young to be 'interested' in reflecting on religion. It is a product of inarticulacy in conventional Christianity, a new 'silence of history', marking the birth of Britain's dechristianised generations in the 1960s.

THE DEMISE OF CHRISTIAN RELIGION

The statistics of British secularisation show by all indicators that the greatest gradient of decline of formal Christian religiosity occurred after 1958. Moreover, for the majority of the indicators, the greatest absolute and proportionate losses of the British people to organised religion occurred after that date.

We saw in Chapter 7 that Christian church connection grew per head of population down to the first decade of the twentieth century, and between 1905 and 1950 entered a period of fluctuation, exacerbated by two world wars, which left many indicators in the mid-1950s higher than in much of the nineteenth century and only marginally lower than at their highest point. Only churchgoing had declined, but this amounted mostly to a thinning of the people's religious worship, not to a massive polarisation between churchgoers and non-churchgoers. Sunday school enrolment and religious marriage showed remarkable strength until the 1930s. Baptism into the Church of England actually grew down to 1927, so that it was at a higher rate throughout the inter-war years than it had been in the Edwardian period. Though most of these indicators showed a downturn in the 1930s, especially in the late 1930s, most of the indicators were still strong by the 1940s.

What was happening was this. Adult church activity was declining but adult church association remained strong and, in the case of baptism, showed periods of growth. Sunday school enrolment, though declining, was doing so at a far slower rate than adult churchgoing. Adults were continuing the late Victorian trend of investing less in activity and more in passive association: through membership, attendance to religious rites of passage, and in ensuring that their children attended Sunday school. With discursive Christianity still strong in the inter-war period, family subscription to religiosity was becoming increasingly concentrated in the family and the community. The family subscribed to the discourses of Christian behaviour less by going to church and more by passive and surrogate association: the family rituals of marriage and baptism, and the attendance of children at Sunday school.

In the light of this, what happened in the 1950s becomes all the more remarkable; the two trends are reversed. Church of England baptism rates and the rate of solemnisation of marriage actually started to fall in the early 1950s, whilst church membership and Sunday school enrolment grew very significantly. In England, Easter day communicants grew 20.1 per cent as a proportion of population between 1947 and 1956; in Scotland, total religious affiliation to all churches grew 7.6 per cent as a proportion of total population, and Sunday school enrolment by 31.3 per cent as a proportion of 5–14 year olds. One consequence was a revival of religious marriage; after declining between the late 1930s and the early 1950s, it then grew between 1952 and 1957 from 69 to 72 per cent of all marriages in England and Wales and from 82 to 83 per cent of marriages in Scotland. The way in which this growth was achieved is best seen from Figure 8.1 which shows the recruitment success during the twentieth century of Britain's two major churches, the Church of England and the Church of Scotland. The number confirmed in the Church of England (usually between the ages of 12 and 16) is measured for each year as a percentage of the number baptised fourteen years previously, and the number becoming new communicants 'by profession' in the Church of Scotland (usually between the ages of 16 and 20) is measured as a percentage of those baptised eighteen years before. The graph shows increasing recruitment success between 1945 and 1956, notably in the Church of Scotland. All British churches benefited to greater or lesser degrees from growth in this period. In short, from 1945 to 1956 British organised Christianity experienced the most rapid rates of growth since statistics started to be collected in the nineteenth century.

From 1956 all indices of religiosity in Britain start to decline, and from 1963 most enter free fall. As Figure 8.1 shows, this fall was very rapid in the 1960s, and after levelling off at haemorrhaging rates of between 22 and 28 per cent during the 1970s and 1980s, fell again in the 1990s to a catastrophic rate of recruiting baptised persons into full membership of only 17 per cent in the Church of Scotland and 20 per cent in the Church of England. All the figures in this and the preceding chapters show the scale of declension: an unremitting decline in membership, communicants, baptisms and religious marriage which, at the start of the third millennium, shows no sign of bottoming out. The Sunday school in particular is close to disappearing as a significant institution. In Scotland, presbyterian Sunday school enrolments represented 39 per cent of Scottish children in 1956, but then fell to 19 per cent in 1973; from an all-time peak of 325,200 children in Church of Scotland Sunday schools in 1956, the numbers had reached only 60,936 in 1994. In England and Wales, the collapse of Sunday schools led to interruptions in the publishing of statistics by the Church of England in 1961, the Methodist Church and the Presbyterian Church in Wales in 1967, and by the Congregationalist Church in 1968 – an interruption which signalled the decay of the 'statistical discourse' which the churches had developed in the nineteenth century. The 'saved' could no longer be counted.

All of the indicators show that the period between 1956 and 1973 witnessed unprecedented rapidity in the fall of Christian religiosity amongst the British people. In most cases, at least half of the overall decline in each indicator recorded during the century was concentrated into those years. That in itself makes the 'long sixties' highly significant in the history of British secularisation. What heightens the significance is the fact that so many indices of religiosity fell simultaneously. Across the board, the British people started to reject the role of religion in their lives – in their marriage,

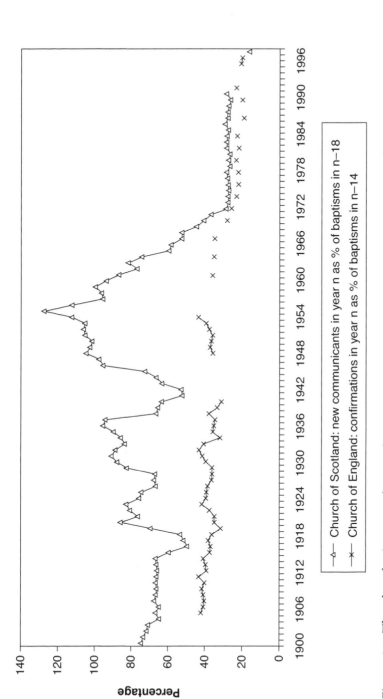

Figure 8.1 The churches' success in recruitment, 1900–98

Sources: Figures calculated from R. Currie, A. Gilbert and L. Horsley, *Churches, Churches and Churchgoers: Patterns of Church Growth in the British Isles since 1700*, Oxford, Clarendon Press, 1977, pp. 167–70; *Church of England Yearbook, 1984–2000; Church of Scotland Yearbook, 1971–99.*

as a place to baptise their children, as an institution to send their children for Sunday school and church recruitment, and as a place for affiliation. The next generation, which came to adulthood in the 1970s, exhibited even more marked disaffiliation from church connection of any sort, and *their* children were raised in a domestic routine largely free from the intrusions of organised religion. The broken, abrupt, dismissive and disinterested responses of young oral interviewees of the 1980s become explicable. They just had no discursive, associational or institutional link with Christianity.

If churchgoing, church recreation, church membership and religious rites of passage started declining in sequence between the 1880s and 1960s, their accelerated fall from the 1960s is probably starting a fifth phenomenon: the decline of Christian belief. Steve Bruce has recently suggested that from the 1960s faith itself – in God, in the afterlife, in the supernatural – has been in decline.[62] Certainly, some social-survey data seems to show not only decline in personal piety (private and daily prayer for instance), but also a fall in the proportion of people who claim to believe in the basic supernatural tenets of Christianity (such as belief in the existence of God, and the existence of heaven and hell).[63] For the generations growing up since the 1960s, new ethical concerns have emerged to dominate their moral culture – environmentalism, gender and racial equality, nuclear weapons and power, vegetarianism, the well-being of body and mind – issues with which Christianity and the Bible in particular are perceived as being wholly unconcerned and unconnected. At the same time, the social implications of conventional religious culture – respectability, sobriety, observance of social convention, observance of the Sabbath – have been rejected *en bloc*. Even where a moral goal appears to have survived (as with sobriety, especially in relation to driving), this has been remoralised in discourse in a form completely divorced from religiosity and Christian ethics.

The result has been that the generation that grew up in the sixties was more dissimilar to the generation of its parents than in any previous century. The moral metamorphosis directly affected the churches' domain: the decline of church marriage, the rise of divorce and remarriage, the rise of cohabitation in place of marriage (notably from the late 1970s), decreasing stigmatisation of illegitimacy, homosexuality and sexual licence, the growing recourse to birth control and abortion, and the irresistible social pressures for government liberalisation of restrictions on drinking, Sunday closing and recreation. The range of the changes in demography, personal relationships, political debate and moral concerns was so enormous that it did not so much challenge the Christian churches as bypass them. Of course, the new cultural environment affected the churches deeply, and transformed them fundamentally. Ecclesiastical change has been enormous: Vatican II and its aftermath, the *Honest to God* debate, the impact of protest against the Vietnam and Biafran wars, ecumenical discourse, feminism, the rise of environmentalism, and awareness of social and 'North–South' issues

Table 8.1 Confirmations in the Church of England, 1900–97

(a) *Numbers of confirmations 1900–97:*

1900	181,154	1960	190,713
1910	227,135	1970	113,005
1920	199,377	1980	97,620
1930	144,323	1990	59,618
1940	142,294	1997	40,881
1950	142,294		

(b) *Confirmations by sex per 1,000 of population aged 12–20 years:*

	Males	*Females*		*Males*	*Females*
1956	28.1	40.8	1968	16.9	26.1
1957	n/a	n/a	1969	15.9	24.8
1958	27.6	40.6	1970	15.3	24.2
1959	n/a	n/a	1971	14.6	23.4
1960	27.6	40.9	1972	13.8	22.4
1961	26.7	39.3	1973	12.8	20.7
1962	24.7	36.7	1974	12.1	19.6
1963	22.0	32.0	1975	12.0	19.1
1964	20.7	31.3	1976	11.3	18.3
1965	19.1	29.5	1977	11.1	18.4
1966	18.8	27.8	1978	11.1	18.6
1967	17.7	27.6	1979	10.7	18.2

Sources: R. Currie, A. Gilbert and L. Horsley, *Churches and Churchgoers: Patterns of Church Growth in the British Isles since 1700*, Oxford, Oxford University Press, 1977, pp. 167–8; *Yearbook of the Church of England*, 1974, 1980–2000, and 1984, Statistical Supplement, p. 41.

(including the recent church involvement in the movement to eradicate Third World debt).[64] These developments have been important, but have had little success in putting the Christian back into British public morality. Since the 1960s, the churches have become increasingly irrelevant in the new cultural and ethical landscape. One example is hostility to abortion, which between the 1960s and late 1980s was perceived almost exclusively as a Christian (and mainly Roman Catholic) restatement of 'traditional' values, thereby uniting socialists, liberals and feminists as an act of faith in the new secular morality (in this case, of a woman's right to choose); by the 1990s, anti-abortion sentiment was developing as a secular and close to environmentalist credo in which the 'sacredness' of life should be protected from human interference just as the planet required protection from global warming.

The greatest impact of the dechristianisation of British morality has been upon women. The residue of Christian female piety, which by the late 1940s and 1950s had been deposited in the extremely vigorous representation of the respectable wife, mother and young girl, was washed away in the cultural revolution of the 1960s. British women secularised the construction of their identity, and the churches started to lose them. The exodus started with the young. As Table 8.1(a) shows, in the Church of England the number of confirmations (usually occurring between the ages of 12 and 18) was still extremely strong as late as 1960 and then started to fall steeply and unremittingly. Table 8.1(b) indicates that female confirmations were always higher than males, but it was in 1961–3 that the proportion of girls taking this ceremony started to fall steeply, halving in the period 1961–74. Even though male confirmations were also falling (and indeed at a faster rate), the critical fact here is that female confirmation was still extremely high in the 1950s whilst male confirmation was already low and falling. Male alienation from religion certainly seems to have been more progressive than female alienation, and men's membership links with churches in the twentieth century may have been held in place in large part as a propriety – in deference to the more resilient religiosity of wives and mothers. Men were partners to religious respectability; when women no longer needed to be 'chaperoned' to church, and indeed did not want to go at all, men no longer had 'to keep up appearances' in the pews. Victorian evangelicals were probably right: when women stopped identifying with church, so did men. The British schoolgirl of the mid-1950s faced playground taunts for proclaiming atheism; by contrast, the 'atheist' schoolgirl of the mid-1960s was rapidly becoming the norm.[65] Freed from religious constraints on 'female respectability', the secularisation of the form of marriage and child baptism (domestic occasions orchestrated conventionally by women) arose from the early 1970s onwards by negotiation between females of different generations (principally between mother and adult daughter). The religious alienation of the next generation of children followed. If this analysis is correct, the keys to understanding secularisation in Britain are the simultaneous de-pietisation of femininity and the de-feminisation of piety from the 1960s.

CHAPTER NINE

THE END OF
A LONG STORY

—— .◆. ——

At the start of the third millennium, we in Britain are in the midst of secularisation. This is not a novel statement, but this book has sought to show that what is taking place is not merely the continuing decline of organised Christianity, but the death of the culture which formerly conferred Christian identity upon the British people as a whole. Whereas previously, men and women were able to draw upon a Christian-centred culture to find guidance about how they should behave, and how they should think about their lives, from the 1960s a suspicion of creeds arose that quickly took the form of a rejection of Christian tradition and all formulaic constructions of the individual. For some scholars what is being described here is the condition of post-modernity – the obliteration of agreement on core realities and metanarratives by which the present and the past are understood. If a core reality survives for Britons, it is certainly no longer Christian.

To make this case, this book has had to show the poverty of existing social-science theory governing the understanding of religious decline. Traditionally in Britain, secularisation has been understood in terms of dichotomies between city and countryside, and between proletarian and bourgeois. These dichotomies were drawn from the evangelical–Enlightenment bipolarities by which so much of nineteenth- and twentieth-century British society was understood. Social science inherited from evangelicalism the ways of perceiving religion and society, and it has thereby constricted the study of the subject within those early nineteenth-century parameters. The metanarrative resulting from this meeting of evangelicalism and Enlightenment failed to explain what happened to religiosity, when it happened or why it happened. Even to this day, many social scientists (especially some sociologists of religion) tend to be disinterested in these questions, including the crucial one of 'when'.[1] Without an interest in the timing of secularisation, there can be no serious identification of causes.

Scholars who have moved significantly away from social-scientific (and indeed scientific) method have already charted part of the route to a new understanding of the end of the Christian religion. The 'philosophical anthropology' of Charles Taylor is important in this regard.² Taylor argues that in the mediaeval and early-modern worlds, religious beliefs 'sank into the background'. He writes: 'In our public and private life of prayer, penance, devotion, religious discipline, we lean on God's existence, use it as the pivot of our action, even when we aren't formulating our belief, as I use the stairs or banister in the course of my focal action'. Taylor proposes that one of the fundamental changes wrought by modernism in the late eighteenth and early nineteenth centuries was the movement of Christian faith from the background to the foreground of the individual's identity; 'theology comes indexed to a personal vision, or refracted through a particular sensibility'. However, he says, this place of religion in personal life was fundamentally and permanently changed in the twentieth century:

> Virtually nothing in the domain of mythology, metaphysics, or theology stands in this fashion as publicly available background today. But that doesn't mean that there is nothing in any of those domains that poets may not want to reach out to in order to say what they want to say, nor moral sources they descry there that they want to open for us. What it does mean is their opening [of] these domains, in default of being a move against a firm background, is an articulation of personal vision. It is one that we might come to partake in as well, as a personal vision; but it can never become again an invoking of public references, short of an almost unimaginable return – some might say 'regression' – to a new age of faith.³

Though Taylor's language is different, and at the risk of being mistaken and committing a disservice, there seems to me in his crafting of religious change a notion of pre-modernity, modernity and post-modernity, following similar contours to those outlined in this book. The last change Taylor ascribes to 'modernism', a timing which he locates in literature and the arts to the turn of the nineteenth–twentieth centuries, and the causes to the 'internalizing move of modern humanism, which recognises no more constitutive goods external to us'. The articulation of good – the very speaking of it – becomes less, he says, since as humanists we are fearful of formulaic responses, historical sham, and a 'moral assurance . . . which actually insulates us from the energy of true moral sources'. We also fall silent about 'the narrative construction of our lives' – in other words, we no longer articulate our lives as moral stories. As a moral philosopher, he says that whilst '[t]here are good reasons to keep silent', he urges us not to be, and to abjure modern (post-modern?) relativism about the absence of absolute good and 'hypergoods'.⁴ What Taylor may seem to be describing is post-modernity, but he calls it modernity.

Indeed, what divides analysis within the academy is the virtue of post-modernism as a theory and method of analysis, and post-modernity as an historical period. The cynics of post-modernity rely on the belief that in the year 2000 it is still modernism that is acting upon us as the agent of secularisation in an unbroken line stretching back to the late eighteenth or early nineteenth centuries. It is still the Enlightenment paradigm that they promulgate, that rationality was hostile to popular religion and the 'religious self'. To the supporters of post-modernity, this is fundamentally wrong. It is a failure to understand the nature of the evangelical age and the duration of its legacy. Instead of rationality and religion clashing in the Enlightenment, it is the story of the Enlightenment's boost to Christian religion, already well told, that needs to be more widely accepted.[5] Meanwhile, there are still too many scholars who misread the secularising impact of industrialisation and urbanisation, despite all the revisionist research of the 1980s and 1990s. The cumulative effect is that scholars from a wide variety of backgrounds falsely conflate our secularisation with what they think was the secularisation of the nineteenth century. They have failed to perceive the robustness of popular religiosity during industrialisation and urban growth between the 1750s and the 1950s.

This failure is caused by a focus on 'structures' (such as churches and social classes) to the neglect of 'the personal' in piety. The 'personal' is intrinsically wrapped up with language, discourses on personal moral worth, the narrative structures within which these are located, and the timing of change to these. Around 1800, with the fading of coercive religion (or what Charles Taylor calls 'background' religion, and 'the great chain of being'), religiosity became overwhelmingly discursive, dependent on bringing an evangelical narrative of the life story to the foreground of personal identity. These discourses were fundamentally gendered as, perhaps, they had always been, but where before 1800 Christian piety had been located in masculinity, after 1800 it became located in femininity. Paeans of praise were heaped on women's innate piety whilst brickbats were hurled at men's susceptibility to temptation. Enforcement of 'hypergoods' (again drawing on Taylor) was transferred from external agencies (the state churches) to the internal of the individual. Identity became something incredibly personal, a matter for deep personal enforcement, negotiation or neglect. In this 'system', women were the key, for it was their religiosity that mattered. It was their influence on children and men, their profession of purity and virtue, their attachment to domesticity and all the virtues located with that, which sustained discursive Christianity in the age of modernity.

This age lasted a century and half, from about 1800 to about 1960. Though these things are never instantaneous, the age of discursive Christianity then quite quickly collapsed. It did so, fundamentally, when women cancelled their mass subscription to the discursive domain of Christianity. Simultaneously, the nature of femininity changed fundamentally, shedding its veneer of piety and respectability, and becoming disjoined from the romance which provided women's personal narrative for femininity and piety. The 'promiscuous girl' of 1970, who was morally indifferent to her sexual activity if not proud of it, marked the end of evangelical discourse. A generation later in the 1990s, this secular moral aggression of young women had been translated into 'girl power'. Women still make up the majority of churchgoers. But they are overwhelmingly older women, raised under the old discourses, and who continue to seek affirmation of their moral and feminine identities in the Christian church. Men are proportionately under-represented as they always have been, but then Sunday church service is still an 'unmanly' site in discourse. The really important group that is missing from church is young women and girls. There is no longer any femininity or moral identity for them to seek or affirm at the British Christian church. It is their absence that marks the end of evangelical femininity and piety, and the fusion between the two.

Before 1800, Christian piety had been a 'he'. From 1800 to 1960, it had been a 'she'. After 1960, it became nothing in gendered terms. More than this, the eradication of gendered piety signalled the decentring of Christianity – its authority and its cultural significance. Scholars are increasingly coming to understand the relationship of Christianity to society in terms of gender, the body and sexuality. The way in which this relationship was configured changed in different ages, in what Foucault called different epistemes. But what has been new and unprecedented in the episteme of post-modernity since the 1960s has been the dissolution of gendered discursive Christianity. The ungendering of British Christianity signalled something greater: the 'absence' of what Jeremy Carrette has called 'a transcendent and normative ideal',[6] resulting in a religious vacuum into which considerable philosophical and theological energy is being poured in a search for a new way of corralling the human religious spirit when there is no centre and no coda. It is precisely because 'the personal' changed so much in the 1960s – and has continued to change in the four decades since – that the churches are in seemingly terminal decay and British Christian culture is in its death throes. Charles Taylor is right; it seems unlikely that there will ever be a return to an age of faith. The evangelical narrative has decayed; the discourses on gendered religiosity have withered. The search for personal faith is now in 'the New Age' of minor cults, personal development and consumer choice. The universal world-view of both Christianity and identity which prevailed until the 1950s seems impossible to recreate in any form.

The way of viewing religion and religious decline in Britain offered in this book – if it is correct – should have wider applicability. It may help to explain the near contemporaneous secularisation of Norway, Sweden, Australia and perhaps New Zealand, and should help to account for the rapid secularisation of much of Catholic Europe since the 1970s. Critically, it may also help to explain the North American anomaly. Throughout secularisation studies from the 1950s to the 1990s, the United States and

Canada have seemed difficult to fit in the British model of religious decline. A supposedly obvious 'secular' society of the twentieth century has sustained high levels of churchgoing and church adherence. Debate on this has gripped American sociologists of religion for decades without apparent resolution. Perhaps the answer lies in seeing the same discursive challenge as Britain experienced *emerging* in North America in the 1960s, but then not *triumphing*. A discursive conflict is still under way in North America. The Moral Majority and the evangelical fight back has been sustained in public rhetoric in a way not seen in Europe. North American television nightly circulates the traditional evangelical narrative of conversionism, with cable and satellite channels broadcasting religious issues in a way quite alien to Europe where, broadly, there is no meaningful audience for them. In the USA and to a lesser extent Canada, a discursive battle rages, and has raged, since the 1960s. Secular post-hippy culture of environmentalism, feminism and freedom for sexuality coexists beside a still-vigorous evangelical rhetoric in which home and family, motherhood and apple pie, are sustaining the protocols of gendered religious identity. Piety and femininity are still actively enthralled to each other, holding secularisation in check. In Foucauldian terms, North America may be experiencing an overlap of epistemes (of modernity and post-modernity).

And what of the British Christian churches? The scholar of religious decline is accustomed to studying churches, but the further from 1960 you look, the less relevant are they to such study. Churchpeople continue to examine religious decline in terms of what the churches are doing – their good and bad management – and have an endearingly optimistic faith in the future. In the midst of religious crisis in the 1960s, 1970s, 1980s and 1990s, churchpeople continued to predict a corner about to be turned in church decline.[7] But it did not happen and seems unlikely to happen. British culture is pioneering new discursive territory. As Foucault demonstrated in his studies of civilisations from the classical to the modern, religious discourses have 'governed' the self through rites which have constituted a series of

> techniques which permit individuals to effect, by their own means, a certain number of operations on their bodies, on their souls, on their own thoughts, on their own conduct, and this in a manner so as to transform themselves, modify themselves, and to attain a certain state of perfection of happiness, of purity, of supernatural power, and so on.[8]

This role of discursive Christianity seems to have stopped effecting these operations on the individual in Britain and much of Europe. The 'religious life' in which individuals imagined themselves, and which gave them the narrative structure for gendered discourses on religiosity to be located in their personal testimony, seems to have vanished. This is not the death of churches, for despite their dramatic decline, they will continue to exist in some skeletal form with increasing commitment from decreasing numbers of adherents.[9] Nor is it the death of belief in God, for though that too has declined, it may well remain as a root belief of people. But the culture of Christianity has gone in the Britain of the new millennium. Britain is showing the world how religion as we have known it can die.

CHAPTER TEN

POSTSCRIPT: THE MORTALITY OF CHRISTIAN BRITAIN RECONSIDERED

—— .◆. ——

INTRODUCTION

'The Church is one generation away from extinction', said Dr George Carey, Archbishop of Canterbury, on budget day 1999, describing Britain as having 'something of an allergy to religion'.[1] Despite many informed commentators having issued dire warnings about the demise of churches or Christianity in this country, the appearance of *The Death of Christian Britain* in December 2000 led a few Christians to want to shoot the herald – or at least they sent me Biblical texts and warnings that I was destined for hell, to be flung by the angels into the lake of fire.[2] A few Christian historians and sociologists, too, have been hostile. One accused me of 'enormous condescension' in having 'written rather pityingly about 1960s' Christians, depicting them as vainly swimming against the tide of historical inevitability – not saving but drowning',[3] whilst another accused me of being 'maybe a little gleeful' with the end of Christianity as a sense of self (and accusing me of using the word 'religiosity' as a 'somewhat pejorative' anti-Christian word).[4] But other Christian responses have been more positive, including several ministers and priests who wrote to me, and some British denominations and divinity colleges called on me to conduct seminars. Meanwhile, online discussion about the book has been vigorous at times, and some Christians have become strongly engaged with its ideas.[5] A few considered me under-committed; Stephen Logan criticised my failure to describe secularisation as 'good or bad', lambasting me for *failing* to celebrate the demise of Christianity.[6]

There may well be valid criticisms of this book – some under-researched issues, and some statements deserving better nuance with wider evidence. I will consider some of its shortcomings in this chapter. But though as a non-Christian, but not secularist, historian I claim not to be 'neutral', yet I am not seeking to take 'sides' (whatever those may be perceived to be) concerning faith, conversions and the place of religion in the present and past affairs of British public life. One reviewer took me in this book to be 'celebrating' and applauding the demise of Christian Britain.[7] I certainly do not celebrate Christian congregations in contraction, parish churches in crisis because of shortage of ministers, and church buildings up for sale. I am saddened by the pain experienced by communities (including my own) and the loss to the cultural fabric of the nation resulting from church closures. But I do celebrate the death of Christian Britain, if 'Christian Britain' is as I have defined it in this book: not as Christianity (and certainly not as the churches), but rather *the dominance of a Christian culture within British society*.[8] This book is about a popular culture that arose in the shadow of the Enlightenment and bifurcated between 'respectable' and 'rough'; the former dominated morally by providing distinctive gender definitions of piety (replacing an early-modern culture with very different definitions) which lasted from around 1800 to around 1960. Largely uncontested discourses of submission to Christian moral codes demanded that people perform protocols of behaviour (which I then went on to describe in their heavily gendered forms in Chapters 3 and 4). The culture was a hegemony maintained by acculturation, not by state enforcement. It might have been much flouted and ignored, but those who did so were branded deviants, miscreants and 'heathens', not just (or even mainly) by church clergy but by their families and communities. This was discursive power. The death of *that* was what my book was about – about locating its timing, its characteristics and circumstances.

I believe that I lived through that 'death' in the 1960s. And yes, I celebrated it both then and, increasingly, since as the magnitude of what happened in the cultural revolution of that decade becomes better appreciated. It freed me and British popular culture as a whole from the relentless misery of an inescapable Christian discourse which governed virtually all aspects of self-identity and expression, community-regulated leisure and domestic life (and to an extent economic life too). It was a culture that had, in its last decades between 1945 and 1960, been backed by the state: through harshly enforced censorship of books and theatres, Sunday closing in many places, of cinemas, public houses, theatres and even children's playparks, the banning of most forms of gambling, the harsh criminalisation of homosexual relations, and many other things besides. By the 1950s organised Christianity had become characterised by the support of a harsh and vindictive state apparatus that oppressed many pleasures without reason, and hurt the lives of many young people – especially women and gays. And it was the first of these who, in the view laid out in this book, took the lead role in and from the 1960s in overturning that regime, taking on the churches and wider cultural and civil institutions. The female discourse of domesticity was ideologically affirmed primarily by Christianity, but conveniently exploited by the law, commerce and many institutions (not least male trade unions). That discourse was also, in the argument of this book, the bulwark to Christian piety in this country: piety and femininity were mutually enslaved discourses. If domesticity died as a dominant discourse, so too did the churches as popular institutions. I believed at both a personal and intellectual level that the death of Christian culture as the dominant discourse of British life took place in the 1960s. This book sought to explore and explain it.

COMPETENCES AND METHODOLOGIES

Over the last forty years, religion has disappeared from much history writing because the 'secular' nature of Britain has been taken as axiomatic.[9] Like other social historians of religion, I am one who has sought to reinstate it in the consciousness of the history discipline. Events and recent developments have changed matters somewhat: the attacks of 9/11 in New York and of 7/7 in London, amongst others, and the rise during the 1990s and 2000s of a new assertive quality to conservative Christianity and its pressure groups on issues like abortion, homosexuality and blasphemy. This new appearance of what has been called 'resurgent' religion in the public sphere is not because British religion is 'growing'; church attendances, membership, baptisms, marriages and virtually all other indicators of religious rites have continued to slide in the period 2000–2008 as they have since the 1960s. In that regard, nothing has changed in the social reality of secularisation in Britain. But a *perception* of resurgence of religion in Britain has been brought on by emerging issues of religion in politics and moral campaigning, increased by the way in which Tony Blair 'came out' on television as a committed Christian in the closing months of his premiership in 2006 and then, on demitting office the following year, converted to Roman Catholicism.[10]

The disappearance of religion from British historiography of the late modern period has occurred side-by-side with declining interest in social class as the category of analysis in British social history. For what was a brief period, social class dominated the heyday of the social history of religion from the late 1950s to the 1970s, giving way in the 1980s and 1990s to a slow slide in interest in both. Whilst there had been slowly growing attention from the late 1980s to gender in religious history (not least in Hugh McLeod's work), there was as yet no noticeable interest in using gender as a *category of analysis* in relation to the general social history of secularisation.[11] Amongst social historians of religion, including the present author, social class was sustained as the only category of analysis worth considering, often passing muster as 'urbanisation' or some such surrogate category.

The analytical backbone to *The Death of Christian Britain* arose in 1996 when I turned to postmodernism and gender (when introduced by my new partner to women's history and discourse analysis, and when inspired by an article by Sarah Williams that rejected the primacy of social class and called for a 'linguistic turn' in the study of religion in Victorian Britain[12]).

Three related observations struck me: that religious decline in Britain only became really serious in the 1960s (a 'fact' known but largely sidestepped by academics), that any change in religious fortunes in that decade could not be explained by changes in social class (as broadly there were none of sufficient magnitude) but might be explained by changes in gender (which were profound), and that the way to demonstrate such a thing could not be through the traditional social-science route of church-led social history, but through a larger linguistic turn into a postmodern-inspired approach of discourse analysis and personal-testimony study.[13] With the addition of statistical analysis, none of these three main research methods was in itself original or novel, but their combined use in religious history was newer.

Novelty has induced some censure. A fair criticism of the discourse analysis is that I paid too little attention to Roman Catholicism, Anglo-Catholicism and non-evangelicalism generally, being 'overly syncretic', identifying similarities amongst British Christians but minimising their differences.[14] This criticism has come from a number of Catholic and Catholic-sensitive reviewers, including Sheridan Gilley, who noted that 'Catholics are treated simply as a species of conversionist Protestants'.[15] In my defence I focussed upon Protestantism, and evangelicalism in particular, because I argued that it was this brand of Christianity that set the pace in ideological, public policy and cultural terms in the nineteenth century, with evangelicals – through their energy, ideas and emphasis on action – having an impact in Britain far in excess of their numbers or civil status.[16] By 1900, evangelicals had attracted an intellectual support (from other church traditions especially), in parallel to popular gendered discourses on piety, which was so strong that the Christian culture they had nurtured proved resilient and seemingly impervious to moral refutation for a further half century; modern Christianity became dominated by these gendered discourses. Moreover, I was influenced, firstly, by Mary Heimann's well-received *Catholic Devotion in Victorian England* (1995) that emphasised the parallels rather than the contrasts between Catholic and Protestant (and which I suspected could be taken further), and, secondly, by the experience recounted by oral respondents and autobiographers between the 1880s and 1940s (some quoted in the book) that showed they attended services of both Catholic and Protestant churches with regularity and 'without discrimination' (the words of one woman from Glasgow). This was something perhaps lost in the 1950s and 1960s. I believe strongly that 'official' church history over-emphasises ecclesiastical separation between laity over the past two hundred years. Following the lead of Patrick Joyce in his shift from emphasising class difference in Victorian popular culture to empathising the shared vision of 'the common people', and acknowledging also Patrick Pasture's similar observations on Christianity from a Belgian context,[17] the people's history suggests a strong common Christian experience from 1800 to 1950. Ecclesiastical history has a tendency to divide the people in this period, cultural history to unite them.

Each can overdo its trend, but there is a different, street-level narrative of religious history still to be written from the cultural perspective, which excludes the starting point of Christian division and starts instead at that of the people's common culture. Shared cultural experiences are exposed in detail in Sarah Williams's work on folk religion in mid-twentieth-century London and Elizabeth Roberts's extensive interview work on women's churching rituals in Lancashire. There was a common religious life of the Christian people that crossed, and even to an extent ignored, church boundaries. I tried to contribute to this 'other' narrative.

The fact that discourse analysis hinted at postmodernism attracted its customary opprobrium, but sometimes it created theoretical confusion as well. One reviewer assumed that 'discourse' meant I was studying what he called 'the elites as the originators of Christian discourse', and ignoring working people and their temperance and teetotal movements (which were actually quite well cited in the book).[18] Another reviewer took me for being opposed to post-structuralism instead of in favour of it,[19] whilst a more general complaint was my 'highfalutin' language of 'discourses' and 'discursiveness', even when it contained valuable argument.[20] Actually, as postmodern method goes, this book is quite jargon-light (opening me to criticism from the theory-sensitive). Yet, those more understanding of the method rightly pointed out that the challenge to the social-scientific model of secularisation does not come solely from postmodernism, hinting at the possibility (as many have suggested) that a book with the same overall argument could have been accomplished by more traditional methods of evidence and argument.[21] Of this I am not sure. Traditional evidence would have pointed to a religious story framed by the same old periodisations around world wars and revolutions, historical changes resulting from the same old materialist causes of poverty and affluence, and would have crystallised as yet another washed-out proto- or post-Marxist approach leaving an unsatisfying inconclusiveness to what caused the 1960s' death of Christian culture. If modern cultural theory is accepted as having the capability of appreciating historical change differently (and in certain circumstances better), then it is worth trialling *in toto*.

It was the coupling of discourse analysis to the analysis of personal testimony – a technique I learned from Penny Summerfield's 1998 book *Reconstructing Women's Wartime Lives* – that I hoped would allow the book to deliver something rather different in the social history of religion (see page 115). Of course, some people are just thoroughly irreconcilable to the scholarly usage of oral testimony – which, one reviewer disdainfully dismissed, 'adds colour but hardly objectivity'.[22] Amongst academic historians this view is thankfully receding, and at least two of the harshest critics of the book's thesis are amongst oral history's most devoted advocates. The use of personal testimony (which includes autobiography, court testimonies and the like) is now better theorised and commands widespread support in the profession. Still, this does not overcome objections that my sample (from existing oral history archives) was either unrepresentative or, more commonly, that my 'reading' of the oral history and autobiographical material was biased or plain wrong. Hugh McLeod thinks that oral testimony by those born in the mid-twentieth century and later does not show any of the signs of reticence and 'stunting' of conceptions of religion that I have suggested.[23] Such difference of interpretation may arise from consulting different testimonies, or 'reading' them in different ways, but I feel that the 'stunting' is a demonstrable and analytically fruitful feature in exploring long-term change in 'religious' testimony. Certainly, the incomprehension I explored between the oral history interviewer and interviewee struck a chord amongst a number of readers who felt that often the Christian position was dismissed because of lack of understanding on the part of the interviewer concerning the nature and content of Christian concepts and ways of speaking. Two members of the clergy wrote to me acknowledging the validity of the notion of increasing 'silence' on religious matters in the language and personal narratives of people since the 1950s.[24]

From the combination of discourse analysis and analysis of personal testimony emerged my notion of 'discursive Christianity'. This seems to have been hated by general readers as jargon, but welcomed by many scholars who found it one of the least problematic innovations in the book.[25] But even those who warmed to the concept may not have appreciated precisely what is meant by it in the context of modern cultural theory. Sarah Williams found that I defined discursive Christianity in terms of a particular ideal type of evangelicalism – what she felt was a monolithic discourse that failed to look at differences within it. I agree it had that quality. But she was wrong to assume that I was looking 'to what extent a particular church-based discourse was absorbed by the culture at large'.[26] I was not trying to do that at all. The discourse was not church-authored nor monopolised, but, in common with all dominant modern discourses, was one refined and hybridised by hundreds of independent Christian organisations, through thousands of authors writing in church, independent and secular journals, novels and obituaries. Indeed, there is hardly an official church source on the subject consulted in the book; I didn't use sermons, and I didn't use church policy documents. And the reason I did not use those things is that the Christian discourse of gendered pieties was never formally formulated by the churches. Whilst some elements (notably male 'heathens') were broadcast by evangelicals in particular, such discourse was not a policy like church welfare or poor-relief policy. Nor is discourse the same as ideology. 'Discursive Christianity' is like neither of these. Discourses, as Foucault and modern theorists have defined them (and as they have been studied by hundreds of cultural historians) are to do with injunctions on conduct formed, circulated and hybridised in culture as a whole – popular culture, religious culture, political culture, but a cultural formation, not a policy one.

But Williams then goes on to a more powerful and insightful point of criticism. She is a scholar who presaged my work in this book with her own excellent research which suggested the need to reconsider the centrality of social class to analysing religious formation and secularisation.[27] So in that sense she backs the task of shifting social class to one side – not dispensing with it, but re-evaluating it in the light of bigger and more connected discourses. But, she says,

> there is a sense in which Brown is in danger of simply replacing one meta-narrative based on themes of modernisation and class with one based on the imposition of a powerful official discourse on the society as whole. 'Social class' has then merely been replaced by 'discursive power' as the key to religiosity. What is missing in this approach is the diversity and complexity of popular definitions of religiosity.[28]

She is surely right when she then went on to say that people were not passive receivers of discourse, but participated actively 'in shaping their own culture in matters of religion' as they did in all other matters. This is an interesting reference to wider debates in cultural history about the manner in which discourse works – one that involves an (unavoidable?) tension between the way discourses limit humans' choices within their own cultures, versus the agency of the individual man or woman to negotiate between, around or past those discourses.[29] But postmodernists get an unfair press on this. In a book on historical theory, I wrote: 'People's minds, conscious or unconscious, are not passive vessels for containing discourses. Rather, the individual constructs their own identity by drawing on the discursive construction of the self available in society at large'.[30] In this regard, in *The Death of Christian Britain*, I did not deny agency to the individual. One example of negotiation of discourse comes in the exceptionally candid oral interview of Ronald Walker (see pages 118–21), whilst other hints at the torture of such negotiation come in the testimony of Paula Queen (see page 184) and her grief at the death of discourse. The agency of the individual is not denied by postmodern method, and certainly not in the way that Marxist approaches of previous decades tended to see social class as an unavoidable economic determinant of religious affiliation and practice. But there is always a tension between the individual and culture. At the end of the day, if discourse analysis is an important tool for the social scientist and historian (and much of my profession agree that it is), then we have to look at how discourse is something cultural – i.e. something exchanged between individuals in mutually recognisable forms – thereby detracting from the role of the individual in constantly creating *individual* cultures. Culture is not the individual; by definition culture transcends the individual. Otherwise, there would be no social exchange and, in this case, no common beliefs of Christians within and between churches. The historian will get nowhere unless he or she looks *to some extent* at how individuals are moulded by cultural forces within the society in which they live and breathe. This is not to deny that individuals participated in this process, as Williams says, but culture is not something that cloaks the individual alone.

WAS THE DEATH ILL-CONCEIVED? CULTURAL CHANGE, SOCIOLOGICAL CHANGE, THEOLOGICAL CHANGE

In 2000, Hugh McLeod wrote that 'historians of many different kinds are agreed that secularisation is the central "story" of Western Europe's modern religious history, but they offer quite different, and sometimes incompatible, versions of how it actually happened.' He wrote a masterly study of European secularisation between the 'crazy' and 'holy and terrible year' of 1848 and 'the even crazier, more terrible and completely unholy year' of 1914. He explained that most historians of the last thirty years of the twentieth century, aware of the severe decline of churches since the 1960s, were tempted to look to the late Victorian and Edwardian period mainly in order to trace the origins of this later decline.[31] For my part, constantly tracing 'origins' seemed to ignore the obvious: that religious decline was a massive event of the 1960s which, in many regards (such as in the scale of gender change and youth revolt, and their impact upon organised Christianity), was in *no way* presaged in the nineteenth century.

This book constituted shifting my own focus – perhaps obsession – on nineteenth-century urbanisation and ecclesiastical adaptation to the twentieth century. It is a move of which many specialist religious historians have approved. Jeremy Morris has noted the power of 'predetermined conclusions as to church decline in the Victorian period which dominated the literature in the 1950s, 60s and 70s, which implicitly or explicitly linked a decline in religion to the modernisation thesis of sociology'.[32] The first historian to really lay out the emptiness of the theory was Jeff Cox in 1982, and his work then and since to expose the 'master' narrative of secularisation in historians' thinking has been an important element in the work of all of us who are concerned to expose theory and extend and validate the importance of evidence.[33] But this has since been taken up by some religious sociologists, such as Grace Davie and the American Peter Berger in his recent disavowal of secularisation theory of which he had previously been a world-leading proponent.[34]

My book raised larger questions about the dominance of secularisation theory, its origins in the very definition of religiosity at the start of the nineteenth century, and thus the built-in nature of the self-proof that theory leads to. David Nash is one who felt that my book contributed towards an undermining of the 'broad and homogenizing process' of secularisation as envisaged by sociologists.[35] He deprecated the sense of inevitability and longevity built into the process, and the way in which it has caused (and continues to cause) historians studying every stage of modern history to be '[b]rowbeaten into thinking that religion must be, by definition, in recession'.[36] Historical inquiry has been compromised, the sting plucked from it by a sociological inevitability and a disinterest in timing and causes. In one sense, the historian has been reclaiming the story of religion from sociology.

Indeed, Nash points to the uses of an older-fashioned historical method to be exploited in chasing out the historical flaws in the history of secularisation. Nash is happy with the advent of a postmodern method, and a focus on lived lives and the narratives that shape and provide self-understanding, but is less happy with the remaining sense of my describing what he calls 'an irremovable moment that has passed'; I may have changed the history of the process, he says, but the inevitable endpoint remains in *The Death of Christian Britain* (the title as well as the text). To better this, he thinks my argument does not go far enough. He calls for an end to endpoints in secularisation studies – to study where religion and religious narratives have survived the 'death of Christian Britain' in, he argues, 'slimming culture in the West' and in therapy and new age culture, in drug and substance-abuse rehabilitation regimes, supported by celebrities who search for 'therapy-based salvation'.[37] Nash is one of a number who point to the residue of Christian narratives of redemption and conversion in post-sixties Britain, indicating, it is proposed, something less than the secularised culture I imagined in this book.[38] I am happy to think about ways of removing endpoints, inevitabilities and the ineluctable from the historical narrative. But the death of a dominant discourse is still that – a death. It might survive as one *competing narrative* in a multicultural society of many faiths and lots of no-faiths (however we label these). But that does not negate the passing of the time when a Christian discourse was hegemonic. And are post-1960s secularised narratives of Christian conversions – including 'therapy-based salvation' – evidence enough to suggest a survival of Christian narrative? These are *residues*, not salient *Christian* narratives that continue to engineer British society and morality; they have been rendered de-Christianised – in some parts atheist, in most parts religiously indifferent. A conversion narrative is merely a structure, not in itself a discourse. Just because Christmas is the structure of a pagan festival does not signify that Britain today worships paganism. The study of changing discourses within rituals and narrative structures has long been a productive area of historical inquiry, and I have gone further recently in exploring the gendered nature of the evangelical conversion narrative and the period when it held indomitable sway.[39] But there is little sensible *religious* comparison to be drawn between, on the one hand, the evangelical Christian conversion and, on the other, a conversion narrative in an atheistic novel, in holistic alternative therapy or (as I will come on to) in feminism. If narratives do not *serve* Christianity, they are not Christian: they have been de-Christianised, and even as a conversion narrative can no longer be claimed as a province of Christendom.

Since 2000, narratives of religious decline have become matters of intensified interest across different disciplines and different countries. Sociologists, philosophers and anthropologists have been chewing on the nature of 'the secular' with renewed vigour.[40] The most ambitious has been Charles Taylor in *A Secular Age*[41] in which, though he affirms with many caveats the secularisation thesis, he envisages the secular age as not an absence of religion but a multiplication of options from within an ever-growing range of spiritualities and religions. Key here for him is a growing search for *authenticity* in the western individual's search for self-expression – one sourced from, but by no means confined by, the aspirations of the sixties in an 'expressive revolution' that has deeply alienated late twentieth-century generations from the churches (which, Taylor rightly observes, find it hard to talk to the millennium generation).[42] In a different approach, Talal Asad in *Formations of the Secular* focusses particularly on the link between religion and the state, and looks at 'the secular' as a product of secularism framed by the colonial issue of a Europe encountering Islam, and by the secular condition as a perfection of the European Enlightenment.[43] Other sociologists, notably Steve Bruce, sustain pretty traditional social-scientific approaches to the inevitable process of religious decline. But sociologists and historians to an extent are talking past each other over secularisation. Historians find difficulty in engaging with quite such sweeping concepts and ideas that are, in their view, at best loosely pinned down empirically, and which often have a poor recognition of the importance of dates and the causes of historical change associated with them. This is why the recent rise of international historical interest in the twentieth century, and especially the 1960s, has been so valuable, bringing together the parallels in experience over religion and secularisation between countries like Australia, Belgium, Britain, Canada, Germany, the Netherlands and Sweden.[44] Behind each of these, to greater or lesser extents, has been a critique of secularisation as an adjunct to modernisation in the period 1750–1950 and a rise of interest in approaches to the 1950–2000 period ranging from the merely statistising to the postmodern and gendered. What Michael Gauvreau says of Canada can extend more broadly: 'The central difficulty with the "modernisation as secularisation" pillar that undergirds the structure of Canadian social history is that it has largely lost any concrete point of reference in actual historical contexts or events.'[45] Underlying it all has been the presumption that the journey from rural to urban society, from agricultural to industrial, has also been, step for step, the journey from a faith-centred, Christian culture to an unbelieving, secularising one. This is now severely disrupted as a pattern of thought amongst historians of secularisation, with cultural historians in Britain having shifted considerably towards denouncing the inevitability of the secularisation theory.[46] The rise of multi-faith societies is equally no longer seen as the necessary accompaniment to secularisation: 'Pluralisation of denominations started in the countryside and then spread to cities, not vice versa.'[47]

If some sociologists (like Peter Berger and Grace Davie) no longer equate secularisation with modernisation, they still seem more reluctant than historians to admit that religious pluralism can be an agent of religious growth.[48] Yet a few sociologists are shifting their ground. David Herbert in his broad sociological review of rethinking religion in the modern world agreed that 'to assess the social significance of religion, secularisation theorists measure the wrong things'.[49] He went on:

> Although one may expect a general correlation between church attendance and the social influence of religion, a far better indication is given by looking at the way religion influences people's lives and a good way to do this is to look at the texts and artefacts of popular culture and oral history.

The same methodology is implied in Davie's use of Hervieu-Léger's concept of a 'chain of memory' that transmits Christian culture between generations and seems to be close to the inter-generational personal testimony I exploited in Chapter 8. However, the critical issue that I posed in this book is recognising when this chain broke down. Many scholars recognise this breach of the continuity in Christian culture – especially between mother and daughter – wrought by the 1960s.[50] But Davie has made an entire hypothesis out of the memory *surviving* that breach of the chain, an issue to which I will return in the last section.

Where I sense that this book has generated more interest for its methodology is in the idea of 'discursive Christianity'. For liberal Christian commentators, what I describe in the decay of discursive Christianity 'is the death of Christianity as a meta-narrative'.[51] David Herbert remarks that this is an important and more fruitful way to measure the social significance of religion, and notes quite rightly the role of education in maintaining discourse (in Foucauldian terms, in circulating it and hybridising it for survival and sustained relevance). This is quite right, and Herbert points to parallel work on Egypt and how 'discursive Islam' survived Islamic de-politicisation in the 1960s.[52] But not all are happy with how well the concept of discursive Christianity is deployed in this book. Jeremy Morris thinks the way I use it 'homogenizes' sources which have subtle differences and show changes in character over the period, and presents 'discursive Christianity' as 'semi-detached' from the social and political mainstream. There is an unavoidable conundrum here. He is right that I present a view of a *core* discursive Christianity over the period from 1800 to 1960, differentiated only by gender and largely not by time period or locality. But this is deliberate and unavoidable, since, in line with much feminist historiography (which stresses continuity in discourse on gendered roles over centuries) and discourse theory (which considers discourse as dominant and hegemonic across society), the fundamental, underlying discourse about male and female roles stayed the same in modernity. Men's place was in the world, women's was in the home. These gendered discourses varied only at the margins, were 'hybridised' by new users and circulators of it, and left very little freedom to the individual author to vary discourse (largely at the level of textual content, not the overall meaning).[53] Now, there may be profound reasons to dispute or modify that argument, and to look to ways in which the protocols of behaviour commanded by discourses varied by time and place. I can think of great variations around Britain in the Victorian period in the expected ways of expressing 'respectability', of religious dress (especially for women) and of Sabbath conduct. But there remained at the heart of these variations a *core* discourse on female domesticity, the innate femininity of the qualities of human piety, and men's constant susceptibility to the temptations of drink, gambling and sex. These *core* discourses were the same in London, Lincoln or Lerwick, and the same in 1850 as in 1950.[54]

Morris and others suggest that my own account of the changing persistence, and in some cases disappearance, of the evangelical discourse (such as from boys' magazines in the inter-war period) indicates secularisation. But discourse is not measured by rises and falls like barometric pressure (or churchgoing changing by percentage points). Discourse is about a *dominance*, and that dominance is not negated by the shifting patterns of its circulation – only by its end. The discourse on gendered piety disappeared from boys' magazines in the 1920s and 1930s, but was sustained strongly in girls' and women's magazines where it survived into the 1950s. This signified the increasing discursive burden being imposed on women, with a hardening in the late 1940s and 1950s evident in the pro-natalism campaign of government and the final blast of the feminisation of religion which was inflicted upon the young women of mid-century.[55] The victory of the traditional discourse on women's roles in the late 1940s, as Penny Summerfield chronicles and I tried to trace in relation to religion, is not to be seen from a post hoc perspective as a trend on the way to secularisation, but as a final and extremely vigorous, and in its time unrelenting, campaign to keep girls in the home. And turning closer to analysis of women's autobiographies for the 1940s and 1950s, the historian feels the intensity of that discourse.[56] Finally, theological and institutional controversy, Morris further suggests, must have had an impact on the contours of popular belief, and I left that out of this book. That is true, but because, as he rightly suggests, I was not producing a comprehensive survey of belief but focussing on secularisation. Religious controversy and scandal I have tackled in a recent book – though it must be said that, whilst the ritual controversy was clearly powerful around 1900, viewed through the lens of popular culture and personal testimony, remarkably little of it (beyond Catholic–Protestant antagonisms) made a lasting impression in the twentieth century.[57]

Despite the reaction of some critics, I do not believe cultural historians should become more like ecclesiastical historians. For decades, many of the latter missed the vitality of faith beyond church walls in the past – its diversity, its folk qualities, its variation into forms that many clergy abhorred or, at best, ignored as unfashionable, uncouth and 'pagan'. Discourse analysis, coupled with personal testimony, is one vital means for penetrating the extra-ecclesiastical dimensions of popular religion, getting into the minds, the bedrooms and the wardrobes of people as they conjured themselves as Christian men and women.

WAS THE DEATH LATE? VISIONS OF THE INDUSTRIAL WORLD

The majority of *The Death of Christian Britain* is about the world of modernity from 1800 to about 1950. It is about characterising this period as one of continuities in the culture of Christian Britain – its faith, discourses and protocols of behaviour. Attacking the notion that industrialisation and urbanisation secularised the British people was quite an acceptable and welcomed argument for many religious historians, who felt it to have long been an error of church and social history. But for others, this was an argument that was wrong in principle or degree – 'too dedicated to revolutionist historiography'[58] or ignoring the evidence of more gradual decline in the observance of religion.

The principle at stake here is that of gradualism in secularisation – the supposed long-term nature of secularisation and its centrality to long-term modernisation. Traditional secularisation theory is founded on gradualism, inevitability and the grinding down of Christianity and religious sensibility in general in the modernising world of Enlightenment thought, industrial work and urban living. Its greatest current sociological exponent is Steve Bruce, who maintains an unrelenting adherence to sociological orthodoxy even as some recent advocates (like Peter Berger) defect,[59] whilst Hugh McLeod, though far from being in favour of secularisation theory, writes that the 'gradual decline of Christendom is one of the central themes in the history of western Europe and North America during the last three centuries'.[60] There were great changes to the way in which religion found social significance between 1800 and 1960 (including during 1870–1930 declining churchgoing but a rising relative importance attached to church membership, baptism of children and the pan-class culture of respectability). Yet this was far from constituting secularisation, but rather a religious readjustment to keep Christian culture dominant; for as long as the hegemony of discursive Christianity remained, the secular society remained a long way off. Evidence for the sustained importance of this culture comes in various forms. My description of 'the last great puritan age' echoes the work of Olaf Blaschke on Germany who, working at the same time as me, argued in 2002 that the 'second confessional age' of the nineteenth and early twentieth centuries should be regarded as a period of immense Christian strength, only collapsing in the 1960s.[61] On a smaller scale, Dorothy Entwistle has shown in a number of studies of working-class Lancashire based on oral history how the church and church rituals remained absolutely central to identities and experiences, not least for children but for adults too, into the 1920s and 1930s; the churches and chapels, she concludes, had an 'enduring attraction'.[62]

Whilst many church historians agree with this book's contention on the strength of Christian culture in the industrial society from the 1800s to the 1950s, many have queried aspects of my characterisation of it – notably of evangelicalism. Mary Clare Martin has criticised me and earlier historians of childhood and the family for contending 'that fear of retribution and pressure to repent were frequent and disturbing features of children's lives between 1740 and 1870, particularly in the early nineteenth century'. She argues from some first-hand recollections of individuals in Walthamstow and Leyton, then two Essex villages, that there was little evidence of children being taught about hell and those that were did not record it 'as harmful'. 'Fear', she says, was used as a sense of awe and reverence rather than terror.[63] From her limited evidence Martin may well be right, and I have no doubt that parents, teachers and others mediated the discursive power of death-bed culture for children. But that part of my study was not dealing with experience; it was dealing with discourse, and there is no doubt (which she did not challenge) that the literature written and published for children by evangelicals, and published in magazines such as those of the Primitive Methodists, and which I quoted from in this book, was designed to induce terror in children by talking of hell, eternal damnation and the dangers of a child dying without repentance (see page 65). This character of evangelical literature for children in the early nineteenth century is hard to deny, and, though it declined from the later nineteenth century, it retained a presence in some evangelical rhetoric (against which many parents even today still protect their children).

The closing years of the puritan age attract special attention. Simon Green does not approve of this book's description of the 1950s; it may have been 'bold social analysis', he says, but 'It is also wholly inadequate social history.' Calling me a 'child of the 1960s', he insinuates that my description of the post-war era as 'the age of austerity' was somehow new and outlandish when, in fact, this title has been much used of the late 1940s and early 1950s.[64] There is rising agreement amongst economic historians that the years 1950 to 1973 were 'the golden years' of British economic growth, and many writers like Sandbrook and Jarvis show that the British people (beyond the 'educated classes, widely understood', as Green quaintly puts it) experienced a rapid rise in prosperity.[65] But the rise in consumption was very much restricted to the late 1950s, from 1957 onwards. With stop–go policies, it was difficult for British working people to make a substantive growth in consumption, and to acquire new homes, and the improvement of working-class life was held in check not from want of employment, but from want of affordable good housing, domestic space and household goods to buy. The rise in consumption figures for workers came late. There were 2 million private taxed cars on British roads in 1950 (with ownership restricted to 14 per cent of households) and this rose to over 3 million (at 28 per cent by 1960), much of it in the boom years of 1957–61 – with a tripling between 1950 and 1966 accounted for in large measure by the sixties boom, not by the 1950s. Television licences rose from 3 million in 1953 to 4 million in 1955, but it took the next five years for them to rise to 10 million, whilst washing machine ownership also rose sharply after 1955.[66] In this way, the 'age of austerity', as a consumer phenomenon, is strongly identified with the late 1940s and early 1950s, and the age of plenty is later and mostly in the 1960s.

But the 1950s were not merely 'austere' in consumption terms. As I made plain in Chapter 8, austerity was also experienced as religious revival for some (especially the young and females) and in the way austerity was experienced as expectation of moral behaviour and deportment. Reactions to this have varied, from those who regard my description as too extreme to those who regard it as not extreme enough. On the one side, Green denied what he considered the 'emerging professional consensus' of historians that the 1950s were marked by religious revival, arguing that church membership fell and that the true character of the decade was of sustained religious decline.[67] McLeod also downgrades the 'revival' image, rehabilitating the 1950s as a decade of gradual liberal intellectual growth, increasing commitment amongst Christians and limited revival amongst teenagers and young adults; he argues that 'it would be hard to justify' my claim that the later 1940s and 1950s witnessed the greatest growth in church members that Britain had experienced since the mid-nineteenth century.[68] Though historians now agree that there was some church growth in the 1950s, Green says it was 'little more than a minor redistribution amongst the practising religious towards the Establishment'[69] in England. In this way, the growth is seen by McLeod and Green to be small-scale and marginal, making little impression on the long-term trend of decline.

I dispute this, and I do so with greater vigour now than I did at the time of writing the first edition. Let me first look to the situation in the churches with the least evidence of revival – the Free Churches (which were called Nonconformist or dissenting churches in the nineteenth century). There was a general stability to the membership of many dissenting churches from the end of the war until 1956–7. The Methodist Church reached a plateau of membership at around 742,000 to 746,000 between 1946 and 1956, and only from 1957 is there a discernible fall.[70] In the Baptist and Congregationalist churches, there were minor falls in membership; in their Scottish branches the falls were small, and in the case of the Congregationalists there was level membership in 1946–56, whilst in England over the same period the Baptists fell from 218,727 to 198,597 and the Congregationalists from 223,634 to 193,341. The biggest falls by far were in Wales, where a crisis of dissent from the inter-war years continued in the 1950s; Wales deserves a detailed study to ascertain the causes of this early and steep collapse of dominant Christian culture.[71]

But these were relatively small churches. In the larger churches in the 1950s there was significant growth. Leaving aside the sustained growth in numbers of practising Roman Catholics (which reached a peak of mass attendance in 1966), the Church of England reached its post-war peak of Easter Day communicants in 1958–62, the Church of Scotland reached a post-war membership peak in 1956, the Presbyterian Church of England in 1960 and the Presbyterian Church in Ireland in 1967.[72] McLeod does not offer any direct evidence against the proposition of rising church membership, and admits a rise of 24 per cent between 1947 and 1956 in Easter Day communicants as a proportion of English adults (a rise of 2.6 per cent per annum).[73] By any standards that was large, and was unprecedented in the twentieth century. But McLeod seeks to challenge this argument of unprecedented church growth principally by switching the argument to something different – churchgoing where he rightly detects stasis in the 1950s. Church membership and churchgoing are two different indicators, and they don't always move together. In relation to adherence, some churches were performing less well than others in the 1950s, but there was no collapse of church membership, no mass haemorrhage of the faithful, whilst in relation to churchgoing there was equally no sudden collapse in the 1950s (as there was to be in the 1960s).

Indeed, there was something of a religious boom in the late 1940s and 1950s.[74] This is borne out by statistics. The Church of England post-war baptism rate stayed buoyant, reaching a peak (amongst the years with recorded data) in 1950 of 632 births per 1,000 (up from 597 in 1947), and only from 1958 does it fall permanently below 600.[75] The growth in youth membership and religious participation is widely attested from statistics and qualitative sources, and McLeod himself produces a table of data that shows that female confirmations per 1,000 of population aged over 12 rose continuously and sharply from 1948 to 1960, with the 1960 peak (at 40.9 per 1,000) being the highest since before 1934, whilst male confirmations also reached a post-war peak (of 28.1) in 1956.[76] This boom in religious recruitment can also be seen in the recruitment success figures (see Figure 8.1, p. 189), with the Church of England's success in turning baptised persons into confirmations rising from 35.8 per cent in 1948 to 43.8 per cent in 1954, its highest recorded figure in the twentieth century, and the Church of

Scotland's rising from 67 per cent in 1938 to its all-time peak of 128 per cent in 1955. This was staggering church growth, of a kind unique in both the Church of England and the Church of Scotland in the late modern era, and not seen in any significant church since the short periods of religious revival affected Methodism in the nineteenth century (when some branches achieved unrepeated figures ranging between 3.4 and 13.6 per cent per annum during the revivals of 1859, 1876 and 1882).[77] After 1918, growth rates in virtually all British Protestant churches were routinely of the order of 1.0 to 2.0 per cent per annum, mostly minus figures. Therefore, what happened during 1945–56 was really remarkable. Even if there had been a fall in indicators of religiosity in the late 1930s and during wartime, and even if not all of the levels of religiosity of that decade were to be repeated, the growth in religiosity come the peace was nonetheless strikingly large and sudden. Fed by a powerful revival of the Sunday School movements in those denominations, what the Church of England and the Church of Scotland achieved between 1945 and 1957 was not only unprecedented in British established churches, but was of a scale unseen since Victorian revival.[78]

Coming from an opposite viewpoint to those critics, Matthew Grimley takes an even wider definition of moral austerity than I did. In his view, even if I described Britain of the period 1945–63 accurately as 'the nation's last Puritan age', I was at fault in limiting this to sexual morality. Grimley writes that '[Brown] misses the important point that it was also a period in which there remained a residual, if a greatly attenuated, sense of Puritanism as a continuing tradition in national culture, a sense that was lost thereafter'. He makes an interesting case for there being something larger at work. He identifies a change in English national identity appearing before the 1960s, in what he calls the 'decline of the language of national providence in the 1950s', marked in part when the notion of Britain as a Protestant country became unacceptable through 'immigration of a substantial non-Christian religious population'.[79] The problem here is twofold. Firstly, his conception of 'Britain' transmogrifies into 'England' at various points, making it a little difficult to pin down what territory, and identity, he is actually referring to. Secondly, his argument misidentifies the periodisation of immigrations. The immigrants of the 1940s, 1950s and 1960s were overwhelmingly Christian, dominated by the movement of peoples from the Caribbean. Asian migration of non-Christian peoples only became comparable in numerical terms in the late 1960s and 1970s. In all, from 1953 to 1961, 240,650 came from the West Indies, but only 69,800 from India and 42,250 from Pakistan (including East Pakistan, which in 1971 became Bangladesh).[80] Yet, despite those caveats, Grimley makes a convincing case for *something* changing in the British/English character in the 1950s, though I think his case is stronger amongst English intellectuals than the population at large for whom the real change came in the next decade.

WAS THE DEATH PREMATURE? THE 1960s IN RELIGIOUS HISTORY

Before *The Death of Christian Britain* appeared, a number of historians had identified the importance of the 1960s to secularisation in different parts of the world. In 1997, David Hilliard broached the subject in an article on Australia, whilst Peter van Rooden did the same for the Netherlands.[81] Since 2000, the identification of the caesura in Christian culture in 1960s' Britain has led to a number of key scholars recognising important aspects of that trauma, and making broader estimations of the applicability of that timing to other nations. Amongst many studies, I would point to Patrick Pasture, writing from a Belgian base, who is in no doubt about the 1960s' impact: 'What really happened is mainly a fundamental break with history.'[82] In Canada, Stuart Macdonald has identified in a statistical study that, though some churches did not follow a British-like pattern, three of the large Protestant denominations did, involving a sudden and dramatic move from growth to a permanent religious decline, whilst work by Michael Gauvreau is absorbing the new attention to the 1960s and to the European experience more generally as a framework for understanding Canadian trajectories of religious transformation.[83] Wim Damberg has shown for German Catholicism that there was a surge of church attendance in the late 1940s, after which a moderate decline set in during the 1950s to accelerate in the early 1960s and, again, during 1968–74.[84] This type of pattern of change in the 1960s is now appearing more commonly from international historical studies.

The question of the suddenness of change to religious culture in Britain has also been emerging as of increasing interest to historians.[85] The most significant study of all, that by Hugh McLeod, is an excellent international examination of the religious crisis of the 'long sixties' from 1958 to 1974. Surveying England, western and northern Europe, North America and Australasia, he concludes: 'In the religious history of the West these years may come to be seen as marking a rupture as profound as that brought about by the Reformation.'[86] Arguably, McLeod's book marks the coming of age of the sixties as the main focus for the historian's interest in secularisation, and I will return to some of his arguments shortly. Elsewhere, interest in the 1960s as a trauma in the cultural life of Britain has generated new synoptic studies, such as Michael Donnelly's, which locates the debates and much of the key evidence.[87] More detailed studies are drawing out the interaction of religion with cultural change, including Mark Roodhouse who has shown that the *Lady Chatterley* trial of 1960 was not just a key event eroding the institutional structures of cultural traditionalism, but that it induced an acrimonious public debate that split Anglican moral theory and undermined the Church of England's wider moral authority in English society – arguably leading to a hastening of the process of secularisation.[88]

But some Christian scholars are less convinced of the 1960s as cultural revolution and consider that I had made 'overblown claims' for that decade of a 'semi-apocalyptic' nature, and have devoted considerable space in a book, *Redefining Christian Britain*, in an attempt to overturn my argument and evidence.[89] Unfortunately, they made some errors. Some contributors tended to think this book was about the decline of Christianity in the 1960s when it was actually about the collapse of dominant Christian culture. The editors confused 'diffusive' with 'discursive' Christianity, and they tried to disagree with what they falsely suggested I had stated about the contraceptive pill in the 1960s – when I never mentioned the pill anywhere in the book. One of the contributors, William Whyte, made an exaggerated critique of the importance of *Jackie* magazine in my arguments about the sixties, when discussion of it filled up only nine sentences, and charged me with signifying that 'this was a generation of women that replaced Jesus with Jackie' (which is not what I said nor meant). He further attributed me with arguing that 'religion had been feminized' when I did not; I spoke variously of 'piety', 'religiosity' and 'Sundays' as being feminised, which are very different things. Another contributor, Holger Nehring seemed to imply that I suggested CND was the product of 'an a-religious generation of young protesters', when I have explicitly located both it and the anti-apartheid movement in the context of religious protest.[90] Overall, the editors and some of the contributors of *Redefining Christian Britain* seemed to be suggesting that in various ways I sought to 'write Christians out' of the important movements, literature and legacies of the 1960s. In one regard, they did this unfairly; the editors disputed my implication of the decline of Christian folk belief and practice by representing evidence cited by another scholar, used by him to *illustrate* the manner of 'the death of Christian Britain thesis', as evidence of that scholar's *dispute* with the thesis.[91] In any event, the evidence for a sudden and dramatic disappearance of much Christian folk belief and practices in the 1960s and 1970s is pretty convincing. Hugh McLeod is quite clear that folk Christian practices such as 'churching', which Sarah Williams fascinatingly found recalled by elderly oral history respondents in the 1990s, was strong in the early 1950s but declining rapidly in the 1960s, and seemed, from the oral testimony he reviewed, to have all but disappeared by the mid-1970s.[92]

It is indeed McLeod who provides the most detailed and nuanced evidence for the depth, geographical breadth, severity and consequences of de-Christianisation in Europe in the 1960s. He feels 1963 is less significant in the downturn in religious statistics (as I suggested on page 1) than 1967 and in overall secularisation by his favoured year, 1968.[93] McLeod identifies strongly with '68ers', especially the Christian contribution to the moral debates over Vietnam and apartheid. But two things are missing: firstly, the statistics of church decline show no distinctive change in 1968, whilst they do in 1963, and, secondly, in Britain '*les évènements*' of 1968 were largely a damp squib: governments rocked in the USA, Prague, Paris and other European nations; Britain gawked but did not tremble.

Yet, though McLeod and I share a great deal in common in terms of understanding the significance of the 1960s to secularisation, he nonetheless has caricatured my treatment of the decade. 'For him', McLeod wrote, 'the 1960s mark a blissful dawn, and the heroines of his story are the millions of women (mostly young) who rejected the definitions of femininity, the moral rules, and the career options prescribed by the churches'.[94] My blissful dawn is displaced by his version in which he places (mostly male) radical priests and theologians centre stage. His heroes are the political and religious radicals of 1968 and especially the Christian liberals and 'pragmatic Christians' who came in to challenge apartheid, the Biafran War and the Vietnam War and support other radical causes that disturbed the British establishment. McLeod follows the line of Gérard Cholvy and Yves-Marie Hilaire, who place religious change in France as being principally driven by developments within the religious world.[95] He points to the evidence of liberal Christian involvement in high political debate on law reforms, emphasising their key role at certain points (including the votes of seven out of twenty-six Anglican bishops on homosexual law reform in the House of Lords[96]). But the struggles in the streets over gay liberation and feminism involved a mighty contest with Christian conservatives (including in Northern Ireland where the Revd Dr Ian Paisley led the 'Save Ulster from Sodomy' campaign, and in Scotland where the humanist Labour MP Robin Cook engineered to decriminalise homosexuality in 1980 in the face of Christian opposition). The fact is that Christian clergy and activists were the loudest opponents of most liberal reforms in the 1960s – including opposing measures to end book, theatre and television censorship, decriminalise suicide, homosexuality and abortion, liberalise divorce and legalise off-course gambling. There was never any doubt in the minds of campaigners who overturned these repressions that their opponents were predominantly Christians in the churches, even when, as McLeod rightly asserts, the campaigners included Christian liberals amongst their number. But the existence of Christian proponents of these reforms cannot detract from the fact that their opponents were Christians in their own churches.[97]

Christian heroes of liberalism there undoubtedly were in the 1960s and religious historians are starting to explore the modernisation of British Christianity. Ian Jones and Peter Webster have begun an important exploration of innovation in church music, and, though the opposition to 'happy clappy music' in many Christian congregations was profound and lasted long into the 1970s, this undoubtedly laid a musical basis for the evolution of other trends in Christianity (including Charismatic Renewal).[98] Yet, in this important work there lies the danger of underestimating just how much the leisure culture of the young swung from church dances and coffee bars to an almost wholly secular raft of pleasures. McLeod is not alone in tending to underplay the impact the sixties had on young people through the media, and emphasises the intellectuals and what he calls the 'highly profiled Protestant avant-garde' – the playwrights and the Christian theologians.[99] He tends to emphasise the *liberal* changes to Christianity in the sixties, and seeks to marginalise conservative change. This he does particularly in relation to Mary Whitehouse because, he says, she 'represented the conservative end of the spectrum of Christian opinion at the time, and was far from representative'.[100] This surely underplays the impact of a woman who had a public profile greater than any liberal Christian leader of the decade, dominating television, newspapers and magazines of the time. As an icon of the conservative Christian laity, she was taken by secular liberals and the young to be leading the churches into their obsession with sexual promiscuity, and to be the personification of the forces against which sixties' rebellion was fighting. McLeod's international account of religious change in the long 1960s is unlikely to be bettered, but it can be nuanced differently from his emphasis on liberal and what he calls 'pragmatic' Christian responsiveness in favour of the conservative Christian retrenchment that left a legacy after the 1970s in the 'family values' political action in the Conservative Party and in the Charismatic Renewal of the so-called 'Thatcher generation' of born-again Christians.[101]

Would any of what happened to Christianity in the 1960s have taken place without youth culture and women's liberation? Would Christian liberal reformers in the House of Lords, in the Free Churches and elsewhere really have accomplished anything as sweeping and revolutionary as the massive decline in the Christian churches that ensued? In 2006, the senior padre in the British armed forces wrote that his department was 'struggling for coherence':

> Britain's rapid secularisation since the 1960s, combined with encroaching professionalism and fiscal accountability, has left chaplains lacking sure legitimacy within a culture that no longer deems Christian discourse normative . . . Civil society has largely embraced secular liberalism, marginalising religion in the public space.[102]

It is this *cultural* collapse of Christendom that in the end needs explaining from the 1960s.

To do this, many historians reach instinctively for the narratives of prosperity, poverty and breakdown of communities with which the history of secularisation has been customarily written in Britain. Sheridan Gilley argued that *The Death of Christian Britain* should have considered the wider breakdown of stable communities, the Blitz, decline of heavy industry and so on in relation to secularisation. My reason for disagreement is that these are the items in the traditional narrative of religious social history, and I tried to show in the book (as Gilley explains) that this narrative is the product of secularisation theory and is essentially useless for explaining the timing or causes of secularisation (just as gender historians have shown that this narrative of events does not explain fundamental change in gender history). Affluence on its own is not a sustainable explanation of the timing and character of religious alienation in Britain when, in America, it led on in the 1970s to a resurgence of conservative religion.

Nor is social class a sustainable explanation. The religiosity of the working classes in the past and present has been an ongoing work of revisionism in which many scholars have participated.[103] But whilst most social historians of religion are now agreed that the working classes were more religious than once thought, McLeod continues to assert for the 1960s that class differences had a greater role to play in religion than did gender.[104] The patterns of the nineteenth century (that I reviewed and itemised on pages 154–6) continued in the later twentieth century, with evidence that, though the lower working classes were poor churchgoers, the skilled upper working class were more numerous and, indeed, invariably dominated most Christian congregations.[105] Come the 1960s, there was no sudden working-class alienation from either the churches or Christian piety different from any middle-class exodus, and which can account for the timing and severity of the decline in organised Christianity in that decade. The rise of affluence and the reforms of Christian intellectuals and 'pragmatic' Christians cannot explain why hundreds of thousands of people stopped going to church, stopped registering their adherence and membership of churches, stopped baptising their babies, started a move towards secular forms of marriage and not getting married at all, and started the slow process – very slow albeit – that has led to a decline in belief in God in Britain (and in most European countries). So great was the cultural transformation that it had all these deep and profound demographic consequences. And at the heart of those demographic changes, I submit, was the changed decision making of young women.

WERE WOMEN TO 'BLAME'? GENDER, SEX AND DE-CHRISTIANISATION

The history of gender is important, not because it shows 'the importance of women', but because it provides a different chronology to history. It does not follow the convenient trajectories, pace and periodisations of conventional history. Thus, key questions in gender history like 'did women have a Renaissance, a Reformation or an Enlightenment?', produce answers in which traditional events feature, but not necessarily as the customary turning points. New events and continuities take precedence: the rise of the female 'witch' in early-modern European culture, coupled with the cementing of masculine conceptions of Christian piety, the feminisation of European Christianity around 1800, first-wave feminism, second-wave feminism and the late twentieth-century trend towards sexual emancipation. Some of these period changes framed this book: 1800 as marking the maturing of feminisation of conceptions of Christian piety and the targeting of the male 'heathen'; 1950–63 as the last hurrah for this conception of the human condition marked by a reinvigorated Puritanism in the form of panics over deviancy (religious, sexual, youth); and 1963 as marking a new era of rising gender equality accompanied by the collapse of popular Christianity (churchgoing, church membership, rites of passage). In these ways, symmetries between gender change and religious change lie at the analytical heart of this book.

The most significant cultural configuration of Christianity in the 1800–1950 period was its gendering.[106] Charles Taylor, in his complex contribution to a 'long secularisation' account, does recognise the feminisation of Christianity in modernity, and notes its wider context: 'Feminization of the culture went parallel to feminization of the faith.'[107] I agree with Taylor completely, but go further (as with many in religious studies) to argue that female subordination has long been a religious issue in which, in most societies, men and women experience their religious identity differently.[108] One fine distinction to how I described this in Chapter 4 comes from Linda Wilson, who, in looking at Nonconformist obituaries, found their spirituality gendered in relation to home but not in relation to personal devotion, which was largely undifferentiated by sex.[109] Still, this does not disturb the contention (pages 60–61) that women's obituaries in Nonconformist journals were privileged over men's in number, prominence and a distinctive reverence for the unsullied character of the subjects, and that these contributed to a wider circulating discourse on the innate virtues of women and the innate potentialities for sinful temptation by men (including clergy).

The significance of the gendering of religion, according to this book, lay in how this discursive Christianity crashed as the dominant culture in the 1960s, triggering rapid secularisation. Few studies have as yet focussed on gender and secularisation in the 1960s. One that has, by Peter van Rooden, was based on a small oral history project to discern the circumstances of the dramatic Christian decline in the Netherlands in the 1960s. Though he attached great importance to institutional factors (the collapse of the 'religious pillars' which had characterised Dutch and also neighbouring countries from the nineteenth century), he wrote that 'the cultural revolution of the 1960s, interpreted as the emergence within mass culture of the expressive and reflexive self, explains the collapse of West-European Christianity'. Yet, he did not detect gender as a specific major factor in religious change: 'Before the 1960s, in the Netherlands, there was no discursive link between religion and women. Femininity and the rules associated with it were not expressed in religious terms, and religion was not a discursive monopoly of women.' Instead, he noted: 'The close link between religion and women that did in fact exist, was not discursive, but practical. Almost all interviews make clear that women played the most important roles in religious socialisation, the supervision of the religious rituals, and the religious involvement of the family.'[110] This still leaves unanswered, of course, how those female-guided religious rituals were buttressed, as they must have been, by a discursive framework which made them so gendered. Ritual without discourse is conceptually problematic.

I placed a great deal of significance on sexual identity in the religious transformation of women in the 1960s. In recent work, I have done this even more.[111] I place the significance of changing sexual mores amongst women at the forefront of my analysis of female revolt against the Christian churches in and from the 1960s. McLeod attacks this proposition in a number of ways. Firstly, he asserts the significance of the 1950s in that 'much of the ground was being prepared' in the form of increased discussion about sex before marriage, and more sexual activity. He cites questionnaire data seeming to indicate a steady rise in female pre-marital sex across the twentieth century, but these data actually are so unspecific about each decade that they reveal nothing about the 1950s.[112] McLeod also places some importance on the growth of birth-control clinics as evidence of rising sexual activity, but misses the evidence of what these clinics were actually doing. Though the Family Planning Association (FPA) expanded the number of birth-control clinics in Britain from 61 in 1938 to 340 in 1961, the clientele were, officially at least, all women who were, or were about to be, married (with only 14 per cent of clients being unmarried at the time the advice was first sought, but marriage being presumed to be imminent). Far from being the agents of sexual experimentation, surveys showed that the FPA's clientele were still strongly conservative, especially the further north from London you moved. And, even for the married, rising success with FPA propaganda was far from certain. One detailed study of Belfast shows that the Marie Stopes Clinic there closed in 1947; a second voluntarily run one in a hospital only saw women in hospital and some women 'smuggled' from outside, and it only saw two or three women per fortnight during the 1950s. In Ulster, of course, the 'religious question' – the opposition of the Catholic Church – was the major factor inhibiting growth, and it was only in the early 1960s that proper publicity for the existence of birth-control advice was even contemplated (the location of the clinics even then not being well revealed). Yet, given that two-thirds of the population was Protestant, a greater success might have been expected. Until the early 1960s attendance at the first Belfast clinic (the Royal Victoria Maternity Hospital) was at the low level of 30–40 women per year, but then rose to 168 in 1964 and 2,000 in 1967.[113] Though Belfast may not be typical in all regards, a general point arises: insofar as the sexual revolution was a revolution amongst single women, the FPA was not in a position before the late 1960s to offer significant levels of advice or contraceptives to women outwith marriage.

In truth, contraception did not lay at the heart of the early stage of the sexual revolution. Though McLeod presents pre-marital sexual activity as growing in the 1950s, it was in the 1960s that this really occurred and before the oral contraceptive pill became available to single women (in 1968).[114] If the sexual revolution of the 1960s was about anything, it was overwhelmingly the revolution in sexual activity before marriage, outwith marriage (i.e. adultery) and after marriage (i.e. in divorce and its consequences), and the growing discourse that pre-marital sex for women was not immoral but exciting and above all fun. Young girls were exposed to magazines and pop songs in which sex, romance and fun with boys were freed from the older discourse circulated in women's magazines about the ideals of domesticity and how to train for it.[115]

And the evidence is strong for pre-marital sex not growing in the 1950s but booming in the 1960s. Figure 10.1 indicates the level of illegitimacy in England and Wales between 1945 and 1975. The illegitimacy rate is taken by demographers, and by Hera Cook specifically, as a good indicator of the extent of pre-marital sex before the arrival of the pill. The graph shows quite clearly that from the end of the war in 1945 until 1955 inclusive there was a decline in illegitimacy, whilst at the same time Church of England Easter Day communicants were rising as a proportion of population. The illegitimacy rate was going down, suggesting the conclusion that pre-marital sex was on the decline. In 1957, the level of illegitimacy was nearly half what it

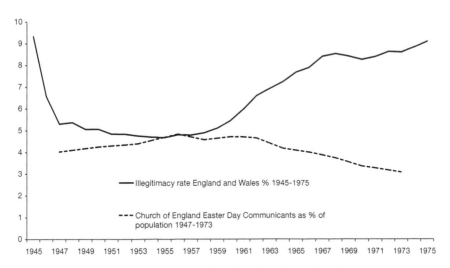

Figure 10.1 Illegitimacy rate and Church of England communicants, 1945–75

Note: The series Church of England Communicants has gaps filled by linear extrapolation between datapoints at 1947, 1950, 1953, 1956, 1958, 1960, 1962, 1964, 1968, 1970 and 1973.

Source: Data are calculated from figures at www.gro.gov.uk and from sources cited in Figure 7.1 (p. 164).

had been in 1945, and even in 1959 it was lower than in 1947 and 1948, and was still showing only a modest upward trend. These data suggest that pre-marital sexual activity was in *decline* down to the mid-1950s, followed by a mild upward trend in the next four years. Far from there being a sexual revolution in the 1950s, this was a decade in which single women reduced sexual intercourse prior to marriage. There may have been a sexual revolution amongst the bohemian and art school set, but it did not surface across society, which, on the contrary, marched in the opposite sexual and demographic direction.

There is much survey, autobiographical and oral evidence for the 1940s and 1950s to support this interpretation. Mass-Observation's so-called 'little Kinsey' report of 1949 seemed to show deeply conservative attitudes. It questioned 2,052 people chosen at random on the streets in a cross-section of British cities. Some 44 per cent of the sample felt that 'standards of sexual morality' were 'declining', and only 17 per cent thought they were improving. On extra-marital relations, it found very decidedly conservative views. Overall, 63 per cent disapproved of extra-marital relations (compared with a much lower 24 per cent on the largely middle-class national M-O panel). In other words, in 1949 there was above-average opposition amongst church-goers to extra-marital sex. Mass-Observation's conclusion of its data was: 'There is certainly no easy or widespread acceptance of sex relations outside marriage in the population as a whole.'[116] Geoffrey Gorer's 1951 inquiry seemed to show much more firmly conservative attitudes, especially amongst churchgoers. Out of his panel of 5,000 people, he found 52 per cent opposed to pre-marital sexual experience and 63 per cent opposed to young women having pre-marital sex. He noted 'the high valuation put on virginity'. Gorer came away with the impression of conservative sexual views and activities of the English people and concluded 'I very much doubt whether the study of any other urban population [in the rest of the world] would produce comparable figures of chastity and fidelity'.[117] This case is reinforced by Kate Fisher's work, which underlines one of the key points made in this book about women's ignorance concerning sex (see pages 135, 183–4). She notes that what sexual information there was in the first six decades of the twentieth century was surrounded with euphemism and oblique reference – what one of her respondents described as 'a curiously sexless world' of the 1950s, instilling a sense of anxiety and incomprehension amongst women.[118] And this extended to knowledge of birth control, and distinctly hampered its use, leaving chastity much more widespread as a method of birth control than previously thought. And this sexual ignorance was highly gendered, with sexual information overwhelmingly a man's domain.[119] Women, Fisher states, asserted their ignorance as a means of reinforcing their virtue.

Only a very small number of precocious young women were open to sexual experimentation in the 1950s, notably at Oxford and Cambridge universities. Joan Bakewell, who in 1951 went to Cambridge from a 'respectable' grammar school for girls in Stockport, quickly fell into the sexually adventurous atmosphere of the town – including the homosexual culture surrounding King's College. But, when she and her boyfriend moved to London in 1954, it was quite impossible to gain lodgings together: 'no landlady would rent a flat, no hotel would let a room to a couple which hadn't evidence of marriage'.[120] Even in metropolitan, *avant garde* London, which was to be the forefront of sexual liberation in the 1960s, it was quite impossible to share lodgings with a man whilst unmarried in 1954 and 1955, and this was also the case in Glasgow.[121] The repressive moral environment of the 1950s was inescapable, except, it seems, in Oxbridge. For the majority, churchgoing and pre-marital sex were two opposing life choices. This seems to be supported by the result of correlating the illegitimacy rate against Anglican Easter Day communicants 1947–73 (the data from Figure 10.1), which produces a figure of −0.8081, suggesting a strong inverse link between these two variables. Thus, there is every reason to believe that sexual activity and churchgoing had a causative connection; the moral and ethical climate in which churchgoers moved before the 1960s tended to make them more likely to *not* have sexual intercourse until marriage or, at the least, until a pregnancy might run to term after a wedding date.

But things were changing after 1960. In Figure 10.1, there is a very marked increase in illegitimacy from 1960 to 1968 (at the very same time that Easter Day communicants start to decline as a proportion of population). Hera Cook rightly takes this as indicative of rising pre-marital sexual intercourse. By 1968, the rate of 8.5 per cent was the highest figure for the whole century, with the exception of one year, 1945. The level of sexual activity was now into new territory. Then in 1969 the surge halts – with a figure of 8.4 per cent at which it stays until 1972, when the figures start to rise again. The cause of this was the removal in 1968 of the BMA's restriction upon British doctors prescribing the pill to unmarried women. The flattening of the line in this graph is the product of the arrival of the pill. In short, the sexual revolution in relation to pre-marital sex was well underway by 1968, *before the pill*. The pill did not start, did not instigate, the surge in pre-marital sex. It was already happening.

What was going on had a profound impact on organised Christianity. By 1968, the newspapers and the television screens of Britain were full of commentary from conservative Christians, clergy and laity alike, about the rise of permissiveness. The 'promiscuous girl' was at the forefront of discussion – including in the *Church Times*, where the leader pages contained almost weekly items on churchmen criticising sexual behaviour.[122]

The control of female sexual activity must be the subject of a different paper, but I adhere to Linda Woodhead's statements in this regard. She has written that it is only in the modern period that sex has 'assumed such central and universal prominence in a Christian agenda', a reaction against permissiveness, the privatisation of Christianity, and the historical Christian concern with sexual regulation. It was, she says, related to the churches' anxiety to regulate women's bodies 'to retain social power in a situation where such power is under increasing retreat'.[123]

And it was young women who made the choice to enter into pre-marital sexual encounters on a massive scale in the 1960s. The change in sexual activity was much more marked for women than for men. In 1964, a survey showed that the level of sexual activity amongst teenage girls was very low: 5 per cent of 16-year-olds, 10 per cent of 17-year-olds, and 17 per cent of 18-year-olds claimed to have had pre-marital sex. But by 1974/5, a similar survey found the figures had risen to 21, 37 and 47 per cent respectively. By comparison, the change in teenage male pre-marital sexual activity was much lower: rises from 14 to 32 per cent of 16-year-olds, 26 to 50 per cent of 17-year-olds, and 34 to 65 per cent of 18-year-olds.[124] So, whilst male sexual activity had about doubled in each age group between 1964 and 1974/5, female sexual activity had tripled or (in the case of 16- and 17-year-olds) quadrupled. This marks yet again how the sexual revolution was overwhelmingly a phenomenon of the sixties, not the fifties, and how it was much more a female than a male revolution. Moreover, the same 1964 data were analysed to show that those with the greatest level of sexual activity were the least likely to be churchgoers; sexual activity was a good predictor of churchgoing.[125] This is clear evidence of the salience of sex to secularisation in Christian Britain in the 1960s.

Leaving sexual activity aside, there have been high levels of scepticism amongst many established church historians and sociologists as to the significance of women's defection from the churches in the Christian crisis of the 1960s. Some base this scepticism on a wider denial of either the suddenness or the severity of the sexual revolution, the women's liberation movement and the impacts these had on religious belief. One group of Christian scholars wrote in response to the present book that, in the 1960s, 'ideas about identity, about gender and about sexuality, and – by implication – about belief, slowly mutated', a mutation 'which only gradually challenged conventions of gender'.[126] The women's revolution of that decade, widely described in feminist and other historiography, is thereby reduced to a slow process of some indeterminate duration.

But the revolt of women in the pews was real. Patrick Pasture finds the case convincing on the abandonment of female piety in the 1960s as women started to go their own way, and thinks it applies across much of western Europe.[127] Historians of Catholicism in Europe speak of the cultural rift between Catholicism and the liberal–pluralist societies of Europe culminating in the rift of Vatican II in the 1960s and the complex changes in religious practice that resulted.[128] But Hugh McLeod has expressed particular doubt as to this hypothesis, and casts doubt on there being any evidence on this matter.[129] In truth, he himself contributes quite a bit of the evidence in his own work. In his recent book on the 1960s, he publishes a table on Anglican

Church confirmations per 1,000 of population over twelve years amongst men and women. This shows two important things. Firstly, it indicates that the growth in church members in the Church of England between 1948 and 1960 was fuelled by young women. In those years, female confirmations rose from 33.6 to 40.9 per 1,000 population (a rise of 28 per cent); by contrast, male confirmations were static at 27.3 and 27.6, showing no meaningful growth whatsoever. This therefore buttresses considerably the case for young women's responsiveness in the 1950s to the last and ferocious blast of the traditional discourse on femininity and piety. Secondly, though from 1960 to 1974 female confirmations fell marginally slower than men's (a drop of 52 per cent compared with 56 per cent), the male figures showed a continuous decline since at least 1934 (of 61 per cent) whilst female decline only *started* in 1960–62.[130] A haemorrhage of male recruitment had thus been established for three decades prior to the 1960s, whilst women's recruitment actually grew over that period. This was creating an ever-increasing imbalance towards a 'woman's church' in the Anglican communion in England. Thus, when decline started, it was the change in female recruitment that was the significant change, not that in male recruitment (as there had been no change). This is shown by correlating confirmations against Church of England Easter Day communicants during 1950–70, which produces a higher figure for women's confirmations (0.9436) than for men's (0.8929).[131] In short, figures for new female recruits correlate better than male recruits with the rise and then the fall of Anglican Church membership in the 1950s and 1960s. This tends to suggest very strongly that the wider collapse of church recruitment, churchgoing and church membership in the early 1960s was triggered by the *sudden* appearance in 1960–62 of female defection from church recruitment, not men's thirty-year-long continued decline.

By the early 1970s, feminism was clearly an important factor in the continued changes to women's lives and identities in Britain. Some women became alienated from organised Christianity as a result of their involvement in the women's movement, but the far greater impact was to put many women off from joining churches. Gerald Parsons has commented that conversion 'does not appear to be a particularly convincing way of describing the decline of the core religious culture of Britain', whilst Hugh McLeod has gone further to state from his review of oral history archives that 'there is no evidence that involvement in the women's movement had been the cause of their rejection of Christianity'.[132] But this evidence is growing. In Scotland, women attracted to feminism in 1968–75 often experienced something akin to the character of a conversion experience, and many came from strong religious backgrounds (Christian and Jewish particularly, including some former nuns) which they were leaving behind. Women's consciousness raising groups, the foundational organisation of feminism in the early 1970s, were based on the idea of 'bearing your testimony', which was brought to the movement by some who were intentionally rejecting, and going on to challenge, oppressive religious backgrounds.[133] In England, there is also testimony to the religious background of the women's liberation movement. Some feminists had difficult experiences of religion in their youth, including Sheila Rowbotham (who was sent by her Methodist-hating father to a Methodist boarding school in North Yorkshire) and Lorna Sage (who at 16 years of age was destined for a Church of England home for unmarried mothers).[134] Other feminist autobiographies speak of the guilt Christianity induced in their youth in the 1950s.[135] Issues with their Christian upbringing in the 1940s and 1950s were an important backdrop to many of those who became feminists in the 1960s and 1970s.

All of this leaves issues to do with men and masculinity. Though a few reviewers felt that this book concentrated too much on femininity and too little on masculinity, parallels outside of Europe have been found for the account of how in Victorian discourse men were expected to submit to female religiosity.[136] But the outcomes of gender interactions in the churches may be complex. In Canada, the Catholic Church lost ground in Quebec after 1965, according to Gauvreau, because of a feminist current within Quebec Catholicism to which conservative forces within the church responded by insisting after 1945 on radically different gender roles and destinies, fostering 'a profound sense of cultural rupture and opposition between men and women'.[137] Certainly, the old truism that Christianity was a 'Ladies' Religion' (see page 93) still has resonance in the twenty-first century; one commentator in an Anglican evangelical journal observed that 'men often remain programmed not to habitually attend church'.[138] But since the 1960s, the loss of the pious femininity in Christian discourse in Britain has left something of a vacuum, being filled from the late 1980s by a greater appearance of masculinity expressed as militancy – something happening not just in Christianity.[139] The outcome of this is unclear, but the greater expression of male religiosity has become something of a trend.

IS DEATH THE ONLY STORY? RELIGION IN MUTATION

There is a growing trend amongst European Christian scholars to deny that secularisation is happening. They generally admit that churchgoing, church membership and most rites of passage (with the exception of Christian funerals) have been declining greatly for forty years. But they have started to become very creative in explaining this as anything but secularisation. Could there be other stories than 'the death of Christian Britain', and do they conflict with it?

This book did not consider in any substantive way other 'religious narratives' of the 1960s and after. It did not reflect in any depth, for example, on the rise of new age spirituality and its impact upon traditional Christianity and the churches. But, since *The Death of Christian Britain* was published, much more history has been written on this subject in Britain and it is starting to be more integrated into the secularisation story.[140] Equally, this volume did not report on the rise of Christian conservativism. Indeed, in 2000 I underestimated, as most liberal commentators did, the extent to which British conservative Christianity would overtake liberal Christianity in political lobbying power, prominence in public debates on ethics and morality, and making themselves militant campaigners in trying to roll back the reforms of the 1960s. This is arguably the most vigorous transformation in Christianity – its bifurcation into extremes of conservatives and liberals, slogging it out for the heartland of the religion. The battles over homosexuality and women clergy are tearing Anglicans apart, and the first of these is seemingly destined to do the same to the Church of Scotland too. As one former Anglican clergyman has observed, the rise of fundamentalism is not just tearing the Church apart, but alienating many of its own members.[141] But these are internecine battles disjoined from a popular culture and political system that has largely passed on; I still think I was right to write in 2000 that since the 1960s 'the churches have become increasingly irrelevant in the new cultural and ethical landscape' inhabited by most people (see page 191). What has become clear since then is that there has been a conservative Christian backlash *because* of that perceived increasing irrelevance. The post-9/11 environment has seen a new vigour amongst conservative Christians, especially where they make common cause with conservatives in other religions (such as with Muslims over abortion), that has contributed to the perceived rise of the 'battle' between faith and secularism. Whilst the power of so-called 'militant secularism' is vastly over-rated (and indeed the very existence of such a 'movement' largely fantasy), religious conservatism has acquired a new public role that belies the absence of significant popular membership.

The cultural historian's knowledge is growing slowly and belatedly about Christian conservativism, especially Pentecostalism and fundamentalism. Pentecostalism, the most vibrant and obvious change in modern Christianity worldwide, may claim the adherence of 12 per cent of the global Christian population, and it causes significant argument about its relationship with fundamentalism.[142] Accounts from religious historians on Charismatic Renewal are detailed on personnel and methods of transmission, whilst information is also growing on other Christian innovations such as the Toronto Blessing and the Alpha courses. But cultural history (as distinct from religious history) accounts of these are still sketchy; we are lacking evidence on the political positioning of such trends in popular culture, the extent of influence and of conversions, and their wider impact on lay attitudes to the churches. For example, some anecdotal evidence suggests that in many places in Britain Charismatic Renewal has affronted traditional Christians, alienating some from their local churches, and more widely it may well be the case that the population at large find their residual Christianity disjoined from this phenomenon.[143] By contrast, Pentecostalism is becoming better understood – a movement which in Britain is predominantly black, and strongly reliant on immigrants from West Africa and the Afro-Caribbean community; this fits with David Martin's recent description of world Pentecostalism as 'the religious mobilization of the culturally despised, outside any sponsorship whatever, whether of their own local intelligentsias, or of the clerical secular intelligentsias of the West'.[144] But it is probably too dismissive to say that, as a cultural revolution, Pentecostalism has no political implications. It is inherently conservative and is drawn inexorably to share a political influence with other religious conservatives in British Christianity, Islam and Judaism. Each of these developments was outwith the purview of this book and, though I have written about some of them elsewhere, religions in the context of a secularising society await the gaze of the cultural historian.[145]

If the cultural historian is cautious about researching the present, others are bolder. An increasing number of Christian sociologists and historians place emphasis on Christianity in Europe (including Britain) undergoing 'mutation' into new forms, rather than decline. Most Christian commentators accepted the truth of the decline of the churches in Britain, but defended this in different ways as 'not secularisation'.[146] One group of Christian scholars has stated of Britain that 'the closure of churches should not be seen as synonymous with decline'.[147] This may be a difficult proposition for the evidence-based historian to agree with; the last forty years have seemed incontrovertibly decades when closing churches went hand-in-hand with loss of members, declining Christian rites, the overturning of Christian influence in the state, and the loss of a culture of Christianity in British communities. This is not to deny that new forms of Christian worship have been emerging for some time: the house church movement and mega-churches are two examples. But arguments are becoming more conceptually elaborate. Sociologist Grace Davie has argued that European religion is mutating, and in this the churches remain important in specific roles (such as education and philanthropy, retaining what she sees as a vital 'memory' for Christianity in Europe). So, the collapse of the churches is thus positive, not negative; even the collapse of state churches is, she says, not due to 'religious causes' but is 'part of the renegotiation of European society as a whole'.[148] In this argument, Christian institutions are stronger than their weakness or disappearance would suggest, and, though active Christian numbers go down, they have a disproportionate impact in charitable and ethical endeavour. Though she notes that this mutation is 'very unlikely' to result in a significant increase in churchgoing in modern Europe, Davie claims that unchurched Europeans 'remain grateful to rather than resentful of their churches' for these 'vicariously' performed tasks – which include rites like funerals and national celebrations – which 'carry' the continent's Christian memory. From this, Davie follows a number of other Christians in proposing that the very definition of religion is widening (to include individual and social health and, to resurrect an older concept of sociology, even civil religion) and in so doing, whilst the decline of conventional forms and measure of religion has to be acknowledged, there is a mutated vicarious religion surviving.[149]

This search for new models of religion is something that is strongest and most diverse amongst Christian scholars (both sociologists and historians). Many are adhering to the concept championed by Charles Taylor of the rise since 1945 of the popular and cultural search for religious 'authenticity', in which tradition and rules in Christianity were interrogated (and in many cases bypassed) in a drive which amongst other things spawned new age spirituality both within and outwith the Christian churches.[150] In this, as Mathew Guest has started to explore, the congregation itself has heightened the drive for 'authenticity' – searching for new forms of meeting, ranging from small house churches to larger 'mega-churches' – in which the liturgy and experience resonated more with people than did tradition and older ritual; this may even signal at one extreme the formation of the temporary congregation in what is mostly a 'churchless faith'.[151]

Some sociologists of religion, such as Steve Bruce, remain sceptical of such arguments.[152] And I do too. The extent and observable trajectory of de-Christianisation in British society since the 1960s needs, it seems to me, to be restated vigorously in the light of the most recent evidence. Churchgoers, church members and religious rites of passage have all continued to dive since 2000, sustaining straight-line graph gradients of declension in formal Christian religion in Britain. A study in 1999–2000 examining the religious lives of three generations born in 1946, 1958 and 1970 showed a steep decline in observance; by the turn of the century, only 8 per cent of 42-year-olds attended church weekly, and 5 per cent of 30-year-olds, with more women than men attending.[153]

Finally, there is a moral dimension to Christian critiques of secularisation. Some have sensed from my book that I took it that the loss of Christian culture in the 1960s introduced a moral vacuum, or as some would have it pejoratively as a 'moral relativism'. Some commentators criticised me for not attempting to tot up the moral losses of de-Christianisation – alleged to include growing violence, crime, suspicion and selfishness; some accused me of succumbing to 'the relativistic spirit of our age . . . evident in the conduct of Brown's own argument'.[154] In this sense, some have falsely approved of my thoughts, because I do not and did not subscribe to this 'moral vacuum hypothesis'. In the first place, I have argued elsewhere that relativism is a moral good of enormous proportions – something to be gloried in, fought for and utilised by the historian, and something whose absence poses enormous dangers for democracy, reason and tolerance (including in the history profession).[155] In the second place, even David Herbert, who otherwise has a very good and insightful understanding of how my work relates to that of others, has possibly misunderstood me on this issue. I do not see the 1960s as undermining morality or moral narratives in British or European culture. I did not say, as Herbert suggests I did, that 'modern individuals can no longer articulate coherent moral stories about themselves, largely as a result of the decline of the social influence of religious narratives'.[156] On the contrary, I contend that the loss of *Christian* moral narratives from the 1960s was very much propelled by vigorous promulgation of *new* narratives which, with amazing suddenness, swept liberal culture: postcolonial narratives, feminism, gay liberation, the green movement and narratives of sexual freedom. Morality was not lost, it was recrafted with spirit and determination into forms that define common culture and values for most Britons in the present day. These were *moral* narratives, however much some conservative and traditional Christians may wish to denigrate them as amoral ones. This process is not at an end. It continues today, for instance, in relation to the issue of euthanasia, where conservatives in the churches are recoiling from popular pressure for the law to be changed to enable the citizen to be supported by others if he or she decides to end his or her life. Now, many philosophers have no doubt contributed towards the intellectualising of this position; but it must be clearly understood that *popular* adoption of this lies at the root of this new position, and that it was not something handed down from above. This is the people's decision – a truly democratic discourse that has emerged with amazing unanimity amongst the British unchurched since around 1990 and, though there may be many who will deny it fervently, also amongst some laity and clergy of the Christian churches who have participated in or approved of assisted suicide.

This brings me full circle to a restatement of the need for the production of a cultural history of secularisation. David Nash is right that historians of religion (which has to include the important role of non-religious historians of the subject) have to place religion centre stage of cultural history of the present as of the near past, and not allow it to be ignored by succumbing to the anachronistic sacred–profane dichotomy which, over many decades, has marginalised religion within our discipline. But in doing this, the cultural historian is looking to the power of the people as agents of change, and should not allow the moral judgments of Christian scholars nor the undue privileging of intellectuals (Christian or otherwise) in the narrative of the process. British secularisation did not involve the leadership of the state (as in France), nor the collapse of denominational 'pillars' (as in Belgium, the Netherlands and to an extent West Germany). It has been above all a product of people's choices, made largely free from intellectuals or a supposed descent into immorality and crime. The death of Christian British culture, or the rupture in Christianity as McLeod puts it, was a real and – I would argue – a cataclysmic event of the 1960s. Sweeping as it may seem, the conclusion of the first edition of this book still stands. I wrote at the end of Chapter 9 that the churches will not die, but would continue to exist in some skeletal form (which is what seems to be suggested by most British Christian sociologists). What I did write is that 'the culture of

Christianity has gone in the Britain of new millennium. Britain is showing the world how religion as we have known it can die'. The emphasis here is upon 'religion as we have known it', and should not be taken as a statement that the rest of the world will follow Britain or that religion itself is ending. From what even my most strident critics are saying, based on the present evidence, mutation is precisely the best the Christian faith can hope for in the circumstances of British secularisation.

NOTES

—— •◆• ——

1 INTRODUCTION

1 Excluding Ireland and Northern Ireland.
2 C. Taylor, *Sources of the Self: The Making of the Modern Identity*, Cambridge, Mass., Harvard University Press, 1989, pp. 491–2.
3 P. Brierley and H. Wraight (eds), *UK Christian Handbook 1998/99*, London, Christian Research Association, 1997, p. 12. This claim rests on a belief-based definition of 'Christian' which poses difficulties for social-survey meaningfulness and reliability: namely, 'acceptance of the historic formulary of the Godhead as the three eternal Persons, in God the Father, God the Son and God the Spirit in an unchanging Essence'.
4 Data from P. Brierley and V. Hiscock (eds), *UK Christian Handbook 1994–95*, London, Christian Research Association, 1993, and 1991 British Social Attitudes Survey, quoted in S. Bruce, *Religion in Modern Britain*, Oxford, Oxford University Press, 1995, pp. 49, 51; *The Scotsman*, 8 April 1999; *The Observer*, 9 November 1997; *The Guardian*, 8 July 2000.
5 Bruce, *Religion in Modern Britain*, pp. 73–94, 101–2, 117–21.
6 *The Guardian*, 11 April 2000; *The Scotsman*, 11 April 2000.
7 *The Guardian*, 5 February 2000.
8 *The Scotsman*, 10 November 1997, 28 December 1998, 8 April 1999; *The Herald*, 19 December 1998; *The Guardian*, 11 August 2000.
9 *The Scotsman*, 30 August 1999; *Scotland on Sunday*, 14 May 2000.
10 *The Observer*, 9 November 1997; *The Scotsman*, 3 April 1999.
11 Grace Davie, quoted in *The Observer*, 9 November 1997. G. Davie, *Religion in Britain since 1945: Believing Without Belonging*, Oxford, Blackwell, 1994.
12 R. Wuthnow, *The Restructuring of American Religion: Society and Faith since World War II*, Princeton, Princeton University Press, 1988, pp. 14–99; C.G. Brown, 'A revisionist approach to religious change', in S. Bruce (ed.), *Religion and Modernization: Sociologists and Historians Debate the Secularization Thesis*, Oxford, Clarendon Press, 1992, pp. 46–8.
13 D. Hilliard, 'The religious crisis of the 1960s: the experience of the Australian churches', *Journal of Religious History*, 1997, vol. 21, p. 211.
14 L. Hölscher, 'Die Religion des Bürgers: Bürgerliche Frömmigkeit und Protestantishe Kirche im 19. Jahrundert', *Historshe Zeitschrift*, 1990, vol. 250, p. 630; H. McLeod, *Religion and the People of Western Europe 1789–1989*, Oxford, Oxford University Press, 1997, pp. 133–40.

15 Statistics in this paragraph are from, or calculated from, R. Currie, A. Gilbert and L. Horsley, *Churches and Churchgoers: Patterns of Church Growth in the British Isles since 1700*, Oxford, Clarendon Press, 1977, pp. 223–9; *Population Trends*, 95 (1999), p. 57; *Annual Report of the Registrar General, Scotland,* 1997; *Church of England Yearbook*, 2000; *Church of Scotland Yearbook*, 1999; C.G. Brown, 'A revisionist approach to religious change', in Bruce (ed.), *Religion and Modernization*, pp. 40–9.

16 Key texts in the 'pessimist' school are: E.R. Wickham, *Church and People in an Industrial City*, London, Lutterworth, 1957; K.S. Inglis, *Churches and the Working Classes in Victorian England*, London, RKP, 1963; B. Wilson, *Religion in Secular Society*, Harmondsworth, Penguin, 1966; P.L. Berger, *The Social Reality of Religion*, London, Longman, 1969; O. Chadwick, *The Secularization of the European Mind in the Nineteenth Century*, Cambridge, Cambridge University Press, 1975; Currie *et al.*, *Churches and Churchgoers*; D. Martin, *A General Theory of Secularization*, Oxford, Basil Blackwood, 1978; A.D. Gilbert, *The Making of Post-Christian Britain: A History of the Secularization of Modern Society*, London, Longman, 1980; S. Bruce, *Religion in the Modern World: From Cathedrals to Cults*, Oxford, Oxford University Press, 1996.

17 Amongst specialists, see R. Wallis and S. Bruce, 'Secularization: the orthodox model', and B.R. Wilson, 'Reflections on a many sided controversy', in Bruce (ed.), *Religion and Modernization*; A.D. Gilbert, 'Secularization and the future,' in S. Gilley and W.J. Sheils (eds), *A History of Religion in Britain*, Oxford, Basil Blackwell, 1994.

18 H. McLeod, *Class and Religion in the Late Victorian City*, London, Croom Helm, 1974, and J. Obelkevich, *Religion and Rural Society: South Lindsey 1825–1875*, Oxford, Clarendon Press, 1976; E.T. Davies, *Religion in the Industrial Revolution in South Wales*, Cardiff, University of Wales Press, 1965; R. Moore, *Pit-men, Preachers and Politics: The Effects of Methodism in a Durham Mining Community*, Cambridge, Cambridge University Press, 1974; and S. Yeo, *Religion and Voluntary Organisations in Crisis*, London, Croom Helm, 1976.

19 Leading the way was J. Cox, *The English Churches in a Secular Society: Lambeth 1870–1930*, Oxford, Oxford University Press, 1982, followed by C.G. Brown, 'Did urbanisation secularise Britain?', *Urban History Yearbook*, 1988; R. Gill, *Competing Convictions*, London, SCM, 1989; C.G. Brown, 'A revisionist approach to religious change', in Bruce (ed.), *Religion and Modernization*; M. Smith, *Religion in Industrial Society: Oldham and Saddleworth 1740–1865*, Oxford, Oxford University Press, 1994; C.G. Brown, 'The mechanism of religious growth in urban societies: British cities since the eighteenth century,' in H. McLeod (ed.), *European Religion in the Age of Great Cities 1830–1930*, London, Routledge, 1995; and S.J.D. Green, *Religion in the Age of Decline: Organisation and Experience in Industrial Yorkshire 1870–1920*, Cambridge, Cambridge University Press, 1996.

20 K.J. Christiano, *Religious Diversity and Social Change: American Cities 1890–1906*, Cambridge, Cambridge University Press, 1987; R. Finke and R. Stark, 'Evaluating the evidence: religious economies and sacred canopies,' *American Sociological Review*, 1989, vol. 54; R. Finke, 'An unsecular America', in Bruce (ed.), *Religion and Modernization*; L. Hölscher, 'Secularization and

urbanization in the nineteenth century: an interpretative model', in McLeod (ed.), *European Religion*.

21 The field sadly lacks a sophisticated comparative literature, other than in the work of Hugh McLeod: see H. McLeod, *Piety and Poverty: Working-class Religion in Berlin, London and New York 1870–1914* , New York, Holmes & Meier, 1996; and H. McLeod, *Religion and the People of Western Europe 1789–1989*, Oxford, Oxford University Press, 1997.

22 McLeod, *Class and Religion*; H. McLeod, 'New perspectives in Victorian working-class religion: the oral evidence', *Oral History Journal*, 1986, vol. 14; Brown, 'Did urbanisation secularise Britain?'; and C.G. Brown and J.D. Stephenson, 'Sprouting wings? Women and religion in Scotland *c*. 1890–*c*. 1950', in E. Breitenbach and E. Gordon (eds), *Out of Bounds: Women in Scotland in the Nineteenth and Twentieth Centuries*, Edinburgh, Edinburgh University Press, 1992.

23 For a model of staggered working-class secularisation in metropolitan cities, see McLeod, *Piety and Poverty*. For a model of religious growth in British cities, see Brown, 'The mechanism of religious growth'.

24 C.G. Brown, 'Essor religieux et sécularisation', in H. McLeod, S. Mews and C. D'Haussy (eds) *Histoire Religieuse de la Grande-Bretagne*, Paris, Editions du Cerf, 1997, pp. 315–37.

25 A phrase popularised by Wilson, *Religion in Secular Society*, p. 14.

26 M. Spufford, 'Can we count the "godly" and the "conformable" in the seventeenth century?', *Journal of Ecclesiastical History*, vol. 36 (1985).

2 THE PROBLEM WITH 'RELIGIOUS DECLINE'

1 The classic formulation of this grand narrative is Peter Laslett's *The World We Have Lost*, London, Methuen, 1965, a book founded on a discourse on the pre-industrial 'otherness' of religiosity which his readers are invited to share. It includes the following hostages to hundreds of doctoral fortunes: 'All our ancestors were literal Christian believers, all of the time.' (p. 71); 'It has been shown only very recently how it came about that the mass of the English people lost their Christian belief, and how religion came to be a middle-class matter.' (p. 72).

2 The classic formulation of this second, post-industrial revolution part of the grand narrative is Alan Gilbert's *The Making of Post-Christian Britain: A History of the Secularization of Modern Society*, London and New York, Longman, 1980. Though more cautious than Laslett, Gilbert felt empowered by the intellectual bravado of 1970s' sociology to vacuum up swathes of history in his own empirically contestable statements: 'Organized religion, everywhere in the British Isles, has failed to cope with the decline of the territorial community and the emergence of pluralistic, partial communities.' (p. 84).

3 J. Walsh, 'Methodism and the mob in the eighteenth century', *Studies in Church History*, 1972, vol. 8, p. 218; C.G. Brown, 'Protest in the pews: interpreting Presbyterianism and society in fracture during the Scottish economic revolution', in T.M. Devine (ed.), *Conflict and Stability in Scottish Society 1700–1850*, Edinburgh, John Donald, 1990.

4   E.J. Evans, *The Contentious Tithe: The Tithe Problem and English Agriculture, 1750–1850*, London, RKP, 1976; A.A. Cormack, *Teinds and Agriculture*, London, Hodder & Stoughton, 1930.

5   Wickham, *Church and People*, pp. 42–3, 47–9, 57–8, 72–3, 114–15, 142–3 and appendix III; C.G. Brown, 'The costs of pew-renting: church management, churchgoing and social class in nineteenth-century Glasgow', *Journal of Ecclesiastical History*, 1987, vol. 38.

6   O. Chadwick, *Victorian Miniature*, London, Futura, 1983, orig., 1960; C.G. Brown, 'The Myth of the Established Church', in J. Kirk (ed.), *Church and State in Scotland*, Edinburgh, Scottish Church History Society, 2000.

7   J. Macinnes, *The Evangelical Movement in the Highlands of Scotland 1688 to 1800*, Aberdeen, Aberdeen University Press, 1951; C.G. Brown, *Up-helly-aa: Custom, Culture and Community in Shetland*, Manchester, Mandolin, 1998.

8   E.P. Thompson, *Customs in Common*, London, Merlin, 1991, pp. 83–96.

9   L. Davidoff and C. Hall, *Family Fortunes: Men and Women of the English Middle Class 1780–1850*, London, Routledge, 1987, pp. 155–6.

10 F.W. Freeman, 'Robert Fergusson: pastoral and politics at mid century', in A. Hook (ed.), *The History of Scottish Literature vol. 2 1660–1800*, Aberdeen, Aberdeen University Press, 1987, pp. 142–9.

11 T. Smollett, *The Expedition of Humphry Clinker*, orig. 1771, Harmondsworth, Penguin, 1967, p. 66.

12 W. Cowper, *The Task* (1785), quoted in B.I. Coleman (ed.), *The Idea of the City in Nineteenth-Century Britain*, London, RKP, 1973, pp. 25–6.

13 W. Wordsworth, *The Prelude* (1805), quoted ibid., pp. 32–3.

14 R. Southey, quoted ibid., p. 41.

15 J. Blackburn, *Reflections on the Moral and Spiritual Claims of the Metropolis*, London, Holdsworth, 1827, pp. 7, 13, 24.

16 M. Maxwell-Arnot, 'Social change and the Church of Scotland', in M. Hill (ed.), *A Sociological Yearbook of Religion in Britain, vol. 7*, London, SCM, 1974, pp. 96–9.

17 Quoted in *Scots Magazine*, January 1787, pp. 15–17.

18 Ibid., December 1787, p. 619.

19 J. Sinclair (ed.), *The Statistical Account of Scotland*, vol. 10, Edinburgh, 1790, p. 560.

20 Ibid., vol. 20, pp. 535–6.

21 Mark Docker, 1817, quoted in Wickham, *Church and People*, pp. 84–5.

22 J.P. Kay, *The Moral and Physical Condition of the Working Classes Employed in the Cotton Manufacture in Manchester*, second edn, London, 1832, p. 112.

23 In relation to Sheffield, Wickham commented in 1957: 'Considering the early evangelical zeal for foreign missions, for the abolition of slavery, and for the care of the poor, it is surprising how late in time there is either public awareness or stirring of conscience about the *missionary* problem at home.' Wickham, *Church and People*, p. 85.

24 Revd S. MacGill, *Our Blessings and Our Duty: Under the Present Circumstances*, Glasgow, 1798, pp. 54–5.

25 Revd Alexander Carlyle, quoted in R. Heron (ed.), *Account of the Proceedings and Debate, in the General Assembly of the Church of Scotland . . . Respecting*

the Propagation of the Gospel among the Heathen, Edinburgh, Lawrie, 1796, p. 37.

26 The Bishop of Llandaff to William Pitt in 1800, quoted in D. Hempton, *Methodism and Politics in British Society 1750–1850*, London, Hutchinson, 1987, p. 78.

27 An apt description of E.T. Davies, *Religion and Society in the Nineteenth Century*, Llandybie, Davies, 1981, p. 39.

28 W. Hanna (ed.), *Memoirs of Thomas Chalmers*, vol. 1, Edinburgh, Constable, 1854, p. 438.

29 Ibid., pp. 445–6.

30 T. Chalmers, *A Sermon delivered in the Tron Church on the occasion of the death of Princess Charlotte*, Glasgow, 1817, pp. 30–1.

31 T. Chalmers, *The Christian and Civic Economy of Large Towns*, Glasgow, 1821, p. 51.

32 Ibid., pp. 25–9.

33 T. Chalmers, *The Right Ecclesiastical Economy of a Large Town*, Edinburgh, 1835, pp. 20–1.

34 Quoted in B. Hilton, *The Age of Atonement: The Influence of Evangelicalism on Social and Economic Thought, 1795–1865*, Oxford, Clarendon, 1988, p. 57.

35 *The Methodist Magazine*, June 1821, pp. 452–5, and July 1821, pp. 517–31.

36 Hilton, *Age of Atonement, passim*, but especially pp. 39, 55–70, 81–91, 115–25, 183–9.

37 Chalmers, *Christian and Civic Economy*, p. 67.

38 *The Watchman*, 11 February 1835, p. 45.

39 B.W. Noel, *The State of the Metropolis Considered*, London, 1835, pp. 26–7.

40 *Census of Great Britain 1851, Religious Worship, England and Wales, BPP*, lxxxix (1852–3), pp. cxxvii, clviii–clxii.

41 *One of the Least Among the Brethren: A Revived Ministry our only Hope for a Revived Church*, London, Jackson & Walford, 1844, p. 27.

42 R. Vaughan, *The Age of Great Cities*, 1843, reprint Shannon, Irish University Press, 1971, esp. pp. 227, 309–10, 319.

43 A. Watt, *The Glasgow Bills of Mortality for 1841 and 1842*, Glasgow, 1844; A. Watt, *The Vital Statistics of Glasgow, for 1843 and 1844*, Glasgow, 1846; W. Logan, *The Moral Statistics of Glasgow*, Glasgow, 1849.

44 *Chamber's Journal*, no. 485, 16 April 1853, p. 253.

45 Ibid., no. 319, 11 February 1860.

46 J. Thomson, *The City of Dreadful Night*, orig. 1880, Edinburgh, Canongate, 1993, pp. 29–31, 52, 56.

47 J.R. Walkowitz, *City of Dreadful Delight: Narratives of Sexual Danger in Late-Victorian London*, London, Virago, 1992.

48 *British Weekly*, 17 December 1886, p. 5.

49 W. Booth, *In Darkest England and the Way Out*, London, Salvation Army, n.d. [1890].

50 C.F.G. Masterman, *The Condition of England*, London, Methuen, 1909, p. 266.

51 H. Drummond, *The City Without a Church*, Stirling, Drummond Tract Enterprise, 1892, pp. 4, 7.

52 E.P. Hennock, *Fit and Proper Persons: Ideal and Reality in Nineteenth-century Urban Government*, London, Edward Arnold, 1973; C.G. Brown, '"To be

aglow with civic ardours": the "Godly Commonwealth" in Glasgow 1843–1914', *Records of the Scottish Church History Society,* 1996, vol. 26.

53　W.H. Fraser, 'From civic gospel to municipal socialism', in D. Fraser (ed.), *Cities, Class and Communication,* Brighton, Harvester, 1990.

54　A.S. Matheson, *The City of God,* London, T. Fisher Unwin, 1910, p. 161.

55　Wickham, *Church and People,* p. 14.

56　Ibid., p. 85.

57　Inglis, *Churches and the Working Classes,* p. 3. Inglis repeatedly quoted Chalmers with approval; see pp. 5, 11, 18, 64.

58　A.F. Winnington-Ingram, *Work in Great Cities,* 1896, p. 22.

59　G.K. Clark, *The Making of Victorian England,* London, Methuen, 1962, p. 181; J. Kent, 'Feelings and festivals', and D.E.H. Mole, 'The Church of England and the working classes in Birmingham', both in H. Dyos and M. Wolff (eds), *The Victorian City,* vol. 2, London, Routledge, 1973, pp. 866, 868, 821.

60　J. Kent, *Holding the Fort: Studies in Victorian Revivalism,* London, Epworth, 1978, p. 362.

61　Examples from Scottish historians of the 1970s and 1980s: 'The social structure of the industrial areas was a pyramid and its broad base was pagan.' 'During the industrial revolution the poor and destitute had been lost to [the churches] and become pagan.' '[T]he bulk of the urbanized masses remained unchurched'; '[T]he decay of Christian fellowship was manifest in the increasing alienation of the "lower orders" from every kind of religious faith and practice'. A.L. Drummond and J. Bulloch, *The Church in Victorian Scotland 1843–1974,* Edinburgh, Saint Andrew Press, 1975, pp. 40–1; A.L. Drummond and J. Bulloch, *The Church in Late Victorian Scotland 1874–1900,* Edinburgh, Saint Andrew Press, 1978, p. 144; S. and O. Checkland, *Industry and Ethos: Scotland 1832–1914,* London, Edward Arnold, 1984, p. 132; A.C. Cheyne, *The Transforming of the Kirk: Victorian Scotland's Religious Revolution,* Edinburgh, Saint Andrew Press, 1983, p. 110.

62　See for instance the chapter on religion in J. Harris, *Private Lives, Public Spirit: Britain 1870–1914,* Harmondsworth, Penguin, 1994.

63　E.P. Thompson, *The Making of the English Working Class,* orig. 1963, Harmondsworth, Penguin, 1968.

64　H. Perkin, *The Origins of Modern English Society 1780–1880,* London, RKP, 1969, p. 196.

65　A.A. MacLaren, *Religion and Social Class: The Disruption Years in Aberdeen,* London, RKP, 1974.

66　J. Foster, *Class Struggle and the Industrial Revolution,* London, RKP, 1974. For a critique of his findings on religion, see Smith, *Religion in Industrial Society,* pp. 243–71.

67　H. McLeod, *Class and Religion in the Late Victorian City,* London, Croom Helm, 1974; S. Yeo, *Religion and Voluntary Organisations in Crisis,* London, Croom Helm, 1976; J. Cox, *The English Churches in a Secular Society: Lambeth 1870–1930,* Oxford, Oxford University Press, 1982; J.N. Morris, *Religion and Urban Change: Croydon 1840–1914,* Woodbridge, Royal Historical Society, 1992; S.J.D. Green, *Religion in the Age of Decline: Organisation and Experience in Industrial Yorkshire 1870–1920,* Cambridge, Cambridge University Press, 1996.

68 R. Currie, A. Gilbert and L. Horsley, *Churches and Churchgoers: Patterns of Church Growth in the British Isles since 1700,* Oxford, Clarendon Press, 1977; A.D. Gilbert, *Religion and Society in Industrial England: Church, Chapel and Social Change 1740–1914*, London, Longman, 1978; Gilbert, *Post Christian Britain.*

69 Cox, *English Churches*, esp. pp. 9–20, 265–76; C.G. Brown, 'Did urbanisation secularise Britain?'.

70 H. McLeod, 'New perspectives in Victorian working-class religion: the oral evidence', *Oral History Journal*, 1986, vol. 14; C.G. Brown and J.D. Stephenson, 'Sprouting wings? Women and religion in Scotland *c.* 1890–*c.* 1950', in E. Breitenbach and E. Gordon (eds), *Out of Bounds: Women in Scotland in the Nineteenth and Twentieth Centuries*, Edinburgh, Edinburgh University Press, 1992; S.C. Williams, *Religious Belief and Popular Culture in Southwark, c. 1880–1939*, Oxford, Clarendon Press, 1999.

71 H. McLeod, *Religion and Society in England 1850–1914*, Basingstoke, Macmillan, 1996, p. 178.

72 L. Davidoff and C. Hall, *Family Fortunes: Men and Women of the English Middle Class, 1780–1850*, London, Routledge, 1987, pp. 73–192, esp. at p. 76.

73 D. Hempton, *The Religion of the People: Methodism and Popular Religion c. 1750–1900*, London, Routledge, 1996, pp. 49–72.

74 Williams, *Religious Belief.*

75 For example, S. Bruce, *Religion in the Modern World: From Cathedrals to Cults*, Oxford, Oxford University Press, 1996.

76 The following three paragraphs draw inspiration from Jean-Francois Lyotard, *The Postmodern Condition* (1984), quoted in K. Jenkins (ed.), *The Postmodern History Reader*, London, Routledge, 1997, pp. 36–7.

77 The best account by far of the way in which Enlightenment rationality merged into evangelicalsim is Hilton, *Age of Atonement.*

78 One who has started this project in relation to non-formal, or folk, religion, is Williams, *Religious Belief.*

79 M. Foucault, *The Archaeology of Knowledge*, London, Routledge, 1989 edn, pp. 73, 183; also useful here is Roland Barthes, 'The discourse of history', in Jenkins (ed.), *Postmodern History Reader*, pp. 120–3.

80 Foucault, *Archaeology*, p. 46.

81 Adapted from ibid., pp. 50–55.

82 'All the writers of the bourgeoisie are unanimous on this point, that the workers are not religious, and do not attend church.' F. Engels, *The Condition of the Working Class in England in 1844*, 1892, p. 125.

83 James, one of the founding specialists in this field, criticised the 'better classes' who feared poverty for 'so unmanly and irreligious a state of opinion'. And he wrote that 'in our Father's house are many mansions, and each of us must discover for himself the kind of religion and the amount of saintship which best comports with what he believes to be his powers and feels to be his truest mission and vocation'. W. James, *The Varieties of Religious Experience: a Study in Human Nature*, orig. 1902, London, Longmans, Green, 1928, pp. 368, 377.

84 C. Taylor, *Human Agency and Language: Philosophical Papers I*, Cambridge, Cambridge University Press, 1985, pp. 1, 3, 103, 216.

85 L. Stanley and S. Wise, *Breaking Out Again: Feminist Ontology and Epistemology*, London and New York, Routledge, 1993, p. 157.

3 THE SALVATION ECONOMY

1 A.T. Bradwell, *Autobiography of a Converted Infidel*, Sheffield, George Chalmers, 1844, pp. 20, 24, 26.

2 B. Hilton, *The Age of Atonement: The Influence of Evangelicalism on Social and Economic Thought, 1795–1865*, Oxford, Clarendon, 1988, p. 8.

3 Ibid., p. 13.

4 E.J. Yeo, *The Contest for Social Science*, London, Rivers Oram, 1996.

5 D. Hempton, *The Religion of the People: Methodism and Popular Religion c. 1750–1900*, London, Routledge, 1996, pp. 73–90.

6 D. Bebbington, *Evangelicalism in Modern Britain*, London, Unwin Hyman, 1989, pp. 42–74; Hilton, *Age of Atonement*; Yeo, *Social Science*.

7 On the meaning of 'conformity' in early modern England, see M. Spufford, 'Can we count the "godly" and the "conformable" in the seventeenth century?', *Journal of Ecclesiastical History*, 1985, vol. 36.

8 In one of these works in 1779, a minister bemoaned 'the Ommission of our worthy Forefathers to transmit to Posterity a full and Circumstantial account' of earlier revivals. J. Robe, 1779, quoted in A. Fawcett, *The Cambuslang Revival*, London, Banner of Truth Trust, 1971, p. 5.

9 R. Currie, A. Gilbert and L. Horsley, *Churches and Churchgoers: Patterns of Church Growth in the British Isles since 1700*, Oxford, Clarendon Press, 1977, p. 139.

10 A point made for overseas missions in C. Hall, *White, Male and Middle Class: Explorations in Feminism and History*, Cambridge, Polity Press, 1992, pp. 218–19.

11 W. Porteous, *The Doctrine of Toleration*, Glasgow, 1778, pp. 8, 14; Edinburgh University Library, Laing MSS, La. II 500, letters from William Porteous to Lord Advocate, 24 January and 20 February 1797; 21 February 1798. *Principal Acts of the General Assembly of the Church of Scotland, 1794–1812*, pp. 38–45.

12 I. Bradley, *The Call to Seriousness*, London, Jonathan Cape, 1976, p. 22.

13 On the associational ideal, see S.J.D. Green, *Religion in the Age of Decline: Organisation and Experience in Industrial Yorkshire 1870–1920*, Cambridge, Cambridge University Press, 1996. On the key role for the doctrine of assurance of salvation in evangelicalism, see Bebbington, *Evangelicalism*, pp. 42–50, 74.

14 This is the slant given to this puritanising process in Bradley, *Call to Seriousness*, esp. pp. 34–56; D. Rosman, *Evangelicals and Culture*, London, Croom Helm, 1984; and L. Davidoff and C. Hall, *Family Fortunes: Men and Women of the English Middle class, 1780–1850*, London, Routledge, 1987, esp. pp. 73–148.

15 J. Dunlop, *Autobiography*, London, 1932, pp. 7, 9, 27.

16 *Chamber's Journal*, vol. 5, no. 210, 6 February 1836.

17 *The General Baptist Repository and Missionary Observer*, new series vol. 1, 1 January 1834, p. 11.

18 Ibid., p. 9

19 E.P. Thompson, *Customs in Common*, London, Merlin, 1991.

20 A. Clark, *The Struggle for the Breeches: Gender and the Making of the British Working Class*, London, Rivers Oram Press, 1995.

21 H. Cunningham, *Leisure in the Industrial Revolution*, London, Croom Helm, 1980.

22 The original and still one of the best expositions of evangelicalism's popularity as a social-reform tool to adapt working men to industrial capitalism is E.P. Thompson, *The Making of the English Working Class*, London, Harmondsworth, 1969 edn, chapters 11 and 12.

23 For one example, see C.G. Brown, 'The religion of an industrial village: the churches in Balfron 1789–1850', *Scottish Local History Society Journal*, 1995, vol. 35, pp. 9–15.

24 J.L. Hammond and B. Hammond, *The Town Labourer 1760–1832: The New Civilisation*, London, Longman's Green, 1917, p. 271.

25 A.A. MacLaren, *Religion and Social Class: The Disruption Years in Aberdeen*, London, RKP, 1974.

26 Clark, *Struggle*, pp. 92–118. James Hammerton, in discussing evangelicalism in the context of *middle-class* experience of domestic conflict, makes a similar point that 'the evangelical emphasis on domesticity elevated motherhood and the moral power of women to a point that was inconsistent with their total subordination.' A. J. Hammerton, *Cruelty and Companionship: Conflict in Nineteenth-century Married Life*, London, Routledge, 1992, p. 71.

27 M. Heimann, *Catholic Devotion in Victorian England*, Oxford, Clarendon Press, 1995, pp. 116–17, 137, 144, 156–7.

28 A term coined by, and a point forcefully made in Bebbington, *Evangelicalism*, pp. 107–8, 129, 149–50, and D. Bebbington, *Victorian Nonconformity*, Bangor, Headstart, 1992, pp. 23, 28.

29 Ibid., pp. 68–9.

30 On the role of association in the churches, and the importance of this to urban society, see Green, *Religion*.

31 'The chapels were ordinarily pulsating with life, drawing in fresh recruits and setting up new daughter congregations.' Bebbington, *Victorian Nonconformity*, p. 23.

32 R. Wardlaw, *The Contemplation of Heathen Idolatry an Excitement to Missionary Zeal*, London, Williams & Co., 1818, p. 23.

33 There is a very wide literature dealing with the development of religious voluntary organisations. Useful examples are S. Mechie, *The Church and Scottish Social Development 1760–1860*, Oxford, Oxford University Press, 1960, which deals with the church origins of penny banks, and C. Binfield, *George Williams and the YMCA*, London, Heinneman, 1973.

34 *Autobiography of a Scotch Lad*, Glasgow, 1887, p. 30.

35 T. Chalmers, *The Christian and Civic Economy of Large Towns*, Glasgow, 1821, pp. 66–7.

36 Ibid., p. 29.

37 *British Messenger* 1 July 1863, p. 81.

38 M.S.S. Herdman, *The Romance of the Ranks: Reminiscences of Army Work*, Stirling, Drummond Tract Enterprise, 1888, pp. 124–5.

39 *Old Age not a 'Convenient Season' for Repentance*, Stirling, Drummond Tracts no. 299, 1871.

40 Quoted in H. McLeod, *Class and Religion in the Late Victorian City*, London, Croom Helm, 1974, p. 53.

41 Quoted in W. Hanna (ed.), *Memoirs of Thomas Chalmers*, vol. 1, Edinburgh, Constable, 1854, p. 440.

42 Revd W. Johnson, *Open-air Preaching*, Stirling, Drummond Tract Enterprise, 1853, p. 2.

43 *British Messenger* 1 January 1862, p. 11.

44 'Why are Ye Idle?' by Charlotte Murray, *Messages from the Master: And Other Poems*, Stirling, Drummond Tract Enterprise, 1880, p. 38.

45 *British Messenger*, 1 August 1862, p. 89.

46 J.C. Gibson (ed.), *Diary of Sir Michael Connal*, Glasgow, 1895, pp. 24, 66.

47 *An Account of the Origin and Progress of the London Religious Tract Society*, London, 1803, p. 9.

48 An American Citizen, *Philosophy of the Plan of Salvation*, London, The Religious Tract Society, *c.* 1837, flyleaf.

49 Uncatalogued correspondence on union of Stirling Tract Enterprise with Monthly Tract Society of London, the Family Worship Union, the Scottish Colportage Society and the Pure Literature Society of Ireland, contained in Stirling University Library, Drummond Collection.

50 *British Messenger*, 1 December 1865, p. 144.

51 Ibid., 1 November 1862, p. 132.

52 V.M. Skinner, *These Seven Years; or the Story of the 'Friendly Letter Mission'*, Stirling, Drummond Tract Enterprise, 1888, p. 11.

53 R.W. Cooper, *Tract Distribution: Something You Can Do, and How To Do It*, Stirling, Drummond Tract Enterprise, *c.* 1935, pp. 1–2.

54 'What a Tract Did', *Good News*, January 1922, p. 2.

55 Cooper, *Tract Distribution*, pp. 7–8.

56 Ibid., pp. 9–10.

57 C. Cook, *Sketches from Life*, Stirling, Drummond Tract Enterprise, 1892.

58 This marked-up bound copy of *British Messenger*, 1 October 1862, is in Stirling University Library, Drummond Collection.

59 *Chamber's Journal*, no. 1, 4 February 1832.

60 *Chamber's Journal*, vol. 5, no. 209, 30 January 1836, p. 1.

61 In 1863, his novel *Rachel Ray* was commissioned by the Revd Norman Macleod, editor of the evangelical magazine *Good Words*, but rejected by him because of its unsympathetic portrayal of an evangelical clergyman. Quoted in D. Skilton (ed.), *The Early and Mid-Victorian Novel*, London, Routledge, 1993, pp. 56–8 n. 2.

62 D. Trotter, *The English Novel in History 1895–1920*, London, Routledge, 1993, p. 63.

63 Ibid., p. 182.

64 On the 'parting of the ways' between 'highbrow' and 'lowbrow' literature in inter-war Britain, see R. Williams, *The English Novel from Dickens to Lawrence*, London, Chatto and Windus, 1970, ch. 5; A. Light, *Forever England: Femininity, Literature and Conservatism between the Wars*, London, Routledge, 1991, p. x.

65 A phrase used in E. Routley, *The Church and Music*, n.p., Duckworth, 1978, p. 185.

66 E. Routley, *The English Carol*, London, Herbert Jenkins, 1958, pp. 173–89.

67 Quoted in H. Cunningham, *Leisure in the Industrial Revolution*, London, Croom Helm, 1980, p. 103.

68 One piano manufacturer, Broadwood's, produced pianos at the rate of 19 per year during 1718–82, 400 per year during 1782–1802, and 1,680 per year during 1802–24. Routley, *English Carol*, p. 169.

69 A.T. Taylor, *Labour and Love: An Oral History of the Brass Band Movement*, London, Elm Tree Books, 1983.

70 *The General Baptist Repository*, 1 January 1824, p. 7.

71 J. Blackburn, *The Salvation of Britain Introductory to the Conversion of the World*, London, Jackson & Walford, 1835, pp. 15–22.

72 *The Christian Miscellany and Family Visitor*, December 1867, pp. 364–5.

73 *British Weekly*, 5 November 1886, p. 1.

74 G.W. Haughton, *Free Salvation; or God's Gift of the Saviour*, Stirling, Drummond Tract Enterprise, 1901, p. 7.

75 Cf. Hugh McLeod, who has written that 'sectarianism provided for large numbers of people the strongest basis for their social identity', resulting in 'self-built ideological ghettos'. H. McLeod, *Religion and the People of Western Europe 1789–1989*, Oxford, Oxford University Press, 1997, p. 36.

76 Heimann, *Catholic Devotion*, pp. 35, 152, 195–9; L.H. Lees, *Exiles of Erin: Irish Migrants in Victorian London*, Manchester, Manchester University Press, 1979, pp. 172–97; B. Aspinwall, 'The formation of the Catholic community in the west of Scotland: some preliminary outlines', *Innes Review*, 1982, vol. 33 pp. 47, 53; B. Aspinwall and J. McCaffrey, 'A comparative view of the Irish in Edinburgh in the nineteenth-century', in R. Swift and S. Gilley (eds), *The Irish in the Victorian City*, London, Croom Helm, 1985, pp. 135–9.

77 *Good News*, January 1923, p. 3.

4 ANGELS: WOMEN IN DISCOURSE AND NARRATIVE 1800–1950

1 N. Auerbach, *Woman and the Demon: The Life of a Victorian Myth*, Cambridge, Mass., Harvard University Press, 1982, pp. 64, 71–108.

2 M.R. Miles, *Carnal Knowledge: Female Nakedness and Religious Meaning in the Christian West*, New York, Vintage, 1991, pp. 53–77; P. Crawford, *Women and Religion in England 1500–1720*, London, Routledge, 1993, p. 25.

3 D. Cressy, *Birth, Marriage and Death: Ritual, Religion and the Life-Cycle in Tudor and Stuart England*, Oxford, Oxford University Press, 1997, esp. pp. 475–82.

4 Crawford, *Women and Religion*, pp. 73–115; C. Larner, *Enemies of God: The Witch-hunt in Scotland*, Oxford, Oxford University Press, 1983.

5 J. Gregory, 'Homo Religiosus: masculinity and religion in the long eighteenth century', in T. Hitchcock and M. Cohen (eds), *English Masculinity 1660–1800*, London, Longman, 1999, p. 105.

6 For this section, I have benefited enormously from Sue Morgan's comments, and from reading S. Morgan, *A Passion for Purity: Ellice Hopkins and the Politics of Gender in the late-Victorian Church*, Bristol, Centre for Comparative Studies in Religion and Gender, 1999, esp. pp. 6–43.

7   B.L. Epstein, *The Politics of Domesticity: Women, Evangelism and Temperance in Nineteenth-Century America*, Middletown, Conn., Wesleyan University Press, 1981; C. Hall, *White, Male and Middle Class: Explorations in Feminism and History*, Cambridge, Polity Press, 1992, pp. 75–93; F. Prochaska, *Women and Philanthropy in Nineteenth Century England*, Oxford, Clarendon Press, 1980; O. Banks, *Faces of Feminism: A Study of Feminism as a Social Movement*, Oxford, Martin Robertson, 1981, pp. 13–27; B. Taylor, *Eve and the New Jerusalem: Socialism and Feminism in the Nineteenth Century*, London, Virago, 1983; L. Davidoff and C. Hall, *Family Fortunes: Men and Women of the English Middle Class 1780–1850*, London, Routledge, 1987, pp. 71–192; Morgan, *Passion for Purity*, esp. pp. 170–1.

8   M. Foucault, *The Archaeology of Knowledge*, London, Routledge, 1989 edn, pp. 50–5.

9   *The General Baptist Repository and Missionary Observer*, July 1848, p. 318.

10 *An Account of the Origin and Progress of the London Religious Tract Society*, London, 1803, pp. 7–8.

11 *The Methodist Magazine*, vol. 34, January 1811, p. 3.

12 Ibid., vol. 34, January 1811, p. 74.

13 *The Methodist Magazine*, vol. 11, February 1832, pp. 156–9.

14 *The Primitive Methodist Magazine* vol. 2, January 1821, pp. 14–15.

15 *The General Baptist Repository*, February 1840, pp. 34–5

16 Ibid., vol. 10, 1848, index.

17 Ibid., vol. 3, 1 January 1824, p. 20.

18 Ibid.

19 Poem by Revd R.M. McCheyne, quoted in J.F. Moncrieff, *The Prize-Winners: An Address to the Young*, Stirling, Stirling Tract Enterprise, *c.* 1911, p. 17.

20 *British Messenger*, vol. 68, February 1920, p. 17.

21 *The Edinburgh Christian Magazine*, vol. 3, 1851, p. 203.

22 *The Day-Star*, vol. 11, 1855, p. 266.

23 Ibid., vol. 10, 1854, p. 112.

24 Ibid., vol. 12, 1856, p. 13.

25 M. Stanley, 'Clubs for working girls', *The Nineteenth Century*, 1889, vol. 25, p. 74.

26 *The General Baptist Repository*, May 1848, pp. 202–3.

27 Ibid., February 1848, pp. 68–9.

28 *British Messenger*, 1 August 1862, p. 90.

29 Quoted in *The Methodist Magazine*, vol. 21, March 1842, pp. 44–6.

30 R. Dodsley, *The Economy of Human Life*, Preston, 1837, p. 23.

31 *The Christian Miscellany and Family Visitor*, 1890, p. 128.

32 Ibid., p. 129.

33 *British Messenger*, vol. 79, November 1930, p. 125.

34 *The Christian Miscellany*, 1890, p. 229.

35 *Girl's Own Paper*, vol. 5, 1883–4, p. 147.

36 *Old Age not a 'Convenient Season' for Repentance*, Stirling, Drummond Tracts no. 299, 1871.

37 *The Christian Miscellany*, 1890, p. 185.

38 Ibid., p. 395.

39 *Be not Deceived*, Stirling, Drummond Tract no. 321, *c.* 1873.

40 *The Christian Miscellany*, vol. 13, January 1867, p. 11.

41 Reprinted from *The Child's Magazine* in *The Primitive Methodist Children's Magazine*, no. 10, October 1827, pp. 151–3.

42 Ibid., new series vol. 1, 1843, pp. 11–13.

43 *A Heroic Child*, Stirling, Drummond Tracts, 1871 First Series, no. 181.

44 Quoted in *The Christian Miscellany*, 1890, p. 394.

45 *The Ball-Room and Its Tendencies: An Affectionate Appeal to Professing Christian Parents of the Upper and Middle Classes*, Stirling, Drummond Tracts no. 31, 1853, pp. 1–2.

46 *A Race-Course Dialogue*, Stirling, Drummond Tract no. 97, 1852, pp. 1–2.

47 *British Messenger,* vol. 68, September 1920, p. 100. See also D. Rapp, 'The British Salvation Army, the early film industry and urban working-class adolescents, 1897–1918', *Twentieth Century British History*, 1996, vol. 7, pp. 157–88.

48 *Light Reading*, Stirling, Drummond Tract no. 124, 1853.

49 *Confession of a Novel-Reader*, Stirling, Drummond Tract no. 126, 1853.

50 *British Weekly*, 2 January 1902.

51 'But I suffer not a woman to teach, nor to usurp authority over the man, but to be in silence.' (King James version.)

52 *The General Baptist Repository*, vol. 3, 1 January 1824, p. 17; 1 March 1824, pp. 94–5.

53 *Free Church Magazine*, 1844, vol. 6, p. 171.

54 B. Stanley, *The Bible and the Flag: Protestant Missions and British Imperialism in the Nineteenth and Twentieth Centuries*, Leicester, Apollos, 1990, pp. 80–1; S. Gill, *Women and the Church of England: From the Eighteenth Century to the Present*, London, SPCK, 1994, pp. 131–98; O. Checkland, *Philanthropy in Victorian Scotland*, Edinburgh, John Donald, 1980, pp. 84–9.

55 Revd G. Everard, *Life for Evermore*, Stirling, Drummond Tract Enterprise, 1902, p. 93.

56 Such as the accounts of 'Miss Fraser' in A.M.C. (pseud.), *Stories of a Men's Class* and *Two Words Did It, and Other Narratives*, both Stirling, Drummond Tract Enterprise, 1903.

57 *British Weekly*, 26 November 1886, p. 15.

58 Ibid., 21 March 1918, p. 454.

59 I. McEwan, *Enduring Love*, London, Vintage, 1998, p. 48.

60 Ibid.

61 M.R. Somers and G.D. Gibson, quoted in P. Joyce, *Democratic Subjects: The Self and the Social in Nineteenth-century England*, Cambridge, Cambridge University Press, 1994, p. 153.

62 Ibid., p. 189.

63 J.R. Walkowitz, *City of Dreadful Delight: Narratives of Sexual Danger in Late-Victorian London*, London, Virago, 1992, esp. pp. 81–120.

64 E.D. Ermarth, *The English Novel in History 1840–1895*, London, Routledge, 1997, p. 125.

65 See for instance D.B. Hindmarsh, *John Newton and the English Evangelical Tradition Between the Conversions of Wesley and Wilberforce*, Oxford, Clarendon Press, 1996, pp. 13–49.

66 *Chamber's* was serialising stories in 1834 before Charles Dickens' experiment in serialised publishing of Pickwick Papers in nineteen monthly parts in 1836–7.

D. Skilton (ed.), *The Early and Mid-Victorian Novel*, London, Routledge, 1993, p. 32, n. 1.

67 Religious polarities of melancholy and happiness constituted the structure of William James' study of the divided self; W. James, *The Varieties of Religious Experience*, London, Longmans, Green, orig. 1902, 1928 imprint, pp. 78–188.

68 Major-General M.H. Synge, quoted in M.S.S. Herdman, *The Romance of the Ranks: Reminiscences of Army Life*, Stirling, Drummond Tract Enterprise, 1888, p. vi.

69 These were: descent from a higher world, descent to a lower world, ascent from a lower world, and ascent to a higher world, where the highest world level is heaven. N. Frye, *The Secular Scripture: A Study of the Structure of Romance*, Cambridge, Mass., Harvard University Press, 1976, pp. 5, 97.

70 Frye's seven phases in the 'revelation' of the Bible were: creation, revolution or exodus, law, wisdom, prophecy, gospel and apocalypse. N. Frye, *The Great Code: The Bible and Literature*, Toronto, Academic Press Canada, 1982, pp. 105–38, 169.

71 U. Eco, *The Role of the Reader*, Bloomington, Ind., University of Indiana Press, 1979, p. 146. For an appreciation of the value of this technique, see D. Strinati, *An Introduction to Theories of Popular Culture*, London, Routledge, 1995, pp. 102–8.

72 Eco, *Role of the Reader*, p. 156.

73 *The General Baptist Repository*, February 1848, p. 69.

74 G. Pettman, *The Unequal Yoke*, Stirling, Stirling Tract Enterprise, *c.* 1938.

75 N. Fabb, *Linguistics and Literature*, Oxford, Blackwell, 1997, pp. 203–6.

76 A.M.C. (pseud.), *Two Words Did It, and Other Narratives*, Stirling, Drummond Tract Enterprise, 1903, pp. 18, 28.

77 A.O. Stott, 'Fanny's Mistake and Its Sequel', in *Good News*, June 1924, no. 751, pp. 21–2.

78 *British Weekly*, 22 July 1887, p. 188–9.

79 *British Messenger*, 1 March 1862.

80 S. Watson, *Catherine Ballard*, Stirling, Drummond Tract Enterprise, 1894, p. 86.

81 Ibid., pp. 154–5.

82 Mrs Harvey-Jellie, 'Saved from Drifting', *Good News*, February 1922, no. 722, p. 2.

83 *British Messenger*, 1 August 1865, p. 85.

84 *The Christian Miscellany*, vol. 13, January 1867, p. 10.

85 G. Pardon, *Love's Healing*, Stirling, Drummond Tract Enterprise, *c.* 1925, p. 16.

86 M. Wynn, *Jennifer-Ann*, Stirling, Drummond Tract Enterprise, *c.* 1946, p. 32. After 1910, Drummond's books were uniformly undated, allowing for their endless reprinting with re-typesetting and new illustrations of the latest ladies' fashions to maintain an air of modernity.

87 H. Kent, *The Doctor's Story: How a Woman Doctor Found her Way to a World of Glad Service through Doors of Sorrow*, Stirling, Drummond Tract Enterprise, *c.* 1930, p. 2.

88 Ibid., p. 16.

89 *Good News*, February 1937, no. 904, pp. 5–6.

90   'The Heavenly Colour', in *Daybreak*, no vol., no date, *c.* 1905, p. 15.

91   E. Poole, *My Garden*, Stirling, Drummond Tract Enterprise, 1889.

92   Cf. P. Branca, *Silent Sisterhood: Middle-class Women in the Victorian Home*, London, Croom Helm, 1975, p. 147.

93   M. Beetham, *A Magazine of Her Own? Domesticity and Desire in the Woman's Magazine, 1800–1914*, London, Routledge, 1996, pp. 36–111, 157–73.

94   *Chamber's Journal*, 6 February 1836.

95   E.D. Ermarth, *The English Novel in History 1840–1895*, London, Routledge, 1997, p. 206.

96   *Chamber's Journal*, 13 February 1832, pp. 19–20.

97   Ibid., 25 August 1832, p. 233.

98   Ermarth, *English Novel*, p. 4.

99   Ibid., p. 40.

100 Ibid., p. 7.

101 Ibid., pp. 22, 27.

102 Ibid., pp. 27–8.

103 Ibid., pp. 31–2.

104 Ibid., pp. 41–65.

105 Quoted in D. Skilton (ed.), *The Early and Mid-Victorian Novel*, London, Routledge, 1993, p. 26.

106 S. Foster, *Victorian Women's Fiction: Marriage, Freedom and the Individual*, Beckenham, Croom Helm, 1985, pp. 7, 15.

107 j. Dixon, *The Romance Fiction of Mills & Boon, 1909–1990s*, London, UCL Press, 1999, pp. 33–4.

108 Ibid., pp. 167–8.

109 Ermarth, *English Novel*, pp. 199–202.

110 Something of this sort is suggested in D. Trotter, *The English Novel in History 1895–1920*, London, Routledge, 1993, p. 183.

111 C.G. Brown, 'Popular culture and the continuing struggle for rational recreation', in T.M. Devine and R.J. Finlay (eds), *Scotland in the Twentieth Century*, Edinburgh, John Donald, 1996.

112 *Mrs Miniver*, starring Greer Garson and Walter Pidgeon (dir William Wyler, MGM Films, 1942, original book by Jan Struther).

113 Quoted in A. Light, *Forever England: Femininity, Literature and Conservatism Between the Wars*, London, Routledge, 1991, p. 117.

114 Ibid., p. 121.

115 Quoted in ibid., p. 123.

116 Ibid., p. 131.

117 Quoted in ibid., p. 146.

118 *Girl's Own Paper*, vol. 7, 3 July 1886, p. 637.

119 Ibid., 10 July 1886, p. 644.

120 Ibid., 31 July 1886, p. 703.

121 Ibid., 4 September 1886, pp. 769–70.

122 Ibid., 8 October 1886, pp. 4–7; vol. 17, 7 March 1896, pp. 362–4.

123 Ibid., 28 March 1896, pp. 458–9.

124 Ibid., vol. 8, 15 January 1887, p. 252; vol. 17, 28 March 1896, pp. 403–4.

125 Ibid., vol. 37, 1916–17, p. 13.

126 Ibid., pp. 13, 21–2.
127 P. Tinkler, *Constructing Girlhood: Popular Magazines for Girls Growing Up in England 1920–1950*, London, Taylor and Francis, 1995, pp. 45–6.
128 *Girl's Own Paper*, vol. 42, 1922, pp. 15, 24–5, 65, 546–9, 563, 567; and vol. 46, 1926, pp. 15, 134.
129 Ibid., vol. 58, 1938, pp. 1–4, 5, 14–15, 55, 67–9, 96, 228, 272.
130 Tinkler, *Constructing Girlhood*, pp. 55–9.
131 D. Kyles, *Should a Girl Smoke? An Appeal to British Womanhood*, Stirling, Drummond Tract Enterprise, 1938, pp. 3–4.

5 HEATHENS: MEN IN DISCOURSE AND NARRATIVE 1800–1950

1 This is a transition outlined in E.A. Foyster, *Manhood in Early Modern England: Honour, Sex and Marriage*, London, Longman, 1999, pp. 207–13.
2 On the dominance of male exemplars before 1800, see J. Gregory, 'Homo Religiosus: masculinity and religion in the long eighteenth century', in T. Hitchcock and M. Cohen (eds), *English Masculinity 1660–1800*, London, Longman, 1999.
3 J. Tosh, *A Man's Place: Masculinity and the Middle-class Home in Victorian England*, New Haven, Yale University Press, 1999, esp. pp. 195–7.
4 N. Vance, *Sinews of the Spirit: The Ideal of Christian Manliness in Victorian Literature and Religious Thought*, Cambridge, Cambridge University Press, 1985; J. Springhall, 'Building character in the British boy: the attempt to extend Christian manliness to working-class adolescents, 1880–1914', in J.A. Mangan and J. Walvin (eds), *Manliness and Morality: Middle-class Masculinity in Britain and America, 1800–1940*, Manchester, Manchester University Press, 1987; P. Walker, ' "I live but not yet I for Christ Liveth in me": Men and masculinity in the Salvation Army, 1865–90', in M. Roper and J. Tosh (eds.), *Manful Assertions: Masculinities in Britain since 1800*, London, Routledge, 1991.
5 *British Weekly*, 27 April 1888, p. 481.
6 Ibid., 18 and 25 May, 17 and 24 August 1888.
7 Ibid., 18 November 1887, p. 39.
8 Ibid., 9 December 1887, p. 99.
9 Ibid., 4 November 1887, p. 1.
10 Ibid., 27 January 1888, p. 243.
11 Ibid., 16 March 1888, p. 356.
12 *The Awful Disclosures of Maria Monk* was a much reprinted and, for its time, supposedly titillating account, reputedly by a former nun, of alleged sexual abuse by priests in a Montreal nunnery. Editions were customarily 'Published for the Trade' and without a publisher's name. It was a work of both anti-Catholic bigotry and ecclesiastical pornography. It is still said to be available from extremist Protestant outlets.
13 *British Weekly*, 23 March 1888.
14 Ebenezer Elliott, quoted in H.N. Fairchild, *Religious Trends in English Poetry, vol. IV: 1830–1880: Christianity and Romanticism in the Victorian Era*, New York and London, Columbia University Press, 1957, p. 88.

15 G. Crossick, 'From gentlemen to the residuum: languages of social description in Victorian Britain', in P.J. Corfield (ed.), *Language, History and Class*, Oxford, Blackwell, 1991, pp. 162–3.

16 C.T. Bateman, 'Missionary efforts in the metropolis', in R. Mudie-Smith (ed.), *The Religious Life of London*, London, Hodder & Stoughton, 1904, p. 314.

17 *The Christian Miscellany and Family Visitor*, vol. 13, 1867, p. 72.

18 P. Bailey, '"Will the real Bill Banks please stand up?" Towards a role analysis of mid-Victorian working-class respectability', *Journal of Social History*, 1979, vol. 12.

19 *The General Baptist Repository and Missionary Observer*, no. 19, July 1840, p. 193.

20 *The Christian Miscellany*, vol. 13, 1867, p. 30.

21 Ibid., vol. 13, 1867, p. 157.

22 *The General Baptist Repository*, no. 19, July 1840, p. 194.

23 Ibid., vol. 3, February 1824, p. 21.

24 *The Methodist Magazine*, vol. 34, January 1811, p. 9.

25 'Elizabeth', writing in *The General Baptist Repository*, vol. 10, May 1848, p. 203.

26 E. Poole, *Shut the Door*, Stirling, Drummond Tract Enterprise, 1890, pp. 6–8.

27 *British Messenger*, January 1878, p. 4.

28 Ibid., February 1878, p. 10.

29 Ibid., March 1878, p. 30, and April 1878, pp. 42–3.

30 M.S.S. Herdman, *The Romance of the Ranks: Reminiscences of Army Work*, Stirling, Drummond Tract Enterprise, 1888, pp. 15, 18, 21, 26, 46, 51, 60–1, 64, 123, 138.

31 *Which?*, Stirling, Drummond Tract Enterprise, tract no. 2, first series.

32 *What is Lost by Strong Drink?*, Stirling, Drummond Tract Enterprise, tract no. 58, first series.

33 *The Spiritual Thermometer*, Stirling, Drummond Tract Enterprise, tract no. 14, first series.

34 *The Street Preacher*, Stirling, Drummond Tract Enterprise, tract no. 7, first series.

35 C. Cook, *Sketches from Life: Tract 1: A Voice from the Convict Cell*, Stirling, Drummond Tract Enterprise, 1892, pp. 8–10.

36 *What thou doest, do quickly*, Drummond Tract Enterprise, tract no. 139, first series.

37 *The Religion We Want*, Drummond Tract Enterprise, tract no. 249, first series.

38 *Who will be at the Theatre?*, Drummond Tract Enterprise, tract no. 112, first series.

39 *The Theatre*, Drummond Tract Enterprise, tract no. 193, first series.

40 *British Messenger*, 1 March 1862, p. 25.

41 *The Ball-Room and Its Tendencies*, Drummond Tract Enterprise, tract no. 31, original series, 1853.

42 *Hell! What is it?* Drummond Tract Enterprise, tract no. 330, first series.

43 *British Messenger*, 1 December 1865, p. 133.

44 C. Murray, *Messages from The Master: And Other Poems*, Stirling, Drummond Tract Enterprise, 1880, p. 67.

45 *British Messenger*, 1 January 1862, p. 9.

46 *Choose Life*, Stirling, Drummond Tract Enterprise, tract no. 64, second series.

47 R.W. Cooper, *Tract Distribution: Something You Can Do, and How To Do It*, Stirling, Drummond Tract Enterprise, *c.* 1935, p. 10.

48 *Good News*, May 1923.

49 J. Springhall, *Youth, Empire and Society: British Youth Movements 1883–1940* London, Croom Helm, 1977.

50 C.G. Brown, 'The Sunday-school movement in Scotland, 1780–1914', *Records of the Scottish Church History Society*, 1981, vol. 21.

51 Vance, *Sinews of the Spirit*, p. 2.

52 The timing of this change in the curriculum is evident in *Glasgow United Y.M.C.A. Annual Reports*, 1877, pp. 14–20, and 1883, p. 15; see also Vance, *Sinews of the Spirit*, p. 168.

53 *Races, Games, and Balls*, Drummond Tract Enterprise, tract no. 339, original series, 1853.

54 A. Nicolson, 'Moody and Sankey in Scotland 1873–1874: "And it's from the old we travel to the new"', unpublished BA Hons. dissertation, Department of History, University of Strathclyde, 1998.

55 *North British Daily Mail*, quoted in R.K. Curtis, *They Called Him Mr. Moody*, New York, 1962, p. 188.

56 *British Messenger*, September 1922, p. 105.

57 P. Bilsborough, 'The development of sport in Glasgow, 1850–1914', unpublished M.Litt. thesis, University of Stirling, 1983, p. 147.

58 J. Clifford, *The Dawn of Manhood*, London, Christian Commonwealth, 1886; J.T. Davidson, *The City Youth*, London, Hodder & Stoughton, 1886; *British Weekly*, 5 November 1886, p. 7.

59 C.G. Brown, 'Sport and the Scottish Office in the twentieth century: the control of a social problem', *European Sports History Review*, 1999, vol. 1, pp. 164–82.

60 *British Weekly*, 8 July 1887, p. 152; 3 February 1888, p. 257.

61 W. Hanna (ed.), *Memoirs of Thomas Chalmers*, vol. 1, Edinburgh, Constable, 1854, p. 433.

62 *British Weekly*, 24 December 1886, p. 5.

63 For instance, see ibid., 12 December 1901.

64 *The Primitive Methodist Magazine*, vol. 2, November 1821, pp. 252–4.

65 C. Harvie, 'The Covenanting tradition', in G. Walker and T. Gallagher (eds), *Sermons and Battle Hymns: Protestant Popular Culture in Modern Scotland*, Edinburgh, Edinburgh University Press, 1990; C.G. Brown, *Religion and Society in Scotland since 1707*, Edinburgh, Edinburgh University Press, 1997, pp. 22–5, 78–83.

66 Stirling General Associate [Antiburgher] Presbytery minutes, 11 February 1783, Stirling Archive Services CH3/286/2.

67 J. Peddie, *A Defence of the Associate Synod against the Charge of Sedition*, Edinburgh, 1800, p. 7.

68 J. Sinclair, *The Statistical Account of Scotland, vol. 8*, Edinburgh, William Creech, 1793, p. 352.

69 J. Galt, *Annals of the Parish*, orig. 1821, reprint Edinburgh, James Thin, 1978, p. 5.

70 W. Adamson, *The Life of the Rev. Fergus Ferguson*, London, Simpkin, 1900, p. 76.

71 J. Brown, *The Life of a Scottish Probationer: Being a Memoir of Thomas Davidson* [1838–70], Glasgow, Maclehose, 1877, pp. 173–4.

72 For example, N. Macleod, *Reminiscences of a Highland Parish,* London, 1867, a bestseller by one minister about his ministerial father and grandfather; D. Macleod, *Memoir of Norman Macleod D.D. two volumes, by his Brother,* London, Daldy, Isbister & Co., 1876; S. Smith, *Donald Macleod of Glasgow: A Memoir and a Study,* London, James Clarke, 1926; R. Ferguson, *George Macleod: Founder of the Iona Community,* London, HarperCollins, 1990, about Norman's grandson.

73 J. Brown, *Life of William B. Robertson, D.D.,* Glasgow, Maclehose, 1889, p. 14.

74 D. Hobbs, *Robert Hood, the Bridgeton Pastor: The Story of His Bright and Useful Life,* Edinburgh, Fairgrieve, 1894, p. 31.

75 *Sunny Stories,* Stirling, Drummond Tract Enterprise, *c.* 1955, p. 16.

76 Hobbs, *Robert Hood,* pp. 33–4

77 Ibid., pp. 45–6.

78 D. Beaton, *Memoir, Diary and Remains of the Rev. Donald Macfarlane, Dingwall,* Inverness, Northern Counties Newspaper, 1929, p. 11.

79 D. Macleod, *Norman Macleod,* p. 103.

80 *British Messenger,* 1 January 1872, pp. 2–3, 1 February 1872, p. 11, 1 March 1872, p. 27.

81 E.D. Ermarth, *The English Novel in History 1840–1895,* London, Routledge, 1997, p. 39.

82 S.R. Crockett, *The Stickit Minister and Some Common Men,* orig. 1893, reprint London, T. Fisher Unwin, 1905.

83 Ibid., pp. 15–16.

84 J.M. Barrie, *Auld Licht Idylls,* orig. 1887, reprint London, Hodder & Stoughton, *c.* 1910, pp. 11–12.

85 Ibid., p. 73.

86 J.M. Barrie, *A Window in Thrums,* orig. 1889, reprint London, Hodder & Stoughton, 1938, p. 152.

87 J.M. Barrie, *The Little Minister,* orig. 1891, reprint London, Cassell & Company, 1909, p. 298.

88 A. Jarvis, *Samuel Smiles and the Construction of Victorian Values,* Stroud, Sutton, 1997, pp. 57, 98–114.

89 Smiles in *Lives of the Engineers,* quoted ibid., p. 75.

90 C. Brady, *The Riches of His Grace,* Stirling, Drummond Tract Enterprise, 1885, p. 129.

91 *The Book of Fire, or the Lake of Fire!,* Stirling, Drummond Tract Enterprise, tract no. 307, first series.

92 *British Weekly,* 22 May 1919, p. 205.

93 C.C.A. Savery, *God Bless Daddy: A Bedtime Book for Sons and Daughters of Soldiers, Sailors, Airmen,* Stirling, Drummond Tract Enterprise, *c.* 1944.

94 J.N. Dick, *Men of Destiny: Christian Messages from Modern Leaders,* Stirling, Drummond Tract Enterprise, 1944.

95 A.S. Swan, 'A Winning Fight', in *British Weekly,* 13 December 1917, p. 207.

96 J. Paterson-Smyth, *God and the War,* London, Hodder & Stoughton, 1915, pp. 62, 69.

97 H.H. Henson, 'The Church of England after the War', in F.J. Foakes-Jackson (ed.), *The Faith and the War,* London, Macmillan, 1915, p. 239.

98 C.G. Brown, 'Piety, gender and war in the 1910s', in C. Macdonald and E. McFarland (eds), *Scotland and the Great War*, East Linton, Tuckwell, 1999.

99 D. Cairns, *The Army and Religion*, London, Hodder & Stoughton, 1919, p. 9.

100 N. Maclean and J.P.P. Sclater, *God and the Soldier*, London, Hodder & Stoughton, 1917, pp. 125–7, 224.

101 Cairns, *Army and Religion*, p. 93.

102 Ibid., p. 97.

103 Ibid., pp. 371–2.

104 W.H. Archer, *Collier Jack*, Stirling, Drummond Tract Enterprise, *c.* 1900.

105 'Jock' in *Good News* no. 752, August 1924, pp. 29–30.

106 Ibid., August 1926, pp. 29–32.

107 *British Messenger*, vol. 89, 1940; vol. 98, 1946 (unpaginated).

108 R. Cunningham, *This Man or His Parents*, Stirling, Drummond Tract Enterprise, *c.* 1930.

109 *British Messenger*, April 1937.

110 *Oh! If I Had Listened*, Stirling, Drummond Tract Enterprise, tract no. 40, second series.

111 *British Messenger*, April 1920, pp. 38–9.

112 J.H. Wilson, *A Bright Sunset: or, Recollections of the Last Days of a Young Football Player*, Stirling, Drummond Tract Enterprise, 1902.

113 E. Poole, *His Mighty Men*, Stirling, Drummond Tract Enterprise, 1891, p. 2.

114 S. Watson, *Disloyal*, Stirling, Drummond Tract Enterprise, 1891, pp. 209–10.

115 P.B. Power, *The Man that Carried the Baby and Other Stories*, Stirling, Drummond Tract Enterprise, Household Series no. 1, 1896, pp. 10, 23.

116 E. Poole, *Shut the Door*, Stirling, Drummond Tract Enterprise, 1890, p. 5.

117 Crossick, 'From gentlemen to the residuum', p. 163.

118 Published by the Society for the Diffusion of Useful Knowledge. Extracts can be viewed at www.history.rochester.edu/pennymag

119 How this problem materialised within Anglicanism is mentioned in S. Gill, *Women and the Church of England: From the Eighteenth Century to the Present*, London, SPCK, 1994, pp. 83–7.

120 *Chamber's Journal*, 13 February 1832, p. 21.

121 Ibid., 25 August 1832, p. 233.

122 Ibid.

123 Ibid., 24 December 1836, p. 377.

124 Ibid., 5 February 1853, p. 95. Another feature article covering the same ground appeared two months later, 16 April 1853, p. 253.

125 Ibid., 11 February 1860, p. 84.

126 Ibid., 5 January 1833.

127 Ibid., 30 January 1836, p. 1.

128 Ibid., 27 February 1836, p. 33.

129 For instance James Payne's 'The Bateman Household', ibid., 7 January 1860.

130 H.N. Fairchild, *Religious Trends in English Poetry, vol IV: 1830–1880: Christianity and Romanticism in the Victorian Era*, New York and London, Columbia University Press, 1957, pp. viii, 559.

131 Charles Kingsley, 'Sunday Morning', quoted ibid., p. 19.

132 Robert Browning, 'Pacchiarotto', quoted ibid., p. 165.

133   See H.N. Fairchild, *Religious Trends in English Poetry: vol. II: 1740–1780: Religious Sentimentalism in the Age of Johnson*, New York and London, Columbia University Press, 1942.

134   This moral turn is chronicled in R.H. MacDonald, 'Reproducing the middle-class boy: from purity to patriotism in the boys' magazines, 1892–1914', *Journal of Contemporary History*, 1989, vol. 24, pp. 519–39.

135   *Boy's Own Paper*, vol. 52, 1929–30.

136   C.G. Brown, 'Popular culture and the continuing struggle for rational recreation', in T.M. Devine and R.J. Finlay (eds), *Scotland in the Twentieth Century*, Edinburgh, Edinburgh University Press, 1996; M. Clapson, *A Bit of a Flutter: Popular Gambling and English Society, c. 1823–1961*, Manchester, Manchester University Press, 1992, p. 67.

6 PERSONAL TESTIMONY AND RELIGION
1800–1950

1   Notable examples are D. Vincent, *Bread, Knowledge and Freedom: A Study of Nineteenth-century Working Class Autobiography*, London, Methuen, 1981, and the study of 4,000 unsolicited letters on religion from the mid-1960s 'Honest to God' debate in R. Towler, *The Need for Certainty: A Sociological Study of Conventional Religion*, London, RKP, 1984.

2   P. Summerfield, *Reconstructing Women's Wartime Lives: Discourse and Subjectivity in Oral Histories of the Second World War*, Manchester, Manchester University Press, 1998, p. 15.

3   A technique pioneered in L. Passerini, *Fascism in Popular Memory: The Cultural Experience of the Turin Working Class*, Cambridge, Cambridge University Press, 1987; and A. Thomson, 'Anzac memories: putting popular memory theory into practice in Australia', *Oral History Journal*, 1990, vol. 18.

4   D. Cameron *et al.*, *Researching Language: Issues of Power and Method*, London and New York, Routledge, 1992, esp. p. 5; an example of reflexivity in action is L. Sitzia, 'Telling Arthur's story: oral history relationships and shared authority', *Oral History Journal*, 1999, vol. 27, pp. 58–67.

5   I am very grateful to Penny Summerfield for leading me down this path.

6   Some oral-history work undertaken by 'religiously-informed' researchers can show signs of more confused intersubjectivity – for instance, of interviewees being asked in detail about religious experiences, and replying that they 'should have had' spiritual or conversionist occurrences but confessing inability to recall them. See R.P.M. Sykes, 'Popular religion in Dudley and the Gornals c. 1914–1965', unpublished Ph.D. thesis, University of Wolverhampton, 1999, pp. 297–8.

7   Vincent, *Bread, Knowledge and Freedom*, pp. 9–10,

8   L. Stanley, *The Auto/Biographical I: The Theory and Practice of Feminist Auto/Biography*, Manchester, Manchester University Press, 1992, pp. 59–88.

9   For conventions adopted for use of real names or pseudonyms of oral-history interviewees in Chapters 6 and 8, see 'Note on Oral History' on page xi.

10 Qualidata Archive [QA], Family Life and Work Experience [FLWE], interviewee 142, p. 4.
11 QA, FLWE, interviewee 142, p. 14.
12 Ibid.
13 Ibid., p. 18.
14 Ibid., p. 19.
15 Ibid.
16 Ibid.
17 Ibid., pp. 20–1.
18 Ibid., p. 21.
19 Ibid., p. 48.
20 Ibid.
21 QA, FLWE, interviewee 11, pp. 37–8.
22 QA, FLWE, interviewee 13, p. 4.
23 QA, FLWE, interviewee 87, pp. 3, 17–18, 25.
24 QA, FLWE, interviewee 90, *passim*, and interviewer's correspondence.
25 University of Lancaster, Centre for North West Regional Studies, Sound Archive [CNWRS, SA] respondent Mr T.3.P (b. 1886), pp. 1, 27, 34, 43, 55.
26 CNWRS, SA respondent Mr M.1.L (b. 1910), p. 10.
27 CNWRS, SA respondent Mrs N.W.B.1.P (b. 1900), p. 14.
28 Vincent, *Bread, Knowledge and Freedom*, pp. 167–78.
29 A. Somerville, *The Autobiography of a Working Man*, orig. 1848, London, MacGibbon & Kee, 1967, pp. 72–3.
30 D. Fraser (ed.), *The Christian Watt Papers*, Inverness, Caledonian Press, 1988.
31 Quoted in Vincent, *Bread, Knowledge and Freedom*, pp. 169–70.
32 P. Taylor, *Autobiography*, Paisley, Gardner, 1903, p. 121.
33 C.A. Whatley (ed.) *The Diary of John Sturrock, Millwright, Dundee 1864–5*, East Linton, Tuckwell, 1996, p. 29.
34 For example, A. Somerville, *Autobiography*; *Chapters in the Life of a Dundee Factory Boy*, Dundee, 1851; and J. Younger, *Autobiography of John Younger, Shoemaker, St. Boswells*, Kelso, 1881.
35 A good example is Mrs Sydney Watson, *A Village Maiden's Career*, London, Partridge & Co., 1895, whose husband wrote evangelical novels featured in Chapters 4 and 5.
36 Vincent, *Bread, Knowledge and Freedom*, pp. 179–81, 188.
37 See the research evidence of different psychologists surveyed in W. James, *The Varieties of Religious Experience: A Study in Human Nature*, orig. 1902, London, Longmans, Green, 1928, pp. 189–258; quotations at p. 200.
38 F. Colquhoun, *Haringay Story*, London, Hodder & Stoughton, 1955, pp. 205–30; *Lewis: Land of Revival: The story of the 1949–52 Lewis Revival as told by the islanders*, cassette tape, Belfast, Ambassador Productions, 1983.
39 W.L Courtney (ed.), *Do We Believe? A Record of a Great Correspondence in "The Daily Telegraph", October, November, December, 1904*, London, Hodder & Stoughton, 1905.
40 Ibid., pp. 193–4.
41 Ibid., pp. 271–2.
42 Ibid., p. 246.
43 Ibid., pp. 204–5.

44 Watson, *Village Maiden's Career*, p. 39.

45 M. Penn, *Manchester Fourteen Miles*, London and Sydney, 1982, pp. 172–87; A. Foley, *A Bolton Childhood*, Manchester, 1973, p. 36.

46 W. Foley, *A Child in the Forest*, London, Futura, 1977, pp. 79, 111.

47 M. Weir, *Best Foot Forward*, London, Collins, 1972, p. 69.

48 Penn, *Manchester Fourteen Miles*, p. 67; F. Thompson, *Larkrise to Candleford*, orig. 1945, Harmondsworth, Penguin, 1983, p. 215.

49 CNWRS, SA respondent Mrs B.1.P (b. 1900), p. 43.

50 CNWRS, SA respondent Mrs A.2.P (b. 1900), p. 16.

51 University of Strathclyde, Department of History, Scottish Oral History Centre Archive [SOHCA], respondent 006/Mrs R.2 (b. 1905), p. 4.

52 SOHCA, respondent 006/Mrs V.1 (b. 1914), p. 8.

53 QA, FLWE, interviewee 65, p. 20.

54 SOHCA, respondent 006/Mrs F.3 (b. 1910), p. 13.

55 SOHCA, respondent 006/Mrs U.1 (b. 1898), p. 8.

56 SOHCA, respondent 006/Mrs E.2 (b. 1905), p. 5.

57 SOHCA, respondent 006/Mrs X.2 (b. 1920), p. 11.

58 M. Weir, *Shoes were for Sunday*, London, Collins, 1994, p. 128.

59 For an example of how this experience affected one young girl, see C.G. Brown and J.D. Stephenson, '"Sprouting wings"? Women and religion in Scotland 1890–1950', in E. Breitenbach and E. Gordon (eds), *The World is Ill Divided: Women's Work in Scotland in the Nineteenth and Early Twentieth Centuries*, Edinburgh, Edinburgh University Press, 1990, pp. 105–6, 115–16.

60 'We were encouraged of course to go to church, we were allowed to go to church, maybe every second Sunday. We wouldn't be allowed to go every Sunday but every second Sunday.' SOHCA, respondent 006/Mrs T.1 (b. 1906), p. 13.

61 'I must have been a little saintlike, for I was chosen to be a Sunday school teacher in the little kindergarten and I told the children lovely bible stories.' D. Scannell, *Mother Knew Best: An East End Childhood*, London, Pan, 1974, p. 127.

62 CNWRS, SA respondent Mrs NW.B.2.B (b. 1931).

63 SOHCA, respondent 006/Mrs W.1 (b. 1913).

64 J. Bullock, *Bower's Row: Recollections of a Mining Village*, London, EP Publishing, 1976, p. 18.

65 Weir, *Best Foot Forward*, p. 285.

66 QA, FLWE, interviewee 71, p. 11.

67 QA, FLWE, interviewee 82, p. 55.

68 QA, FLWE, interviewee 145, p. 53.

69 SOHCA, respondent 006/Mrs K.3 (b. 1906), p. 16.

70 D.A. Reid, 'Weddings, weekdays, work and leisure in urban England 1791–1911: the decline of Saint Monday revisited', *Past and Present*, 1996, no. 153, pp. 147, 150–3, 157.

71 QA, FLWE, interviewee 14, p. 39.

72 Quoted in H. McLeod, *Class and Religion in the Late Victorian City*, London, Croom Helm, 1974, p. 50.

73 CNWRS, SA respondent Mr A.2.B (b. 1904), p. 38.

74 A. Blair, *Tea At Miss Cranston's*, London, Shepheard-Walwyn, 1985, pp. 91–2; SOHCA, respondent 006/Mrs H.2 (b. 1900), p. 4.

75 SOHCA respondent 006/Mrs W.2 (b. 1916), p. 3.
76 P. Camporesi, *The Magic Harvest: Food, Folklore and Society*, London, Polity, 1998, p. 186.
77 SOHCA, respondent 006/Mrs R.1 (b. 1912).
78 QA, FLWE, interviewee 64, p. 34.
79 E. Hall, *Canary Girls and Stockpots*, Luton, 1977, p. 16.
80 G. Foakes, *My Part of the River*, London, 1976, p. 22; R. Gamble, *Chelsea Child*, London, Ariel, 1982, pp. 33, 184, 188–90, 192; H. Forrester, *Liverpool Miss*, London and Glasgow, Collins, 1982, p. 15; D. Noakes, *The Town Beehive: A Young Girl's Lot: Brighton 1910–34*, Brighton, QueenSpark, 1980, p. 65.
81 Foley, *Child in the Forest*, p. 253.
82 QA, FLWE, interviewee 156, p. 38.
83 C.G. Brown, *Up-helly-aa: Custom, Culture and Community in Shetland*, Manchester, Mandolin, 1998, pp. 65–71.
84 Roberts noted the key role of his mother's corner shop as a venue for gossip about women's respectability; R. Roberts, *The Classic Slum*, Harmondsworth, Penguin, 1973, p. 43.
85 J. Seabrook, *The Unprivileged*, Harmondsworth, Penguin, 1973, p. 72.
86 S.C. Williams, *Religious Belief and Popular Culture in Southwark c. 1880–1939*, Oxford, Oxford University Press, 1999, p. v.
87 Williams, p. 90.
88 D. Cressy, *Birth, Marriage and Death: Ritual, Religion and the Life-Cycle in Tudor and Stuart England*, Oxford, Oxford University Press, 1997, pp. 197–229; Sykes, 'Popular religion', pp. 181–4; Williams, *Religious Belief*, pp. 88–9, 96–7. This theme is extensively addressed in Elizabeth Roberts' oral testimony in CNWRS, SA.
89 Oral testimony in Shetland Archive SA/3/1/77/2.
90 Williams, *Religious Belief*, p. 104. See also Sykes, 'Popular religion', pp. 95–298, and D. Clark, *Between Pulpit and Pew: Folk Religion in a North Yorkshire Fishing Village*, Cambridge, Cambridge University Press, 1982.
91 L. Stanley and S. Wise, *Breaking Out Again: Feminist Ontology and Epistemology*, London and New York, Routledge, 1993, pp. 110, 195.
92 QA, FLWE, interviewee 77, p. 13.
93 QA, FLWE, interviewee 342, p. 35.
94 Stories of this practice were recounted at the Ecclesiastical History Conference, New College, Edinburgh, September 1999, by Dr William Griffith, University of Wales at Bangor, and Professor Donald Meek, University of Aberdeen.
95 Scannell, *Mother Knew Best*, p. 111.
96 QA, FLWE, interviewee 34, p. 11.
97 QA, FAM, interviewee QD3/100/FAM/23.
98 QA, FLWE, interviewee 240, p. 17.
99 Brown and Stephenson, '"Sprouting Wings"?', pp. 22–3.
100 CNWRS, SA respondent Mr B.1.B (b. 1897), p. 63.
101 Quoted in McLeod, *Class and Religion*, p. 51.
102 QA, FLWE, interviewee 99, p. 17.
103 QA, FLWE, interviewees 142, p. 19; 77; 90 p. 34; 99.

104 QA, FLWE, interviewee 130, p. 15.

105 QA, FLWE, interviewee 34, pp. 8, 11.

106 Prosecutions for playing football in the streets were still common in Scotland until the 1950s. C.G. Brown, 'Popular culture and the continuing struggle for rational recreation', in T.M. Devine and R.J. Finlay (eds), *Scotland in the Twentieth Century*, Edinburgh, John Donald, 1996, p. 228–9.

107 There were 15 major restrictive parliamentary acts between the Public Houses (Scotland) Act, 1853 and the Sunday Entertainments Act, 1932.

108 See M. Clapson, *A Bit of a Flutter: Popular Gambling and English Society c. 1823–1961*, Manchester, Manchester University Press, 1992; M. Hilton, '"Tags", "Fags" and the "Boy labour problem" in late Victorian and Edwardian Britain', *Journal of Social History*, 1996, vol. 28, pp. 587–607; Brown, 'Popular culture'.

109 H. McLeod, 'New perspectives on Victorian working-class religion: the oral evidence', *Oral History Journal*, 1986, vol. 14, p. 33.

110 The Qualidata Family Life collection of 498 interviews took 46 informants from Scotland, of whom 10 were from Shetland, 6 from Barra and 3 from Lewis – all highly religious communities. Calculated from index cards to QA, FLWE.

111 Brown and Stephenson, '"Sprouting Wings"?', pp. 100–1.

112 Ibid.

113 QA, FLWE, interviewee 26, p. 34.

114 QA, FLWE, interviewee 90, p. 44.

115 QA, FLWE, interviewee 130, p. 17.

116 QA, FLWE, interviewee 191, p. 16

117 Ibid.

118 CNWRS, SA respondent Mrs B.1.P (b. 1900), p. 42.

119 QA, FLWE, interviewee 14, p. 8.

120 QA, FLWE, interviewee 65, pp. 32–3.

121 McLeod, *Class and Religion*, pp. 55–7.

122 QA, FLWE, interviewee 70, pp. 16, 24.

123 On Protestant parents sending children to Sunday school as a 'conscience salver', see R. Roberts, *A Ragged Schooling*, Manchester, Manchester University Press, 1976, p. 102.

124 QA, FLWE, interviewee 73, p. 17.

125 QA, FLWE, interviewees 82, pp. 17, 19, 32–3, 52–6.

126 QA, FLWE, interviewee 145, p. 53.

127 QA, FLWE, interviewee 146, p. 23.

128 QA, FLWE, interviewee 147.

129 QA, FLWE, interviewee 148, p. 18.

130 The pattern was evident in QA, FLWE, interviewees 53, 64, 70, 82, 99, 145, 146, 147, 148, 161, 191, 201, 225, 240.

131 This cycle is also suggested in R. Chadwick, 'Church and people in Bradford and district 1880–1914: The protestant churches in an urban industrial environment', unpublished D.Phil. thesis, University of Oxford, 1986, p. 173.

132 Though Wigley recounts the slowness of legislative change to Sunday law to 1972, he probably exaggerates the degree of change to Sunday behaviour

between 1900 and 1939. J. Wigley, *The Rise and Fall of the Victorian Sunday*, Manchester, Manchester University Press, 1980, pp. 192–8.

133 C. Davies, *Clean Clothes for Sunday*, Lavenham, Terence Dalton, 1974, p. 25.

134 See the accounts of Women's Institute members in *Norfolk Within Living Memory*, Newbury and Norwich, Countryside Books, 1995, pp. 34–9.

7 'UNIMPEACHABLE WITNESSES': THE STATISTICS OF 'CHRISTIAN PROGRESS' 1800–1950

1 R. Mudie-Smith (ed.), *The Religious Life of London*, London, Hodder & Stoughton, 1904, pp. 6–7.

2 T. Chalmers, *The Christian and Civic Economy of Large Towns*, Glasgow, 1821, p. 111.

3 Ibid., p. 112.

4 Ibid., p. 109.

5 Census of Great Britain, 1851: Religious Worship, England and Wales, *British Parliamentary Papers*, lxxxix (1852–3), pp. clviii, clxvii.

6 W.S.F. Pickering, 'The 1851 religious census – a useless experiment?', *British Journal of Sociology*, 1967, vol. 18, p. 403.

7 H. Perkin, *The Origins of Modern English Society 1780–1880*, London, Routledge and Kegan Paul, 1969, p. 201.

8 H. McLeod, 'Class, community and region: the religious geography of nineteenth century England', in M. Hill (ed.), *Sociological Yearbook of Religion in Britain*, vol. 6, 1973; H. McLeod, 'Religion', in J. Langton and R.J. Morris (eds), *Atlas of Industrializing Britain 1780–1914*, London, Methuen, 1986.

9 K.D.M. Snell, *Church and Chapel in the North Midlands: Religious Observance in the Nineteenth Century*, Leicester, Leicester University Press, 1991, pp. 25–6.

10 H. McLeod, 'Religion', p. 212; R.J. Morris, 'Urbanisation and Scotland', in W.H. Fraser and R.J. Morris (eds), *People and Society in Scotland, vol. 2 1830–1914*, Edinburgh, John Donald, 1990, p. 92.

11 C.G. Brown, 'Did urbanisation secularise Britain?' *Urban History Yearbook* 1988, pp. 6–8.

12 S. Bruce, 'Pluralism and religious vitality', in S. Bruce (ed.), *Religion and Modernization: Sociologists and Historians Debate the Secularization Thesis*, Oxford, Oxford University Press, 1992, pp. 182–5. See the criticism of Bruce's methods in C.G. Brown, *Religion and Society in Scotland since 1707*, Edinburgh, Edinburgh University Press, 1997, p. 65, n. 7.

13 I am grateful to Hugh McLeod for this point.

14 On this latter point, see Snell, *Church and Chapel*, pp. 26–7.

15 Census of Great Britain, 1851, clviii, clxvii.

16 McLeod, 'Religion', p. 214.

17 F.M.L. Thompson, *Hampstead: Building a Borough, 1650–1964*, London, RKP, 1974, p. 387.

18 P. Hillis, 'Presbyterianism and social class in mid-nineteenth-century Glasgow: a study of nine churches', *Journal of Ecclesiastical History*, 1981, vol. 32, p. 54.

19 J. Kent, 'Feelings festivals: an interpretation of some working-class religious attitudes', in H. Dyos and M. Wolff (eds), *The Victorian City*, London, Routledge, 1973, vol. 2, pp. 858, 868.

20 E.R. Norman, *Church and Society in England 1770–1970: A Historical Study*, Oxford, Clarendon Press, 1976, p. 124.

21 D.E.H. Mole, 'Challenge to the Church: Birmingham 1815–65', in Dyos and Wolff (eds.), *The Victorian City*, p. 829.

22 H. McLeod, *Class and Religion in the Late Victorian City*, London, Croom Helm, 1974, pp. 28–9.

23 Ibid., pp. 299–303.

24 McLeod, 'Religion', pp. 214, 216.

25 The poor reliability of social indicators (including those used by McLeod) are indicated by the following correlations between them. For the 28 boroughs of Metropolitan London (excluding the City): % population living in over-crowded houses v. % population living in houses of 8 or more rooms = –0.4865. Percentage of population living in overcrowded houses v. domestic indoor servants as percentage of households = –0.3702. For 25 boroughs of Greater London with significant levels of factory employees: percentage of occupied males in industries characterised by large-scale production v. domestic indoor servants as percentage of households = 0.1138.

26 This resulted in certain boroughs which were highly socially mixed (like Stoke Newington) being awarded undeservingly high scores.

27 J. Cox, *The English Churches in a Secular Society: Lambeth, 1870–1930*, Oxford, Oxford University Press, 1982; A.B. Bartlett, 'The Churches in Bermondsey 1880–1939', unpublished Ph.D. thesis, University of Birmingham, 1987; M. Smith, *Religion in Industrial Society: Oldham and Saddleworth 1740–1865*, Oxford, Oxford University Press, 1994; S.J.D. Green, *Religion in the Age of Decline: Organisation and Experience in Industrial Yorkshire 1870–1920*, Cambridge, Cambridge University Press, 1996; H. McLeod, *Religion and Society in England 1850–1914*, Basingstoke, Macmillan, 1996; C.G. Brown, *Religion and Society in Scotland since 1707*, Edinburgh, Edinburgh University Press, 1997.

28 Bartlett, 'The Churches in Bermondsey', p. 393.

29 R.E. Chadwick, 'Church and people in Bradford and District 1880–1914: the Protestant churches in an urban industrial environment', unpublished D.Phil. thesis, University of Oxford, 1986, pp. 84, 90–5.

30 Figures calculated by using a variable for church attendance rate constructed by taking the difference between percentages of total city population and total city attendances in each ward. The last two series, along with death rate and imr rates, are contained in Chadwick, 'Church and people', pp. 84, 90, 93.

31 A.D. Gilbert, *Religion and Society in Industrial England: Church, Chapel and Social Change 1740–1914*, London, Longman, 1976, p. 63

32 Hillis, 'Presbyterianism'.

33 Snell, *Church and Chapel*, p. 44; C.D. Field, 'The social structure of English Methodism, eighteenth–twentieth centuries', *British Journal of Sociology*, 1977,

vol. 28, p. 203, table II, from which I have aggregated artisans, colliers and labourers for these figures.

34 Chadwick, 'Church and people', pp. 156–8.

35 Calculated from L. Jeffrey, 'Women in the churches of nineteenth-century Stirling', unpublished M.Litt. thesis, University of Stirling, 1996, p. 115.

36 E. Hopkins, 'Religious dissent in Black Country industrial villages in the first half of the nineteenth century', *Journal of Ecclesiastical History*, 1983, vol. 34, pp. 411–24.

37 Calculated from Jeffreys, 'Women in the churches', pp. 116, 150.

38 Calculated from data in R. Dennis, *English Industrial Cities of the Nineteenth Century: A Social Geography*, Cambridge, Cambridge University Press, 1984, p. 282.

39 B.S. Rowntree, *Poverty: A Study of Town Life*, London, Macmillan, 1901, p. 347; B.S. Rowntree, *Poverty and Progress: A Second Survey of York*, London, Longmans, 1941, p. 423.

40 Field, 'The social structure', pp. 210, 216.

41 P.L. Sissons, *The Social Significance of Church Membership in the Burgh of Falkirk*, Edinburgh, Saint Andrew Press, 1973, pp. 60, 71, reanalysed in C.G. Brown, 'Religion and secularisation', in A. Dickson and J.H. Treble (eds), *People and Society in Scotland, vol. 3 1914–1990*, Edinburgh, John Donald, 1992, p. 63. See also L. Burton, 'Social class in the local church: a study of two Methodist churches in the Midlands', in M. Hill (ed.), *A Sociological Yearbook of Religion*, no. 8, London, 1975, pp. 20, 27.

42 Using data on the churchgoing censuses held in 28 boroughs of London (excluding the City) on different dates in 1902–3. It is possible that the variables could still have affected changes in attendance levels *within* each borough. The weather variable was constructed on a six-point scale, from 1 (fine) to 6 (heavy rain), and the date variable was constructed on a 12-point scale representing January to December. Calculated from data in Mudie-Smith (ed.), *Religious Life*, p. 87.

43 Chadwick, 'Church and people', p. 52.

44 I performed this regression on data provided, ibid., pp. 84, 90, 93.

45 Averages calculated from data in Dennis, *English Industrial Cities*, table 9.3, p. 281.

46 West London included St. Marylebone, Kensington, Paddington and Chelsea. Women made up 55 per cent of the population of Bradford and 57 per cent of West London. Figures from and calculated from C.D. Field, 'Adam and Eve: Gender in the English Free Church constituency', *Journal of Ecclesiastical History*, 1993, vol. 44, pp. 63–79; Chadwick, 'Church and people', pp. 144–5; Mudie-Smith (ed.), *Religious Life*.

47 Jeffrey, 'Women in the churches', p. 131. Linda Jeffrey's work on Stirling is an important counterweight to Chadwick's on Bradford, showing that while in the English town the difference between the percentages of males and females who were in church membership with their spouses was 37 per cent, in Stirling it was only 21 per cent, indicating a much greater degree of husband-wife church membership (especially amongst the working classes) in the Scottish town.

48 All the data for London in 1902–3 in this section, including the tables, were calculated from Mudie-Smith (ed.), *Religious Life*.

49 Correlations of 0.3782 and –0.3782 respectively, based on the seven boroughs of St. Marylebone, Westminster, Kensington, Chelsea, Paddington, Hammersmith and Fulham.

50 r = +0.8812, R² = 0.7766.

51 A. Sherwell, 'The problem of west London', in Mudie-Smith (ed.), *Religious Life*, pp. 91–2.

52 Mission stations include those of the Church of England, Baptists, Congregationalists, Wesleyan Methodists, Presbyterian Church, and evangelical mission services. Figures calculated from Mudie-Smith (ed.), *Religious Life*, p. 271.

53 By the 1930s, Catholic churches in London and Liverpool typically had five masses on Sunday morning, and one either on Saturday or Sunday evening, in addition to any weekday services on offer. I am grateful to Mary Heimann for advice on this point.

54 H. McLeod, *Religion and Society in England 1850–1914*, Basingstoke, Macmillan, 1996, p. 13. C.G. Brown, 'Religion', in R. Pope (ed.), *Atlas of British Social and Economic History since c. 1700*, London, Routledge, 1989, pp. 211–12.

55 This is the plausible scenario suggested by Smith for Lancashire and which certainly seems true of Scotland. M. Smith, *Religion in Industrial Society*, pp. 250–3.

56 W.L. Courtney (ed.), *Do We Believe? A Record of a Great Correspondence in "The Daily Telegraph", October, November, December, 1904*, London, Hodder & Stoughton, 1905, pp. 265–6; R.M. Goodridge, 'Nineteenth-century urbanization and religion: Bristol and Marseilles 1830–1880', in D. Martin (ed.), *A Sociological Yearbook of Religion in Britain*, no. 2, London, 1969, pp. 126–7.

57 McLeod, 'Class, community and region', p. 43; Chadwick, 'Church and people', p. 76.

58 J.T. Stoddart, 'The Daily News census of 1902–3 compared with the British Weekly census of 1886', in Mudie-Smith (ed.), *Religious Life* pp. 282–8; R. Gill, *The Myth of the Empty Church*, London, SPCK, 1990, pp. 299–322; McLeod, *Class and Religion*, pp. 232–8.

59 Graphs of church membership per capita, with discussion of the data, appear in C.G. Brown, 'A revisionist approach to religious change', in Bruce (ed.), *Religion and Modernization*, pp. 31–58; and C.G. Brown, 'Religion, class and church growth', in Fraser and Morris (eds), *People and Society*, pp. 311–16.

60 Data from or calculated for English and Welsh churches from R. Currie, A. Gilbert and L. Horsley, *Churches and Churchgoers: Patterns of Church Growth in the British Isles since 1700*, Oxford, Clarendon Press, 1977, p. 65; Gilbert, *Religion and Society*, p. 37; and for Scottish churches from the author's running datasets of Scottish churches' membership.

61 The church membership data at decennial intervals 1800–1950 was set against census population data for years 1801–1951 (with a figure for 1941 calculated by linear extrapolation); data from Currie, Gilbert and Horsley, *Churches and Churchgoers*, p. 25; and from B.R. Mitchell and P. Deane (eds), *Abstract of British Historical Statistics*, Cambridge, Cambridge University Press, 1962, p. 6.

62 Calculated from the author's running datasets on Scottish church membership.
63 C.G. Brown, 'Religion and secularisation', in Dickson and Treble (eds), *People and Society*, pp. 48–55.
64 Brown, *Religion and Society*, p. 54; in England there was a rise during 1919–34 from 1.57 to 1.77 per cent of marriages being performed by non-mainstream churches; calculated from data in Currie, Gilbert and Horsley, *Churches and Churchgoers*, p. 224, 'others' column.
65 Calculated from the author's datasets on Scottish church members and church attendance censuses.
66 S.C. Williams, *Religious Belief and Popular Culture in Southwark, c. 1880–1939*, Oxford, Oxford University Press, 1999, pp. 54–104.
67 Cf. McLeod, *Religion and Society*, p. 60.

8 THE 1960S AND SECULARISATION

1 One of the few to note the significance of the fifties is G. Parsons, 'Contrasts and continuities: the traditional Christian churches in Britain since 1945', in G. Parsons (ed.), *The Growth of Religious Diversity: Britain from 1945, vol. 1*, London, Routledge, 1993, pp. 46–55. For examples of how 1950s' church growth has been largely ignored or downgraded, see B. Wilson, *Religion in Secular Society*, Harmondsworth, Penguin, 1966; G. Davie, *Religion in Britain since 1945: Believing Without Belonging*, Oxford, Blackwell, 1994, pp. 30–3.
2 L. Heron (ed.), *Truth, Dare or Promise: Girls Growing up in the Fifties*, London, Virago, 1985, p. 5.
3 P. Summerfield, *Women Workers in The Second World War*, London, Croom Helm, 1984, p. 184.
4 Ibid., pp. 188–9.
5 Ibid., p. 190; C.L. White, *Women's Magazines 1693–1968*, London, Michael Joseph, 1970, chapter 6; S. Rowbottom, *A Century of Women: The History of Women in Britain and the United States*, London, Viking, 1997, pp. 242–9, 280–4.
6 Heron (ed.), *Truth, Dare or Promise*, p. 4.
7 P. Summerfield, *Reconstructing Women's Wartime Lives*, Manchester, Manchester University Press, 1998, p. 259.
8 *Brief Encounter*, starring Celia Johnson and Trevor Howard (dir. David Lean, Pinewood Films 1945).
9 Quoted in C.L. White, *The Women's Periodical Press in Britain 1946–1976*, London, HMSO, 1977, p. 10.
10 Nestlé advertisement, 1951, quoted ibid.
11 Ibid., p. 11.
12 Monica Dickens in *Women's Own*, 28 January 1961, quoted ibid., p. 11
13 Ibid.
14 F. Colquhoun, *Harringay Story: A Detailed Account of the Greater London Crusade 1954*, London, Hodder & Stoughton, 1955; T. Allan, *Crusade in Scotland – Billy Graham*, London, Pickering & Inglis, 1955; D.P. Thomson, *Visitation Evangelism in Scotland 1946–1956*, Crieff, no pub., c. 1956; Parsons, 'Contrasts and continuities', pp. 46–9.

15 Colquhoun, *Harringay Story*, pp. 232–3; Allan, *Crusade in Scotland*, pp. 8, 108. In the Mission England crusade of 1984, 61 per cent were under 25 years of age; D. Williams, *One in a Million: Billy Graham with Mission England*, Berkhamsted, Word Books, 1984, p. 184.

16 Children were special targets. Ten thousand Glasgow state-school pupils were marshalled by the Education Authority to a daytime meeting to hear Graham preach. Allan, *Crusade in Scotland*, p. 19.

17 Comment to the author by his cousin, 1998. The aunt was the author's mother.

18 Haringay attendances were 1.756 million, Greater London population (1951 census) was 8.3 million; Glasgow attendances in 1955 were 830,670, Glasgow city population (1951) was 1.09 million. The demographics of later missions were interestingly different. Billy Graham events in London in 1966–7 (700,000 attenders) and a six-city Mission England event in 1984 (1.026 million attenders) achieved far lower penetration of the media and density of popular participation, but achieved significantly higher rates of coming forward – 9.4 per cent in 1984 compared to 2 per cent in 1954–5; Williams, *One in a Million*, p. 184. The recession and the coal strike of 1984 created an encouraging economic backdrop for attendance and conversion amongst those who still retained a discursive 'memory' of Christianity. If the argument of this book is correct, missions of the new millennium will fail amongst the young because of their unfamiliarity with discursive Christianity due to its disappearance from the family and youth media, and the young's absence from Sunday schools.

19 J. Pascal, 'Prima ballerina absoluta', in Heron (ed.), *Truth, Dare or Promise*, p. 29.

20 S. Pixner, 'The oyster and the shadow', ibid., p. 85.

21 B. Miles, *Paul McCartney: Many Years from Now*, London, Vintage, 1998, p. 32; C. Steedman, *Landscape for a Good Woman: A Story of Two Lives*, London, Virago, 1986, p. 71.

22 I. Macdonald, *Revolution in the Head: The Beatles' Records and the Sixties*, London, Pimlico, 1995, p. 6.

23 V. Walkerdine, 'Dreams from an ordinary childhood', in Heron (ed.), *Truth, Dare or Promise*, p. 65.

24 Ibid., p. 72.

25 C. Steedman, 'Landscape for a Good Woman', ibid., p. 117.

26 In addition to three of The Beatles, the art colleges produced Eric Clapton, David Bowie, Pete Townsend of The Who, all of Pink Floyd, Keith Richards, Ron Wood, Ray and Dave Davies of the Kinks, Jeff Beck and Eric Burdon. Macdonald, *Revolution in the Head*, p. 13; A. Marwick *The Sixties*, Oxford, Oxford University Press, 1998, pp. 57–9.

27 Miles, *Paul McCartney*, p. 40.

28 E. Roberts, *Women and Families: An Oral History, 1940–1970*, Oxford, Blackwell, 1995, p. 159.

29 A.H. Halsey, *Trends in British Society since 1900*, London, Macmillan, 1972, p. 311.

30 QA, FAM, interviewee QD3/100/FAM/74.

31 Steedman, 'Landscape for a Good Woman', in Heron (ed.), *Truth, Dare or Promise*, p. 105.

32 Marwick, *The Sixties*, pp. 145–6, 265, 357, 679–724; B. Osgerby, *Youth in Britain since 1945*, Oxford, Blackwell, 1998, pp. 82–103.

33 T. Ali, *1968 and After: Inside the Revolution*, London, Blond and Briggs, 1978; Marwick, *The Sixties*, p. 4.

34 On historians and postmodernity, see K. Jenkins (ed.), *The Postmodern History Reader*, London, Routledge, 1997, esp. pp. 3–5.

35 Jean-Francois Lyotard, 'The postmodern condition', ibid., p. 37.

36 A. McRobbie, 'Jackie: An Ideology of Adolescent Femininity', Centre for Contemporary Cultural Studies, University of Birmingham, Occasional Paper no. 53, April 1978, pp. 1, 3, 14, 17–19, 25.

37 White, *Women's Periodical Press*, p. 27.

38 Ibid., p. 15.

39 Ibid., pp. 56–8.

40 It is impressive what a high proportion of television and radio comedy material in the sixties was aimed at the military.

41 'In the electric age man seems to the conventional West to become irrational.' M. McLuhan, *Understanding Media: The Extensions of Man*, orig. 1964, Cambridge, Mass., MIT Press, 1994, p. 15.

42 This analysis involved classifying the lyrics of 167 Beatles songs into romance/non-romance, using the lyrics of the songs (excluding instrumental pieces) by Lennon–McCartney and Harrison in *The Beatles Complete* (London, Wise Publications, n.d.). The classification focused on the 'obvious' theme or signification of the lyrics to a non-expert in the 'real' or 'hidden' meanings of the lyric writer. I was much assisted in this by consulting Macdonald, *Revolution in the Head*.

43 *The Beatles Complete* p. 178. 'She's Leaving Home'. Words and music by John Lennon and Paul McCartney © 1967 Northern Songs. Used by permission of Music Sales Ltd. All rights reserved. International copyright secured.

44 Ray Davies speaking on the compact disc, *Ray Davies: The Storyteller*, 1998, Guardian Records, EMI Records Ltd., end of track 13.

45 A. Myrdal and V. Klein, *Women's Two Roles: Home and Work*, London, RKP, 1956, p. 26.

46 A clash evocatively recounted in J. Winterson, *Oranges are Not the Only Fruit*, London, Pandora, 1985.

47 *Reports to the General Assembly of the Church of Scotland*, 1970, pp. 399–410. After 1972, the Committee confined itself largely to alcoholism, gambling and domestic violence.

48 QA, FAM, interviewee QD3/100/FAM/23.

49 QA, FAM, interviewee QD3/100/FAM/24.

50 QA, FAM, interviewee QD3/100/FAM/25.

51 In order, the testimony of QA, FAM, interviewees QD3/100/FAM/115 (b. 1922), /74 (b. 1945) and /75 (b. 1969).

52 A good example is QA, FLWE interviewee 99, pp. 13–50, who stopped going to church at the age of thirteen in the 1910s.

53 QA, FLWE interviewee 65, p. 15.

54 SOHCA, respondents 006/Mrs G.3 (b. 1925) and Mrs I.2 (b. 1907).

55 SOHCA, respondent 006/Mrs C.2 (b. 1912), pp. 22–3.

56 W. Foley, *A Child in the Forest*, London, Futura, 1977; L. Beckwith, *The Hills is Lonely, The Sea for Breakfast*, London, Arrow, 1972, several others about the Highlands, and her *About My Father's Business*, London, Arrow, 1973 about Cheshire; F. Thompson, *Larkrise to Candleford*, orig. 1945, Harmondsworth, Penguin, 1973.

57 V. Massey, *One Child's War*, London, BBC, 1983; E. Hall, *Canary Girls and Stockpots*, Luton, 1977; M. Hobbs, *Born to Struggle*, London, 1973.

58 C. Taylor, *Sources of the Self: The Making of the Modern Identity*, Cambridge, Mass., Harvard University Press, 1989, pp. 491–2; and advance publicity sheet for Charles Taylor's Gifford Lectures at the University of Edinburgh, April–May 1999.

59 L. Passerini, *Fascism in Popular Memory: The Cultural Experience of the Turin Working Class*, Cambridge, Cambridge University Press, 1987; R. Hutton, 'The English Reformation and the evidence of folklore', *Past and Present*, 1995, no. 148, p. 114.

60 R. Towler, *The Need for Certainty: A Sociological Study of Conventional Religion,* London, RKP, 1984.

61 See for instance J. Green, *Days in the Life: Voices from the English Underground 1961–1971*, London, Pimlico, 1998.

62 S. Bruce, 'Religion in Britain at the close of the 20th century: a challenge to the silver lining perspective', *Journal of Contemporary Religion*, 1996, vol. 11, 269–71.

63 (A. Robertson), *Lifestyle Survey*, Edinburgh, Church of Scotland, 1987.

64 See for instance H. McLeod, *Religion and the People of Western Europe 1789–1989*, Oxford, Oxford University Press, 1997, 134–43; P.A. Welsby, *A History of the Church of England 1945–1980*, Oxford, Oxford University Press, 1984, pp. 97–106; D. Hilliard, 'The religious crisis of the 1960s: the experience of the Australian churches', *Journal of Religious History*, 1997, vol. 21; I. Machin, 'British churches and moral change in the 1960s', in W.M. Jacob and N. Yates (eds), *Religion and Society in Northern Europe since the Reformation*, Woodbridge, Boydell Press, 1993; S. Gilley and W.J. Sheils (eds), *A History of Religion in Britain*, Oxford, Blackwell, 1994, esp. pp. 467–521.

65 In Falkirk in the 1960s only 40 per cent of non-churchgoing teenagers expressed a belief in God compared to 75 per cent for churchgoers; boys were even more secularised, with bizarre scores of 37 per cent for churchgoers and 47 per cent for non-churchgoers. P.L. Sissons, *The Social Significance of Church Membership in the Burgh of Falkirk,* Edinburgh, Church of Scotland, 1973, p. 325.

9 THE END OF A LONG STORY

1 The most recent and jarring example of this failure is Steve Bruce, who writes: 'Social historians of religion disagree about the precise shape of the curve [of religious growth and decline] and the placing of the peak, but, whatever objection they may raise to this or that measure, they are agreed that there are now far fewer church members and church-goers than there were in 1950, 1900, 1850, or 1800.' S. Bruce, *Religion in the Modern World: From Cathedrals to Cults*, Oxford, Oxford University Press, 1996, p. 31.

2 On his argument against modelling 'the study of man on the natural sciences', see C. Taylor, *Human Agency and Language: Philosophical Papers I*, Cambridge, Cambridge University Press, 1985, pp. 1–3, 103.

3 C. Taylor, *Sources of the Self: The Making of the Modern Identity*, Cambridge, Mass., Harvard University Press, 1989, pp. 491–2.

4 Ibid., pp. 93–4, 97–107.

5 For those who understand this for Britain, see B. Hilton, *The Age of Atonement: The Influence of Evangelicalism on Social and Economic Thought, 1795–1865*, Oxford, Clarendon Press, 1988; and D. Bebbington, *Evangelicalism in Modern Britain*, London, Unwin Hyman, 1989, esp. pp. 50–63. For one who understands precisely the same for Norway at the same period, see N. Witoszek, 'Fugitives from Utopia: the Scandinavian Enlightenment reconsidered', in O. Sorensen and B. Strath (eds), *The Cultural Construction of Nordern*, Oslo, Scandinavian University Press, 1997.

6 J.R. Carrette, *Foucault and Religion: Spiritual Corporality and Political Spirituality*, London, Routledge, 2000, p. 152. For a collection of views from the world of religious studies, see P. Heelas (ed.), *Religion, Modernity and Postmodernity*, Oxford, Blackwell, 1998.

7 Ian Bradley, Church of Scotland minister and Head of Religious Broadcasting at BBC Scotland, posited in 1992 that 'the nineties will be a religious decade'. I. Bradley, *Marching to the Promised Land: Has the Church a Future?*, London, John Murray, 1992, p. 204.

8 Foucault quoted in Carrette, *Foucault*, p. 149.

9 See for example p. 229, n. 18.

10 POSTSCRIPT: THE MORTALITY OF CHRISTIAN BRITAIN RECONSIDERED

1 www.time.com/time/magazine/article/0,9171,35306,00.html.

2 Letter to the author, 12 January 2003.

3 M. Grimley, book review, *Twentieth Century British History*, vol. 19, 2008, pp. 383–4.

4 Monica Furlong, book review, *Journal of Ecclesiastical History*, vol. 54, 2003, pp. 184–5.

5 See for instance 'A not so critical response to Callum Brown's *Death of Christian Britain*', at http://unsanitaryjesus.wordpress.com.

6 Book review, *The Spectator*, 14 April 2001.

7 Sarah Williams, www.gospel-culture.org.uk, *Newsletter* 33, Spring 2002.

8 One of the best understandings and elaborations of my book and its arguments is from the course material for the Open University course AA307, 'Religion in History', and notably G. Parsons, *AA307 Study Guide 4: The Death of Christian Britain: Exploring a Thesis*, Milton Keynes, Open University, 2005.

9 Note the absence of any chapter on religion, or indeed any meaningful reference to religion or churches, amongst the thirty chapters in Paul Addison and Harriet Jones (eds), *A Companion to Contemporary Britain, 1939–2000*, Oxford, Blackwell Publishing, 2005.

10 C.G. Brown, '"Best not to take it too far": how the British cut religion down to size', www.opendemocracy.net/globalization-aboutfaith/britain_religion_3335 .jsp, 8 March 2006.

11 For the theory of gender as a category of analysis, see J. Scott, *Gender and the Politics of History*, New York, Columbia University Press, 1988.

12 S. Williams, 'The language of belief: an alternative agenda for the study of Victorian working-class religion', *Journal of Victorian Culture*, vol. 1, 1996, pp. 303–17.

13 After an initial outing of these ideas in a conference paper in 1997, the book was researched during late 1997 and 1998 and the first draft completed in March 1999. The revised paper appeared later as C.G. Brown, 'The secularisation decade: what the 1960s have done to the study of religious history', in H. McLeod and W. Ustorf (eds), *The Decline of Christendom in Western Europe 1750–2000*, Cambridge, Cambridge University Press, 2003, pp. 29–46.

14 Book review, *Histoire Sociale – Social History*, vol. xxxvi, 2003, pp. 257–60; J. Morris, 'The strange death of Christian Britain: another look at the secularization debate', *Historical Journal*, vol. 46, 2003, pp. 963–76, at pp. 970–6; Monica Furlong, book review, *Journal of Ecclesiastical History*, vol. 54, 2003, pp. 184–5; David Fergusson, book review, *Scottish Economic and Social History*, vol. 21, 2001, p. 75.

15 Sheridan Gilley, *Reviews in History*, December 2001, www.history.ac.uk/ reviews/paper/gilleys.html.

16 D.W. Bebbington, *Victorian Nonconformity*, Bangor, Headstart, 1992.

17 P. Joyce, *Visions of the People: Industrial England and the Question of Class, 1848–1914*, Cambridge, Cambridge University Press, 1991; P. Pasture, 'The role of religion in social and labour history', in L.H. van Voss and M. van der Linden (eds), *Class and Other Identities: Gender, Religion and Ethnicity in the Writing of European Labour History*, New York and Oxford, Berghahn Books, 2002, pp. 116–17. See also Pasture's Introduction in L.H. van Voss, P. Pasture and J. De Maeyer (eds), *Between Cross and Class: Comparative Histories of Christian Labour in Europe 1840–2000*, Bern, Peter Lang, 2005.

18 Gerald Wayne Olsen, book review, *Histoire Sociale – Social History*, vol. xxxvi, 2003, pp. 257–60.

19 Logan, *The Spectator*, 14 April 2001.

20 Gilley, *Reviews in History*; letter to the author dated 11 February 2001.

21 D. Nash, 'Reconnecting religion with social and cultural history: secularization's failure as a master narrative', *Cultural and Social History*, vol. 1, 2004, pp. 302–35, at p. 319.

22 R.D. Kernohan, *Contemporary Review*, April 2002, p. 246.

23 H. McLeod, *The Religious Crisis of the 1960s*, Oxford, Oxford University Press, 2007, p. 243.

24 Letter to the author, 30 May 2006.

25 J. Garnett, M. Grimley, A. Harris, W. Whyte and S. Williams (eds), *Redefining Christian Britain: Post 1945 Perspectives*, London, SCM Press, 2006, p. 5.

26 Williams, www.gospel-culture.org.uk.

27 Williams, 'The language of belief'.

28 Williams, www.gospel-culture.org.uk.

29 See also M.E. Ruff, 'The postmodern challenge to the secularization thesis', *Schweizerische Zeitschrift für Religion- und Kulterheschichte*, vol. 99, 2005, pp. 385–401.

30 C.G. Brown, *Postmodernism for Historians*, Harlow, Longman, 2005, p. 127; see also pp. 66–7, 134–8.

31 H. McLeod, *Secularisation in Western Europe 1848–1914*, Basingstoke, Macmillan, 2000, pp. 4, 9, 29–30.

32 Morris, 'Strange death', p. 965.

33 J. Cox, 'Master narratives of long-term religious change', in H. McLeod and W. Ustorf (eds), *The Decline of Christendom in Western Europe 1750–2000*, Cambridge, Cambridge University Press, 2003, pp. 201–17.

34 G. Davie, *Religion in Modern Europe: A Memory Mutates*, Oxford, Oxford University Press, 2000, pp. 1, 24–37; P. Berger, 'The desecularization of the world: a global overview', in P.L. Berger (ed.), *The Desecularization of the World*, Washington, DC, Ethics and Public Policy Center, 1999.

35 Nash, 'Reconnecting religion', p. 304.

36 Ibid., p. 309.

37 Ibid., pp. 319–21.

38 See also B. Martin, 'Dark materials? Philip Pullman and children's literature', in J. Garnett *et al.*, *Redefining Christian Britain*, pp. 178–89.

39 C.G. Brown, 'The unconverted and the conversion: gender relations in the salvation narrative in Britain 1800–1960', in J.N. Bremner, W.J. van Bekkum and A.L. Molendijk (eds), *Paradigms, Poetics and Politics of Conversion*, Leuven, Peeters, 2006, pp. 183–99.

40 See, e.g., B. Martin, *A Sociology of Contemporary Cultural Change*, Oxford, Basil Blackwell, 1981.

41 C. Taylor, *A Secular Age*, Cambridge, Mass., Belknap Press, 2007.

42 Ibid., pp. 427, 492, 495.

43 T. Asad, *Formations of the Secular: Christianity, Islam, Modernity*, Stanford, Stanford University Press, 2003.

44 See, e.g., H. McLeod, *Religion and the People of Western Europe 1789–1989*, 2nd edn, Oxford, Opus, 1997; O. Blaschke (ed.), *Konfessionen im Konflikt: Deutschland zwischen 1800 und 1970 ein zweites konfessionelles Zeitalter*, Göttingen, Vandenhoeck & Ruprecht, 2002; P. Pasture, 'Christendom and the legacy of the sixties: between the secular city and the age of Aquarius', *Review d'Histoire Ecclesiastique*, vol. 99, 2004, pp. 82–117.

45 M. Gauvreau, 'Introduction', in M. Gauvreau and O. Hubert (eds), *The Churches and Social Order in Nineteenth- and Twentieth-century Canada*, Montreal, McGill-Queen's University Press, 2006, p. 9.

46 Nash, 'Reconnecting religion', and J. Morris, 'Strange death', p. 963. Unaccountably, Robin Gill has accused me of proposing church decline as the product of 'some invisible but ineluctable process of secularization', when all my work for thirty years has been to oppose this: R. Gill, *The 'Empty' Church Revisited*, Aldershot, Ashgate, 2003, p. 159.

47 M. Gauvreau, 'Introduction', in Gauvreau and Hubert, *The Churches and Social Order*, p. 11.

48 Berger, 'The desecularization of the world', p. 196.

49 D. Herbert, *Religion and Civil Society: Rethinking Public Religion in the Contemporary World*, Aldershot, Ashgate, 2003, p. 22.

50 Ibid.

51 *Christianity and Society*, April 2004, pp. 30–31.

52 Herbert, *Religion and Civil Society*, p. 22.

53 Morris, 'Strange Death', p. 969; Brown, *Postmodernism*, pp. 66–7; though, on the present, cf. Z. Bauman, *Liquid Life*, Cambridge, Polity, 2005.

54 Actually, the Lerwick case is complex and exceptional in Britain; see L. Abrams, *Myth and Materiality in a Woman's World: Shetland 1800–2000*, Manchester, Manchester University Press, 2003.

55 D. Riley, '"The free mothers": pronatalism and working women in industry at the end of the last war in Britain', *History Workshop Journal*, Spring 1981, pp. 59–118. Employers had a different attitude, wanting cheap female labour to make good the shortfall of male workers.

56 C.G. Brown, 'Gendering secularisation: locating women in the transformation of British Christianity in the 1960s', forthcoming, in G. Stedman Jones and I. Katznelson (eds), Title tba.

57 C.G. Brown, *Religion and Society in Twentieth-century Britain*, Harlow, PearsonLongman, 2006, pp. 44–5, 101, 149–50, 153–61.

58 *Histoire Sociale – Social History*, vol. xxxvi, 2003, pp. 257–60.

59 See also A. Crockett and D. Voas, 'Generations of decline: religious change in 20th-century Britain', *Journal for the Scientific Study of Religion*, vol. 45, 2006, pp. 567–84.

60 McLeod, *Religious Crisis*, pp. 16–18. See the critique of Pasture and the present author in H. McLeod, 'The crisis of Christianity in the west', in H. McLeod (ed.), *The Cambridge History of Christianity, vol. 9: World Christianities, c.1914–c.2000*, Cambridge, Cambridge University Press, 2006, pp. 328–9.

61 Blaschke (ed.), *Konfessionen im Konflikt*.

62 D. Entwistle, '"Hope, Colour and Comradeship": loyalty and opportunism in early twentieth-century church attendance among the working class in north west England', *Journal of Religious History*, vol. 25, 2001, pp. 20–38, at p. 38.

63 M.C. Martin, 'Relationships human and divine: retribution and repentance in children's lives, 1740–1870', in K. Cooper and J. Gregory (eds), *Retribution, Repentance and Reconciliation*, London, Boydell Press, 2004, pp. 253–65, at pp. 253–4, 264.

64 See M. Sissons and P. French (eds), *The Age of Austerity, 1945–51*, London, Hodder and Stoughton, 1963; and D. Kynaston, *Austerity Britain 1945–51*, London, Bloomsbury, 2007.

65 D. Sandbrook, *Never Had It So Good: A History of Britain from Suez to the Beatles*, London, Little Brown, 2005; M. Jarvis, *Conservative Governments, Morality and Social Change, 1957–64*, Manchester, Manchester University Press, 2005.

66 Data from Sandbrook, *Never Had It So Good*, pp. 114, 360–61; www. dft.gov.uk/pgr/roads/environment/cvtf/theenvironmentalimpactsofroa3793? page=2; and www.statistics.gov.uk/STATBASE/xsdataset.asp?More=Y&vlnk =1459&All=Y&B2.x=84&B2.y=10.

67 S.J.D. Green, 'Was there an English religious revival in the 1950s?', *Journal of the United Reformed Church History Society*, vol. 7, 2006, pp. 517–38, at p. 520.

68 See p. 170; also McLeod, *Religious Crisis*, p. 38.

69 Green, 'English religious revival', p. 529.

70 R. Currie, A. Gilbert and L. Horsley, *Churches and Churchgoers: Patterns of Church Growth in the British Isles since 1700*, Oxford, Clarendon Press, 1977, pp. 164–5.
71 The distinctive pattern of religious decline in Wales is raised in Brown, *Religion and Society*, pp. 155–7, and Morris, 'Strange death,' p. 974. See also the sociological case studies in P. Chambers, *Religion, Secularization and Social Change in Wales*, Cardiff, University of Wales Press, 2005.
72 Currie *et al.*, *Churches and Churchgoers*, pp. 134–5.
73 McLeod, *Religious Crisis*, p. 38.
74 This argument is further explored in Brown, *Religion and Society*, pp. 177–223.
75 David Voas thinks this is a freak 'spike' and that the decline is really from the 1930s. But so many data, measuring different religious indicators, 'spike' in the 1950s suggesting something far more than a freak baptism figure. D. Voas, 'Intermarriage and the demography of secularization', *British Journal of Sociology*, vol. 54, 2003, pp. 83–108, at p. 89.
76 McLeod, *Religious Crisis*, p. 40.
77 A.D. Gilbert, *Religion and Society in Industrial England: Church, Chapel and Social Change, 1740–1914*, London and New York, Longman, 1976, pp. 188–9.
78 Some oral history evidence from the Netherlands tends to suggest that the 1950s were 'more religious and churchly' than the 1930s. See P. van Rooden, 'Oral history en het vreemde sterven van het Nederlands christendom', *Bijdragen en Mededelingen betreffende de Geschiedenis der Nederlanden*, vol. 119, 2004, pp. 524–51, available online as 'Oral history and the strange demise of Dutch Christianity', at www.xs4all.nl/~pvrooden/Peter/publicaties/oral%20 history.htm.
79 M. Grimley, 'The religion of Englishness: Puritanism, providentialism, and "national character", 1918–1945', *Journal of British Studies*, vol. 46, 2007, pp. 884–906, at p. 906. See also M. Grimley, 'Civil society and the clerisy: Christian elites and national culture, c.1930–1950', in J. Harris (ed.), *Civil Society in British History*, Oxford, Oxford University Press, 2003, pp. 231–47.
80 Figures calculated from data in Z. Layton-Henry, *The Politics of Immigration: Immigration, 'Race' and 'Race' Relations in Post-war Britain*, Oxford, Blackwell, 1992, p. 13.
81 D. Hilliard, 'The religious crisis of the 1960s: the experience of the Australian churches', *Journal of Religious History*, vol. 21, 1997; P. van Rooden, 'Secularisation, deChristianisation and reChristianisation in the Netherlands', in H. Lehmann (ed.), *Dechristianisierung und Rechristianisierung im neuzeitlichen Europa und in Nordamerika: Bilanz und Perspektiven der Forschung: Veröffentlichungen des Max-Planck-Instituts für Geschichte 130*, Göttingen, Vandenhoeck & Ruprecht, 1997, pp. 131–53, and online at www.xs4all.nl/ ~pvrooden/Peter/publicaties/1997a.htm.
82 Pasture, 'Christendom', p. 113.
83 S. Macdonald, 'Death of Christian Canada? Do Canadian church statistics support Callum Brown's timing of church decline?', *Historical Papers: Canadian Society of Church History*, 2006, pp. 135–56; M. Gauvreau and O. Hubert, 'Beyond Church history: recent developments in the history of religion in Canada', in M. Gauvreau and O. Hubert (eds), *The Churches and Social Order in Nineteenth- and Twentieth-century Canada*, Montreal, McGill-Queen's University Press, 2006.

84 W. Damberg, 'Pfarrgemeinden und katholische Verbände vor dem Konzil', in G. Wassilowsky (ed.), *Zweites Vatikanum: vergessene Anstösse, gegenwärtige Fortschreibungen*, Freiburg, Herder, 2004, pp. 11, 17.

85 Death 'confronts us in a stark manner with the rapidity and radicalism of recent secularisation,' Williams, www.gospel-culture.org.uk.

86 McLeod, *Religious Crisis*, p. 1.

87 M. Donnelly, *Sixties Britain: Culture, Society and Politics*, London, Pearson Education, 2005.

88 M. Roodhouse, 'Lady Chatterley and the monk: Anglican radicals and the Lady Chatterley trial of 1960', *Journal of Ecclesiastical History*, vol. 59, 2008, pp. 475–500. For new details on the trial and its aftermath, see A. McCleery, '*Lady Chatterley's Lover* recovered', *Publishing History*, vol. 59, 2006, pp. 61–84.

89 Garnett *et al.*, *Redefining Christian Britain*, pp. 5, 116.

90 Ibid., pp. 64, 116, 118, 128–9, 138, 289. Brown, *Religion and Society*, p. 208.

91 They do this for evidence cited by Gerald Parsons in a paragraph where he speaks of 'the decline of even residual belief in specifically Christian concepts and doctrines'. Compare what is said at J. Garnett *et al.*, *Redefining Christian Britain*, p.118, with what is said at G. Parsons, 'How the times they are a'changing: exploring the context of religious transformation in Britain in the 1960s', in J. Wolffe (ed.), *Religion in History: Conflict, Conversion and Coexistence*, Manchester, Manchester University Press/Open University, 2004, p. 174.

92 Garnet *et al.*, *Redefining Christian Britain*, p. 118; McLeod, *Religious Crisis*, pp. 108–10; S.C. Williams, *Religious Belief and Popular Culture in Southwark, c.1880–1939*, Oxford, Oxford University Press, 1999.

93 Though he seems to equivocate over his chosen year by then suggesting that the 'ten years from 1965 to 1975' were important in relation to the loss of habit of churchgoing. McLeod, *Religious Crisis*, pp. 141–60, 188.

94 Ibid., p. 13.

95 For a summary of their views, see McLeod, *Religious Crisis*, pp. 8–13. For a hint of McLeod's own part in liberal 1960s' Christianity, see p. 228.

96 McLeod, *Religious Crisis*, p. 224.

97 On my account of the mid-1960s, McLeod erroneously claims that I suggest 'that the interest in religious debate in this period was limited to "the elderly"'. I pointed correctly to a study that showed how elderly Christians sent many letters to John Robinson after the publication of *Honest to God*. McLeod, *Religious Crisis*, p. 84 fn. 2; see also p. 186.

98 I. Jones, with P. Webster, 'Expressions of authenticity: music for worship', in J. Garnett *et al.*, *Redefining Christian Britain*, pp. 50–62.

99 McLeod, *Religious Crisis*, p. 87.

100 Ibid., p. 89. For my own account of Whitehouse's significance, see Brown, *Religion and Society*, pp. 248–52.

101 W. Thompson, 'Charismatic politics: the social and political impact of renewal', in S. Hunt, M. Hamilton and T. Walter (eds), *Charismatic Christianity: Sociological Perspectives*, Basingstoke, Macmillan, 1997.

102 A. Totten, 'Coherent chaplaincy', *Journal of the Royal Army Chaplains' Department*, vol. 45, 2006, p. 6.

103 For Canada, see the review in N.F. Christie and M. Gauvreau, 'Modalities of social authority: suggesting an interface for religious and social history', *Histoire Sociale – Social History*, vol. xxxvi, no. 71, May 2003, pp. 8–18.

104 McLeod, *Religious Crisis*, pp. 52–5.

105 For some of this evidence, see E. Ferri, J. Bynner and M. Wadsworth (eds), *Changing Britain, Changing Lives: Three Generations at the Turn of the Century*, London, Institute of Education, 2003, p. 271; C.G. Brown, 'Religion and secularisation', in A. Dickson and J.H. Treble (eds), *People and Society in Scotland: vol. 3, 1914–1990*, Edinburgh, John Donald, 1992.

106 Recent important contributions include J. Wolffe, *The Expansion of Evangelicalism: The Age of Wilberforce, More, Chalmers and Finney*, Downers Grove, Ill., InterVarsity Press, 2007, especially pp. 126–58; N.F. Christie (ed.), *Households of Faith: Family, Gender and Community in Canada 1760–1969*, Montreal, McGill-Queen's University Press, 2002. See also D.W. Bebbington, *The Dominance of Evangelicalism: The Age of Spurgeon and Moody*, Leicester, InterVarsity Press, 2005, pp. 202–12.

107 Taylor, *Secular Age*, p. 494. One Christian historian imagined that I was out of line with this type of work: Whyte, who claims to detect 'more than a whiff of Whiggery about Brown's account', misreported that my contention was 'that in the Victorian era men abandoned the church, leaving piety the preserve of women'. W. Whyte, 'The *Jackie* Generation: girls' magazines, pop music, and the discourse revolution', in Garnet *et al.*, *Redefining Christian Britain*, pp. 128, 131.

108 U. King and T. Beattie (eds), *Gender, Religion and Diversity: Cross-cultural Perspectives*, London, Continuum, 2004.

109 L. Wilson, *Constrained by Zeal: Female Spirituality amongst Nonconformists, 1825–1875*, Carlisle, Paternoster Press, 2000.

110 Van Rooden, 'Oral history'.

111 Brown, *Religion and Society*, pp. 225–70; idem., 'Secularisation, the growth of militancy and the spiritual revolution: religious change and gender power in Britain 1901–2001', *Historical Research*, vol. 80, 2007, pp. 393–418; Brown, 'Gendering secularisation'.

112 McLeod, *Religious Crisis*, p. 57.

113 F. Laffitte, 'The users of birth control clinics', *Population Studies*, vol. 16, 1962, pp. 12–30, at p. 12; L. McCormick, '"The Scarlet Woman in Person": The establishment of a family planning service in Northern Ireland, 1950–1974', *Social History of Medicine*, vol. 21, no. 2, 2008, pp. 345–60.

114 McLeod, *Religious Crisis*, pp. 161, 163. H. Cook, *The Long Sexual Revolution: English Women, Sex and Contraception 1800–1975*, Oxford, Oxford University Press, 2004, pp. 1–2; K. Fisher, *Birth Control, Sex and Marriage in Britain, 1918–1960*, Oxford, Oxford University Press, 2006, p. 8. A number of women and reviewers wrote to me about failing to mention the pill in the first edition of this book; the omission was an accident when a paragraph was deleted before publication. McLeod suggested in a private communication that a rise in the use of condoms in the 1950s might have achieved a reduction in the illegitimacy rate, but so far I have seen no demographer make this argument.

115 Though Whyte seems to think that the rise of *Jackie* from 1964 with just this revolutionary core message was not somehow overturning traditional discourses of training for marriage: Whyte, '*Jackie* Generation', pp. 132–3.

116 Quoted in D. Kynaston, *Austerity Britain*, London, Bloomsbury, 2007, pp. 374–5.

117 G. Gorer, *Exploring English Character*, London, Cresset Press, 1955; Kynaston, *Austerity Britain*, p. 375.

118 Fisher, *Birth Control*, pp. 48–50.

119 Ibid., pp. 56, 68. The 'silence about sex' syndrome has also been discerned from oral testimony on religion in the Netherlands: van Rooden, 'Oral History'.

120 J. Bakewell, *The Centre of the Bed*, London, Sceptre, 2003, p. 125.

121 C.G. Brown, A. McIvor and N. Rafeek, *The University Experience 1945–1975: An Oral History of the University of Strathclyde*, Edinburgh, Edinburgh University Press, 2004, p. 100.

122 McLeod, *Religious Crisis*, p. 195, fn. 25, suggests the *Church Times* in the 1960s made few complaints about sex on TV. On the contrary, amidst that paper's prominent reporting of the wider Anglican obsession with promiscuity, there were regular items on this. This started as early as 18 January 1963, when there are complaints about the BBC's turn 'towards cheapness and vulgarity' in abolishing restrictions on jokes about sex. Besides references to MRA (Moral Re-Armament)'s campaigns against the media (e.g. 20 September 1963), items on sex, promiscuity and television seemed to peak in 1967: for example 13 January 1967, 24 January 1967, 16 June 1967 and 15 September 1967.

123 L. Woodhead, 'Sex and secularisation', in Gerard Loughlin (ed.), *Queer Theology: Rethinking the Western Body*, Oxford, Blackwell, 2007, pp. 230–44, at p. 230; See also L. Woodhead, 'Gender differences in religious practice and significance', in J. Beckford and N.J. Demerath III (eds), *The Sage Handbook of the Sociology of Religion*, Los Angeles, Sage, 2007, pp. 550–70. Both are available at www.lindawoodhead.org.uk/recent_chapters_articles.

124 J. Lewis and K. Kiernan, 'The boundaries between marriage, nonmarriage, and parenthood: changes in behaviour and policy in postwar Britain', *Journal of Family History*, vol. 21, 1996, pp. 372–87, at p. 374.

125 McLeod, *Religious Crisis*, p. 164.

126 Garnett *et al.*, *Redefining Christian Britain*, p. 123.

127 Pasture, 'Christendom', p. 114.

128 See e.g. W. Damberg, 'Entwicklungslinien des europäischen Katholizismus im 20.Jahrhundert', *Journal of Modern European History*, vol. 3, 2005, pp. 164–82; and N. Atkin and F. Tallett, *Priests, Prelates and People: A History of European Catholicism since 1750*, London, I.B. Tauris, 2003, pp. 330–33.

129 McLeod, *Religious Crisis*, p. 186.

130 Ibid., p. 40.

131 Correlation of female and male Church of England confirmations per 1,000 population (12-years-old and over) against Church of England Easter Day communicants as a percentage of population, using only years for which complete data were available: 1950, 1953, 1956, 1958, 1960, 1962, 1964, 1966, 1968 and 1970. Confirmation data used in the correlation were taken from Table 8.1(b), p. 191, and EDC data calculated (using intercensal population estimates for England) from figures in Currie *et al.*, *Churches and Churchgoers*, p. 129.

132 Parsons, 'How the times', p. 183; McLeod, *Religious Crisis*, p. 182.

133 I am grateful for this insight to my doctoral student Sarah Browne at the University of Dundee, who is researching the Scottish women's liberation movement.

134 S. Rowbotham, *Promise of a Dream: Remembering the Sixties*, London, Verso, 2001, pp. 2, 4, 6; L. Sage, *Bad Blood*, London, Fourth Estate, 2001, pp. 89, 237, 244.

135 See pages 174–5; and Bakewell, *The Centre*, pp. 72–5.

136 C. Gribben, book review, *Church and Society*, April 2004, p. 31; D. Nash, book review, *New Humanist*, Summer 2001; Herbert, *Religion and Civil Society*, p. 23.

137 M. Gauvreau, *The Catholic Origins of Quebec's Quiet Revolution 1931–1970*, Montreal, McGill-Queen's University Press, 2005, p. 177.

138 L. Barley, book review, *Anvil*, vol. 19, no. 2, 2002, p. 144.

139 Brown, *Religion and Society*, pp. 297–314.

140 P. Heelas and L. Woodhead, *The Spiritual Revolution*, Oxford, Blackwell, 2005; S. Sutcliffe, *Children of the New Age: A History of Spiritual Practices*, London, Routledge, 2003; Nash, 'Reconnecting religion', p. 321; J. Carrette and R. King, *Selling Spirituality: The Silent Takeover of Religion*, London, Routledge, 2005, p. 170.

141 M. Hampson, *Last Rites: The End of the Church of England*, London, Granta, 2006.

142 D. Bebbington, *Evangelicalism in Modern Britain: A History from the 1730s to the 1980s*, London, Unwin Hyman, 1989, pp. 240–48; D. Martin, *Pentecostalisms: The World Their Parish*, Oxford, Blackwell, 2002, esp. pp. 1–7.

143 Bebbington, *Evangelicalism*, pp. 229–33, 240–48; A. Anderson, 'The Pentecostal and Charismatic movements', in H. McLeod (ed.), *The Cambridge History of Christianity, vol. 9: World Christianities, c. 1914–c.2000*, Cambridge, Cambridge University Press, 2006, pp. 89–106; N. Scotland, 'Evangelicalism and the Charismatic Movement (UK)', in C. Bartholomew, R. Parry and A. West (eds), *The Futures of Evangelicalism*, Leicester, InterVarsity Press, 2003, pp. 271–301. On alienation of worshippers from new liturgies, see Parsons, 'How the times', pp. 177–8.

144 Martin, *Pentecostalisms*, p. 167.

145 Brown, 'Secularization'; see also Brown, *Religion and Society*, pp. 278–319.

146 Book review, *Scottish Economic and Social History*, vol. 21, 2001, p. 75.

147 Garnett *et al.*, *Redefining Christian Britain*, p. 165.

148 Davie, *Religion in Modern Europe*, p. 51.

149 Ibid., pp. 56, 59.

150 C. Taylor, *The Ethics of Authenticity*, Cambridge, Mass., Harvard University Press, 1991; Garnett *et al.*, *Redefining Christian Britain*, pp. 12; 19–112.

151 M. Guest, 'Reconceiving the congregation as a source of authenticity', in Garnett *et al.*, *Redefining Christian Britain*, pp. 63–72.

152 S. Bruce, book review, *Twentieth Century British History*, vol. 19, 2008, pp. 246–8.

153 Ferri *et al.*, *Changing Britain*, pp. 270–71.

154 *The Spectator*, 14 April 2001.

155 Brown, *Postmodernism*, p. 175.

156 Herbert, *Religion and Civil Society*, p. 95.

SOURCES

_____ •◆• _____

ORAL TESTIMONY

CNWRS, SA Centre for North West Regional Studies, Sound Archive, oral-history collection, University of Lancaster.

FAM, Family Intergenerational Interviews, Qualidata Archive, University of Essex.

FLWE, Family Life and Work Experience before 1918 Collection, Qualidata Archive.

SOHCA, Stirling Women's Oral History Project interviews, Scottish Oral History Centre Archive, Department of History, University of Strathclyde.

PRIMARY MANUSCRIPT SOURCES

Edinburgh University Library, Laing MSS, La. II 500, letters from William Porteous to Lord Advocate, 24 January and 20 February 1797, 21 February 1798.

Stirling Archive Services CH3/286/2, Stirling General Associate [Antiburgher] Presbytery minutes, 11 February 1783.

PRIMARY PUBLISHED SOURCES

Adamson, W., _The Life of the Rev. Fergus Ferguson_, London, Simpkin, 1900.

Allan, T., _Crusade in Scotland – Billy Graham_, London, Pickering & Inglis, 1955.

Autobiography of a Scotch Lad, Glasgow, 1888.

Bakewell, J., _The Centre of the Bed_, London, Sceptre, 2003.

Barrie, J.M., _Auld Licht Idylls_, orig. 1887, reprint London, Hodder & Stoughton, 1938.

——, _A Window in Thrums_, orig. 1889, reprint London, Hodder & Stoughton, 1938.

——, _The Little Minister_, orig. 1891, reprint London, Cassell & Company, 1909.

Bateman, C.T., 'Missionary efforts in the metropolis', in Mudie-Smith (ed.), q.v.

Beatles Complete, The, London, Wise Publications, n.d.

Beaton, D., _Memoir, Diary and Remains of the Rev. Donald Macfarlane, Dingwall_, Inverness, Northern Counties Newspaper, 1929.

Beckwith, L., _The Hills is Lonely, The Sea for Breakfast_, London, Arrow, 1972.

——, *About My Father's Business*, London, Arrow, 1973.

Blackburn, J., *Reflections on the Moral and Spiritual Claims of the Metropolis*, London, Holdsworth, 1827.

——, *The Salvation of Britain Introductory to the Conversion of the World*, London, Jackson & Walford, 1835.

Blair, A., *Tea At Miss Cranston's*, London, Shepheard-Walwyn, 1985.

Booth, W., *In Darkest England and the Way Out*, London, Salvation Army, n.d. [1890].

Bradwell, A.T., *Autobiography of a Converted Infidel*, Sheffield, George Chalmers, 1844.

Brown, J., *The Life of a Scottish Probationer: Being a Memoir of Thomas Davidson*, Glasgow, Maclehose, 1877.

——, *Life of William B. Robertson, D.D.*, Glasgow, Maclehose, 1889.

Bullock, J., *Bower's Row: Recollections of a Mining Village*, London, EP Publishing, 1976.

Cairns, D., *The Army and Religion*, London, Hodder & Stoughton, 1919.

Census of Great Britain 1851, Religious Worship, England and Wales, *British Parliamentary Papers* lxxxix (1852–3).

Chalmers, T., *A Sermon delivered in the Tron Church on the occasion of the death of Princess Charlotte*, Glasgow, 1817.

——, *The Christian and Civic Economy of Large Towns*, Glasgow, 1821.

——, *The Right Ecclesiastical Economy of a Large Town*, Edinburgh, 1835.

Chapters in the Life of a Dundee Factory Boy, Dundee, 1851.

Clifford, J., *The Dawn of Manhood*, London, Christian Commonwealth, 1886.

Colquhoun, F., *Harringay Story: A Detailed Account of the Greater London Crusade 1954*, London, Hodder & Stoughton, 1955.

Courtney, W.L., (ed.), *Do We Believe? A Record of a Great Correspondence in "The Daily Telegraph," October, November, December, 1904*, London, Hodder & Stoughton, 1905.

Crockett, S.R., *The Stickit Minister and Some Common Men*, orig. 1893, reprint London, T. Fisher Unwin, 1905.

Davidson, J.T., *The City Youth*, London, Hodder & Stoughton, 1886.

Davies, C., *Clean Clothes for Sunday*, Lavenham, Terence Dalton, 1974.

Dodsley, R., *The Economy of Human Life*, Preston, 1837.

Drummond, H., *The City Without a Church*, Stirling, Drummond Tract Enterprise, 1892.

Dunlop, J., *Autobiography*, London, 1932.

Engels, F., *The Condition of the Working Class in England in 1844*, 1892.

Ferguson, R., *George Macleod: Founder of the Iona Community*, London, HarperCollins, 1990.

Foakes, G., *My Part of the River*, London, Shepheard-Walwyn, 1976.

Foley, A., *A Bolton Childhood*, Manchester, WEA, 1973.

Foley, W., *A Child in the Forest*, London, Futura, 1977.

Forrester, H., *Liverpool Miss*, London and Glasgow, Collins, 1982.

Fraser, D. (ed.), *The Christian Watt Papers*, Inverness, Caledonian Press, 1988.

Galt, J., *Annals of the Parish*, orig. 1821, Edinburgh, James Thin, 1978.

Gamble, R., *Chelsea Child*, London, Ariel, 1982.

Gibson, J.C. (ed.), *Diary of Sir Michael Connal*, Glasgow, 1895.

Glasgow United Y.M.C.A. Annual Report, 1877.

Gorer, G., *Exploring English Character*, London, Cresset Press, 1955.

Green, J., *Days in the Life: Voices from the English Underground 1961–1971*, London, Pimlico, 1998.

Hall, E., *Canary Girls and Stockpots*, Luton, 1977.

Hampson, M., *Last Rites: The End of the Church of England*, London, Granta, 2006.

Hanna, W. (ed.), *Memoirs of Thomas Chalmers*, vol. 1, Edinburgh, Constable, 1854.

Henson, H.H., 'The Church of England after the War', in F.J. Foakes-Jackson (ed.), *The Faith and the War*, London, Macmillan, 1915.

Heron, L. (ed.), *Truth, Dare or Promise: Girls Growing up in the Fifties*, London, Virago, 1985.

Heron, R. (ed.), *Account of the Proceedings and Debate, in the General Assembly of the Church of Scotland . . . Respecting the Propagation of the Gospel among the Heathen*, Edinburgh, Lawrie, 1796.

Hobbs, D., *Robert Hood, the Bridgeton Pastor: The Story of His Bright and Useful Life*, Edinburgh, Fairgrieve, 1894.

Hobbs, M., *Born to Struggle*, London, 1973.

Kay, J.P., *The Moral and Physical Condition of the Working Classes Employed in the Cotton Manufacture in Manchester*, London, second edn, 1832.

Lewis: Land of Revival: The story of the 1949–52 Lewis Revival as told by the islanders, cassette tape, Belfast, Ambassador Productions, 1983.

Logan, W., *The Moral Statistics of Glasgow*, Glasgow, 1849.

MacGill, Revd S., *Our Blessings and Our Duty: Under the Present Circumstances*, Glasgow, 1798.

Maclean, N., and Sclater, J.P.P., *God and the Soldier*, London, Hodder & Stoughton, 1917.

Macleod, D., *Memoir of Norman Macleod D.D. two volumes, by his Brother*, London, Daldy, Isbister & Co., 1876.

Macleod, N., *Reminiscences of a Highland Parish*, London, 1867.

Massey, V., *One Child's War*, London, BBC, 1983.

Masterman, C.F.G., *The Condition of England*, London, Methuen, 1909.

Matheson, A.S., *The City of God*, London, T. Fisher Unwin, 1910.

Miles, B., *Paul McCartney: Many Years from Now*, London, Vintage, 1998.

Mudie-Smith, R. (ed.), *The Religious Life of London*, London, Hodder & Stoughton, 1904.

Noakes, D., *The Town Beehive: A Young Girl's Lot: Brighton 1910–34*, Brighton, Queenspark, 1980.

Noel, B.W., *The State of the Metropolis Considered*, London, 1835.

Norfolk Within Living Memory, Newbury and Norwich, Countryside Books, 1995.

One of the Least Among the Brethren: A Revived Ministry our only Hope for a Revived Church, London, Jackson & Walford, 1844.

Paterson-Smyth, J., *God and the War*, London, Hodder & Stoughton, 1915.

Peddie, J., *A Defence of the Associate Synod against the Charge of Sedition*, Edinburgh, 1800.

Penn, M., *Manchester Fourteen Miles*, London and Sydney, 1982.

Porteous, W., *The Doctrine of Toleration*, Glasgow, 1778.

Principal Acts of the General Assembly of the Church of Scotland, 1794–1812.

Reports to the General Assembly of the Church of Scotland, 1966–72.

Roberts, R., *The Classic Slum*, Harmondsworth, Penguin, 1973.

——, *A Ragged Schooling*, Manchester, Manchester University Press, 1976.

Rowntree, B.S., *Poverty: A Study of Town Life*, London, Macmillan, 1901.

——, *Poverty and Progress: A Second Survey of York*, London, Longmans, 1941.

Scannell, D., *Mother Knew Best: An East End Childhood*, London, Pan, 1974.

Seabrook, J., *The Unprivileged*, Harmondsworth, Penguin, 1973.

Sinclair, J. (ed.), *The Statistical Account of Scotland*, Edinburgh, 1790.

Smith, S., *Donald Macleod of Glasgow: A Memoir and a Study*, London, James Clarke, 1926.

Somerville, A., *The Autobiography of a Working Man*, orig. 1848, London, MacGibbon & Kee, 1967.

Stanley, M., 'Clubs for working girls', *The Nineteenth Century*, 1889, vol. 25.

Steedman, C., *Landscape for a Good Woman: A Story of Two Lives*, London, Virago, 1986.

Taylor, P., *Autobiography*, Paisley, Gardner, 1903.

Thompson, F., *Larkrise to Candleford*, orig. 1945, Harmondsworth, Penguin, 1983.

Thomson, D.P., *Visitation Evangelism in Scotland 1946–1956*, Crieff, no pub., *c.* 1956.

Thomson, J., *The City of Dreadful Night*, orig. 1880, Edinburgh, Canongate, 1993.

Vaughan, R., *The Age of Great Cities*, 1843, reprint Shannon, Irish University Press, 1971.

Wardlaw, R., *The Contemplation of Heathen Idolatry an Excitement to Missionary Zeal*, London, Williams & Co., 1818.

Watson, Mrs S., *A Village Maiden's Career*, London, Partridge & Co., 1895.

Watt, A., *The Glasgow Bills of Mortality for 1841 and 1842*, Glasgow, 1844.

——, *The Vital Statistics of Glasgow, for 1843 and 1844*, Glasgow, 1846.

Weir, M., *Best Foot Forward*, London, Collins, 1972.

——, *Shoes were for Sunday*, London, Collins, 1994.

Whatley, C.A. (ed.) *The Diary of John Sturrock, Millwright, Dundee 1864–5*, East Linton, Tuckwell, 1996.

Williams, D., *One in a Million: Billy Graham with Mission England*, Berkhamsted, Word Books, 1984.

Winterson, J., *Oranges are Not the Only Fruit*, London, Pandora, 1985.

Younger, J., *Autobiography of John Younger, Shoemaker, St. Boswells*, Kelso, 1881.

RELIGIOUS TRACTS

All tracts are Drummond Tract Enterprise, Stirling, except where otherwise stated.

A Heroic Child, 1871.

A Race-Course Dialogue, 1852.

A.M.C. (pseud.), *Stories of a Men's Class*, 1903.

——, *Two Words Did It, and Other Narratives*, 1903.

American Citizen, An, *Philosophy of the Plan of Salvation*, London, The Religious Tract Society, *c.* 1837.

An Account of the Origin and Progress of the London Religious Tract Society, London, 1803.

Archer, W.H., *Collier Jack*, c. 1900.

The Ball-Room and Its Tendencies, 1853.

Be not Deceived, n.d.

The Book of Fire, or the Lake of Fire!, n.d.

Brady, C., *The Riches of His Grace*, 1885.

Choose Life, n.d.

Confession of a Novel-Reader, 1853.

Cook, C., *Sketches from Life: Tract 1: A Voice from the Convict Cell*, 1892.

Cooper, R.W., *Tract Distribution: Something You Can Do, and How To Do It*, c. 1935.

Cunningham, R., *This Man or His Parents*, c. 1930.

Dick, J.N., *Men of Destiny: Christian Messages from Modern Leaders*, 1944.

Everard, Revd G., *Life for Evermore*, 1902.

Haughton, G.W., *Free Salvation; or God's Gift of the Saviour*, 1901.

Hell! What is it?, n.d.

Herdman, M.S.S., *The Romance of the Ranks: Reminiscences of Army Work*, 1888.

Johnson, Revd W., *Open-air Preaching*, 1853.

Kent, H., *The Doctor's Story: How a Woman Doctor Found her Way to a World of Glad Service through Doors of Sorrow*, c. 1930.

Kyles, D., *Should a Girl Smoke? An Appeal to British Womanhood*, 1938.

Light Reading, 1853.

Moncrieff, J.F., *The Prize-Winners: An Address to the Young*, c. 1911.

Murray, C., *Messages from the Master: And Other Poems*, 1880.

Oh! If I Had Listened, n.d.

Old Age not a 'Convenient Season' for Repentance, 1871.

Pardon, G., *Love's Healing*, n.d.

Pettman, G., *The Unequal Yoke*, c. 1938.

Poole, E., *Shut the Door*, 1890.

——, *His Mighty Men*, 1891.

——, *My Garden*, 1892.

Power, P.B., *The Man that Carried the Baby and Other Stories*, 1896.

Races, Games, and Balls, 1853.

The Religion We Want, n.d.

Savery, C.C.A., *God Bless Daddy: A Bedtime Book for Sons and Daughters of Soldiers, Sailors, Airmen*, c. 1944.

Skinner, V.M., *These Seven Years; or the Story of the 'Friendly Letter Mission'*, 1888.

The Spiritual Thermometer, n.d.

The Street Preacher, n.d.

Sunny Stories, c. 1955.

The Theatre, n.d.

Watson, S., *Disloyal*, 1894

——, *Catherine Ballard*, 1894

What is Lost by Strong Drink?, n.d.

What thou doest, do quickly, n.d.

Which?, n.d.

Who will be at the Theatre?, n.d.

Wilson, J.H., *A Bright Sunset: or, Recollections of the Last Days of a Young Football Player*, 1902.
Wynn, M., *Jennifer-Ann*, c. 1946.

MAGAZINES

Boy's Own Paper, 1886–1930.
British Messenger, 1862–72, 1920–55.
British Weekly, 1886–1919.
Chamber's Journal, 1832–6, 1853–60.
The Christian Miscellany and Family Visitor, 1867, 1890.
Christian Reformer, 1815.
Daybreak, no dates, c. 1900–10.
The Day-Star, 1855–6.
The Edinburgh Christian Magazine, 1851.
Free Church Magazine, 1843–8.
The General Baptist Repository and Missionary Observer, 1824–48.
Girl's Own Paper, 1886–7, 1896, 1916–17, 1922, 1926, 1938.
Good News, 1860–75.
The Methodist Magazine, 1811–52.
The Primitive Methodist Children's Magazine, 1827, 1843–5.
The Primitive Methodist Magazine, 1821.
Scots Magazine, 1787.
The Watchman, 1835–6.

FILMS

Brief Encounter, starring Celia Johnson and Trevor Howard (dir. David Lean, Pinewood Films 1945).
Mrs Miniver, starring Greer Garson and Walter Pidgeon (dir. William Wyler, MGM Films, 1942, original book by Jan Struther).

SECONDARY SOURCES

Abrams, L., *Myth and Materiality in a Woman's World: Shetland 1800–2000*, Manchester, Manchester University Press, 2003.
Addison, P., and Jones, H. (eds), *A Companion to Contemporary Britain, 1939–2000*, Oxford, Blackwell Publishing, 2005.
Ali, T., *1968 and After: Inside the Revolution*, London, Blond and Briggs, 1978.
Anderson, A., 'The Pentecostal and Charismatic movements', in H. McLeod (ed.), *The Cambridge History of Christianity, vol. 9: World Christianities, c. 1914–c.2000*, Cambridge, Cambridge University Press, 2006.
Asad, T., *Formations of the Secular: Christianity, Islam, Modernity*, Stanford, Stanford University Press, 2003.
Aspinwall, B., 'The formation of the Catholic community in the west of Scotland: some preliminary outlines', *Innes Review*, 1982, vol. 33.

——, and McCaffrey, J., 'A comparative view of the Irish in Edinburgh in the nineteenth-century', in R. Swift and S. Gilley (eds), *The Irish in the Victorian City*, London, Croom Helm, 1985.

Atkin, N., and Tallett, F., *Priests, Prelates and People: A History of European Catholicism since 1750*, London, I.B. Tauris, 2003.

Auerbach, N., *Woman and the Demon: The Life of a Victorian Myth*, Cambridge, Mass., Harvard University Press, 1982.

Bailey, P., '"Will the real Bill Banks pleas stand up?" Towards a role analysis of mid-Victorian working-class respectability', *Journal of Social History*, 1979, vol. 12.

Banks, O., *Faces of Feminism: A Study of Feminism as a Social Movement*, Oxford, Martin Robertson, 1981.

Bauman, Z., *Liquid Life*, Cambridge, Polity, 2005.

Bebbington, D., *Evangelicalism in Modern Britain: A History from the 1730s to the 1980s*, London, Unwin Hyman, 1989.

Bebbington, D.W., *Victorian Nonconformity*, Bangor, Headstart, 1992.

——, *The Dominance of Evangelicalism: The Age of Spurgeon and Moody*, Leicester, InterVarsity Press, 2005.

Beetham, M., *A Magazine of Her Own? Domesticity and Desire in the Woman's Magazine, 1800–1914*, London, Routledge, 1996.

Berger, P.L., *The Social Reality of Religion*, London, Longman, 1969.

——, 'The desecularization of the world: a global overview', in P.L. Berger (ed.), *The Desecularization of the World*, Washington, DC, Ethics and Public Policy Center, 1999.

Binfield, C., *George Williams and the YMCA*, London, Heinemann, 1973.

Blaschke, O. (ed.), *Konfessionen im Konflikt: Deutschland zwischen 1800 und 1970 ein zweites konfessionelles Zeitalter*, Göttingen, Vandenhoeck & Ruprecht, 2002.

Bradley, I., *The Call to Seriousness*, London, Jonathan Cape, 1976.

——, *Marching to the Promised Land: Has the Church a Future?*, London, John Murray, 1992.

Branca, P., *Silent Sisterhood: Middle-class Women in the Victorian Home*, London, Croom Helm, 1975.

Brown, C.G., 'The Sunday-school movement in Scotland, 1780–1914', *Records of the Scottish Church History Society*, 1981, vol. 21.

——, 'The costs of pew-renting: church management, church-going and social class in nineteenth-century Glasgow', *Journal of Ecclesiastical History*, 1987, vol. 38.

——, 'Did urbanisation secularise Britain?', *Urban History Yearbook* 1988.

——, 'Protest in the pews: interpreting presbyterianism and society in fracture during the Scottish economic revolution', in T.M. Devine (ed.), *Conflict and Stability in Scottish Society 1700–1850*, Edinburgh, John Donald, 1990.

——, 'Religion, class and church growth', in Fraser and Morris (eds), q.v.

——, 'Religion and secularisation', in A. Dickson and J.H. Treble (eds), *People and Society in Scotland, vol. 3, 1914–1990*, Edinburgh, John Donald, 1992.

——, 'A revisionist approach to religious change', in Bruce (ed.), q.v.

——, 'The mechanism of religious growth in urban societies: British cities since the eighteenth century', in McLeod, H. (ed.), q.v.

——, 'The religion of an industrial village: the churches in Balfron 1789–1850', *Scottish Local History Society Journal*, 1995, vol. 35.

——, 'Popular culture and the continuing struggle for rational recreation', in T.M. Devine and R.J. Finlay (eds), *Scotland in the Twentieth Century*, Edinburgh, John Donald, 1996.

——, '"To be aglow with civic ardours": the "Godly Commonwealth" in Glasgow 1843–1914', *Records of the Scottish Church History Society*, vol. 26, 1996.

——, 'Essor religieux et sécularisation', in H. McLeod, S. Mews and C. D'Haussy (eds), *Histoire Religieuse de la Grande-Bretagne*, Paris, Editions du Cerf, 1997.

——, *Religion and Society in Scotland since 1707*, Edinburgh, Edinburgh University Press, 1997.

——, *Up-helly-aa: Custom, Culture and Community in Shetland*, Manchester, Mandolin, 1998.

——, 'Piety, gender and war in the 1910s', in C. Macdonald and E. McFarland (eds), *Scotland and the Great War*, East Linton, Tuckwell, 1999.

——, 'Sport and the Scottish Office in the twentieth century: the control of a social problem', *European Sports History Review*, vol. 1, 1999.

——, 'The Myth of the Established Church', in J. Kirk (ed.), *Church and State in Scotland*, Edinburgh, Scottish Church History Society, 2000.

——, 'The secularisation decade: what the 1960s have done to the study of religious history', in H. McLeod and W. Ustorf (eds), *The Decline of Christendom in Western Europe 1750–2000*, Cambridge, Cambridge University Press, 2003.

——, *Postmodernism for Historians*, Harlow, Longman, 2005.

——, '"Best not to take it too far": how the British cut religion down to size', www.opendemocracy.net/globalization-aboutfaith/britain_religion_3335.jsp, 8 March 2006.

——, *Religion and Society in Twentieth-century Britain*, Harlow, PearsonLongman, 2006.

——, 'The unconverted and the conversion: gender relations in the salvation narrative in Britain 1800–1960', in J.N. Bremner, W.J. van Bekkum and A.L. Molendijk (eds), *Paradigms, Poetics and Politics of Conversion*, Leuven, Peeters, 2006, pp. 183–99.

——, 'Secularisation, the growth of militancy and the spiritual revolution: religious change and gender power in Britain 1901–2001', *Historical Research*, vol. 80, 2007, pp. 393–418.

——, and Stephenson, J.D., '"Sprouting wings"? Women and religion in Scotland c. 1890–c. 1950', in E. Breitenbach and E. Gordon (eds), *Out of Bounds: Women in Scotland in the Nineteenth and Twentieth Centuries*, Edinburgh, Edinburgh University Press, 1992.

——, McIvor, A., and Rafeek, N., *The University Experience 1945–1975: An Oral History of the University of Strathclyde*, Edinburgh, Edinburgh University Press, 2004.

Bruce, S., 'Pluralism and religious vitality', in S. Bruce (ed.), q.v.

—— (ed.), *Religion and Modernization: Sociologists and Historians Debate the Secularization Thesis*, Oxford, Clarendon Press, 1992.

——, *Religion in Modern Britain*, Oxford, Oxford University Press, 1995.

——, *Religion in the Modern World: From Cathedrals to Cults*, Oxford, Oxford University Press, 1996.

——, 'Religion in Britain at the close of the 20th century: a challenge to the silver lining perspective', *Journal of Contemporary Religion*, 1996, vol. 11.

Burton, L., 'Social class in the local church: a study of two Methodist churches in the Midlands', in M. Hill (ed.), *A Sociological Yearbook of Religion*, no. 8, London, 1975.

Cameron, D. *et al.*, *Researching Language: Issues of Power and Method*, London and New York, Routledge, 1992.

Camporesi, P., *The Magic Harvest: Food, Folklore and Society*, London, Polity, 1998.

Carrette, J.R., *Foucault and Religion: Spiritual Corporality and Political Spirituality*, London, Routledge, 2000.

——, and King, R., *Selling Spirituality: The Silent Takeover of Religion*, London, Routledge, 2005.

Chadwick, O., *Victorian Miniature*, London, Futura, 1983, orig., 1960.

——, *The Secularization of the European Mind in the Nineteenth Century*, Cambridge, Cambridge University Press, 1975.

Chambers, P., *Religion, Secularization and Social Change in Wales*, Cardiff, University of Wales Press, 2005.

Checkland, O., *Philanthropy in Victorian Scotland*, Edinburgh, John Donald, 1980.

Checkland, S., and Checkland, O., *Industry and Ethos: Scotland 1832–1914*, London, Edward Arnold, 1984.

Cheyne, A.C., *The Transforming of the Kirk: Victorian Scotland's Religious Revolution*, Edinburgh, Saint Andrew Press, 1983.

Christie, N.F. (ed.), *Households of Faith: Family, Gender and Community in Canada 1760–1969*, Montreal, McGill-Queen's University Press, 2002.

——, and Gauvreau, M., 'Modalities of social authority: suggesting an interface for religious and social history', *Histoire Sociale – Social History*, vol. xxxvi, no. 71, May 2003, pp. 8–18.

Christiano, K.J., *Religious Diversity and Social Change: American Cities 1890–1906*, Cambridge, Cambridge University Press, 1987.

Clapson, M., *A Bit of a Flutter: Popular Gambling and English Society, c. 1823–1961*, Manchester, Manchester University Press, 1992.

Clark, A., *The Struggle for the Breeches: Gender and the Making of the British Working Class*, London, Rivers Oram Press, 1995.

Clark, D., *Between Pulpit and Pew: Folk Religion in a North Yorkshire Fishing Village*, Cambridge, Cambridge University Press, 1982.

Clark, G.K., *The Making of Victorian England*, London, Methuen, 1962.

Coleman, B.I. (ed.), *The Idea of the City in Nineteenth-Century Britain*, London, RKP, 1973.

Cook, H., *The Long Sexual Revolution: English Women, Sex and Contraception 1800–1975*, Oxford, Oxford University Press, 2004.

Cormack, A.A., *Teinds and Agriculture*, London, Hodder & Stoughton, 1930.

Cox, J., *The English Churches in a Secular Society: Lambeth 1870–1930*, Oxford, Oxford University Press, 1982.

——, 'Master narratives of long-term religious change', in H. McLeod and W. Ustorf (eds), *The Decline of Christendom in Western Europe 1750–2000*, Cambridge, Cambridge University Press, 2003.

Crawford, P., *Women and Religion in England 1500–1720*, London, Routledge, 1993.

Cressy, D., *Birth, Marriage and Death: Ritual, Religion and the Life-Cycle in Tudor and Stuart England*, Oxford, Oxford University Press, 1997.

Crockett, A., and Voas, D., 'Generations of decline: religious change in 20th-century Britain', *Journal for the Scientific Study of Religion*, vol. 45, 2006, pp. 567–84.

Crossick, G., 'From gentlemen to the residuum: languages of social description in Victorian Britain', in P.J. Corfield (ed.), *Language, History and Class*, Oxford, Blackwell, 1991.

Cunningham, H. *Leisure in the Industrial Revolution*, London, Croom Helm, 1980.

Currie, R., Gilbert, A., and Horsley, L., *Churches and Churchgoers: Patterns of Church Growth in the British Isles since 1700*, Oxford, Clarendon Press, 1977.

Curtis, R.K., *They Called Him Mr. Moody*, New York, 1962.

Damberg, W., 'Pfarrgemeinden und katholische Verbände vor dem Konzil', in G. Wassilowsky (ed.), *Zweites Vatikanum: vergessene Anstösse, gegenwärtige Fortschreibungen*, Freiburg, Herder, 2004.

——, 'Entwicklungslinien des europäischen Katholizismus im 20.Jahrhundert', *Journal of Modern European History*, vol. 3, 2005, pp. 164–82.

Davidoff, L., and Hall, C., *Family Fortunes: Men and Women of the English Middle Class, 1780–1850*, London, Routledge, 1987.

Davie, G., *Religion in Britain since 1945: Believing Without Belonging*, Oxford, Blackwell, 1994.

——, *Religion in Modern Europe: A Memory Mutates*, Oxford, Oxford University Press, 2000.

Davies, E.T., *Religion and Society in the Nineteenth Century*, Llandybie, Davies, 1981.

Dennis, R., *English Industrial Cities of the Nineteenth Century: A Social Geography*, Cambridge, Cambridge University Press, 1984.

Dixon, j., *The Romance Fiction of Mills & Boon, 1909–1990s*, London, UCL Press, 1999.

Donnelly, M., *Sixties Britain: Culture, Society and Politics*, London, Pearson Education, 2005.

Drummond, A.L., and Bulloch, J., *The Church in Victorian Scotland 1843–1974*, Edinburgh, Saint Andrew Press, 1975.

——, *The Church in Late Victorian Scotland 1874–1900*, Edinburgh, Saint Andrew Press, 1978.

Eco, U., *The Role of the Reader*, Bloomington, Ind., University of Indiana Press, 1979.

Entwistle, D., '"Hope, Colour and Comradeship": loyalty and opportunism in early twentieth-century church attendance among the working class in north west England', *Journal of Religious History*, vol. 25, 2001, pp. 20–38.

Epstein, B.L., *The Politics of Domesticity: Women, Evangelism and Temperance in Nineteenth-Century America*, Middletown, Conn., Wesleyan University Press, 1981.

Ermarth, E.D., *The English Novel in History 1840–1895*, London, Routledge, 1997.

Evans, E.J., *The Contentious Tithe: The Tithe Problem and English Agriculture, 1750–1850*, London, RKP, 1976.

Fabb, N., *Linguistics and Literature*, Oxford, Blackwell, 1997.

Fairchild, H.N., *Religious Trends in English Poetry: vol. II: 1740–1780: Religious Sentimentalism in the Age of Johnson*, New York and London, Columbia University Press, 1942.

——, *Religious Trends in English Poetry, vol IV: 1830–1880: Christianity and Romanticism in the Victorian Era*, New York and London, Columbia University Press, 1957.

Fawcett, A., *The Cambuslang Revival*, London, Banner of Truth Trust, 1971.

Ferri, E., Bynner, J., and Wadsworth, M. (eds), *Changing Britain, Changing Lives: Three Generations at the Turn of the Century*, London, Institute of Education, 2003.

Field, C.D., 'The social structure of English Methodism, eighteenth–twentieth centuries', *British Journal of Sociology*, vol. 28, 1977.

——, 'Adam and Eve: Gender in the English Free Church constituency', *Journal of Ecclesiastical History*, vol. 44, 1993.

Finke, R., 'An unsecular America', in Bruce (ed.), q.v.

——, and Stark, R., 'Evaluating the evidence: religious economies and sacred canopies', *American Sociological Review*, vol. 54, 1989.

Fisher, K., *Birth Control, Sex and Marriage in Britain, 1918–1960*, Oxford, Oxford University Press, 2006.

Foster, J., *Class Struggle and the Industrial Revolution*, London, RKP, 1974.

Foster, S., *Victorian Women's Fiction: Marriage, Freedom and the Individual*, Beckenham, Croom Helm, 1985.

Foucault, M., *The Archaeology of Knowledge*, London, Routledge, 1989.

Foyster, E.A., *Manhood in Early Modern England: Honour, Sex and Marriage*, London, Longman, 1999.

Fraser, W.H., 'From civic gospel to municipal socialism', in D. Fraser (ed.), *Cities, Class and Communication*, Brighton, Harvester, 1990.

——, and Morris, R.J. (eds), *People and Society in Scotland, vol. 2, 1830–1914*, Edinburgh, John Donald, 1990.

Freeman, F.W., 'Robert Fergusson: pastoral and politics at mid century', in A. Hook (ed.), *The History of Scottish Literature, vol. 2, 1660–1800*, Aberdeen, Aberdeen University Press, 1988.

Frye, N., *The Secular Scripture: A Study of the Structure of Romance*, Cambridge, Mass., Harvard University Press, 1976.

——, *The Great Code: The Bible and Literature*, Toronto, Academic Press Canada, 1982.

Garnett, J., Grimley, M., Harris, A., Whyte, W., and Williams, S. (eds), *Redefining Christian Britain: Post 1945 Perspectives*, London, SCM Press, 2006.

Gauvreau, M., *The Catholic Origins of Quebec's Quiet Revolution 1931–1970*, Montreal, McGill-Queen's University Press, 2005.

——, and Hubert, O. (eds), *The Churches and Social Order in Nineteenth- and Twentieth-century Canada*, Montreal, McGill-Queen's University Press, 2006.

Gilbert, A.D., *Religion and Society in Industrial England: Church, Chapel and Social Change, 1740–1914*, London and New York, Longman, 1976.

——, *Religion and Society in Industrial England: Church, Chapel and Social Change 1740–1914*, London, Longman, 1978.

——, *The Making of Post-Christian Britain: A History of the Secularization of Modern Society*, London, Longman, 1980.

——, 'Secularization and the future', in S. Gilley and W.J. Sheils (eds), *A History of Religion in Britain*, Oxford, Basil Blackwell, 1994.

Gill, R., *Competing Convictions*, London, SCM, 1989.

——, *The Myth of the Empty Church*, London, SCM, 1992.

——, *The 'Empty' Church Revisited*, Aldershot, Ashgate, 2003.

Gill, S., *Women and the Church of England: From the Eighteenth Century to the Present*, London, SPCK, 1994.

Gilley, S., and Sheils, W.J. (eds), *A History of Religion in Britain*, Oxford, Basil Blackwell, 1994.

Goodridge, R.M., 'Nineteenth-century urbanization and religion: Bristol and Marseilles 1830–1880', in D. Martin (ed.), *A Sociological Yearbook of Religion in Britain*, no. 2, London, 1969.

Green, J., *Days in the Life: Voices from the English Underground 1961–1971*, London, Pimlico, 1998.

——, *All Dressed Up: The Sixties and the Counterculture*, London, Pimlico, 1999.

Green, S.J.D., *Religion in the Age of Decline: Organisation and Experience in Industrial Yorkshire 1870–1920*, Cambridge, Cambridge University Press, 1996.

——, 'Was there an English religious revival in the 1950s?', *Journal of the United Reformed Church History Society*, vol. 7, 2006, pp. 517–38.

Gregory, J., 'Homo Religiosus: masculinity and religion in the long eighteenth century', in T. Hitchcock and M. Cohen (eds.), *English Masculinity 1660–1800*, London, Longman, 1999.

Grimley, M., 'Civil society and the clerisy: Christian elites and national culture, c.1930–1950', in J. Harris (ed.), *Civil Society in British History*, Oxford, Oxford University Press, 2003.

——, 'The religion of Englishness: Puritanism, providentialism, and "national character", 1918–1945', *Journal of British Studies*, vol. 46, 2007, pp. 884–906.

Guest, M., 'Reconceiving the congregation as a source of authenticity', in J. Garnett *et al.* (eds), q.v.

Hall, C., *White, Male and Middle Class: Explorations in Feminism and History*, Cambridge, Polity Press, 1992.

Hammerton, A.J., *Cruelty and Companionship: Conflict in Nineteenth-century Married Life*, London, Routledge, 1992.

Hammond, J.L., and Hammond, B., *The Town Labourer 1760–1832: The New Civilisation*, London, Longman's Green, 1917.

Harris, J., *Private Lives, Public Spirit: Britain 1870–1914*, Harmondsworth, Penguin, 1994.

Harvie, C., 'The Covenanting tradition', in G. Walker and T. Gallagher (eds), *Sermons and Battle Hymns: Protestant Popular Culture in Modern Scotland*, Edinburgh, Edinburgh University Press, 1990.

Heelas, P. (ed.), *Religion, Modernity and Postmodernity*, Oxford, Blackwell, 1998.

——, and Woodhead, L., *The Spiritual Revolution*, Oxford, Blackwell, 2005.

Heimann, M., *Catholic Devotion in Victorian England*, Oxford, Clarendon Press, 1995.

Hempton, D., *Methodism and Politics in British Society 1750–1850*, London, Hutchinson, 1987.

——, *The Religion of the People: Methodism and Popular Religion, c. 1750–1900*, London, Routledge, 1996.

Hennock, E.P., *Fit and Proper Persons: Ideal and Reality in Nineteenth-century Urban Government*, London, Edward Arnold, 1973.

Herbert, D., *Religion and Civil Society: Rethinking Public Religion in the Contemporary World*, Aldershot, Ashgate, 2003.

Hilliard, D., 'The religious crisis of the 1960s: the experience of the Australian churches', *Journal of Religious History*, vol. 21, 1997.

Hillis, P., 'Presbyterianism and social class in mid-nineteenth-century Glasgow: a study of nine churches', *Journal of Ecclesiastical History*, vol. 32, 1981.

Hilton, B., *The Age of Atonement: The Influence of Evangelicalism on Social and Economic Thought, 1795–1865*, Oxford, Clarendon, 1988.

Hilton, M., '"Tags", "Fags" and the "Boy labour problem" in late Victorian and Edwardian Britain', *Journal of Social History*, vol. 28, 1996.

Hindmarsh, D.B., *John Newton and the English Evangelical Tradition Between the Conversions of Wesley and Wilberforce*, Oxford, Clarendon Press, 1996.

Hölscher, L., 'Secularization and urbanization in the nineteenth century: an interpretative model', in McLeod, H. (ed.), q.v.

—— , 'Die Religion des Bürgers: bürgerliche Frömmigkeit und Protestantische Kirche im 19. Jahrundert', *Historsche Zeitschrift*, vol. 250, 1990.

Hopkins, E., 'Religious dissent in Black Country industrial villages in the first half of the nineteenth century', *Journal of Ecclesiastical History*, vol. 34, 1983.

Hutton, R., 'The English Reformation and the evidence of folklore', *Past and Present*, no. 148, 1995.

Inglis, K.S., *Churches and the Working Classes in Victorian England*, London, RKP, 1963.

James, W., *The Varieties of Religious Experience: a Study in Human Nature*, orig. 1902, London, Longmans, Green, 1928.

Jarvis, A., *Samuel Smiles and the Construction of Victorian Values*, Stroud, Sutton, 1997.

Jarvis, M., *Conservative Governments, Morality and Social Change, 1957–64*, Manchester, Manchester University Press, 2005.

Jenkins, K. (ed.), *The Postmodern History Reader*, London, Routledge, 1997.

Jones, I., with Webster, P., 'Expressions of authenticity: music for worship', in J. Garnett *et al.* (eds), q.v.

Joyce, P., *Visions of the People: Industrial England and the Question of Class, 1848–1914*, Cambridge, Cambridge University Press, 1991.

—— , *Democratic Subjects: The Self and the Social in Nineteenth-century England*, Cambridge, Cambridge University Press, 1994.

Kent, J., 'Feelings and festivals', in H. Dyos and M. Wolff (eds), *The Victorian City*, vol. 2, London, Routledge, 1973.

—— , *Holding the Fort: Studies in Victorian Revivalism*, London, Epworth, 1978.

King, U., and Beattie, T. (eds), *Gender, Religion and Diversity: Cross-cultural Perspectives*, London, Continuum, 2004.

Kynaston, D., *Austerity Britain 1945–51*, London, Bloomsbury, 2007.

Laffitte, F., 'The users of birth control clinics', *Population Studies*, vol. 16, 1962, pp. 12–30.

Larner, C., *Enemies of God: The Witch-hunt in Scotland*, Oxford, Oxford University Press, 1983.

Laslett, P., *The World We Have Lost*, London, Methuen, 1965.

Layton-Henry, Z., *The Politics of Immigration: Immigration, 'Race' and 'Race' Relations in Post-war Britain*, Oxford, Blackwell, 1992.

Lees, L.H., *Exiles of Erin: Irish Migrants in Victorian London*, Manchester, Manchester University Press, 1979.

Lewis, J., and Kiernan, K., 'The boundaries between marriage, nonmarriage, and parenthood: changes in behaviour and policy in postwar Britain', *Journal of Family History*, vol. 21, 1996, pp. 372–87.

Light, A., *Forever England: Femininity, Literature and Conservatism between the Wars*, London, Routledge, 1991.

McCleery, A., '*Lady Chatterley's Lover* recovered', *Publishing History*, vol. 59, 2006.

McCormick, L., '"The Scarlet Woman in Person": The establishment of a family planning service in Northern Ireland, 1950–1974', *Social History of Medicine*, vol. 21, no. 2, 2008, pp. 345–60.

Macdonald, I., *Revolution in the Head: The Beatles' Records and the Sixties*, London, Pimlico, 1995.

MacDonald, R.H., 'Reproducing the middle-class boy: from purity to patriotism in the boys' magazines, 1892–1914', *Journal of Contemporary History*, vol. 24, 1989.

Macdonald, S., 'Death of Christian Canada? Do Canadian church statistics support Callum Brown's timing of church decline?', *Historical Papers: Canadian Society of Church History*, 2006, pp. 135–56.

McEwan, I., *Enduring Love*, London, Vintage, 1998.

Machin, I., 'British churches and moral change in the 1960s', in W.M. Jacob and N. Yates (eds), *Religion and Society in Northern Europe since the Reformation*, Woodbridge, Boydell Press, 1993.

Macinnes, J., *The Evangelical Movement in the Highlands of Scotland 1688 to 1800*, Aberdeen, Aberdeen University Press, 1951.

MacLaren, A.A., *Religion and Social Class: The Disruption Years in Aberdeen*, London, RKP, 1974.

McLeod, H., 'Class, community and region: the religious geography of nineteenth century England', in M. Hill (ed.), *Sociological Yearbook of Religion in Britain*, vol. 6, 1973.

——, *Class and Religion in the Late Victorian City*, London, Croom Helm, 1974.

——, 'New perspectives in Victorian working-class religion: the oral evidence', *Oral History Journal*, vol. 14, 1986.

——, 'Religion', in J. Langton and R.J. Morris (eds), *Atlas of Industrializing Britain 1780–1914*, London, Methuen, 1986.

—— (ed.), *European Religion in the Age of Great Cities 1830–1930*, London, Routledge, 1995.

——, *Piety and Poverty: Working-class Religion in Berlin, London and New York 1870–1914*, New York, Holmes & Meier, 1996.

——, *Religion and Society in England 1850–1914*, Basingstoke, Macmillan, 1996.

——, *Religion and the People of Western Europe 1789–1989*, Oxford, Oxford University Press, 1997.

——, *Religion and the People of Western Europe 1789–1989*, 2nd edn, Oxford, Opus, 1997.

——, *Secularisation in Western Europe 1848–1914*, Basingstoke, Macmillan, 2000.

——, 'The crisis of Christianity in the west', in H. McLeod (ed.), *The Cambridge History of Christianity, vol. 9: World Christianities, c. 1914–c.2000*, Cambridge, Cambridge University Press, 2006.

——, *The Religious Crisis of the 1960s*, Oxford, Oxford University Press, 2007.

McLuhan, M., *Understanding Media: The Extensions of Man*, orig. 1964, Cambridge, Mass., MIT Press, 1994.

McRobbie, A., 'Jackie: An Ideology of Adolescent Femininity', Centre for Contemporary Cultural Studies, University of Birmingham, Occasional Paper no. 53, April 1978.

Martin, B., *A Sociology of Contemporary Cultural Change*, Oxford, Basil Blackwell, 1981.

——, 'Dark materials? Philip Pullman and children's literature', in J. Garnett *et al.* (eds), q.v.

Martin, D., *A General Theory of Secularization*, Oxford, Basil Blackwood, 1978.

——, *Pentecostalisms: The World Their Parish*, Oxford, Blackwell, 2002.

Martin, M.C., 'Relationships human and divine: retribution and repentance in children's lives, 1740–1870', in K. Cooper and J. Gregory (eds), *Retribution, Repentance and Reconciliation*, London, Boydell Press, 2004.

Marwick, A., *The Sixties*, Oxford, Oxford University Press, 1998.

Mason, M., *The Making of Victorian Sexual Attitudes*, Oxford, Oxford University Press, 1994.

Maxwell-Arnot, M., 'Social change and the Church of Scotland', in M. Hill (ed.), *A Sociological Yearbook of Religion in Britain, vol. 7*, London, SCM, 1974.

Mechie, S., *The Church and Scottish Social Development 1760–1860*, Oxford, Oxford University Press, 1960.

Miles, M.R., *Carnal Knowledge: Female Nakedness and Religious Meaning in the Christian West*, New York, Vintage, 1991.

Mitchell, B.R., and Deane, P. (eds), *Abstract of British Historical Statistics*, Cambridge, Cambridge University Press, 1962.

Mole, D.E.H., 'The Church of England and the working classes in Birmingham', in H. Dyos and M. Wolff (eds), *The Victorian City*, vol. 2, London, Routledge, 1973.

Moore, R., *Pit-men, Preachers and Politics: The Effects of Methodism in a Durham Mining Community*, Cambridge, Cambridge University Press, 1974.

Morgan, S., *A Passion for Purity: Ellice Hopkins and the Politics of Gender in the late-Victorian Church*, Bristol, Centre for Comparative Studies in Religion and Gender, 1999.

——, 'Writing the male body: sexual purity and masculinity in *The Vanguard 1884–1894*', in A. Bradstock, *et al.* (eds), *Male Models: Men, Masculinity and Spirituality in Victorian Culture*, London, Macmillan, 2000.

Morris, J.N., *Religion and Urban Change: Croydon 1840–1914*, Woodbridge, Royal Historical Society, 1992.

——, 'The strange death of Christian Britain: another look at the secularization debate', *Historical Journal*, vol. 46, 2003, pp. 963–76.

Morris, R.J., 'Urbanisation and Scotland', in W.H. Fraser and R.J. Morris (eds), q.v.

Myrdal, A., and Klein, V., *Women's Two Roles: Home and Work*, London, RKP, 1956.

Nash, D., 'Reconnecting religion with social and cultural history: secularization's failure as a master narrative', *Cultural and Social History*, vol. 1, 2004, pp. 302–35.

Norman, E.R., *Church and Society in England 1770–1970: A Historical Study*, Oxford, Clarendon Press, 1976.

Obelkevich, J., *Religion and Rural Society: South Lindsey 1825–1875*, Oxford, Clarendon Press, 1976.

Osgerby, B., *Youth in Britain since 1945*, Oxford, Blackwell, 1998.

Parsons, G., 'Contrasts and continuities: the traditional Christian churches in Britain since 1945', in G. Parsons (ed.), *The Growth of Religious Diversity: Britain from 1945*, vol. 1, London, Routledge, 1993.

——, 'How the times they are a'changing: exploring the context of religious transformation in Britain in the 1960s', in J. Wolffe (ed.), *Religion in History: Conflict, Conversion and Coexistence*, Manchester, Manchester University Press/Open University, 2004.

——, *AA307 Study Guide 4: The Death of Christian Britain: Exploring a Thesis*, Milton Keynes, Open University, 2005.

Passerini, L., *Fascism in Popular Memory: The Cultural Experience of the Turin Working Class*, Cambridge, Cambridge University Press, 1987.

Pasture, P., 'The role of religion in social and labour history', in L.H. van Voss and M. van der Linden (eds), *Class and Other Identities: Gender, Religion and Ethnicity in the Writing of European Labour History*, New York and Oxford, Berghahn Books, 2002, pp. 116–7.

——, 'Christendom and the legacy of the sixties: between the secular city and the age of Aquarius', *Review d'Histoire Ecclesiastique*, vol. 99, 2004, pp. 82–117.

——, 'Introduction' in L.H. van Voss, P. Pasture and J. De Maeyer (eds), q.v.

Perkin, H., *The Origins of Modern English Society 1780–1880*, London, RKP, 1969.

Pickering, W.S.F., 'The 1851 religious census – a useless experiment?', *British Journal of Sociology*, vol. 18, 1967.

Prochaska, F., *Women and Philanthropy in Nineteenth Century England*, Oxford, Clarendon Press, 1980.

Rapp, D., 'The British Salvation Army, the early film industry and urban working-class adolescents, 1897–1918', *Twentieth Century British History*, vol. 7, 1996.

Reid, D.A., 'Weddings, weekdays, work and leisure in urban England 1791–1911: the decline of Saint Monday revisited', *Past and Present*, no. 153, 1996.

Riley, D., '"The free mothers": pronatalism and working women in industry at the end of the last war in Britain', *History Workshop Journal*, Spring 1981, pp. 59–118.

Roberts, E., *Women and Families: An Oral History, 1940–1970*, Oxford, Blackwell, 1995.

Robertson, A., *Lifestyle Survey*, Edinburgh, Church of Scotland, 1987.

van Rooden, P., 'Secularisation, deChristianisation and reChristianisation in the Netherlands', in H. Lehmann (ed.), *Dechristianisierung und Rechristianisierung im neuzeitlichen Europa und in Nordamerika: Bilanz und Perspektiven der Forschung: Veroffentlichungen des Max-Planck-Instituts für Geschichte 130*, Göttingen, Vandenhoeck & Ruprecht, 1997, pp. 131–53.

——, 'Oral history en het vreemde sterven van het Nederlands christendom', *Bijdragen en Mededelingen betreffende de Geschiedenis der Nederlanden*, vol. 119, 2004, pp. 524–51.

Roodhouse, M., 'Lady Chatterley and the monk: Anglican radicals and the Lady Chatterley trial of 1960', *Journal of Ecclesiastical History*, vol. 59, 2008.

Routley, E., *The English Carol*, London, Herbert Jenkins, 1958.

——, *The Church and Music*, n.p., Duckworth, 1978.

Rowbotham, S., *A Century of Women: The History of Women in Britain and the United States*, London, Viking, 1997.

——, *Promise of a Dream: Remembering the Sixties*, London, Verso, 2001.

Ruff, M.E., 'The postmodern challenge to the secularization thesis', *Schweizerische Zeitschrift für Religion- und Kultergeschichte*, vol. 99, 2005, pp. 385–401.

Sage, L., *Bad Blood*, London, Fourth Estate, 2001.

Sandbrook, D., *Never Had It So Good: A History of Britain from Suez to the Beatles*, London, Little, Brown, 2005.

Scotland, N., 'Evangelicalism and the Charismatic Movement (UK)', in C. Bartholomew, R. Parry and A. West (eds), *The Futures of Evangelicalism*, Leicester, InterVarsity Press, 2003.

Scott, J., *Gender and the Politics of History*, New York, Columbia University Press, 1988.

Sissons, M., and French, P. (eds), *The Age of Austerity, 1945–51*, London, Hodder and Stoughton, 1963.

Sissons, P.L., *The Social Significance of Church Membership in the Burgh of Falkirk*, Edinburgh, Saint Andrew Press, 1973.

Sitzia, L., 'Telling Arthur's story: oral history relationships and shared authority', *Oral History Journal*, vol. 27, 1999.

Skilton, D. (ed.), *The Early and Mid-Victorian Novel*, London, Routledge, 1993.

Smith, M., *Religion in Industrial Society: Oldham and Saddleworth 1740–1865*, Oxford, Oxford University Press, 1994.

Smollett, T., *The Expedition of Humphry Clinker*, orig. 1771, Harmondsworth, Penguin, 1967.

Snell, K.D.M., *Church and Chapel in the North Midlands: Religious Observance in the Nineteenth Century*, Leicester, Leicester University Press, 1991.

Springhall, J., *Youth, Empire and Society: British Youth Movements 1883–1940*, London, Croom Helm, 1977.

——, 'Building character in the British boy: the attempt to extend Christian manliness to working-class adolescents, 1880–1914', in J.A. Mangan and J. Walvin (eds), *Manliness and Morality: Middle-class Masculinity in Britain and America, 1800–1940*, Manchester, Manchester University Press, 1987.

Spufford, M., 'Can we count the "godly" and the "conformable" in the seventeenth century?', *Journal of Ecclesiastical History*, vol. 36, 1985.

Stanley, B., *The Bible and the Flag: Protestant Missions and British Imperialism in the Nineteenth and Twentieth Centuries*, Leicester, Apollos, 1990.

Stanley, L., *The Auto/Biographical I: The Theory and Practice of Feminist Auto/Biography*, Manchester, Manchester University Press, 1992.

——, and Wise, S., *Breaking Out Again: Feminist Ontology and Epistemology*, London and New York, Routledge, 1993.

Strinati, D., *An Introduction to Theories of Popular Culture*, London, Routledge, 1995.

Summerfield, P., *Women Workers in The Second World War*, London, Croom Helm, 1984.

——, *Reconstructing Women's Wartime Lives: Discourse and Subjectivity in Oral Histories of the Second World War*, Manchester, Manchester University Press, 1998.

Sutcliffe, S., *Children of the New Age: A History of Spiritual Practices*, London, Routledge, 2003.

Taylor, A.T., *Labour and Love: An Oral History of the Brass Band Movement*, London, Elm Tree Books, 1983.

Taylor, B., *Eve and the New Jerusalem: Socialism and Feminism in the Nineteenth Century*, London, Virago, 1983.

Taylor, C., *Human Agency and Language: Philosophical Papers I*, Cambridge, Cambridge University Press, 1985.

——, *Sources of the Self: The Making of the Modern Identity*, Cambridge, Mass., Harvard University Press, 1989.

——, *The Ethics of Authenticity*, Cambridge, Mass., Harvard University Press, 1991.

——, *A Secular Age*, Cambridge, Mass., Belknap Press, 2007.

Thompson, E.P., *The Making of the English Working Class*, orig. 1963, Harmondsworth, Penguin, 1968.

——, *Customs in Common*, London, Merlin, 1991.

Thompson, F.M.L., *Hampstead: Building a Borough, 1650–1964*, London, RKP, 1974.

Thompson, W., 'Charismatic politics: the social and political impact of renewal', in S. Hunt, M. Hamilton, and T. Walter (eds), *Charismatic Christianity: Sociological Perspectives*, Basingstoke, Macmillan, 1997.

Thomson, A., 'Anzac memories: putting popular memory theory into practice in Australia', *Oral History Journal*, vol. 18, 1990.

Tinkler, P., *Constructing Girlhood: Popular Magazines for Girls Growing Up in England 1920–1950*, London, Taylor & Francis, 1995.

Tosh, J., *A Man's Place: Masculinity and the Middle-class Home in Victorian England*, New Haven, Yale University Press, 1999.

Totten, A., 'Coherent chaplaincy', *Journal of the Royal Army Chaplains' Department*, vol. 45, 2006.

Towler, R., *The Need for Certainty: A Sociological Study of Conventional Religion*, London, RKP, 1984.

Trotter, D., *The English Novel in History 1895–1920*, London, Routledge, 1993.

Vance, N., *Sinews of the Spirit: The Ideal of Christian Manliness in Victorian Literature and Religious Thought*, Cambridge, Cambridge University Press, 1985.

Vincent, D., *Bread, Knowledge and Freedom: A Study of Nineteenth-century Working Class Autobiography*, London, Methuen, 1981.

Voas, D., 'Intermarriage and the demography of secularization', *British Journal of Sociology*, vol. 54, 2003, pp. 83–108.

van Voss, L.H., Pasture, P., and De Maeyer, J. (eds), *Between Cross and Class: Comparative Histories of Christian Labour in Europe 1840–2000*, Bern, Peter Lang, 2005.

Walker, P., '"I live but not yet I for Christ Liveth in me": Men and masculinity in the Salvation Army, 1865–90', in M. Roper and J. Tosh (eds.), *Manful Assertions: Masculinities in Britain since 1800*, London, Routledge, 1991.

Walkowitz, J.R., *City of Dreadful Delight: Narratives of Sexual Danger in Late-Victorian London*, London, Virago, 1992.

Wallis, R., and Bruce, S., 'Secularization: the orthodox model', in S. Bruce (ed.), q.v.

Walsh, J., 'Methodism and the mob in the eighteenth century', *Studies in Church History*, vol. 8, 1972.

Welsby, P.A., *A History of the Church of England 1945–1980*, Oxford, Oxford University Press, 1984.

White, C.L., *Women's Magazines 1693–1968*, London, Michael Joseph, 1970.

——, *The Women's Periodical Press in Britain 1946–1976*, London, HMSO, 1977.

Wickham, E.R., *Church and People in an Industrial City*, London, Lutterworth, 1957.

Wigley, J., *The Rise and Fall of the Victorian Sunday*, Manchester, Manchester University Press, 1980.

Williams, R., *The English Novel from Dickens to Lawrence*, London, Chatto and Windus, 1970.

Williams, S., 'The language of belief: an alternative agenda for the study of Victorian working-class religion', *Journal of Victorian Culture*, vol. 1, 1996, pp. 303–17.

Williams, S.C., *Religious Belief and Popular Culture in Southwark, c.1880–1939*, Oxford, Oxford University Press, 1999.

Wilson, B.R, *Religion in Secular Society*, Harmondsworth, Penguin, 1966.

——, 'Reflections on a many sided controversy', in S. Bruce (ed.), *Religion and Modernization: Sociologists and Historians Debate the Secularization Thesis*, Oxford, Clarendon Press, 1992.

Wilson, L., *Constrained by Zeal: Female Spirituality amongst Nonconformists, 1825–1875*, Carlisle, Paternoster Press, 2000.

Witoszek, N., 'Fugitives from Utopia: the Scandinavian Enlightenment reconsidered', in O. Sorensen and B. Strath (eds), *The Cultural Construction of Nordern*, Oslo, Scandinavian University Press, 1997.

Wolffe, J., *The Expansion of Evangelicalism: The Age of Wilberforce, More, Chalmers and Finney*, Downers Grove, Ill., InterVarsity Press, 2007.

Woodhead, L., 'Sex and secularisation', in Gerard Loughlin (ed.), *Queer Theology: Rethinking the Western Body*, Oxford, Blackwell, 2007, pp. 230–44.

——, 'Gender differences in religious practice and significance', in J. Beckford and N.J. Demerath III (eds), *The Sage Handbook of the Sociology of Religion*, Los Angeles, Sage, 2007.

Wuthnow, R., *The Restructuring of American Religion: Society and Faith since World War II*, Princeton, Princeton University Press, 1988.

Yeo, E.J., *The Contest for Social Science*, London, Rivers Oram, 1996.

Yeo, S., *Religion and Voluntary Organisations in Crisis*, London, Croom Helm, 1976.

UNPUBLISHED THESES

Bilsborough, P., 'The development of sport in Glasgow, 1850–1914', unpublished M.Litt. thesis, University of Stirling, 1983.

Bartlett, A.B., 'The Churches in Bermondsey 1880–1939', unpublished Ph.D. thesis, University of Birmingham, 1987.

Chadwick, R.E., 'Church and people in Bradford and District 1880–1914: the Protestant churches in an urban industrial environment', unpublished D.Phil. thesis, University of Oxford, 1986.

Jeffrey, L., 'Women in the churches of nineteenth-century Stirling', unpublished M.Litt. thesis, University of Stirling, 1996.

Nicolson, A., 'Moody and Sankey in Scotland 1873–1874: "And it's from the old we travel to the new"', unpublished BA Hons. dissertation, Department of History, University of Strathclyde, 1998.

Sykes, R.P.M., 'Popular religion in Dudley and the Gornals c. 1914–1965', unpublished Ph.D. thesis, University of Wolverhampton, 1999.

INDEX

—— ·◆· ——